140, 167-183

THE PRINCIPAL

FOURTH EDITION

THE PRINCIPAL

Creative Leadership for Effective Schools

GERALD C. UBBEN
University of Tennessee, Knoxville

LARRY W. HUGHES
University of Houston

CYNTHIA J. NORRIS
University of Tennessee, Knoxville

ALLYN AND BACON
Boston ▪ London ▪ Toronto ▪ Sydney ▪ Tokyo ▪ Singapore

Series Editor: *Arnis E. Burvikovs*
Vice President, Editor in Chief, Education: *Paul A. Smith*
Editorial Assistant: *Patrice Mailloux*
Marketing Managers: *Brad Parkins and Kathleen Morgan*
Editorial-Production Administrator: *Annette Joseph*
Editorial-Production Coordinator: *Holly Crawford*
Editorial-Production Service: *Lynda Griffiths, TKM Productions*
Composition Buyer: *Linda Cox*
Electronic Composition: *TKM Productions*
Manufacturing Buyer: *Julie McNeill*
Cover Administrator: *Brian Gogolin*
Cover Designer: *Suzanne Harbison*

A Pearson Education Company
160 Gould Street
Needham Heights, MA 02494

Internet: www.abacon.com

Library of Congress Cataloging-in-Publication Data

Ubben, Gerald C.
The principal : creative leadership for effective schools / Gerald C. Ubben, Larry W. Hughes, Cynthia J. Norris.-- 4th ed.
p. cm.
ISBN 0-205-32211-5
1. School principals--United States. 2. School management and organization--United States. 3. School supervision--United States. 4. School personnel management--United States. I. Hughes, Larry W. II. Norris, Cynthia J. III. Title.
LB2805.U2 2001
371.2'012--dc21 00-042143

Printed in the United States of America

10 9 8 7 6 5 4 3 2 RRD-VA 05 04 03 02 01

Credit: The listing of the six ISLLC standards in the Preface and in Parts I through IV, certain end-of-chapter questions, and Appendix B are printed with permission from Council of Chief State School Officers (1996), *Interstate School Leaders Licensure Consortium: Standards for School Leaders* (Washington DC: Author).

CONTENTS

CHAPTER THREE

Decision Processing and Decision Making at the School Site 45

CHAPTER FOUR

School Improvement through Systematic Planning 69

CHAPTER EIGHT
Special Students and Special Services 167

CHAPTER NINE
Human Resources Development 184

CHAPTER THIRTEEN
Creative Budgeting, Fiscal Accounting, and Building Management 273

CHAPTER FOURTEEN
Technology Applications for School Management 297

PREFACE

This fourth edition of *The Principal* is organized around the new Interstate School Leaders Licensure Consortium (ISLLC) model standards developed specifically for school leaders. The standards present a common core of knowledge, dispositions, and performances that will help link leadership more forcefully to productive schools and enhanced outcomes.

The book continues to be based on the research about the linkages between school leadership and productive schools, especially in terms of outcomes for children and youth. It supports the understanding that formal leadership in schools is a complex multifaceted task that requires continual learning and that effective school leaders must be strong educators anchoring their work on the central issues of learning, teaching, and school improvement. School leaders must also be moral agents and social advocates for the children and communities they serve. Additionally, they must make solid connections with stakeholders, empowering them to create learning communities that value and care for others as individuals and as members of the educational community.

Numerous strategies are being used to strengthen the quality of leadership in our schools today. Many states have strengthened licensing requirements for school leaders, and universities have carried out extensive revisions of their preparation programs. In 1996, the Council of Chief State School Officers (CCSSO) created the Interstate School Leaders Licensure Consortium and charged them with the responsibility to develop a new set of model standards for school leaders. The standards were drafted by personnel from 24 state education agencies and representatives from various professional associations and designed to be compatible with the new National Council for the Accreditation of Teacher Education (NCATE) curriculum guidelines for school administration.

Since the 1987 publication of the *Leaders for America's Schools* by the National Commission on Excellence in Educational Administration, all major professional associations, both practitioner and university based, have devoted major effort to this issue of standards. The National Policy Board for Educational Administration (NPBEA) was created largely in response to this need and in an effort to generate a better and more coordinated approach to this task. The efforts of ISLLC have moved standards to the next level to form a framework that provides an excellent base for the organization of school leader preparation programs.

The six ISSLC standards focus only on the key issues that form the heart and soul of effective leadership. Constant attention is given to issues of learning and teaching and the creation of powerful learning environments. Each of the six standards begins with the words *A school administrator is an educational leader who promotes the success of all students by. . . .* Each standard is, in turn, supported by a framework of knowledge, dispositions, and performances that provide greater specificity to each standard. (A complete list of all six standards along with their associated knowledge, dispositions, and performances is located in Appendix B.)

This book is organized into four parts centered on the six ISLLC standards developed specifically for school leaders. Each of the four major parts of the book is framed with one or two of the standards as its major theme. The parts are as follows:

Part I: Creating a Vision of Leadership and Learning

Standard 1: A school administrator is an educational leader who promotes the success of all students by facilitating the development, articulation, implementation, and stewardship of a clear vision of learning that is shared and supported by the school community.

Standard 5: A school administrator is an educational leader who promotes the success of all students by acting with integrity, fairness, and in an ethical manner.

Part II: Developing a Positive School Culture

Standard 2: A school administrator is an educational leader who promotes the success of all students by advocating, nurturing, and sustaining a school culture and instructional program conducive to student learning and professional growth.

Part III: Managing the Organization

Standard 3: A school administrator is an educational leader who promotes the success of all students by ensuring management of the organization, operations, and resources for a safe, efficient, and effective learning environment.

Part IV: Interacting with the External School Environment

Standard 4: A school administrator is an educational leader who promotes the success of all students by collaborating with families and community members, responding to diverse community interests and needs, and mobilizing community resources.

Standard 6: A school administrator is an educational leader who promotes the success of all students by understanding, responding to, and influencing the larger political, social, economic, legal, and cultural context.

We continue to try to put between two covers of the book a proper balance so that aspiring and practicing administrators may find intellectual challenge as well as cause to reflect on what, with effort and analysis, "might be." It is our hope that we have provided good balance between the theoretical and the practical and the bridge that connects them.

In this fourth edition, we introduce you to a new coauthor: Dr. Cynthia Norris. Her range of experience and her writing style combine well with the earlier editions. For a number of years, she worked as a coinstructor with Dr. Hughes at the University of Houston, and more recently, she has joined ranks with Dr. Ubben at the University of Tennessee. So, philosophically, Dr. Norris blends nicely with the team and adds an excellent understanding of the theoretical frameworks of transformational leadership and the creation of learning communities. We welcome her to the team.

As before, we continue to hope that the readers will find this book to be useful now and on the job. Let us know.

G. C. U.
L. W. H.
C. J. N.

THE PRINCIPAL

PART I

CREATING A VISION OF LEADERSHIP AND LEARNING

The school leaders of the twenty-first century must have knowledge and understanding of the purpose of education and the role of leadership in modern society as well as various ethical frameworks and perspectives on ethics, the values of the diverse school community, professional codes of ethics, and the philosophy and history of education. They should also believe in, value, and be committed to the ideal of the common good, the principles in the Bill of Rights, the right of every student to a free quality education, bringing ethical principles to the decision-making process, subordination of one's own interest to the good of the school community, accepting the consequences for upholding one's principles and actions, using the influence of one's office constructively and productively in the service of all students and their families, and development of a caring school community. The Interstate School Leaders Licensure Consortium (ISLLC) Standard Five supports these standards.

> **Standard 5: A school administrator is an educational leader who promotes the success of all students by acting with integrity, fairness, and in an ethical manner**.

Likewise, the educational leader must have knowledge and understanding of the goals of learning in a pluralistic society; the principles of developing and implementing strategic plans; systems theory; information sources, data collection, and data analysis strategies; effective communication; and effective consensus-building and negotiation skills. They must also believe in, value, and be committed to the educability of all; a school vision of high standards of learning; continuous school improvement; the inclusion of all members of the school community; ensuring that all students have the knowledge, skills, and values needed to become successful adults; a willingness to continuously examine one's own assumptions, beliefs, and practices; and doing the work required for high levels of personal and organization performance. ISLLC Standard One supports these standards.

> **Standard 1: A school administrator is an educational leader who promotes the success of all students by facilitating the development, articulation, implementation, and stewardship of a clear vision of learning that is shared and supported by the school community.**

Part I addresses these two standards and the knowledge, dispositions, and performances that accompany them.

CHAPTER ONE

THE PRINCIPAL

A Creative Blend of Substance and Style

Leadership, in the final analysis, is the ability of humans to relate deeply to each other in the search for a more perfect union. Leadership is a consensual task, a sharing of ideas and a sharing of responsibilities, where a "leader" is a leader for the moment only, where the leadership exerted must be validated by the consent of followers, and where leadership lies in the struggles of a community to find meaning for itself.

—B. Foster[1]

The perception of the school principal has changed dramatically in recent years. No longer are school leaders viewed as mere reactive managers of the status quo whose task is to implement policies created at higher levels of the bureaucratic hierarchy. Instead, today's school principals have been charged with the task of shaping their schools to become outstanding beacons of productive learning. They are challenged to clarify their own values, beliefs, and positions and to engage proactively with others in the redesign and improvement of their schools. They are expected to establish conditions that foster personal empowerment and enhanced development of organizational members and to orchestrate shared power and decision making among an array of individuals both internal and external to the school setting. At the same time, they are encouraged to build a community of leaders and learners who will effectively shape the school environment to champion increased productivity among students. Truly, it is an exciting time to be a school principal! It is a time, as well, that calls for the courageous, insightful, and dedicated leader, for while there are many opportunities, there are also many constraints that challenge that leadership. In this chapter we will consider the school as a context for leadership, the principalship within that context, and the individual within the principal's role. We begin with a discussion of organizational context.

THE SCHOOL: THE CONTEXT FOR LEADERSHIP

The responsibilities of school leadership are best understood when viewed within the *organizational context* in which that leadership occurs. Leaders emerge to guide organizations, defined as "group(s) of people who come together to fulfill a purpose."[2] Leaders are in service to organizations, to the individuals who comprise those organizations, and to the clients that that organization serves. The defined purpose of any organization is shaped to a large degree by the organizational frameworks, or structures, that determine its context. One way of viewing various organizational contexts is to consider them from the viewpoint of metaphors. Morgan has presented three metaphors of organizational context: machines, organisms, and brains. These metaphors help one understand the differences between rationally designed organizations and natural systems and present an initial look at the type of leadership that emerges from each setting.[3]

Schools as Machines

Schools, viewed as machines, exhibit many qualities reflective of the Scientific Management Era, where efficiency and highly structured tasks characterized much of the organization's daily operation. Schools designed in this fashion are closed systems, unaware of, or unresponsive to, the changing needs of their internal and external environments. Characterized by a bureaucratic hierarchy, these schools are tightly coupled, policy-driven settings that tend to stifle the initiative and creativity of organizational members. Leaders of such schools attempt to control both power and knowledge and "manage" the organization and its people so that order, predictability, and tradition are maintained. While on the surface all may seem balanced and smooth running, there is a tendency in such stagnant environments for decay to occur. These organizations face real danger of becoming outdated and obsolete. When organizations are designed as machines, there is a tendency to manage rather than lead, for there is comfort in stability. Even schools that normally would exhibit more open environments can become machine driven. Under threat, these schools and their leaders sometimes revert back to a machine-type model as they attempt to tighten up their standards and be "accountable" in the face of criticism.

Schools as Organisms

Schools, characterized as organisms, or natural systems, exhibit growth and adaptive qualities. Centered on interdependence and collaboration, these schools emphasize individuality, uniqueness, and self-renewal. Such educational settings are responsive, open organizations that meet the changing needs of their internal and external environments. In such schools, principals serve as facilitators of a shared mission that unites organizational members through purposeful commitment. Standardization of method is far less important than the results achieved or the impact realized. Human needs are acknowledged and met while growth is facilitated.

Schools as Brains

Learning organizations, characterized as thinking/learning models, reflect the brain metaphor. Schools of this type emphasize reflective, problem-finding approaches for the improvement of current conditions and practices. The image is one of holistic thought, where both the rational and intuitive dimensions of problem solving come into play. Knowledge, as well as power, is widely dispersed throughout the organization. This enables adaptation to occur and new designs and approaches to be generated. These schools are characterized by community; knowledge is not only shared and stored but it is generated. Principals are facilitators who enable the free flow of communication and exchange of ideas and who set forth conditions that foster the empowerment of others.

Reflection

Viewing these metaphorical contexts from the perspective of schools, it is helpful to explore a series of questions that help paint a vivid picture of each setting. As you reflect on these environmental contexts, it is important to consider some important questions concerning each one. In each context:

1. What would be the purpose of education?
2. What would be the role of the principal? (Director, facilitator, developer?)
3. What would be the role of the teacher? (Laborer, craftsperson, professional, artist?)
4. What would be the role of the learner?
5. What would learning look like?

There is embedded in organizational context both implicit and explicit expectations of what the organizations should accomplish and what the leader should provide to the process of goal fulfillment. As noted:

> Existing structure of a setting or culture defines the permissible ways in which goals and problems will be approached. Not so obvious, particularly to those who comprise the structure, is that existing structure is but one of many alternative structures possible in that setting and the existing one is a barrier to recognition and experimentation with alternative ones.[4]

As you answered each of the previous questions, you did, in fact, explore organizational beliefs and platforms from which leadership is cast. A formal platform is comprised of a series of statements reflecting beliefs, values, and visions for education. Platforms help people clarify personal and organizational expectations.[5] But what are the influences that shape these expectations and that determine those platforms?

School Expectations

In the case of schools, organizational expectations are influenced by various sources: the school community, school district mandates and policy, state and federal policies and directives, court decisions, the general public, the educational profession itself, and various interest and professional groups. Individuals and subgroups within organizations also have their own set of expectations that grow out of their own unique experiences, their personalities and individual needs, and, in many cases, their political agendas. All play a part in shaping organizational expectations, as well as the expectations the organization holds for its leaders.

Expectations for schools tend to become generalized and perpetuated over time by one's past experiences in school settings. For instance, an "overexposure" to a certain organizational context might result in a feeling of comfort that "this is the way things are done around here." While this does enable the preservation of many important traditions and structures, it can also have negative results. In many cases, these past experiences create expectations, which may cause schools to become outdated and obsolete in their purpose. Sarason addressed this issue when he suggested that schools are very difficult to change because most everybody at some point has *been there.*[6] Recognizing this danger and being cognizant of the need to restructure schools to better meet the needs of changing society, many groups have endeavored to change outdated expectations and to redesign the environmental context, or structure that surrounds the school. In recent years, some professional organizations have given a more concentrated effort toward raising and standardizing school expectations and the expectations for its leaders. School expectations have been challenged by the research in effective schools as well as by national reports, such as *A Nation at Risk*[7] and *The Carnegie Report.*[8] The expectations for school principals as leaders of restructured schools have also been challenged. Two major leaders in this arena, the National Policy Board[9] and the Interstate School Leaders Licensure Committee (ISLLC),[10] have developed national standards that attempt to bring greater clarity and direction to the role of school principal.

Tightly Coupled and Loosely Coupled Organizations

Often, there is great difference of opinion as to what constitutes "good schooling" and good leadership within that arena. As a result, schools often find themselves trying to muddle through their task with little true sense of direction or clear understanding of expectations. The very nature of schools and schooling make it difficult to come to agreement on expectations, even within a particular school setting. Weick[11] has referred to this in terms of the "tightly coupled" vs. "loosely coupled" phenomenon. Organizations that are tightly coupled are characterized by four important qualities: (1) there are clear rules and expectations, (2) rules and expectations are disseminated and understood by all organizational members, (3) monitoring of performance is consistent and frequent, and (4) corrective feedback results from assessment results. There is balance and order within the structure that is set; it is a rational system. This tightly drawn system is reflective of the machine metaphor, which carries with it expectations for structure, standardization, and control.

Schools, in contrast to such organizations, are not rational entities, although many people would like them to be. They are, instead, much more loosely coupled and unpredictable. Although there are general expectations for all schools, each school must redefine those expectations based on the things that are not always "clear cut" and predictable. Principals in such settings have greater opportunity to personalize their organizations and voice their own expectations and the expectations of others within their organizations than do principals in more rationally ordered settings. Although there are broad general expectations for all schools, there is great variety among schools in interpretation of those expectations based on their own unique needs. Each school must redefine its own expectations based on the influences it encounters within its own unique setting and on the changing needs of those individuals within the setting.

Leadership Perspectives

It is easy to govern schools based on a set of "standardized expectations"; it is a far greater challenge to examine those expectations according to the needs of the individuals within the setting. Leaders become either reactive or proactive in response. The reactive mode requires only management of a prescribed order; the proactive one requires leadership. The managerial style, often referred to as *transactional leadership,* is reminiscent of the machine metaphor and places all power and responsibility in the hands of the principal. Adherence to the purpose is based on a reactive response supported by positional and coercive power. It is an exchange of "a day's work for a day's pay" with little thought to purposeful commitment.

Certainly, the administrator should be a custodian and preserver of the basic traditions, values, goals, and history of the organization as well as a guardian of all that is good and productive. In that sense, the leader operates as a manager. At the same time, if the organization is to maintain its vitality and meet the needs of its people and of the larger context it serves, the leader must also be a proactive questioner of current practices and a transformer of policies, procedures, and practices that are counterproductive for the organization and its members. The leader must facilitate schools that are not only productive disseminators of knowledge, but schools that guard and preserve the democratic rights of all individuals within that context. The leader must help to elevate and orchestrate higher purposes for the good of all. It that sense, the leader is transformational. The organistic model and the brain model come into play. The *transformational leader* shares power, inspires others to leadership, and encourages participation and involvement of all members in executing the school's purpose.

Single-Loop and Double-Loop Learning

A learning model by Arygris[12] helps in better understanding these different perspectives. He defined two kinds of learning: a single-loop and a double-loop process.[13] "*Single-loop learning* rests in an ability to detect and correct error in relation to a given set of operating norms."[14] It is a three-step process:

1. A norm, or a standard, for operation is established.
2. Monitoring occurs to determine if any discrepancies exist between current conditions and the established norm.

3. Corrective action is taken to ensure that conditions are congruent with the previously established norm.

The single-loop process promotes stability and predictability based on an established norm. It is assumed that what the organization is trying to accomplish is what it *should be* doing. Little consideration is given to the evolving nature of the internal and external school environment. The organization operates as a closed system.

"*Double-loop learning* depends on being able to take a 'double look' at the situation by questioning the relevance of operating norms."[15] It is a four-step process:

1. A norm, or a standard, for operation is established.
2. Monitoring occurs to determine compliance with the established norm.
3. If a discrepancy exists, leaders ask "Why?"
4. Corrective action takes place, which may
   a. bring conditions back in line with the norm, or
   b. establish a new norm.

Double-loop learning encourages growth and development, for it responds to the inevitable changes that occur within the school's internal and external environment. Rather than accepting a goal or norm as being "correct," time is spent in questioning that norm in light of changing needs.

Single-loop learning is a *problem-solving process.* Double-loop learning is both problem solving and *problem finding.*

The Organizational Iceberg

The realization of organizational expectations is not always easy, because schools are occupied with real people who stamp each role and task with their own individuality. Another way of thinking about organizational behavior is to picture an iceberg (see Figure 1.1), with the visible part of the iceberg representing formal organizational expectations. This is the public part of the organization that is manifested in the stated goals and objectives, the organizational chart, the job descriptions—all those things that are official.

Not readily apparent is that part of the organization that lies below the surface—the personal or informal dimension. Manifested in this dimension are the perceptions of organization members about the organization, the differing influence and power patterns that exist irrespective of formal title, the informal reward and sanctioning systems, feelings of trust and confidence, and incipient individual or group paranoia. The below-the-surface organization greatly affects the degree to which the above-the-surface organization is really as it appears and the degree to which the organization reaches its stated and legitimate goals.

The Social Systems Theory

A school principal must consider the individual expectations and needs that govern social behavior when attempting to gain the cooperation of staff. An important model

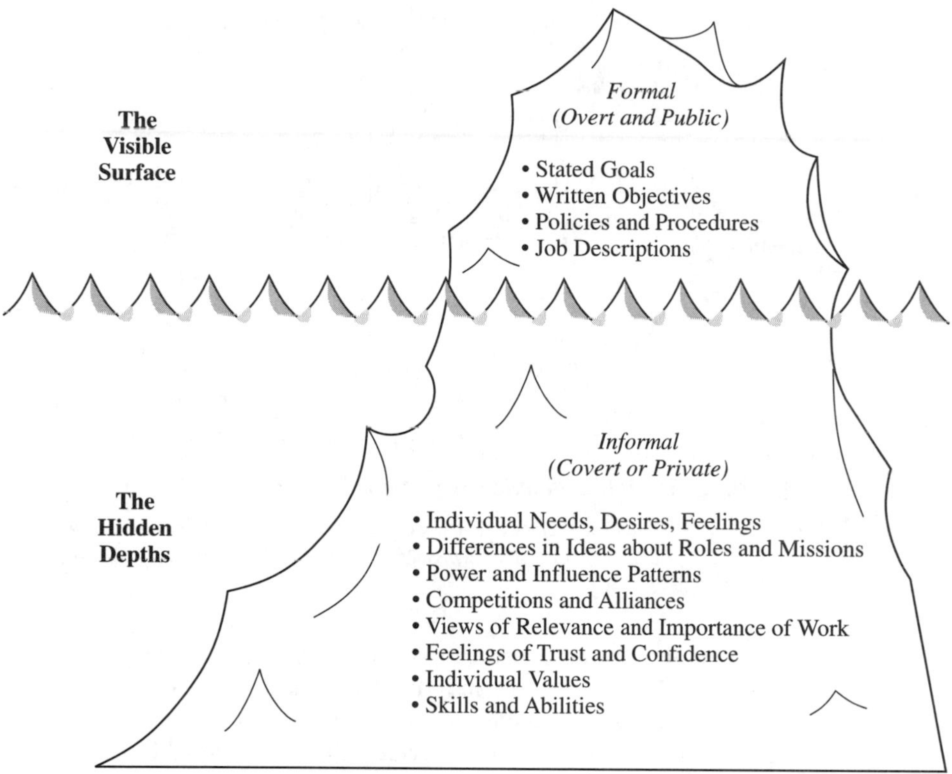

FIGURE 1.1 The Organizational Iceberg

Source: Larry W. Hughes and Gerald C. Ubben, *The Elementary Principal's Handbook: A Guide to Effective Action,* 4th ed. Boston: Allyn and Bacon, 1994, p. 24. Used with permission.

to assist in understanding this interplay of institutional and individual expectations is the social systems model, shown in Figure 1.2.

The work of Getzel and Guba is fundamental to the application of social systems theory in schools. Essentially, they posited two dimensions to the organization: the nomothetic (institutional) dimension and the idiographic (personal) dimension.[16]

Institution refers to the fact that all organizations have necessary functions that must be carried out according to certain expectations. *Roles* are the official positions and offices that have been established to carry out the school's purpose and functions. The behaviors that are to comprise a role are called *role expectations*. Every role has certain normative responsibilities and these will differ by role. It is the interaction of the institutional and idiographic dimensions within that role that results in the observed behavior of individuals in the organization. The principal's responsibility is to serve as the agent for productive interaction. It is not enough to have a stated purpose and expectations for the organization; there must be cooperation by those involved to accomplish the task.

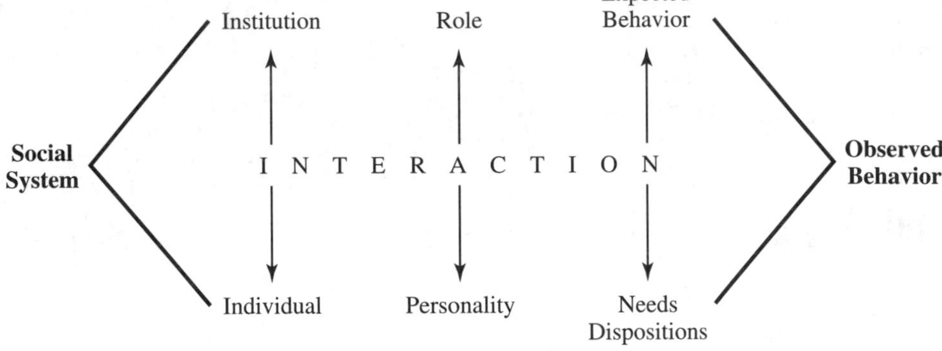

FIGURE 1.2 Depiction of a Social Systems Theory

Source: Larry W. Hughes and Gerald C. Ubben, *The Elementary Principal's Handbook: A Guide to Effective Action,* 4th ed. Boston: Allyn and Bacon, 1994, p. 22. Used with permission.

Personality in the context of the social systems model may be defined as the "dynamic organization within an individual of those 'needs-dispositions' that govern his unique reactions to the environment."[17] In other words, each individual is a complex of previous experiences that have provided him or her with differing orientations to life, to organizations, and to other people. These experiences affect a person's sense of what is pleasurable, important, and real. Personality is to needs disposition as role is to role expectation.

In order for the principal to understand (and reasonably predict) the behavior of a teacher or other staff members, it is essential that the principal know both the role expectation of the particular job and the needs disposition of the individual. In productive organizations, much attention is directed toward helping all workers understand what the organizational expectations are.

The challenge to the principal is to try to address both individual and organizational needs to achieve as much congruence as possible. The greater the congruence, the more satisfied and productive the worker is. This congruence creates interdependence between the individuals and the organization that results in enhanced growth for the individual and greater productivity for the organization.

Viewed systemically, organizational expectations represent the collective expectations of individual members. These expectations can also be viewed from an individual or subgroup perspective. This raises various questions, such as:

1. What does the group expect the organization to accomplish, and what expectations does the group have for the individual within the leadership role?
2. What do individual members and subgroups expect from the organization and its leader and from each other?

3. What does the leader expect from the organization, its members, and himself or herself as the leader?

We turn now to an examination of the expectations for the school principal by considering the nature of the principalship.

THE PRINCIPALSHIP: THE ROLE IN CONTEXT

Schools vary in size and complexity. Similarly, the role of the principal will vary from place to place, as a result of organizational and community expectations. Nevertheless, the *functions* that must be managed by the principal are similar, irrespective of where the position is located or how many students there are.

Five functional aspects comprise the principalship. Four of these take place inside the school; the other occurs in interaction with the outside world. The "inside" functions include staffing and instructional improvement, curriculum development, student services, and resource procurement and building utilization, including budgeting and maintenance. The "outside" function is public relations.

The dimensions of leadership and management cut across these five functions. Leadership is the way principals *use themselves* to create a school climate characterized by student productivity, staff productivity, and creative thought. Think of good management as the systematic application of an array of skills to provide for an orderly and efficient school environment. Figure 1.3 depicts the relationship of the five functions and the two dimensions.

Management

It is without question that productive schools require a high degree of consistency and not a little certitude, as manifest in well-understood policies to guide the daily operation. This is true of all organizations. Organizational members expect that routine matters will be dealt with in firm and expeditious ways. Many aspects of the school must remain in a stable state so that the other aspects can change in a way that is not chaotic. In this sense, the status quo keeps the organization in a stable state, enabling its members to understand what is required of them in achieving organizational goals.[18] Good management, then, is both positive and necessary.

Research and development efforts of such professional organizations as the National Association of Secondary School Principals (NASSP)[19] and the National Association of Elementary School Principals (NAESP)[20] have uncovered discreet skills, the presence of which determines effectiveness. Research done by NASSP[21] reveals six abilities that are important to a successful school administrator. More recently, the National Policy Board has incorporated many of these skills as part of their national standards for school principals.[22] The six NASSP abilities include the following:

- The ability to plan and organize work
- The ability to work with and lead others

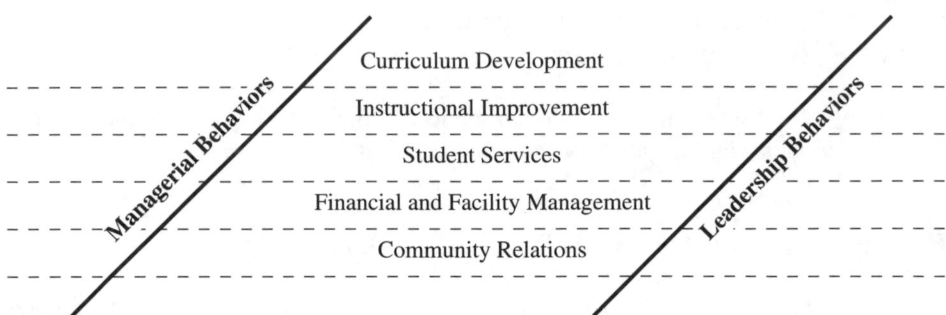

FIGURE 1.3 The Five Functions and Two Dimensions of the Principalship

Source: Larry W. Hughes and Gerald C. Ubben, *The Elementary Principal's Handbook: A Guide to Effective Action,* 4th ed. Boston: Allyn and Bacon, 1994, p. 5. Used with permission.

- The ability to analyze problems and make decisions
- The ability to communicate orally and in writing
- The ability to perceive the needs and concerns of others
- The ability to perform under pressure

Identification of these skills is the result of extensive and intensive job and task analyses of what it is that principals have to do and be good at in order to manage the enterprise effectively.

Management offers to followers "specified external rewards and privileges in exchange for the completion of duties and responsibilities outlined by the organization."[23] The transactions involve relationships between both the school and the larger organization and between the principal (leader) and his or her staff. Managers get things done by making tasks clear and providing reward (favors, pats on the back, good evaluations, awards, released time, etc.) to staff members who perform appropriately and well—that is, those who behave congruently with organizational expectations.

Management in this sense is often referred to as *transactional leadership*. It is based on an exchange between leader and follower to gain cooperation and ensure task completion.

As we discussed in the beginning section of this chapter, leadership and management do not occur without context. Effectively managing and leading any organization requires daily interaction with a large number of groups and the wide variety of individuals comprising these groups. Teachers, parents, children, administrators, classified personnel, merchants, and a host of other "outsiders" and "insiders" all become important reference points. Moreover, persons within these groups, although often sharing common goals, rarely behave similarly or see the same things similarly. People have varying perceptions of the nature of schooling and their own role in the schooling process. They are influenced and motivated in different ways and by different means.

Management and Leadership

Good management creates a necessary state of orderliness and certitude to aspects of the school organization but not to the exclusion of a necessary state of turmoil as new goals and processes are established and as the school family addresses new challenges and struggles to create an even more productive future.

This begins to describe the difference between leadership and management. Management is status quo oriented and assumes a highly stable environment. As Arygris[24] explained in the single-loop process discussed earlier, the job of the manager is to keep things moving correctly according to the norm that has already been set. There is an assumption made that the standards or norms that have been previously established are appropriate ones and the task is to see that conditions are aligned with the established goals. If things are not operating effectively, it is the job of the manager to see that corrective action is taken to bring things back into balance. Management operates from a problem-solving perspective with little attention given to questioning the appropriateness of established norms.

The notion of leadership is much different. Leaders build on the status quo, to be sure, but go well beyond it. As in a double-loop process, they continually reexamine the norm to determine if what the organization *is doing* is what it *should be doing*. As Foster stated, "Leaders always have one face turned toward change."[25] There is a constant reexamination of current conditions and a formulation of new possibilities. Leadership is a problem-finding as well as problem-solving approach. It is a dynamic process that challenges the organization to higher levels of consciousness and growth.

Certainly, good principal leaders also manage, but they manage with a leadership perspective! A different mental set characterizes the leader-manager. These principals use their perceptions of changes that are needed to work both inside and outside the organization to map new directions, to secure new resources and refocus existing resources, and to respond to the realities of a very unstable present and, at times, an unforeseeable future. To such leaders, change is inevitable—the challenge is to make the most of it in increasingly more productive ways. This brings us to the concept of vision and the role it plays in the leadership process. The following section focuses on what has been pondered, puzzled about, and seen.

Leadership and Vision

The quality of *vision* has been pondered frequently, as it seems to relate to effective leadership behavior. Important, also, are the notions of *shared vision* and *transformational leadership.* Vision seems to distinguish leaders from those who are simply good managers. It has been defined as "the capacity to create and communicate a view of the desired state of affairs that induces commitment among those working in the organization."[26]

Create, communicate, and *commitment* are the key words. Organizational study after study, whether that organization is in the public sector or the private sector, a school or a business, reveals that leaders have vision. Bennis[27] found that the key ingredient among executives of highly successful organizations was "compelling vision."

Others, both before and after the Bennis inquiry, have found much the same thing. Norris,[28] for example, called it "creative leadership" and wrote,

> Leadership is creative to the extent that the leader:
>
> - Has a wide knowledge of educational theory and principles
> - Possesses the ability to analyze current situations in light of what should be
> - Can identify problems
> - Can conceptualize new avenues for change

She continued, "Creative leadership requires that the leader make full use of the analytical as well as the intuitive mind."[29] Visionary leaders ask such questions as: Who are the human beings that inhabit the school setting? What are the needs of these individuals? What unique problems face them as they seek to bring meaning to their lives? Vision, then, is asking questions about what might be, standing for something, making certain others know what that "thing" is, and determining appropriate courses of action for getting to expressed goals. Unfortunately, vision is an uncommon quality.

Shared Vision and Authority

Increasingly important is the notion of *shared vision* and the part that the principal plays in fostering the empowerment of others. Commitment to any endeavor is strengthened greatly when others have the freedom to express their own visions of what should be and are encouraged to contribute their unique talents and ideas to the resolution of important issues that concern them. The principal encourages responsibility by allowing the autonomy and authority to match the task.

Contrasting the Transactional and Transformational Leader

In his classic work, *Leadership*,[30] Burns coined the terms *transactional* and *transformational* leadership. These two leadership approaches are, from his perspective, completely different styles that have little to do with each other. He sees these styles as being opposite ends of a continuum, with the leader having certain dispositions that governed their style. The transactional leader operates from a power base of rewards and punishments and endeavors to gain the cooperation of followers on an "exchange" basis. Little personal commitment results from this exchange, since it is dependent on merely understanding the duties and making sure they are accomplished as directed. Leadership in this sense is viewed as a function of organizational position. It is concerned with reacting to presented problems by orchestrating people and tasks to accomplish stated goals. Viewed from this perspective, the school principal focuses on tightly coupled objectives, curriculum, teaching strategies, and evaluation. The teacher is viewed as a "laborer" with administration determining not only the "what," but the "how." The machine metaphor is very much in place.

Transformational leadership, on the other hand, inspires others toward collaboration and interdependence as they work toward a purpose to which they are deeply committed. It is a leadership style based on influence and is accomplished when leaders "delegate and surrender power *over* people and events in order to achieve power over accomplishments and goal achievement."[31] Sergiovanni has referred to transformational leadership as a "value-added" approach, since the focus is on a tightly coupled purpose that determines the "why" rather than the "what" and "how." The teacher is seen as a "craftsman, professional, or artist" rather than laborer,[32] with the organizational context being organistic or brain metaphor oriented. Foster[33] agrees with Burns[34] that these two styles are cut from a different cloth; yet there are others who view the skills as being closely related and building on the other.

Representative of those who see this connection is Bass[35] who has presented a first- and second-order change theory. It is Bass's contention that leaders must manage before they can lead. During first-order change, the leader is concerned with understanding subordinates' needs, providing them appropriate rewards for their contributions, and helping them clarify the connection between their goals and those of the organization. It is only after this is accomplished, Bass suggests, that the leader really inspires others to greater values awareness, encourages their commitment to the goals of the organization, or fosters their personal or professional growth. It is during this later stage that the leader becomes transformational.

The question now becomes: Where does transformational leadership take place? Are all persons in leadership positions transformational leaders? Is only the "designated leader," or the school principal, a transformational leader? Is transformational leadership equated with school effectiveness as determined by stated goals and objectives? Is it possible to be a transformational leader and not manage?

These questions become fertile ground for debate. Both Sergiovanni[36] and Foster[37] have provided a perspective. In Sergiovanni's model of the effective instructional leader (discussed in Chapter 2 of this text), a continuum of leadership skills is presented. The lower three skills—technical, human, and educational—are viewed as basic skills for determining competence as a leader. In other words, these are the necessary skills for good management of the organizational setting and establishment of the basic foundation for effective educational productivity. A school principal would need to attend to all of these skills in adequate fashion to be considered competent; to do less would denote incompetence. The highest two skills—symbolic and cultural—need to be in place before a principal is considered effective (or, in our terminology, "transformational"). This hierarchy is reflective of the theory expressed by Bass[38] and suggests that if an individual is to be transformational *within the principalship role,* he or she must, in fact, have in place a foundation of good management practice to do so. To be an effective symbolic and cultural principal-leader assumes that the foundation of competent management is already in place. However, as Burns suggested, "Leadership is *not merely* a managerial tool."[39]

Foster takes transformational leadership beyond the role of the principal by suggesting that transformational leadership results from "mutual negotiations and shared leadership roles."[40] He continued, "Leadership cannot occur without followership and many times the two are exchangeable. . . . Leaders normally have to negotiate visions and ideas with potential followers, who may in turn become leaders themselves, renegotiating the particular agenda."[41] Certainly, Sergiovanni's[42] notion of the four substitutes for leadership that will be discussed in Chapter 2 supports this idea.

Ethical Responsibilities of Transformational Leadership

Foster suggests that transformational leaders operate from four important characteristics. First, they are *educative*. They help the organization learn. They assist organizational members in important discoveries:

- What has taken place in the school's history?
- What guiding values have helped to shape its culture?
- What is the school's purpose?
- How is power distributed throughout the organization?

Second, they are *critical*. They help organizational members examine current conditions and question their appropriateness for all individuals. They encourage individuals to make a difference in the situations that seem unjust or inappropriate by taking action in positive ways.

Third, transformational leaders are *ethical*. They encourage self-reflection, democratic values, and moral relationships. They strive to influence people to higher levels of values consciousness.

Fourth, they are *transformative*. Their leadership is aimed toward social change through elevation of human consciousness. They seek to build a community of individuals who believe they can make a difference.

THE PRINCIPAL: THE LEADER WITHIN THE ROLE

Developing Leadership Artistry

Leadership is an *art!* Kouzes and Posner see it as a performing art and believe that "in the art of leadership, the artist's instrument is the *self*."[43] Leadership development, then, according to Kouzes and Posner, is "a process of self-discovery and development."[44] Others, such as Barnard, have echoed this idea by suggesting that leadership "is a matter of art rather than science,"[45] that it is "aesthetic and moral rather than logical,"[46] and that it consists of feeling, judgment, sense, balance, and appropriateness. Still others, such as Selznick, believe that "the art of the creative leader is the art of institution building."[47]

Just how is leadership artistry developed and what pathway does self-discovery take? It is suggested by these researchers and others that personal awareness includes an understanding of what one values and believes and not only an affirmation of values, but a confidence in one's ability to persuade others to embrace those values and to reach toward higher purposes. This confidence is the result of careful analysis of one's own strengths and weaknesses in the leadership arena. This analysis begins with an understanding of just what one does believe and why.

Clarifying Values

Values do not just happen. They are influenced over time by the experiences that one encounters, by what one learns and sees modeled, and by what is rewarded or reinforced in one's personal and professional life. As we will discuss later in this text, an individual might enter an organization with a certain set of values that are reinforced by the organizational context. Within a compatible context, the individual would feel validated and surer in his or her position relative to those values. There would be a comfortable feeling that he or she was a real part of the group.

In another situation, the individual might possess a set of values quite different from the values of the organization. The organizational context might cause the individual to relinquish his or her true values in favor of the values voiced by the group—or to conform. In many cases, this might be an actual lowering of standards on the part of the individual. Similarly, the individual might recognize the differences in values that exist between the organization and himself or herself but choose to remain with the organization and try to influence its members to embrace those values of a higher order. In that case, the individual's personal values would be strengthened and the influence of leadership would be felt. Leaders and followers in that sense "raise one another to higher levels of values consciousness."[48]

Leadership as Philosophy in Action

When school principals enter their schools, they bring with them their values, beliefs, and philosophies. Principals lead from their values! The impact of the principal's values is felt, and the positive influence of that impact is dependent on the quality of those values, the clarity with which those values are held, and the strength of the commitment to those values. Earlier, we discussed the individual and organizational (nomothetic) expectations for the various roles within an organization. Regardless of the organization's expectations for the role of "principal," or the expectations held by various individuals or subgroups within the organization, the individual within the role must weigh his or her own expectations against those demands and determine how the role will be shaped. What the principal personally values gives form and substance to the role of principal.

Values shape the direction of leadership, provide the distinctive character of that leadership, and determine the passion that influences others to follow. Leadership, then, becomes a relationship forged on the anvil of respect and personal regard. Leadership is nurtured by the values that ultimately unite individuals, from however dissonant their perspectives.

The principal's values impact the school in two very important ways. First, the principal's values determine *preservation and guardianship.*[49] His or her values will determine what he or she allows to remain stable or unchanged. The principal's values will, likewise, determine what he or she becomes committed to change.

Second, the principal's values will determine the *nature of transformation and change.* His or her values will determine what he or she recognizes as being unjust or inappropriate for the human beings they serve, the nature of the problems he or she identifies and seeks to solve, the quality of his or her critique (or questioning of current practice), and the direction that change will take.[50] Norris stated that "values shape personal dreams and visions"[51] and Kouzes and Posner suggested that these values are "the guiding principles in our lives with respect to personal and social ends we desire and with respect to moral conduct and personal competence such as honesty and imagination."[52]

Espoused Values and Values in Use

Values are both espoused, or voiced, and demonstrated in one's actions. What principals believe is their *espoused theory*. What they demonstrate that they believe through their actions is their *theory in use*.[53] It is important that there be congruence between what principals *say* is important, or that is valued, and what they actually *do* or demonstrate is important by their actions. A congruence between these two is the basis of leader *credibility*.[54] A discrepancy between what leaders say and do leads to mistrust and an inability to influence the behavior of others.

Leadership is dependent on credibility! Credibility, then, has everything to do with values, but to fully appreciate this fact, it is important that one has a clear understanding of the nature of values. The following section will present a model for interpreting the level of one's value consciousness.

Leadership from a Values Perspective

The values that an individual leader possesses are placed on a continuum that ranges from a transactional style (or managerial mindset) to a transformational (leadership) one. In understanding how values shape these perspectives, it is helpful to consider values development as classified through the work of Hall.[55] In Hall's view, values acquisition is a developmental process that proceeds through six distinct cycles of growth:

- *The primal cycle* characterized by security, self-interest, and physical survival
- *The familial cycle* symbolized by the family as protector and legitimate authority
- *The institutional cycle* focused on adherence to legitimate authority symbolized in institutions
- *The intrapersonal cycle* focused on the self and individual values as the basis of interpretation
- *The communal/collaborative cycle* defined by clear personal values emphasizing humanistic concerns
- *The mystical cycle* characterized by integration of the individual, self-actualization, and justice

These six cycles have been reconfigured into four *phases of consciousness*. Hall has suggested that movement from one phase to the next requires that an individual become conscious (aware) of that stage by (1) understanding the world from that perspective, (2) perceiving himself or herself as functioning within that world, or (3) having human needs he or she wishes to satisfy within that phase. A stage of values consciousness is governed not only by the goals or needs the individual seeks to satisfy within that phase but also by the means, or skills, necessary to actualize those goals.

Hall has theorized that full consciousness at each phase does not emerge unless the means are in place to support those goals. This fact becomes a major implication for leadership enactment and the shaping of organizational context. A leader will only lead to the level of his or her phase of consciousness. An organizational context will reflect the level of values consciousness of its members and will be elevated only as those individuals are given the skills, or means, to fulfill those goals.

Hall's Phases of Consciousness

Phase One. The major emphasis at this phase of consciousness is survival. The individual is highly motivated to remain safe and to preserve things in a stable, secure manner. There is a great need during this phase to ensure that life is predictable and that it conforms to known patterns. During periods of increased stress or uncertainty, there is enhanced need for self-preservation and less tolerance for ambiguity. Since structure, predictability, and control give the illusion of "safety," principals who operate from this phase of values consciousness often seek comfort in the tried and true and find the machine metaphor compatible with their needs. Individuals at this phase of consciousness are consumed with their own self-interests and have less empathy for others.

Phase Two. The need for social interaction becomes prevalent at this stage of consciousness. The individual reaches beyond his or her need for self-preservation to appreciate the needs of others. There is an increasing desire to belong at this stage—not only within family and social groups but also to organizations. Organizational affiliation is viewed as adherence to rules, policies, and procedures; therefore, an administrator at this phase strives to operate "by the book," yet at the same time project a caring, considerate attitude toward subordinates. Since schools are viewed as "families," there is emphasis on collegiality and a desire to foster a sense of belonging among the staff.

Phase Three. Individuality emerges during this phase as a creative response to life that takes the place of institutional conformity. During this phase, the individual begins to become his or her "own person." There is increased motivation for self-actualization and a more genuine recognition of the dignity and worth of others. Empathy and a deeper respect for human life are present. Leaders at this phase of values consciousness find the organistic metaphor a compatible view of organizational context. They emphasize the uniqueness of individuals and their need for continued development.

Phase Four. Individuals at this phase begin to think from a more global, systemic perspective. There is an increased desire for harmony, community, and the integration of values, beliefs, and ideas. Principals begin to view the world beyond the borders of the school with a deepening appreciation for the larger community and for societal issues. Principals take on a proactive stance, becoming more involved in the critical questioning of current practice. There is a transformational aspect to leadership that seeks to make a difference in education and in the lives of others. A strong desire to build community in its truest sense emerges.

Implications for Leadership Development

Through personal reflection, leaders encounter their beliefs, strengthen their convictions, and challenge their thinking toward higher levels of moral commitment. Self-awareness initiates this developmental journey that proceeds from values awareness, to aspiration, to action. Each step in development of values consciousness provides a deeper understanding of one's moral responsibility to others and enables a stronger foundation for inspiring others to contribute to an organization's responsiveness to human needs. Truly leadership does become a transformational process.

A Backward Glance

As one considers the nature of present-day theories of leadership, it is important to take a brief look backward at some of the evolving concepts of leadership that have helped to shape one's current thought. We will begin our backward glance with a look at leadership beginning some 50 years ago. That exploration will take us to the present-day focus on transformational leadership.

THE LEADERSHIP BACKGROUND

It is useful to consider the plethora of research about leadership and management in work organizations that has been conducted in the near past and in both the private and public sectors. This research base has much implication to the practice of school administration and specifically to the principal.

Historical Perspective

The Ohio State Leadership Studies. An array of leadership studies was conducted at The Ohio State University in the early 1950s. Individuals in various kinds of organizations were asked to describe their leaders. Two primary behavior categories ultimately were uncovered and these were labeled *consideration* and *initiating structure*.[56]

Consideration was defined as the degree to which a leader acts in a warm supporting way and shows concern for subordinates. Being approachable, accepting of suggestions, looking out for the welfare of subordinates, consulting with subordinates before making decisions, and other similar qualities comprise this category.

Initiating structure was defined as the degree to which leaders define and structure their own roles and the roles of subordinates toward the attainment of the organization's formal goals. Examples of specific behaviors in this category include criticizing unsatisfactory work, letting subordinates know what is expected of them, maintaining definite standards of performance, offering new approaches to problems, and other similar qualities.

The Michigan Studies. Additional leadership studies were conducted at the University of Michigan, also in the 1950s, largely under the direction of Rensis Likert and the Institute of Social Research.[57, 58] Behavioral comparisons of ineffective and effective managers revealed that effective managers had a task orientation that generally focused on such administrative functions as planning, coordinating, and facilitating work. This did not occur at the expense of good interpersonal relations, however. Effective managers were more likely to treat subordinates considerately and to allow some degree of autonomy in deciding how to conduct their work and at what pace. Importantly though, effective managers set high performance goals for subordinates and used group methods of supervision. Also discovered was that high morale (defined as the total satisfaction a worker gets from a work situation) does *not* necessarily result in high productivity. However, the kind of managerial practice that results in high productivity also tends to result in high morale.[59] High morale may describe what Blake and Mouton (to follow) call a 1,9 management style orientation characterized by great concern for people but with no evident thrust toward productivity.

Blake and Mouton. Conceptually related to, but independent from, both The Ohio State leadership studies and the Michigan leadership studies is the work of Blake and Mouton. Their concept resulted in the Managerial Grid.© The grid is based on two dimensions (attitudes) about the workplace: *concern for people* and *concern for production.* Concern for people closely parallels the concept of *consideration* and concern for production parallels *initiating structure.*

The concept is useful for analyzing what managerial attitudes might get in the way of the best job getting done. Is there balance? Is one or the other of the dimensions being emphasized to the exclusion or near exclusion of the other? Is neither emphasized enough? The answers to these questions permit the development of managerial training programs that are skill focused and developmental, so that a managerial deficiency that will deter the effectiveness of the organization can be, if not totally corrected, at least positively addressed.[60]

From Traditional Leadership Theory to Contingency Theory

As supportive of effective schools research findings as are the leadership studies at Ohio State and Michigan and the research applications of Blake and Mouton, none of these take into account the difference in situations demanding leadership nor the expectations and normative behavior of subordinates and superordinates. The dominant trend in leadership theory over the past several years has been toward the development of a situational or "contingency" theory of leadership. Fiedler's work is basic to this trend.[61]

Fiedler's Contingency Model. The reason it is difficult to describe the ideal leader may be best clarified by the seminal work of Fiedler. His model suggests that there is a situational nature to effective leader behavior. It helps explain why some studies have shown that a highly directive, task-oriented leadership style promoted effective work group performance, while other studies have revealed that a nondirective, "human relations" orientation worked best, and still others found some sort of balance resulted in high performance.[62]

From a large number of studies, Fiedler concluded that the interaction of three factors will determine leader effectiveness:

1. *Leader-Member Relations*. This refers to the leader's feeling of being accepted by subordinates. A leader's authority depends at least partly on the acceptance of the group to be led. A person who is respected by and inspires loyalty in the work group needs few of the vestments of rank to get the group to perform the task at hand in a willing and competent manner.

2. *Task Structure*. This is the degree to which the subordinate's tasks are routine and precisely defined as opposed to being relatively unstructured and loosely defined. (On a continuum of "tight" to "loose," one could posit that teaching would tend to be on the loose end.)

3. *Power Position*. This refers to the power inherent in the leadership position and includes the means available to the leader from those at higher administrative levels and authority. This is the extent to which the leader possesses reward, coercive, and legitimate power. The ability to hire, discipline, transfer, provide salary increases, and other less direct rewards and punishments affect the power position.

In measuring the style of the leader, Fiedler returned to the product of The Ohio State University studies. He used two styles as his points of measurement: task oriented (initiating structure) and relationship oriented (consideration). Fiedler's research indicated that the behavior of effective leaders varies according to the nature of three contingency variables: leader-group relations, the degree of structure in the task, and the power position of the leader.

Fiedler hypothesized that the nature of group productivity resulted from a match between leader orientation (task or relationship orientation) and the favorableness of the particular work situation (a mix of personal traits, group beliefs, and situational variables). He concluded that one could not simply speak of effective and ineffective leadership practices, but only of effective and ineffective practices in one situation or another.[63]

Although his methodologies and conclusions have been criticized by some, a great contribution of Fiedler's work is his questioning that there is one best way to lead. Fiedler has established the usefulness of the contingency approach to the study of leadership. He provided an expanded way of thinking about the need for varying leader behavior and introduced the notion that successful leaders will manifest more *or* less in the way of relationship- and task-oriented behavior given certain situations and certain kind of work groups. However, the theory really doesn't have very much to say about how a leader ought to go about successfully managing a work group. A contingency concept advanced by Hersey and Blanchard does examine the specific behavior that is most likely to result in successful problem solving and group productivity.[64]

Hersey and Blanchard and Situational Leadership. Four distinct leadership styles are posited by Hersey and Blanchard: telling, selling, participating, and delegating. Each is viewed as an appropriate style depending on the particulars in the situation. The key variable in the situation is what Hersey and Blanchard call the "maturity" of the work group, which is defined as the readiness to tackle the task facing the group. (Readiness might include attitude as well as ability.)

Groups that are highly mature respond best to delegation; immature groups respond to a high degree of direction (telling). As the group grows in maturity, the leader is most effective next by selling the group; then, as greater maturity occurs, by engaging in practices that call for group participation. Hersey and Blanchard's guiding principle is that as subordinates acquire greater experience, ability, and commitment to the tasks that confront them, better productivity will be attained through greater sharing of decision making. This concept seems reasonable and is consistent with other theories, in that power sharing through delegation and participation should result in greater productivity in groups that have demonstrated mature attitudes and high skills.

The Hersey-Blanchard model basically suffers from an inadequate research base. Neither the model itself nor any of its components has been validated. Perhaps the best-researched contingency model has been that of Robert House's path-goal theory of leadership.[65]

Path-Goal Theory of Leadership. This theory was expounded by House in 1971 and refined and extended by a number of others in subsequent years in an effort to explain how a leader's behavior makes a difference in the motivation and the satisfaction of his or her subordinates. House wrote, "The motivational function of the leader consists of increasing personal payoffs to subordinates for work-goal attainment, and making the path to those payoffs easier to travel by clarifying it, reducing roadblocks and pitfalls, and increasing the opportunities for personal satisfaction en route."[66]

The effect of leader behavior on satisfaction and motivation to work toward organizationally productive ends depends on the situation. Characteristics of subordinates, such as ability and personality, and characteristics of the organizational environment, such as type of task and importance of the work, are the key determinates. Situational variables also determine the kind of leadership behavior preferred by the work group.

House identified four categories of leader behavior.[67] *Supportive leadership* is leadership that includes giving consideration to the needs of subordinates, displaying concern for their welfare, and creating a friendly climate in the work unit. *Directive leadership* lets subordinates know what they are expected to do, gives specific guidance, asks subordinates to follow rules and procedures, formulates schedules, and coordinates the work. *Participative leadership* is consultative and takes subordinates' opinions and suggestions into account when making decisions. *Achievement-oriented leadership* sets challenging goals, seeks performance improvements, emphasizes excellence in performance, and shows confidence that subordinates will attain high standards. It is more than interesting to note how closely this combination of categories relates to certain correlates of leadership in effective schools: climate, clear expectations, emphasis on excellence, and decision-making practices.

Leader behavior has an impact on subordinate performance in several ways. In situations where there is role ambiguity and/or task ambiguity, directive leadership that clarifies the roles and tasks will increase motivation and performance because it will increase the expectancy of subordinates that their efforts will lead to higher performance.

In situations where the tasks to be accomplished are tedious, boring, or stressful, supportive leadership behaviors are most likely to increase satisfaction and performance. By being considerate, offering kind words and moral and physical support, and trying to minimize the negative aspects of the work that needs to get done, the leader makes the situation more tolerable.

Achievement-oriented leadership results in subordinates who have more confidence in their ability to attain high goals, and thus increases the likelihood that there will be a serious and sustained effort. House described two conditions that make participative leadership appropriate: (1) when subordinates are assigned a challenging task that is also ambiguous and (2) in other tasks when subordinates have a high need for independence or are "antiauthoritarian" in their personalities.

SUMMARY

School leadership is best understood in relation to the context in which that leadership takes place. In this chapter we have explored organizational context based on the metaphors of machines, organisms, and brains. Through that exploration, we have examined individual and group expectations and the part they play in determining the nature of the principalship as well as the principal's role within that context.

The concepts of transactional and transformational leadership have also been explored as a way of understanding the importance of principals' values and ethical responsibilities within their role. We have stressed the importance of principals becoming reflective leaders concerned with their own development and leadership artistry.

ACTIVITIES

1. Review Case Study 1 at the end of this book. Apply the concepts expressed in this chapter. What implications do the various views of transformational leadership have for managing and leading? What relevance has social systems theory? Which, if any, of Morgan's metaphors might describe the organization in the case?
2. Turn to the ISLLC Standards found in Appendix B. Review the knowledge, dispositions, and performances listed with Standards One and Five. Reflect on which of the standard items relate directly to the material presented in this chapter. Do these Standards better reflect the concepts of transformational or transactional leadership? Identify one knowledge area, one disposition, and one performance from each standard to link directly to a concept or idea discussed in Chapter 1.

ENDNOTES

1. William Foster, "Toward a Critical Theory of Educational Administration" in *Leadership and Organizational Culture,* ed. T. J. Sergiovanni and J. E. Corbally (Urbana: University of Illinois Press, 1984).

2. *Webster's Dictionary.*

3. Garath Morgan, *Images of Organizations* (Cambridge, MA: Sage, 1986).

4. Seymour Sarason, *Revisiting the Culture of the School and the Problem of Change* (New York: Teachers College Press, 1996), p. 27.

5. Thomas Sergiovanni, "Leadership as Cultural Expression" in *Leadership and Organizational Culture,* ed. T. J. Sergiovanni and J. E. Corbally (Urbana: University of Illinois Press, 1984). Sergiovanni presents a rationale for platform building and discusses its importance in helping future leaders develop and clarify their own personal beliefs.

6. Sarason, *Revisiting the Culture of the School and the Problem of Change.*

7. In its 1983 report, *A Nation at Risk,* the National Commission on Excellence in Education challenged the schools to overcome what they saw as a "rising tide of mediocrity."

8. The Carnegie Foundation for the Advancement of Teaching, *An Imperiled Generation: Saving Urban Schools* (Princeton, NJ: Princeton University Press, 1988). This report discusses the negative environmental factors within school settings that hinder learning in the urban areas.

9. The National Policy Board (NPBEA) is sponsored and supported by the Association of Colleges for Teacher Education, Association of School Business Officials, Council of Chief State School Officers, National Association of Secondary School Principals, National Association of Elementary School Principals, American Association of School Administrators, Association for Supervision and Curriculum Development, National Boards Association, National Council of Professors of Educational Administration, and University Council for Educational Administration.

10. The Interstate School Leaders Licensure Committee is a program of the Council of Chief State School Officers. Representatives from 24 state education agencies and various professional associations drafted the standards that have been developed by this committee. They were written to be compatible with the new National Council for the Accreditation of Teacher Education (NCATE) *Curriculum Guidelines for School Administration.*

11. Karl Weick, "The Significance of Culture," in *Organizational Culture,* ed. P. Frost, L. Moore, M. Lewis, C. Lundenberg, and J. Martin (Beverly Hills: Sage, 1985).

12. Chris Arygris, *Reasoning, Learning and Action* (San Francisco: Jossey-Bass, 1982).

13. Ibid.

14. Morgan, *Images of Organizations,* p. 88.

15. Ibid.

16. Jacob W. Getzels and Egon G. Guba, "Social Behavior and the Administrative Process," *School Review 65* (Winter 1957): 423–441.

17. Ibid.

18. Charles Achilles, John Keedy, and Reginald High, "The Political World of the Principal," in *The Principal as Leader,* ed. Larry W. Hughes (New York: Macmillan, 1994).

19. NASSP has available a variety of descriptive materials and research reports, including validation studies. Write to NASSP, 1904 Association Drive, Reston, VA 22091. The NASSP process is designed for the K–12 spectrum; the skills identified are generic and applicable for elementary as well as secondary school principals.

20. NAESP has developed a similar set of skills for elementary school principals.

21. In the NASSP there are actually 12 discrete skills and attributes: problem analysis, judgment, organizational ability, decisiveness, leadership, sensitivity, stress tolerance, oral and written communication, personal motivation, educational values, and range of interests. What is described here are the more general categories of skills.

22. The National Policy Board distinguished between the academic knowledge base and the professional knowledge base by organizing subject content into work-relevant patterns that make expert knowledge functional.

23. Foster, "Toward a Critical Practice of Leadership."

24. Arygris, *Reasoning Learning and Action.*

25. Foster, "Toward a Critical Theory of Educational Administration."

26. Warren Bennis, "Transformation Power and Leadership," in *Leadership and Organizational Culture,* ed. T. J. Sergiovanni and J. E. Corbally (Urbana: University of Illinois Press, 1984).

27. Ibid.

28. Cynthia Norris, "Developing Visionary Leaders for Tomorrow's Schools," *NASSP Bulletin 74* (May 1990): 6–10.

29. Ibid., p. 7.

30. Burns, *Leadership.*

31. Ibid.

32. Linda Darling-Hammond, "Teacher Evaluation in the Organizational Context: A Review of the Literature," *Review of Educational Research 53,* no. 3 (Fall 1983): 285–328.

33. Foster, "Toward a Critical Theory of Educational Administration."

34. Burns, *Leadership.*

35. Bernard Bass, *Leadership and Performance Beyond Expectations* (New York: Free Press, 1985).

36. Thomas Sergiovanni, "Leadership and Excellence in Schooling," *Educational Leadership 41* (February 1984): 4–13.

37. Foster, "Toward a Critical Theory of Educational Administration."

38. Bernard Bass and Bruce Avolio, eds. *Improving Organizational-Effectiveness through Transformational Leadership* (Thousand Oaks, CA: Sage, 1993).

39. Burns, *Leadership.*

40. Foster, "Toward a Critical Theory of Educational Administration."

41. Ibid., p. 42.

42. T. J. Sergiovanni, *Moral Leadership: Getting to the Heart of School Improvement* (San Francisco: Jossey-Bass, 1992).

43. James Kouzes and Barry Posner, *The Leadership Challenge* (San Francisco: Jossey-Bass, 1987).

44. Ibid.

45. Chester I. Barnard, *The Functions of the Executive* (Cambridge, MA: Harvard University Press, 1938).

46. Ibid.

47. Peter Selznick, *Leadership and Administration: A Sociological Interpretation* (New York: Harper and Row, 1957).

48. Burns, *Leadership.*

49. Christopher Hodgkinson, *The Philosophy of Leadership* (Oxford, England: Basil Blackwell Publisher Limited, 1983).

50. Ibid.

51. Cynthia Norris, "Cultivating Creative Cultures," in *Principal as Leader,* 2nd ed. ed. Larry W. Hughes (Columbus, OH: Merrill, 1994).

52. Kouzes and Posner, *The Leadership Challenge.*

53. Ibid.

54. Kouzes and Posner, *The Leadership Challenge.*

55. Brian Hall, *The Development of Consciousness: A Confluent Theory of Values* (New York: Paulist Press, 1986).

56. Andrew W. Halpin and B. J. Winer, "A Factorial Study of the Leader Behavior Descriptions," in *Leader Behavior in Description and Measurement,* ed. R. M. Stogdill and A. E. Coons (Columbus, OH: Bureau of Business Research, The Ohio State University, 1957).

57. Rensis Likert, *New Patterns of Management* (New York: McGraw-Hill, 1961).

58. Rensis Likert, *The Human Organization: Its Management and Value* (New York: McGraw-Hill, 1967).

59. Rensis Likert, *Motivation: The Core of Management* (New York: American Management Association, Personnel Series #155, 1953). For a highly specific application of Likert to school administration, see Thomas Sergiovanni and R. J. Starratt, *Emerging Patterns of Supervision: Human Perspectives,* 3rd ed. (New York: McGraw-Hill, 1988).

60. Robert R. Blake and Jane S. Mouton, *The Managerial Grid III: The Key to Leadership Excellence* (Houston: Gulf Publishing, 1985). See also Blake and Mouton, *The Managerial Grid* (Houston: Gulf Publishing, 1964); and Blake and Mouton, *Corporate Excellence through Grid Organization Development* (Houston: Gulf Publishing, 1968).

61. Fred E. Fiedler, *A Theory of Leadership Effectiveness* (New York: McGraw-Hill, 1967).

62. Fred E. Fiedler, *Leadership* (New York: General Learning Press, University Program Module Series, 1971). Readers interested in pursuing this further may find the work of Hersey and Blanchard helpful: Paul Hersey and Kenneth H. Blanchard, *Management of Organizational Behavior,* 3rd ed. (New York: McGraw-Hill, 1977).

63. Fiedler, *Leadership.* See also F. E. Fiedler and M. M. Chemers, *Leadership and Effective Management* (Glencoe, IL: Scott, Foresman, 1974).

64. Paul Hersey and Kenneth Blanchard, *Management of Organizational Behavior: Utilizing Human Resources,* 4th ed. (Englewood Cliffs, NJ: Prentice-Hall, 1982).

65. Robert J. House, "A Path-Goal Theory of Leader Effectiveness," *Administrative Science Quarterly 16* (1971): 321–338.

66. Ibid., p. 324.

67. R. J. House and T. R. Mitchell, "Path-Goal Theory of Leadership," *Contemporary Business 3* (Fall 1974): 81–91.

SELECTED READINGS

Bass, Bernard M. *Transformational Leadership Development* (Palo Alto, CA: Consulting Psychologist Press, 1990).

Burns, James McGregor. "Prologue." In *Leadership* (New York: Harper, 1978).

DePree, Max. *Leadership Is an Art* (New York: Dell Publishing, 1990).

Fisher, James L. "Reflections on Transformational Leadership." *Educational Record 75,* no. 3 (Summer 1994): 54, 60–65.

Foster, William. *Paradigms and Promises: New Approaches to Educational Administration* (Buffalo, NY: Prometheus Books, 1986).

Gardner, John W. *On Leadership* (New York: Free Press, 1990).

Greenleaf, Robert K. "Servant as Leader," in *Servant Leadership: A Journey into the Nature of Legitimate Power and Greatness* (New York: Paulist Press, 1977), pp. 7–48.

Hughes, Larry W. *The Principal as Leader* (New York: Macmillan, 1999).

Keedy, John L. "Creative Insubordination: Autonomy for School Improvement by Successful High School Principals." *The High School Journal 76,* no. 1 (September 1992): 17–23.

Maxcy, Spencer. *Educational Leadership: A Critical Pragmatic Perspective* (New York: Bergin and Garvey, 1991).

Morgan, Gareth. *Images of Organization* (Newbury Park, CA: Sage, 1986).

Murphy, Joseph. *The Landscape of Leadership Preparation: Reframing the Education of School Administrators* (Newbury Park, CA: Corwin Press, 1992).

Murphy, Joseph, and Karen Seashore-Louis. *Reshaping the Principalship: Insights from Transformational Efforts* (Thousand Oaks, CA: Corwin Press, 1994).

Nanus, Burt. *Visionary Leadership: Creating a Compelling Sense of Direction for Your Organization* (San Francisco: Jossey-Bass, 1992).

Senge, Peter. *The Fifth Discipline: The Art and Practice of the Learning Organization* (New York: Doubleday, 1990).

Sergiovanni, Thomas J. *Moral Leadership: Getting to the Heart of School Improvement* (San Francisco: Jossey-Bass, 1992).

Sergiovanni, Thomas J. *Value-Added Leadership: How to Get Extra-Ordinary Performance in Schools* (San Diego: Harcourt Brace Jovanovich, 1990).

Thompson, Scott E., ed. *Principals for Our Changing Schools: The Knowledge and Skill Base* (Fairfax, VA: National Policy Board for Educational Administration, 1993).

Wheatly, Margaret. *Leadership and the New Science* (San Francisco: Berrett-Koehler, 1992).

CHAPTER TWO

THE LEARNING COMMUNITY

Individuals are intricately interwoven into groups and groups are reflections of individuals. Individuals are supported, affirmed, and inspired in groups; they are transformed. In turn, individuals transform groups through their collective efforts and commitment to a meaningful purpose. Groups empower individuals; individuals empower groups. It is a reciprocal process known as COMMUNITY.

—C. Norris and B. Barnett[1]

The greatest challenge facing principals today is development. Individual development and organizational development are both part of this challenge. The two are not mutually exclusive, since each contributes to the growth of the other. In essence, the principal must be a nurturer, a challenger, a builder, and a catalyst for growth. But before a principal can inspire the growth and development of others, self-development must occur. In Chapter 1, we addressed the need for leader self-development by connecting personal awareness and growth to leadership artistry. This chapter focuses on ways that the school principal can employ leadership artistry to foster both individual and organizational growth.

A word closely related to the term *development* is *empowerment,* which means "to enable." We believe it is the responsibility of the school principal to ensure that conditions are set forth that will enable individuals and organizations to reach their highest potential. Although empowerment must come from within the individual person, the principal can ensure that the school offers a climate conducive to risk taking, personal contribution, and challenge so that all may be inspired to maximize their unique potential.

We take the position that the most conducive climate for inspiring individual and organizational development is the *learning organization.* In the following discussion, we build the concept of a *learning community* and talk about the conditions that facilitate its enactment.

LEARNING COMMUNITIES

Learning communities, or organizations, are concerned with growth and continuous self-renewal. A principal, then, is "responsible for *building organizations* where people are continually expanding their capabilities to shape their future—that is, leaders are responsible for learning."[2] Learning organizations never "fully arrive"; their self-actualized mode keeps them always searching for new possibilities and opportunities for growth. The characteristics of a learning organization are reflected in the brain metaphor discussed in Chapter 1. Not only does this context enable the assimilation and storage of past knowledge but it also generates new knowledge through the shared experiences, ideas, and perceptions of all group members. Each individual becomes a resource of knowledge for all others and the organization becomes a catalyst for thinking and learning.

Senge's Model

Senge has suggested that learning organizations are distinguished by five important qualities that provide their direction.[3] These qualities are:

Systems Thinking. The whole organization is made up of many parts; these parts form integrated subsystems that affect, and are affected by, each other. What happens in any one part of the organization impacts all other parts. Any decision has a ripple effect. In a learning organization there is a free flow of communication that assists the organization in the integration of knowledge and ideas.

Personal Mastery. Considered by Senge to be the cornerstone of the organization, this "spiritual foundation" is the collective commitment that gives purpose and passion to the work of the organization. It is the quality that gives individuals a sense of belonging and ownership to an organization.

Mental Models. Challenge assumptions! This characteristic encourages organizational members to question current practices, to search for discrepancies that may exist between what *is* and what *ought to be.* It encourages them, as well, to examine group expectations based on their underlying assumptions and to consider what is right and just for all.

Shared Values. Conceptualizing a school vision or sense of direction is a shared responsibility based on the shared values of the group. A vision that encompasses not only the vision of the leader but also the visions of individuals within the group is a vision that is more likely to ensure a pathway that will be followed.

Team Learning. New knowledge and understanding is achieved as individuals share their individual knowledge and experience with each other. Sharing information promotes new connections and new understandings that result in the construction of new knowledge. Perspectives are broadened as individuals see beyond the confines of their own classrooms and consider the organization as a whole.

But what are the implications for schools that do not operate as learning communities?

Disengagement

The opposite of empowerment is, of course, disengagement. There are many examples today of schools that foster a sense of isolation and disengagement that prevents the full development of individual and organizational potential. Many students, teachers, and administrators feel a sense of isolation and disconnectedness within the school setting. Examples of ways in which disengagement is expressed among students include underachievement, school drop-outs, truancy, behavior problems, drug abuse, and gang-related problems. There are also situations of students who just go through the motions and their educational experience is one of quiet desperation.

Among staff, there is evidence of a mass exodus of young teachers after their first year of teaching and burnout among more seasoned staff. Disengagement, too, is reflected in incompetence, lack of motivation, insecurity or lack of confidence, absenteeism, and resignation. Even among administrators, there is sometimes loneliness, isolation, school transfer, early retirement, and feelings of hopelessness.

Certainly, there is a great need in today's schools to build a sense of community! In understanding how to begin such a task, it is important to understand the nature of groups themselves. We will begin by considering their sociological and psychological nature.

Sociological and Psychological Nature of Groups

Groups have both a sociological and a psychological dimension. The sociological dimension is concerned with how the group itself develops and how it, in turn, interfaces with other groups. Applied to school settings, then, the school would be considered a group that contains within it many subgroups. Examples of these subgroups include departments, teams, schools within schools, study groups, cooperative learning groups, and others. Each subgroup interacts with the larger school, with other subgroups within the school, and with groups in the larger environment. In turn, the larger group, or the school, must interface with all the individual subgroups and with other schools, as well as with the umbrella group, or school district. Even beyond the parameters of the official school district, there are other groups that react with the school and its subgroups. Parent groups, support agencies, and state departments of education are but a few examples. Ways of working with many of these groups are discussed in the later chapters concerning public relations, special education, and legal issues.

The psychological nature of groups is concerned with the individual *within* the group. Of particular interest is the nature of the individual's development and how it is affected by the dynamics of the group. What factors create or impede individual development? Of interest, as well, is the impact that the individual, in turn, has on the group. How does the individual influence group development? How might the individual lessen the effectiveness of the total group? How might the group impede the development of the individual? All of these concerns are dealt with as we consider learning communities.

Reciprocity

A major concept that needs to be considered in understanding groups and individuals is the notion of *reciprocity*. Based on the word *reciprocate,* which means to "give back,"[4] it enables individuals and groups to respond in productive ways to the influence of each other. As one entity grows and is strengthened, it provides influence and opportunity to the other for mutual development. This is an exciting notion that lies at the center of what a learning community is all about. Researchers have explored the idea of reciprocity by examining groups, called *cohorts,*[5] which are becoming typical service-delivery models in educational administration programs throughout major universities. We discuss some major findings from this research and provide a cohort model that has implications for learning communities.

Cohort Model

The model shown in Figure 2.1 is the result of researchers'[6] work with cohorts across four university settings over a six-year period. This research suggests that cohorts that operate as true groups are characterized by four important qualities: interaction, purpose, interdependence, and individual growth. The first three qualities determine the

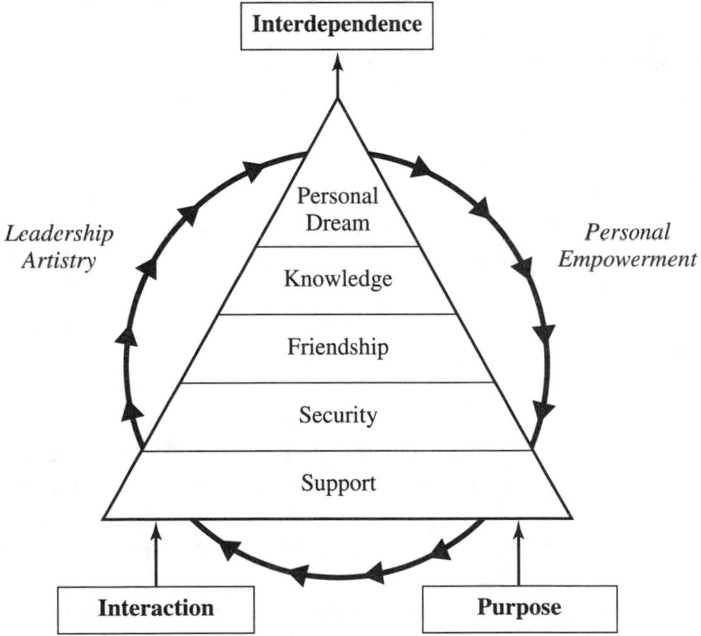

FIGURE 2.1 The Cohort Model

strength or cohesiveness of the group, or cohort. The outer points of the triangle demonstrate this interconnection. The inner portion of the triangle represents the individual development that tends to happen when groups become cohesive, interdependent entities. Individual development includes the following characteristics believed to occur in developmental fashion: support, security, friendship, knowledge, and realization of the personal dream. This model has implications for school settings and suggests that as individuals work in collegial fashion toward a common purpose, they build a learning community that supports and contributes to the individual growth of its members. To the degree that individuals develop, their growth fosters the continued development of the organization. It is truly a reciprocal process known as community.

Empowerment

Empowerment is "the act of increasing either one's own or other's influence over life's circumstances and decisions."[7] "It conveys a psychological sense of personal control or influence and a concern with social influence." Not only does empowerment concern personal influence but it also radiates from the individual a sense of self-actualized behavior that Maslow terms the *creative ego*.[8] These behaviors include:

1. *An Openness to Experience*. There is a lack of rigidity of beliefs, perceptions, and ideas. The individual has a greater tolerance for ambiguity and a receptive attitude toward possibilities.
2. *An Internal Locus of Evaluation*. There is an internal ability to self-evaluate and to rely on one's own judgment in determining personal worth.
3. *The Ability to Toy with Elements and Concepts*. There is a spontaneous exploration of thoughts and ideas as well as a creative response to situations.
4. *A Lack of Fear*. Self-acceptance and confidence are present. There is a greater willingness to venture forth and to try new ideas.

But what exactly can a principal do to enhance conditions that will facilitate such individual empowerment and, in turn, influence greater productivity within the organization? Rath has suggested three theories[9] as being the basis for fostering the empowerment of others.

First, is the theory of *needs*. As pointed out by such theorists as Maslow[10] and Alderfer,[11] emotional security is a basic need that provides a foundation for other higher-level needs. Emotional security is greatly dependent on the climate and conditions under which one works. Effective schools research is but one example of the bulk of literature supporting the need for a positive climate that allows for freedom of expression, risk taking, and exploration. Coleman[12] has discussed the important relationship between *interpersonal intelligence* and *academic achievement*, or professional success. According to Coleman, without the full development of emotional intelligence, academic growth will not be maximized.

This has tremendous implications for the school principal as the person who sets a positive and supportive tone for the organization by allowing others the freedom to risk and to grow. This need for empowerment is at all levels of the organization. It is just as true for the students in a school as for the staff.

As demonstrated by research on groups and cohorts, emotional security also develops most effectively when individuals feel that they have a support group. Learning communities seem to promote this sense of emotional security so necessary for empowerment to occur.

A second theory that supports empowerment is the *values* theory. We have already discussed the importance of principals becoming aware of their own values and visions for education. Without a clear purpose and clarification of one's values, it is difficult to lead with *credibility* and to have the vision required for leadership. It is important that teachers and students also have opportunities to clarify their values and to share in development of the vision and purpose for the school. Opportunities for discussion groups, thinking meetings,[13] and values clarification activities can enhance the students' emotional intelligence and provide a closer bond between the students and the school. In a later chapter on curriculum, we discuss this concept as part of humanistic curriculum theory. It is revisited again in the chapter on school discipline, when we consider the formation of advisory groups and other counseling services. Teachers, too, should be provided opportunities to explore their values through such avenues as platform development,[14] study groups, and work on school improvement plans.

Finally, the theory of *thinking* has a major impact on setting conditions for individual empowerment. Opportunities need to be provided for individuals to share ideas, to elaborate on their own thoughts, and to consider the ideas of others. The thinking/learning organization provides an atmosphere for free exchange of ideas facilitated through critical analysis of issues. Examples of ways in which school principals might inspire this analysis might be through total quality management (TQM), study groups, inquiry, and action based research efforts. All of these are examples of current staff-development delivery systems discussed in a later chapter.

As previously noted, students involved in cohort studies[15] reported an enhanced learning experience through the opportunities they received to share ideas and experiences with each other. How, then, can personal empowerment influence professional empowerment and, in turn, ensure more productive organizational development?

Teacher Empowerment

In considering the need for personal and professional empowerment within school settings, it is time that teachers are "seen in a new way."[16] McLaughlin and Yee[17] help put this notion into perspective by distinguishing between two views of a teacher's career: an institutional view and an individual view. Although the institutional view of a career is the all too common view, it is the responsibility of leaders to ensure that conditions are present that will enable teachers to view their careers from an individual, or more intrinsic perspective. In the following discussion, these views are considered.

Institutional versus Individual View of a Career

The *institutional view of a career* is one in which effectiveness in the profession is judged by self and or others as a measure of one's ability to climb various rungs of the bureaucratic ladder. Reflective of the machine metaphor, it allows the bureaucratic hierarchy to become the measurement of excellence in the profession. Basically, it places the teacher in a subservient role and reinforces compliance and followership. The hierarchy becomes the measure of achievement, and the value of "teacher" is viewed as secondary to being an administrator. It is an externally imposed measure of competence, which carries with it the ultimate goal of getting out of the classroom as quickly as one can move ahead. Moving ahead means basically conforming to a set pattern designed by someone higher in authority and perceived to be more knowledgeable than the teacher in matters of teaching and learning. Years ago, Argyris[18] cautioned organizations against such a perspective, as he suggested the pathway to adult maturity is greatly hampered in bureaucratic organizations that foster this orientation. Organizations keep individuals in an immature state by not allowing them the freedom to exercise their abilities and to make their own decisions.

In contrast to this view is the *individual view of a career* that is intrinsically motivating and encourages the teacher to seek development and opportunities for maximizing potential for its own sake—to become the most effective and contributing teacher that one is capable of becoming. It creates a joy in teaching and a far greater benefit to the profession than does the institutional view. The tendency toward *institutionalizing effectiveness* through the hierarchy has been recognized in efforts to recognize, support, and reward excellent performance in the classroom through such efforts as teacher career ladders and merit pay. This alone, however, will not change teachers' attitudes. The real efforts toward motivation must take place at the building level. Principals will need to recognize and encourage teacher potential and provide opportunities for growth and self-discovery. McLaughlin and Yee[19] suggested that individual effectiveness, satisfaction, and growth are cultivated by two factors: level of opportunity and level of capacity.

Level of opportunity is the real determiner of the degree to which individuals can develop their highest levels of professional competence. These writers consider three factors to be especially important in encouraging this development. The first of these factors is *stimulation.* Research paints the picture of the typical classroom teacher to be one of loneliness, isolation, and despair.[20] Little chance is provided for meaningful interchange of ideas, for camaraderie, or for cultivating a sense of belonging and contribution. The sense of collegiality is missing; the opportunity for collaboration is nonexistent. Through learning communities, principals can help eliminate many of the conditions that create disengagement for teachers.

Second, it is important that teachers receive *challenge.* It is not enough that teachers master a set of minimum competencies and then rest on their laurels. They need to be provided a chance to maximize their potential. Refining their strengths and developing artistry in their profession should become the focus. Often, these opportunities come by contributing to the growth of others through peer coaching or mentoring or by serving as a team leader. In any case, teachers are given opportunities that excite them and motivate their need for self-actualization. Certainly, the research by Maslow,[21] Herzberg,[22] Alderfer, and others suggest that it is the higher levels of need that motivate.

Finally, teachers need *feedback.* Confirmation of their successes reinforces not only their enthusiasm but also the refinement of their skills. Awareness of areas needing improvement provides teachers with information necessary to focus their efforts more successfully in later attempts. Often, principals have little time for intensive feedback sessions with teachers; therefore, they must provide opportunities for others within the school to assist. Professional development and teacher growth then become a joint responsibility.

Not only is it imperative that teachers be given levels of opportunity to increase their individual effectiveness, satisfaction, and growth but they also must be provided similar opportunities to increase their *level of capacity.* In other words, they must be given *power*. Such power includes not only their access to resources but also their ability to mobilize and utilize them, as well as the capability to influence the goals and directions of their institutions.[23] Lightfoot[24] suggested that such empowerment is a mindset, or point of view, that results in behaviors that provide autonomy to teachers to help solve campus issues and concerns. As McLaughlin and Yee stated, "Teachers with a sense of capacity tend to pursue effectiveness in the classroom, express commitment to the organization and career, and report a high level of professional satisfaction."[25]

There are leaders who grant teachers "professional authority" based on "seasoned craft knowledge and personal expertise"[26] rather than relying on traditional authority based on a traditional power base. Sergiovanni has referred to this practice as providing "substitutes for leadership."[27]

Substitutes for Leadership

Sergiovanni considered the use of substitutes for leadership to be a moral leadership process whereby individuals are given the authority and responsibility to apply their own professional knowledge to the decisions that relate to their own educational responsibilities. It is a concept that treats teachers as professionals who operate from an intrinsic, or individual, view of their career. It is a value-added approach, which is dependent on four basic "substitutes" for leadership being in place. They are:

1. *School Norms.* A shared covenant unites individual members in a committed effort to realize common values and beliefs.
2. *The Professional Ideal.* Organizational members accept their individual responsibility for student learning and for their own professional development.
3. *Collegiality.* Individuals collaborate in mutual support and yet assume individual responsibility for their own growth and leadership.
4. *Rewarding Work.* Work is meaningful and individuals feel accountable for their own success and the success of their students.

Instructional Leadership

Even though the original models of instructional leadership were driven by an effective schools concept that placed the school principal at the apex of learning, there is still relevance in considering the dimensions of that leadership as guides for establishing a shared leadership effort in which the principal serves as a *facilitator of the process*. An effective principal must exercise a series of specific instructional leadership behaviors.

Sergiovanni listed five leadership forces or behaviors available to a principal: technical, human, educational, symbolic, and cultural.[28]

Earlier writers organized administrative skills into three skill areas: technical, human, and conceptual. Sergiovanni expanded the third area, conceptual skills, into a series of behavioral forces described as educational, symbolic, and cultural.

Technical. Technical forces include being a good manager and applying good planning, organizing, coordinating, and controlling techniques to ensure optimum effectiveness of the organization. This includes such things as efficient office management practices, good scheduling techniques, and appropriate use of goals and objectives. Technical behaviors are basically the things that would ensure good, efficient management (about which we wrote in the first chapter).

Human Forces. These behaviors emphasize human relations skills, implementing good motivational techniques, and building good morale within the organization. The appropriate use of participatory management is an integral part of this behavior. These skills become major contributors to the climate of the school.

Educational Forces. These behaviors focus on the conceptual knowledge of education. Skills include the ability to diagnose educational problems, carry out the functions of clinical supervision, evaluate educational programs, help develop curriculum, implement staff-development activities, and develop good individual educational programs for individual children.

Symbolic Forces. These behaviors demonstrate to others those things that the leader believes important and of value to the organization. It involves *purposing*—"that continuous stream of actions by an organization's formal leadership which has the effect of inducing clarity, consensus, and commitment regarding the organization's basic purposes."[29]

Symbolic actions also can be expressed by principals modeling behavior they wish to emphasize. When a principal teaches a reading class, for instance, the importance of that activity is being emphasized by example. The key is the signal sent out by the principal regarding what is considered important.

Cultural Forces. The cultural leader functions as the "high priest" of the school. In this role, the leader seeks to strengthen the values and beliefs that make the school unique. He or she attempts to build traditions of the school around those things most highly valued. This is done by sharing with others what the school most values; by orientation of new members of the group—students, staff, and parents—to the values and beliefs of the organization; by telling stories of past glories to reinforce these traditions; or simply by explaining the standard operating procedure that is expected to be used. The cultural leader also publicly rewards those who reflect the desired culture and are its most ardent followers.

The cultural force of leadership bonds students, parents, and teachers together as true believers in the school. It takes on almost a religious fervor and a special sense of personal worth and importance grow out of membership in the organization. The cultural life of a school is "constructed" by someone, hopefully the instructional leaders of the school, and reflects a proper set of values, beliefs, and traditions that provide the foundation for school excellence. It is possible to have a strong or weak culture as measured by the amount of influence it has on participants.

HIGH-PERFORMANCE ORGANIZATIONS

Learning organizations and communities produce more effective high-performance schools. We turn our attention now to some of the characteristics of high-performing organizations. The phrase *high-performance organization* has now come into common usage. We first discovered it in an unfortunately obscure work by Marshall.[28] He described five conditions as characteristic of schools that could be labeled high performing:

1. A supportive outcome-based learning environment in which high standards of education, social development, and health are achieved by all learners
2. An outcome-based environment in which the system of instructional decision making and delivery responds to each learner's needs, interests, abilities, talents, styles of learning, and styles of living
3. An outcome-based environment in which curriculum assessment and human resources development are mutually reinforcing
4. An outcome-based environment in which the resources for learning are planned, focused, and managed by teams of educators with input from parents and other citizens
5. An outcome-based environment in which communication and community involvement are an integral part of the human resource and economic development of the community

Sergiovanni observed that a high-performance school and the principal therein deemphasizes "top down hierarchies and detailed scripts that tell people what to do." Rather, "one gets control by connecting people to outcomes rather than rules. . . . The key to effective leadership is to connect workers tightly to ends, but only loosely to means."[30]

Senge has offered a perspective and a structure for the improvement of the instructional processes.[31] His thesis is fundamental to principals who wish to lead their schools to new heights of performance. He described the skills needed to build what he labels "learning organizations." In such an organization, the leader's responsibility is to provide opportunities for the staff to engage in "generative" learning. As organizational members learn, their capabilities and perceptions expand. In a similar vein, Cordeiro pointed out, "An organization that generates learning is able to grow and develop in an infinite number of ways. Most organizations are adaptive but not also generative. Schools have become proficient at adapting [others'] models."[32]

Others' models or another school's problem solution may not in any way appropriately address problems and challenges confronting one's own school. Adaptation may simply result in frustration and in a local problem not solved. In the learning organization, people ask *why* a condition is the way it is and devise ways to address the "whys." The focus is on the problem, not on the symptoms.

Goal Setting

High-performing organizations are characterized by committed, energetic people who sit down together, examine problems confronting their organization, and figure out ways to overcome these problems. Tanner called this "breaking the bonds of isolation" and creating a "climate of professional inquiry."[33] The principal's job is to facilitate this exchange. The questions to be answered are:

- Why are we doing what we are doing? (a goals question)
- What are we doing? How are we going about achieving our goals? (a process question)
- Can it be done a better way? (an evaluation question)

Principals engage staff, students, and community in goal setting and problem solving because all are stakeholders and each, to one degree or another, has a contribution to make and responsibilities to assume for why things are as they are. Four assumptions guide the principal:

1. People at the working level tend to know the problems best.
2. The face-to-face work group is the best unit for diagnosis and change.
3. People will work hard to achieve objectives and goals they have helped develop.
4. Initiative and creativity are widely distributed in the population.

These assumptions undergird the high-performance organization.

It is axiomatic that any effective organization must have a clear sense of direction. Once developed, the goals need to be explicated by specific objectives and the accomplishment of these objectives must be manifest in instructional activities in the classroom.

Well-understood, well-advertised goals for schools and classrooms are absolutely essential. School climate, consistency in decision making, and accountability for what happens in the instructional delivery system—three very different aspects of schools that aspire to high performance—result from the nature of the goals that are established and *the nature of the goal-setting process.* Stated simply, "The glue that holds together the myriad actions and decisions of highly effective principals . . . [are] the goals that they and their staff have developed for the school and a sense of what their schools need to look like and to do in order to accomplish those goals."[34]

High Expectations, Praise, and Hoopla: The Motivating Work Environment

High standards of accomplishment are characteristic of productive schools. Research about productive educational settings has shown that invariably present is a leader who has high expectations, advertises these expectations, facilitates efforts to achieve the expectations, and monitors progress. This has been so, whether the leader is a teacher in a single classroom working with children or a principal with a staff to manage.

High expectations result in high performance. Even where excellence is not obtained, the result is far higher than what might ever have been predicted. Moreover, staff and principal have a benchmark from which to move to the next higher level, and a diagnostic basis to determine how to get there.

Hoopla. Effective organizations celebrate success! Good leaders use every device at their disposal to call attention to excellent work and great accomplishments (so do good teachers). Recognition lunches, awards banquets, T-shirts emblazoned with "We're Number 1," gold stars, trophies, public announcements, acknowledged favors and special privileges, "Teacher of the Week," "Student of the Day," "Custodian of the Month," school-created important sounding titles, whatever and whenever—when such devices are well intended and well merited, they enhance school productivity. In writing about such activities in highly successful private sector organizations. Peters and Waterman called this "unabashed hoopla and people respond to it."

> When we first looked at this phenomenon, we thought large doses of hoopla and celebration might be limited to companies like Tupperware, where the president and his senior managers are said to participate for thirty days a year in Jubilees, aimed at feting the success of their top 15,000 salespersons and managers. But we found hoopla going on in high tech companies as well.... And at Caterpillar we were told of an event to introduce new equipment where huge pieces of earth-moving machinery were dressed in costume.
>
> ...The people orientation also has its tough side. The excellent companies are measurement-happy and performance oriented, but this toughness is born of mutually high expectations and peer review rather than emanating from table-pounding managers and complicated control systems.[35]

Total Quality Management

A current guiding phrase to describe leadership in the high-performing organization is *total quality management*. The phrase comes from the work of W. Edwards Deming, who was credited with rebuilding the Japanese economy after World War II. Only in the past few years has he become a prophet in his own land. His "14 points" have much relevance to the development of the high-performance school and the leadership behavior characteristic therein. Figure 2.2 is a recapitulation of the essence of the management system proposed by Deming and applied here by us to the school organization.

Fundamental to the theory is a clear and well-understood sense of purpose at all levels of the organization, teamwork and empowerment of all workers, and a prevailing

FIGURE 2.2 The High-Performance School

Total Quality Management: Deming's Fourteen Essentials Applied to the School Organization

Point 1: *Create a constancy of purpose for improvement of products and services.* This means that the focus must be on helping students reach their maximum potential by providing a basis for students and teachers to work together continuously to improve.

Point 2: *Adopt a new philosophy*. Continuous improvement will occur through greater empowerment of teacher-student teams. Instructional decisions and decisions regarding scoping and sequencing of learning events are to be joint efforts involving all the stakeholders.

Point 3: *Cease dependence on mass inspection to achieve quality.* Using test scores as the primary way to assess student achievement and progress is wasteful and frequently unreliable. The end of a unit or a term is too late to assess student process. Tests should be diagnostic and help prescribe new learning events rather than used as summative evidence of the achievement of short-term goals. Also, students must be taught to assess their own work and progress.

Point 4: *Stop awarding business on the basis of price tag alone.* Use high-quality instructional materials—the best available. Free or cheap materials are too often that way because they do not serve learners well.

Point 5: *Improve constantly the system of production and service.* The litany of the school organization should be "Why are we doing what we are doing?" (a goals question), "What are we doing?" (an examination of the way we are trying to do "it"), and "Can it be done a better way?" (an evaluation question). All in the organization need to be empowered to both ask and answer these questions.

Point 6: *Institute training on the job.* In-house programs for both new and old staff members should characterize the work environment. Educators must show students and community what being a good learner is all about. Skills improvement for all in the school organization should be the goal and mechanisms to ensure this must be in place.

Point 7: *Institute leadership.* Leadership acts should be encouraged irrespective of title or position. Leadership consists of working with all members of the school organization and the community as coach and mentor. Leading is helping others achieve worthwhile goals.

Point 8: *Drive out fear.* Fear is counterproductive. In a free society and in a productive school no one is motivated by fear. Positive institutional changes result from shared responsibilities, shared power, and shared rewards.

Point 9: *Break down barriers between departments (and grade levels).* Synergy is required, not just collective energy. Competition between departments dissipates energy that should be directed toward common ends. Create cross-department and multilevel teams devoted to quality. Implement link-pin task forces to break down role and status barriers.

Point 10: *Eliminate slogans, exhortations, and targets.* Educators, students, and community members may collectively arrive at slogans and symbols that harness energy and cause them to pursue common goals and celebrate success, but these will develop out of their working together. Externally imposed sloganeering is hollow, however, and to little result.

Point 11: *Eliminate numerical quotas.* It is not possible to summarize all the ways a person can grow and learn in the barest symbol of languages—a number or a letter—so, stop trying to do this. When a grade or a score becomes the basic symbol of success, short-term gains replace long-term learning and development.

Point 12: *Remove barriers to pride of workmanship.* Humans generally want to do good work, and when they do, feel pride in it. They should be helped to do so. Self-fulfillment is a strong motivator. Realistic and cooperatively established goals result in satisfaction and pride.

Point 13: *Institute a vigorous program of education and self-improvement.* Educators and students require continuous learning programs. Self-renewal must be goal oriented, systematic, and regular, and the effective organization provides the mechanisms for this to take place within the workplace.

Point 14: *Put everybody in the organization to work to accomplish the transformation.* Teachers, administrators, staff, students, and community are stakeholders and should contribute to the realization of the new philosophy. Top-level commitment and community commitment are required. Teachers and students cannot do it alone, nor can an administrator.

drive to serve the customer. The customer is anyone inside or outside the organization to whom members of the organization provide services and products.

A Model for Instructional Leadership

Effective instructional leadership requires a complex set of relationships between principals and their beliefs and the surrounding environment of the school. The principal's values and previous experiences, as well as the expectations of the community and the institution in which the principal finds the school, all must be taken into account.

Values and Beliefs of the Principal. What a principal values and believes should be passed on to all children are the things that become the principal's contribution to the school. Most often, when asked, "What do you think is most important for children to learn?" the principal will have a particular area of interest high on the priority list about which he or she is most willing to talk. Most principals will emphasize basic skills as being important. But beyond the basic skills emphasis, the priorty list can become very diverse.

A principal's beliefs about the ability of all children to learn is extremely important. In most of the research about high-performing schools, principals have a strong belief in and commitment to the ability of all children to learn regardless of race, social conditions, or gender. These beliefs are extremely important because staff members will become attuned to what they believe the principal considers important. This contributes strongly to the establishment of a school culture characterized by high expectations for all.

Community Influences and Expectations. The local community also exerts great pressure on a principal's behavior. Principals of inner-city schools find a high percentage of their time being spent on student behavioral problems that are a direct outgrowth of community and domestic problems at home. High unemployment and high crime rates, poverty, and hunger directly affect the school and expectations for the school. The principal of the highly affluent suburban school is heavily influenced by community demands and expectations of high achievement. National Merit Scholarships, high SAT scores, entrance into the Ivy League colleges, and the athletic stature of the school all become pressures on the principal.

The demands and expectations for a school can change, however. Academic demands for a school can be expressed by a call for high test scores. Some communities will even demand academic excellence that goes beyond mere competence to call for the development in children of attributes such as arts appreciation, curiosity, creativity interpersonal competence, problem-solving skills, critical thinking skills, strong work ethics, and communication skills.

Communities also influence a principal's behavior by their willingness to directly contribute resources to the school in the form of funds and services. If large amounts of money must be raised outside of regular revenue channels by such means as school-based fund-raising activities by children or volunteers, the funds often will be directed to particular interest areas. Parents and community volunteers contributing their time directly to various projects in the school program can be another major influence.

Good instructional leaders are able to harness the interests of the community, taking advantages of its strengths while at the same time focusing on its needs. Over time, an effective instructional leader will even mold the community's expectations for the school, changing satisfaction with mediocrity or special interests to expectations for excellence in the entire program.

Institutional Influences. Every school is influenced by the organization of which it is a unit. A local school is one part of an intricate network of units nested together into districts, regions, and states. The autonomy of the local school varies greatly from school district to school district and, interestingly, even within districts. While all schools have mandates relative to federal, state, and local programs, some principals are much more effective than others in tailoring these programs to meet the needs of their local schools. For example, in one school district, the principal complained about the effort of the central office to impose a districtwide curriculum on his school, citing how the district was presently highly decentralized, allowing the judgment of the local staff to prevail in curriculum matters. He went on to complain how imposing a districtwide curriculum would reduce his role to simply that of a curriculum manager instead of a leader. Another principal in the district, however, saw the same set of circumstances as an opportunity to bring together additional resources to meet the problems of her school. She got most of her teachers onto the curriculum committees and volunteered her school as a pilot for the project. She also commented that her school's enthusiastic participation in some projects gave her increased power to say no to other influences when necessary.

Institutional influences on the local school also are found in the availability of both materials and human resources. School principals often find their time consumed with raising money for this project or that, detracting from their major role as instructional leaders. Efforts to obtain grants that relate directly to the good of the school can often be legitimate, but funding activities through candy sales and bazaars are generally misdirected efforts and consume valuable time.

The quality of the faculty and staff of a school represents another major institutional constraint or influence. Most often, upon assuming a principalship, principals inherit a staff from their predecessors. Efforts to influence the staff may initially be limited to organizational and staff-development activities. Yet, positively influencing the quality of the staff through the selection process may be the most important long-term action of the principal. In fact, some research suggests that principals are effective because they have a staff that allows them to behave as they do. The level of authority given to a principal in employing staff becomes a major factor over time in the principal's ability to influence the development of the staff.

SUMMARY

The focus of this chapter has been on the principal as builder of a learning community that contributes to a high-performance school. The principal has been cast as a facilitator of the learning process. We have stressed, however, that leadership in instructional and curricular endeavors is not the sole province of the principal. Indeed, high performance can occur only as leadership is encouraged to emerge from stakeholders—staff, students, and the community. Setting high standards and exemplifying these is an essential leadership act of the principal, nonetheless. It is the principal who is in the position to facilitate staff development, orchestrate time, and schedule factors so that teachers have opportunities to work together to solve instructional and curricular problems.

ACTIVITIES

1. Review the elements of a learning community. Apply each of the five characteristics to your own school and indicate by example the degree to which your school exemplifies these qualities. What strategies would you, as principal, engage in to overcome any weaknesses?

2. Review Case Studies 2, 3, and 5 at the end of this book. For any or all, analyze the problem presented and, applying the concepts developed in this chapter, set forth a strategy for overcoming the problem. You do not have to solve the problem, but you must accept it as *your* problem and, based on reasonable (and stated) assumptions, provide a framework wherein you expect the problem would be mitigated, if not solved.

3. Turn to the ISLLC Standards found in Appendix B. Review the knowledge, dispositions, and performances listed with Standards One and Five. Reflect on which of the standard items relate directly to the material presented in this chapter. How is the concept of empowerment reflected in ISLLC Standard One? Identify one knowledge area, one disposition, and one performance to link directly to a concept or idea discussed in Chapter 2.

ENDNOTES

1. Cynthia Norris and Bruce Barnett, *Cultivating a New Leadership Paradigm: From Cohorts to Communities*. Paper presented at the University Council for Educational Administration Annual Meeting, Philadelphia, PA, 1994.

2. Peter Senge, *The Fifth Discipline* (New York: Doubleday, 1990), p. 9.

3. Ibid.

4. *Merriam Webster Dictionary, New Edition* (Springfield, MA: Merriam-Webster, Incorporated), 1994.

5. Cynthia Norris, Bruce Barnett, Margaret Bassom, and Dianne Yerkes, "The Cohort: A Model for Developing Transformational Leadership," *Theory Into Practice 27,* no. 3/4 (Fall/Winter 1996): 146–164.

6. Ibid.

7. Neal Gross, "Basic Issues in the Management of Educational Change Efforts," in *The Dynamics of Planned Educational Changes,* ed. R. E. Herriott and N. Gross (Berkeley, CA: McCutchan, 1979), pp. 20–46.

8. Abraham Maslow, "Toward a Psychology of Being," in *The Creativity Question,* ed. A. Rothernburg and C. Housman (Durham, NC: Duke University Press, 1976), pp. 296–305.

9. Louis Raths, Merrill Harmin, and Sidney B. Simon, *Values and Teaching,* (2nd ed.) (Columbus, OH: Merrill, 1978), pp. 27–28.

10. Maslow, "Toward a Psychology of Being."

11. C. P. Alderfer, *Existence, Relatedness, and Growth: Human Needs in Organizational Settings* (New York: Free Press, 1972).

12. Daniel Goleman, *Emotional Intelligence* (New York: Bantam Books, 1995).

13. William Glasser, *School Without Failure* (New York: Harper and Row, 1969) and *Control Theory in the Classroom* (New York: Harper and Row, 1986). Both of these books share considerable insight into ways that values clarification can be facilitated

14. Thomas Sergiovanni and Robert Starratt, *Supervision: A Redefinition* (6th ed.). (New York: McGraw-Hill, 1998).

15. Norris, Barnett, Bassom, and Yerkes, "The Cohort: A Model for Developing Transformational Leadership."

16. Gene Maeroff, "A Blueprint for Empower Teachers, *Phi Delta Kappan,* vol. 69 (March 1988): 473.

17. Milbrey McLaughlin and Sylvia Yee, "School as a Place to Have a Career," in *Building a Professional*

Culture in Schools, ed. Ann Liberman (New York: Teachers College Press, 1988).

18. Chris Argyris, *Personality and Organizations* (New York: Harper and Row, 1957).

19. McLaughlin and Yee, "School as a Place to Have a Career," *Building a Professional Culture in Schools* (New York: Teachers College Press, 1988).

20. Dan Lortie, *Schoolteacher* (Chicago: University of Chicago Press, 1975).

21. Maslow, "Toward a Psychology of Being."

22. Frederick Herzberg, Bernard Mausner, and Barbara Bloch Snyderman, *The Motivation to Work* (New York: John Wiley & Sons, 1959).

23. McLaughlin and Yee, "School as a Place to Have a Career."

24. Sara Lawrence Lightfoot, *The Good High School* (New York: Basic Books, 1983).

25. McLaughlin and Yee, "School as a Place to Have a Career."

26. Thomas Sergiovanni, *Moral Leadership: Getting to the Heart of School Improvement* (San Francisco: Jossey-Bass, 1992).

27. Ibid.

28. R. Marshall, *Restructuring the American Work Place: Implications for the Public Sector* (Eugene, OR: Labor Education Research Center, University of Oregon, 1992). LERC Monograph Series.

29. Thomas J. Sergiovanni, "Leadership and Excellence in Schools," *Educational Leadership 41* (1984): 4–13.

30. Senge, *The Fifth Discipline.*

31. Thomas Sergiovanni, "The Roots of School Leadership," *Principal, 74,* no. 2 (November 1994): 6–9.

32. Ibid., p. 7.

33. Laurel N. Tanner, "The Practical Affairs of Improving Teaching," in *The Principal as Leader,* ed. Larry W. Hughes (New York: Macmillan), pp. 190, 194.

34. Kenneth Leithwood, "The Principal's Role in Teacher Development," in *Changing School Culture through Staff Development: 1990 Yearbook of the Association for Supervision and Curriculum Development.* ed. Bruce Joyce (Alexandria, VA: ASCD, 1990), pp. 71–90.

35. Thomas J. Peters and Robert H. Waterman, *In Search of Excellence* (New York: Harper and Row, 1982), p. 240.

SELECTED READINGS

Blasé, Joseph, and Peggy C. Kirby. *Bringing Out the Best in Teachers: What Effective Principals Do* (Newbury Park, CA: Corwin Press, 1991).

Daresh, John C., and Marcia A. Playko. *Supervision as a Proactive Process: Concepts and Cases* (Prospect Heights, IL: Waveland Press, 1995).

DeFour, Richard, and Robert Eaker. *Professional Learning Communities at Work: Best Practices for Enhancing Student Achievement* (Bloomington, IL: National Educational Service, 1998).

Griffin, Gary A. Leadership for Curriculum Improvement: The School Administrator's Role," in *Critical Issues in Curriculum. The 87th Yearbook of the National Society for the Study of Education,* ed. Laurel Tanner (Part 1, pp. 244–266) (Chicago: University of Chicago Press, 1988).

Hammond, Linda Darling. *The Right to Learn* (San Francisco: Jossey-Bass, 1997).

Hoy, Wayne K. C., John Tarter, and Robert B. Kottkamp. *Open Schools/Healthy Schools* (Newbury Park, CA: Sage, 1991).

Norris, Cynthia. "Cultivating Creative Cultures," in *The Principal as Leader,* ed. Larry W. Hughes (2nd ed.) (New York: Macmillan, 1999).

Norris, Cynthia, Bruce Barnett, Peggy Bassom, and Diane Yerkes. *The Learning Community: A Model for Developing Transformational Leaders* (New York: Teachers College Press, in press).

Lambert, Linda. *Building Leadership Capacity in Schools* (Arlington, VA: Association for Supervision and Curriculum Development [ASCD], 1998).

Leithwood, Kenneth A. "The Principal's Role in Teacher Development," in *Changing School Culture through Staff Development: 1990 Yearbook of the Association for Supervision and Curriculum Development,* ed. Bruce Joyce (pp. 71–90) (Alexandria, VA: Association for Supervision and Curriculum Development [ASCD], 1990).

Senge, Peter. *The Fifth Discipline* (New York: Doubleday, 1990).

Sergiovanni, Thomas J. "The Roots of School Leadership." *Principal 74,* no. 2 (November 1994): 6–9.

CHAPTER THREE

DECISION PROCESSING AND DECISION MAKING AT THE SCHOOL SITE

Teacher leadership has become a key element of recent initiatives [to improve schools]. [These initiatives] have come from the formation of school improvement teams of teachers and administrators, teacher instructional support groups, and teacher-led principal advisory councils. They have also come from efforts of administrators to share and decentralize decision making related to teacher staff development, curriculum development, and program and personnel evaluation.

—M. A. Smythe and J. Brownlee-Conyers[1]

Decision making remains the essential act of the school executive but the manner in which a principal arrives at this essential act will determine the effectiveness of the decision. Decentralized decision making means providing ample opportunities for teachers and other nonadministrators to help make decisions that have to do with the learning outcomes of the students. If this sort of empowerment also means structured avenues for parent and community engagement to help solve local school problems, then that is simply consistent with the ethos on which school systems are based in a democratic society.

But, as Hughes and Ubben have written before:

> If "empowerment" conjures notions of schools or any other operating unit being managed by committees of persons who at best only mean well and at worst do not, then such a practice should be denounced, for it does not bode well for good schooling in general and learners specifically.
>
> Managing, leading and policy analysis; educational change and productive innovation—these require more than good intentions. These require skill and insight.[2]

This chapter is about how to gain that skill and insight. Decision processing is distinguished from decision making. Decision processing is about the way one goes about arriving at the maximum feasible decision—the decision that will work and that groups will work hard to implement.

DECISION MAKING: A PERSPECTIVE

We think of decision making as the result of a problem-solving process rather than simply a final visible act. To achieve good decisions, it is necessary to engage in problem analysis and select the best decision process. Even seemingly simple problems require some thought and anticipation of consequences. This need not take a long time—no one wants to be known as a person who takes the hemorrhoid approach, just sitting on the problem—but delaying action even for a few moments to mull an issue can save a lot of heartburn. Consider the following case.

Del Hollis, a veteran bus driver, came into my office one morning about 10:00A.M. I had begun my first superintendency of this 2,300-student district just over two months earlier. It was now the end of September.

> "Chief," he said, "We've got a problem on the Bus 5 route I drive." I told Del to sit down and asked him what *our* problem was. [Mistake number 1; I was not the one who makes up the bus routes.]
>
> He continued, "As you know [I didn't know], when Bus 5 begins its route, it soon gets to the grade-level crossing at North Thomas Street. Every morning at the time I'm starting out to pick up the children, there is a regularly scheduled freight train that blocks the crossing. I wait and wait. What happens is that this makes me late to Southeast Elementary School, which is where I finish my route. The principal and teachers are complaining because the kids are reaching school after the final bell.
>
> "What I want to do is start my route by going in the other direction—the direction that I would normally be coming in on at the end of my route. Then I could avoid the freight train delay because the tracks would be clear then and the kids would be to school on time. Can do?"
>
> My response was, "Makes sense to me Del, go ahead. Just tell your riders so they know what is happening." A simple problem was solved and I went on to the other work of the day.

It was not a simple problem and things were not as they seemed. In fact, the immediate result was a lot of unnecessary pain, confusion, and embarrassment. The pain involved me, the transportation supervisor, some parents, and ultimately Del Hollis. (But it was I who inflicted the pain on Hollis.) The embarrassment was mine only. Why? The facts came out:

- There was no regular morning freight on the North Thomas Street crossing.
- Small as it was, the school system did have a transportation supervisor.
- Del changed the direction of the route in the morning. So, those children who were picked up first were left off last in the afternoon.

- There was an arterial highway on the route. The route had been structured originally to provide pick up on the home side of these children. Now they had to cross the road.
- Del was having a feud with three of the parents of the children served by his bus. These children were early boarders and lived on the arterial highway.

These first four facts were easily obtainable but that's not the important point. The important issue was that the decision was not mine to make! The first step in any rational decision process is to decide to whom the decision "belongs." Was this my problem to begin with? Nope. It belonged to the transportation supervisor who would have sorted it out in a minute.

As it developed, my hasty decision—made without any information search—also caused a rift with the transportation supervisor. We didn't know each other well; we hadn't worked together long enough to have developed a trusting relationship. He was rumored to have wondered aloud what I thought were the kind of decisions he should be making—how to reorganize the curriculum, perhaps. (It took a lot of time and reassurance to repair that relationship.) And the result was also a lot of angry parents, children placed in a hazardous position, and much time that had to be spent with an insubordinate bus driver. That's a high price to pay for quick action and a stupid decision.

This chapter is organized into four parts. Decision making as a problem-solving process is discussed. A rational problem-solving model is presented and discussed. Next, we will describe two kinds of decision settings (routine and multialternative). The Maier model and the Vroom-Jago decision tree are presented as ways to select a decision process. An examination is made of work groups—departments, grade levels, other staff members, administrators, and entire school faculties—as problem-solving units. The chapter concludes with a section on how to stay out of the garbage can model of decision making.

DECISION MAKING AS PROBLEM SOLVING

A problem exists when there is a state of uncertainty caused by either an unwelcome event or by the need to choose a course of action to achieve certain predetermined goals. Thus, something is a problem when there is a difference between what is currently occurring (the real situation) and what would desirably be happening (ideal situation).

Viewing decision making as problem solving has the advantage of delaying an act or judgment until there is a reasonable basis for that act or judgment. Moreover, not all problems are worthy of responses. Some problems, on just a little reflection, will be solved only at the price of creating a larger problem; other problems are not important and are best ignored; still other problems belong to someone else and should be redirected to the appropriate person. The first decision that needs to be made is about the nature and severity of the problem.

Figure 3.1 depicts a rational problem-solving/decision-making model. Whether the problem is complex, such as how to respond to a school pressure group, or relatively simple, such as what to do with a sick student, the intellectual process is the same.

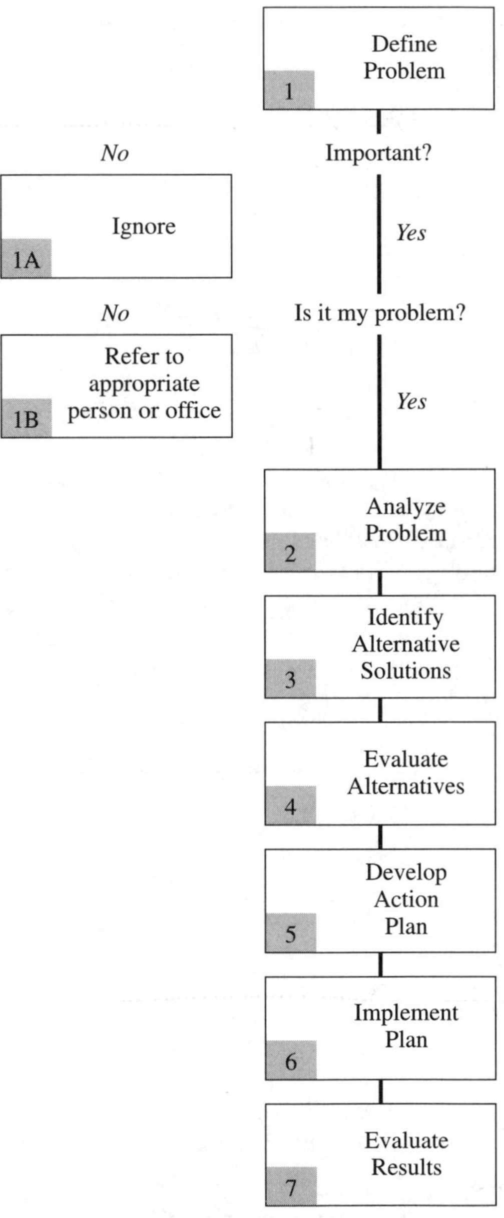

FIGURE 3.1 Rational Decision Making: Steps in Systematic Problem Solving

How to deal with a sick student may not take very much time, but assuming that the student is really ill and that it is the principal's problem, clearly the rest of the process makes sense. In the analysis of the problem, one considers the legal ramifications and school district policy. This provides a framework. Alternative solutions might include sending the student back to class but requiring no participation in class activities, sending the student to the health room until school is over, sending the student home, calling an ambulance and removing the student to a hospital, as well as other possible alternatives.

Each of these alternatives can be quickly evaluated in light of the severity of the problem, the feasibility of the solution, the age of the person, the time of day, and anticipated consequences of any particular action. It will make a difference, too, whether there is a responsible adult present in the home.

Once a judgment is made about the best alternative and it is implemented, the results should be evaluated. Did it work? If not, why not? Was the principal or the school, and especially the student, better off or worse off? Thus, a basis for nonrepetitive error is established.

How long should such a process take? In the instance of the sick student, probably no more than five minutes, less for an experienced principal who knows the policies and the students. A relatively quick diagnosis and a phone call or two will do it. In the instance of a citizens' group upset about a curricular issue or upset about grade placement policy, the process may require more study and time, but the steps are the same and the purpose is the same—to reach a sound judgment in a timely manner that will result in a solution that is in the best interests of all concerned.

DECISION SETTINGS

Problems occur in a variety of forms; they differ in content, in the process by which the problem is addressed, and in the kind of impact made on the organization and the people in the organization. When should one make a straightforward unilateral decision? When should one involve groups in the agonizing process of consensus?

The answer is not difficult to see in the extreme. If the situation is a fire in the basement, an order is issued to clear the building; one does not call a committee together to achieve consensus on which fire exits to use. (However, it would not be inappropriate to involve affected groups or individuals in advance in the development of policies and procedures for how to cope with such emergencies.) It is more useful to think about decision settings than about specific decisions. Problems may fall into two general decision settings: structured settings (routine, recurring issues) and multialternative, unstructured, or innovative settings.

Structured Decision Settings

Many things that happen in the school organization are recurring in nature. The basis for an orderly, goal-oriented school is an array of proven, reliable, productive activities that are instituted, monitored, and terminated by an appropriate set of habituated decisions.

The range of responses to any given issue may be clearly limited by law, policy, and/or custom as well as by time constraints and the maturity of the group affected by the decisions. The principal can expect certain kinds of problems to recur frequently and regularly, given a particular environment or set of circumstances. Routine response mechanisms to these are expected by members of the staff so that they can go about their work with a minimum of disruption. To the maximum degree possible, the decisions and decision processes that respond to recurring activities should be routinized.

Need for Written Policies. Arranging conditions in the school so that recurring problems are resolved with a minimum of disruption and false starts can be readily achieved. A school building policy and rules and regulations manual developed with the assistance of staff and students is called for.

Such a manual should contain statements of basic responsibilities of teachers, counselors, administrators, and classified personnel in each of five functional aspects of the school: pupil personnel services, staffing and staff relations, building management and financial operations, public relations, and curriculum and instructional development. The roles and responsibilities of various personnel with respect to matters pertaining to the functional aspects are carefully delineated, lines of communication are spelled out, and common procedural questions are answered. Importantly, too, the document should also spell out student responsibilities—the rules and regulations by which every student is expected to live.

In such a document, the delegation of specific management tasks to designated people will ensure a necessary degree of stability because it clarifies the "who is to do what" question and because it permits the principal to manage by exception rather than by direct participation in all decisions.

The Importance of Routine Decision Processes. In a well-managed school, routine day-to-day activities are carried on without the constant involvement of the principal. The primary responsibility of the principal is not the routine operation of the building but rather the creation of organizational conditions whereby school operations may be readily modified to meet changing demands and opportunities.

Thus structured or routine decision making, while encompassing problem situations running from the highly important to the mundane, is best formalized to the extent that relatively little stress on individuals or the organization occurs as decisions are promulgated and implemented. Such is often not the case in those settings wherein a variety of responses are available *(multialternative)* or in those settings where no acceptable alternatives are apparent *(unstructured or innovative).*

Multialternative, Unstructured, and Innovative Settings

Even though many of the decisions that need to be made in and about the school are structured and only a limited number of options are available, frequently there are issues for which a wide array of alternative actions is available, and the principal may be confronted with a seemingly endless number of possibilities. Many of these alternatives may appear nearly equal in value *or* there may be an inadequate information base from which to determine the efficacy of the alternatives.

Unanticipated problems, unique situations, and fast-changing conditions are characteristics of organizational life. Decisions in such situations often require "leaps into the unknown"—creative problem resolution that by its very nature produces both individual and organizational stress. In these decision settings, one needs to move from rational decision making to creative decision making. The principal and/or the decision-making group changes from primarily left-brain use to right-brain use.

It is not a once-and-for-all change, however. Generating creative responses to unstructured problems requires some structuring and a return to rational processes when the alternatives are ultimately weighed and an action plan is developed. The generation of alternatives and creative responses requires the combination of some rational processes, frequent abrupt changes to creative processes, and then a return to the rational process. Problem definition, for example, is a rational process, and goal setting or mission statements require rational processes. On the other hand, the development of alternative solutions is an intensely creative process.

It is not an either/or proposition. Groups or individuals do not have to be either creative or rational. Problem-solving groups, or individuals, make use of both orientations and must do so to be effective. Creative processes in the work organization need a structure or framework to be useful. Totally nongoal-oriented "think tanks" are a luxury most organizations cannot afford on an ongoing basis. Organizational creativity is goal oriented.

Techniques for Unstructured, Innovative Decision Making. Several techniques can be used to address problems of an unstructured nature. Three of these—brainstorming, structured absent group, and nominal group—are generally descriptive of the possibilities.

Brainstorming. Brainstorming has as its only purpose the generation of ideas, no matter how impractical the ideas may seem at first consideration. Whereas the usual kinds of meetings or conferences tend to be noncreative, a brainstorming group devotes itself *solely to creative thinking*. To function properly, the group remains, during the period of the brainstorm, completely divorced from the mundane world. The role of the group leader is one of facilitator rather than gatekeeper.

The best method is to record ideas on a flip chart. Using flip charts keeps the ideas visible and thus stimulates other ideas. Moreover, when the session ends, the paper can be given to a secretary for duplication and subsequent circulation to group members.

At some point following the brainstorming session, the group reconvenes for the purpose of judging and modifying the ideas. This session is one of analysis. The purpose is to select those ideas that singly or in combination with other ideas seem to provide a creative solution to the problem.

From the analysis session, the group decides on the four or five solutions that offer a basis for the systematic resolution of the problem. At this point, a group may engage in any number of systematic planning approaches and work the solutions into an implementation phase.

A criticism of the brainstorming technique is that the results may be affected by peer pressure (or hierarchical pressure if it is a vertically organized group). Also, unless the leader is especially well skilled, a few outspoken members may dominate and thus reduce the number of contributions from other members. To avoid this, many leaders turn to either the structured absent group or to the nominal group technique.

Structured Absent Group. This technique does not require a group to convene. Individuals are asked to participate in a simulation activity in which each is presented a case study describing an organizational issue. Included is a modest amount of descriptive data. The organization may be fictitious, but the issue is real. Individuals are asked to respond to three items:

1. Given the issue, what do you think is the problem? What might be some subproblems?
2. What might be two or three actions of a short-term nature that could be expected to reduce the intensity of the problem?
3. Suggest at least two actions or processes that might ultimately resolve the problem.

The responding individuals submit their suggestions to the person charged with ultimately working on the problem. A variation on this is to have the individuals actually meet as a problem-solving group to share their solutions and arrive at an action plan. This latter is similar to the nominal group technique described next.

Nominal Group Technique. As in brainstorming, a small group convenes to focus on an organizational problem. However, the use of this technique requires that although members of the group work on an identified problem in the presence of each other, they do so without immediate interaction.

Once the problem is explained by the convenor, group members are given a few minutes, individually, to write as many alternative solutions to the problem as possible. After the time has elapsed, a presentation of alternatives occurs. Participants give one alternative solution at a time, which is posted on flip chart paper. This continues in round-robin fashion until all alternatives are posted. No discussion of alternatives takes place until all of the alternatives have been recorded.

The value of the process is that divergence is encouraged because alternatives are developed privately. A disadvantage, of course, is that, unlike brainstorming, there is no way for one individual's idea to spark another individual. However, a "creative tension" occurs because participants are aware that others are working on the same problem and they also know that everyone's product will be displayed.

DECISION PROCESSING

An array of problem-solving processes is at the disposal of the school administrator, ranging from a unilateral "This is what must be done" telling process to engaging work groups in consensus decision making. The effective principal uses a range of techniques and processes to arrive at the maximum feasible decision.

The Maier Model

Maier and Verser[3] have discussed the need for decision makers to consider two discrete elements: the requirement that a decision be one that is of high quality and that the decision be one that carries with it the likelihood that subordinates will accept it.

Decision quality refers to objective decisions in the problem-solving process that have to do with achieving organizational goals and maintaining control, aside from any consideration of subordinate motivation. Is the decision technically sound? Is it based on the best information available? A high-quality decision occurs when the best available alternative is selected. (Unfortunately, it is often only through retrospective analysis that one knows whether or not this was so.)

Decision acceptance refers to the degree of commitment required of subordinates to implement the decision. Acceptance is crucial when the administrator is dependent on subordinates to implement a decision. Although it is not possible to know unerringly when to involve others in a decision-making process, who those others should be, or what the nature of their involvement should be, there is always a need to consider the feelings, attitudes, and skills of those who will be charged with implementing the decision. Any decision that will require behavioral change will probably require work-group commitment. The nature of work-group involvement will depend in great part on the complexity of the problem to be solved, the degree to which those affected by the decision will be required to behave differently in order for the decision to be properly implemented, and the degree to which subordinates will accept a unilateral decision.

The Q/A Interaction. Using the two factors of technical expertise needed (quality of decision required) and need for group acceptance (hearty compliance and/or behavior change required) as prime determinants, a quadrant model can be developed to help determine the answer to the involvement question. Figure 3.2 displays such a model.

That quadrant in which both the quality of the decision and the need for work-group commitment is high (Q∗A, the upper right quadrant) presents the greatest challenge to the leader. Into this quadrant fall those decisions that require much in the way of technical expertise and knowledge in order for a good decision to be reached. But it also describes a situation wherein no matter how technically superior the solution may be, in order for that solution to be put into effect much work-group acceptance will be necessary. That is, the decision must fall within the work group's "zone of hearty compliance." Without consideration of the needs and opinions of the group, compliance may not occur. This may be so for several reasons: because an apparent solution is contrary to present practice or present attitudes; because it requires work-group members to perform in ways that are initially more difficult or for which they have not been trained; because of the simple lack of agreement about the efficacy of the decision; or for any number of other reasons, including threat, fear, distrust of administrators, or anger. If any of the previous conditions can be assumed, then something beyond a simple unilateral decision process probably will be required.

What kinds of issues might fall within this quadrant? Any curricular change certainly would, as would budget development. Changes in school policies affecting large numbers of students and school constitutional questions would also seem to fit here.

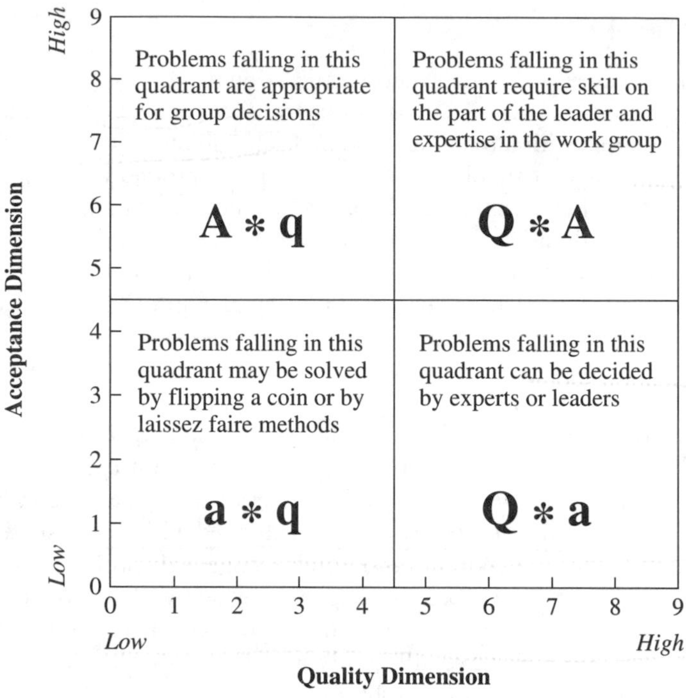

FIGURE 3.2 The Maier Model

Source: Maier, R. F. and Gertrude C. Verser, *Psychology in Industrial Organizations,* Fifth Edition.

Operating in this quadrant will require good human relations skills as well as technical competence in the subject under review.

The upper left quadrant (A∗q) depicts those situations where group feelings may be intense, but great technical expertise is not required because the subject is not a complex one. Any number of resolution schemes are available; the appropriate one must be that which is fair and sensitive to the needs and desires of the work group. Assignment of unpaid extracurricular duties, balanced work schedules for routine duties, and school calendar development, among myriad other decision situations, might fall into this category. Among appropriate ways to handle problems in this quadrant would be the formation of advisory committees, delegation of decision making to standing or ad hoc bodies, or informal consultation with leaders of the groups affected.

The Q∗a quadrant contains those kinds of decisions that affect the quality of the organization in a technical sense but do not have a great impact on the human side of the enterprise. Equipment selection, design of conflict-free schedules, and the design of a management information system, among other examples, might fall into this quadrant.

In the remaining quadrant (a∗q), neither great technical competence nor sensitive human relations is a critical consideration. What is needed is a concrete act to resolve a simple problem. Time is the only critical element. A decision has to be made in a timely fashion, so that people in the organization can go about their work in an orderly, efficient, and knowledgeable manner.

The Maier model is a good analytical tool. It emphasizes that selection of the best decision process will result from an analysis of the nature of the problem and the nature of the work group.

Vroom and Yetton,[4] and Vroom and Jago,[5] have extended these concepts and provided a basis for choosing the decision process most likely to result in the maximum feasible decision. Effective leadership, as manifested in good decision making, depends on understanding the conditions of a problem situation, assessing correctly how much participation or "power sharing" is required to be successful, and establishing the form that the participation should take.[6]

The Vroom-Yetton Decision Process Model

Vroom and Yetton have placed five available decision processes on a continuum from no subordinate influence to maximum subordinate influence:*

The AI Procedure. The leader solves the problem alone using whatever information is available at the time. (The available information is considered to be sufficient.)

The AII Procedure. The leader obtains the necessary information from subordinates who may or may not be told about the problem or why the information is requested. The subordinates' role in this procedure is simply that of providing data, not in developing or evaluating alternatives.

The CI Procedure. The leader shares the problem with one or more subordinates *individually*, asking for ideas, suggestions, and alternatives, but does *not* bring, the relevant subordinates together to do this. The leader then makes the decision which may or may not take into account the ideas of the subordinates.

The CII Procedure. The leader calls the appropriate subordinates together and shares the problem with the group, soliciting ideas, suggestions, and alternatives. Then the leader makes the decision which may or may not take into account the ideas of the subordinates.

The GII Procedure. The leader shares the problem with subordinates as a group. The group as a whole generates and evaluates alternatives, with the ascribed leader's role that of peer. The process is consensus decision making. The leader serves as chair or convenor of the meeting but does not attempt to exert "official" influence in the direction of any specific decision. The leader is willing to agree to and implement any solution which has the support of the group.[7]

The Vroom-Yetton process offers much more guidance to the leader in selecting an appropriate decision process than the Maier model. Both AI and GII may appear at first to be the "riskiest" of the procedures, but neither is any more or less risky than the

*Reprinted from *Leadership and Decision-Making,* by Victor H. Vroom and Philip W. Yetton, by permission of the University of Pittsburgh Press. © 1973 by University of Pittsburgh Press.

others, and when used appropriately each will provide the best route to the maximum feasible decision. How does one choose among the processes?

The relative utility of the five procedures depends on several aspects of the situation within which the problem exists. It depends, as well, on leader judgments about the nature of these aspects:

1. A clear definition of the problem (i.e, what is it that is not what is desired?).
2. The amount of information possessed by the leader and subordinates or, if the information is not currently possessed, whether or not it is known where to find the needed information. This is the degree to which the problem is "structured." An unstructured problem would be one for which inadequate information is available and it is uncertain where to find the needed information or one for which there are a variety of possible actions. A highly structured problem would be one where policy guidance exists.
3. Whether or not it is likely that subordinates will accept a unilateral decision from the leader.
4. Whether or not it is likely that subordinates will cooperate—with the leader or with each other—in trying to collectively reach a good decision (i.e., one that would be in the best interests of the organization).
5. The amount and intensity of disagreement the leader perceives exist among subordinates about preferred alternatives.

Vroom and Jago: The "New" Model

Continuing research has led to refinements and enhancements in the original Vroom-Yetton model. The conceptual framework and the basic assumptions remain unchanged, however. An important enhancement is that the model has been extended to include considerations about the extent to which a given problem solution is either *time driven* or one in which good opportunity for work-group development exists; that is, it is *development driven.* (*Note:* The model handles either problem situations involving a work group and superordinate or individual subordinate/superordinate problems. Our discussion here focuses only on group situations.) Consideration must be given to two aspects: the time available to resolve the issue and the opportunity the issue provides to help a group develop problem-solving skills.

Time-Driven Considerations. The available time to resolve an issue may impinge greatly on the degree to which members of a work group can be involved in problem solving and the form that this involvement takes. CII and GII decision procedures require an investment of time considerably greater than the other procedures. Is the problem important enough—that is, is group commitment necessary and is a high-quality decision required—to justify the expenditure of the labor hours that will be required?

Even if the quality of the decision is not crucial (i.e., there are a number of alternatives, any one of which would adequately resolve the issue), but acceptance is critical and not likely to result from a unilateral decision, then an investment of time will be worth the trouble.

Judicious use of time is an important consideration, however. CII and GII decision processes do use up both the time and the energy of subordinates and peers. A 4-hour group meeting between the principal and an advisory group of eight others consumes 36 labor-hours of work time. What other important activities had to be delayed or not done because of the meeting?

Development-Driven Considerations. Much may be gained from broad participation in decision making by a school staff and school community. Such involvement encourages idea sharing, trust, high performance standards, and work group effectiveness. It also capitalizes on the abilities of the informal leaders on the staff.

However, skills in decision making need to be nurtured and work groups need to be helped to improve these skills. Consider a school or a department with many new personnel or a school suddenly functioning under a mandate for site-based management and similarly a mandated teacher and/or community advisory council. If group members have heretofore been relatively uninvolved and unfamiliar with decision making in an organizational context, there is work to be done by the principal.

Thus, the principal might employ a CII or a GII process on less intense problems with a new group as a way to provide a basis for group members to learn to work together. Later in this chapter there is a discussion about how to set an appropriate framework for group decision making.

The Decision Tree. Help in selecting the most likely process to lead to the maximum feasible decision is available in the form of a decision tree. Eight questions to be answered yes or no comprise the branches of the tree. These questions are addressed *only* after the problem to be solved has been satisfactorily defined.

1. How important is the technical quality of this decision?
2. How important is subordinate commitment to the decision?
3. Does the leader have sufficient information to make a high-quality decision?
4. Is the problem well structured?[8]
5. If the leader were to make the decision alone, is it reasonably certain that subordinates would be committed to the decision?
6. Do subordinates share the organizational goals to be attained in solving this problem?
7. Is conflict among subordinates over preferred solutions likely?
8. Do subordinates have sufficient information to make a high-quality decision?

Figures 3.3 and 3.4 depict the decision tree. Figure 3.3 would be used in instances where the principal considered group development the driving factor; Figure 3.4 would be used where time was the primary concern.

Implications of Decision Processing Models

Using such tools as the Maier model or the Vroom-Jago decision tree for problem analysis does not remove the need for sensitive judgment. Indeed, the effective use of these

QR	Quality Requirement:	How important is the technical quality of this decision?
CR	Commitment Requirement:	How important is subordinate commitment to the decision?
LI	Leader's Information:	Do you have sufficient information to make a high-quality decision?
ST	Problem Structure:	Is the problem well structured?
CP	Commitment Probability:	If you were to make the decision by yourself, is it reasonably certain that your subordinate(s) would be committed to the decision?
GC	Goal Congruence:	Do subordinates share the organizational goals to be attained in solving this problem?
CC	Subordinate Conflict:	Is conflict among subordinates over preferred solutions likely?
SI	Subordinate Information:	Do subordinates have sufficient information to make a high-quality decision?

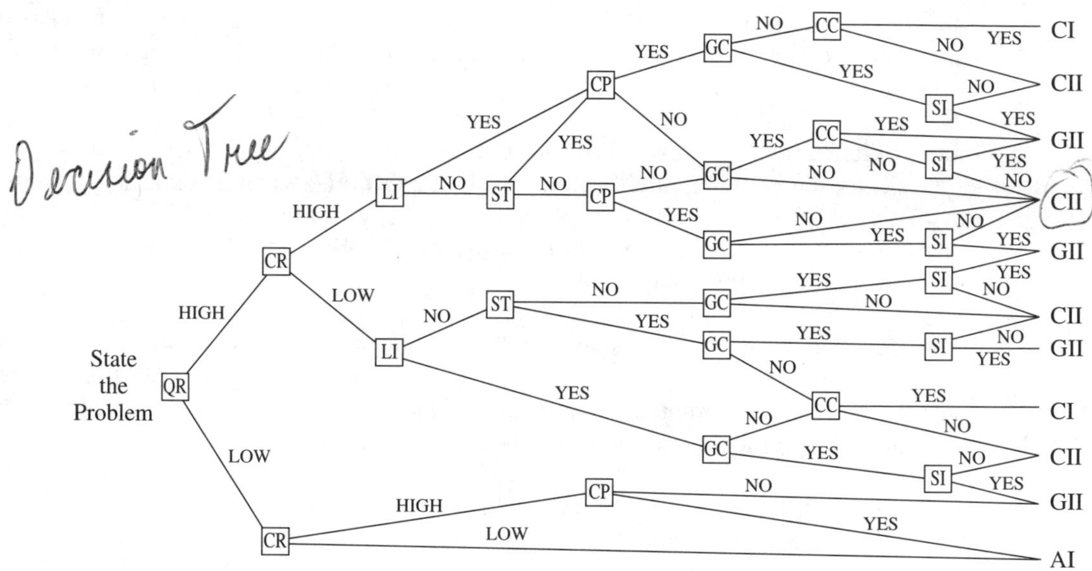

FIGURE 3.3 Vroom-Jago Development-Driven Decision Tree: Group Problems

Source: Reprinted from *The New Leadership: Managing Participation in Organizations* by Victor H. Vroom and Arthur G. Jago, 1988, Englewood Cliffs, NJ: Prentice-Hall. Copyright 1987 by V. H. Vroom and A. G. Jago. Used with permission of the authors.

models requires the highest order of sensitivity. The administrator is after the maximum feasible decision—the decision that offers promise of long-term problem resolution or problem mitigation *and* the one that those most affected will work to carry out. The processes described here are designed to take the administrator to this sort of decision.

What one has, with the rational decision processes just presented, is a basis for reducing the risks and analyzing the strengths and weaknesses of relative positions. The decision tree, the Maier model, and any of a number of other rational processes are tools for the manager to use to arrive at a maximum feasible decision. The models are not a substitute for thinking; they are to stimulate thinking to provide the basis for sound judgments.

QR Quality Requirement:	How important is the technical quality of this decision?
CR Commitment Requirement:	How important is subordinate commitment to the decision?
LI Leader's Information:	Do you have sufficient information to make a high-quality decision?
ST Problem Structure:	Is the problem well structured?
CP Commitment Probability:	If you were to make the decision by yourself, is it reasonably certain that your subordinate(s) would be committed to the decision?
GC Goal Congruence:	Do subordinates share the organizational goals to be attained in solving this problem?
CC Subordinate Conflict:	Is conflict among subordinates over preferred solutions likely?
SI Subordinate Information:	Do subordinates have sufficient information to make a high-quality decision?

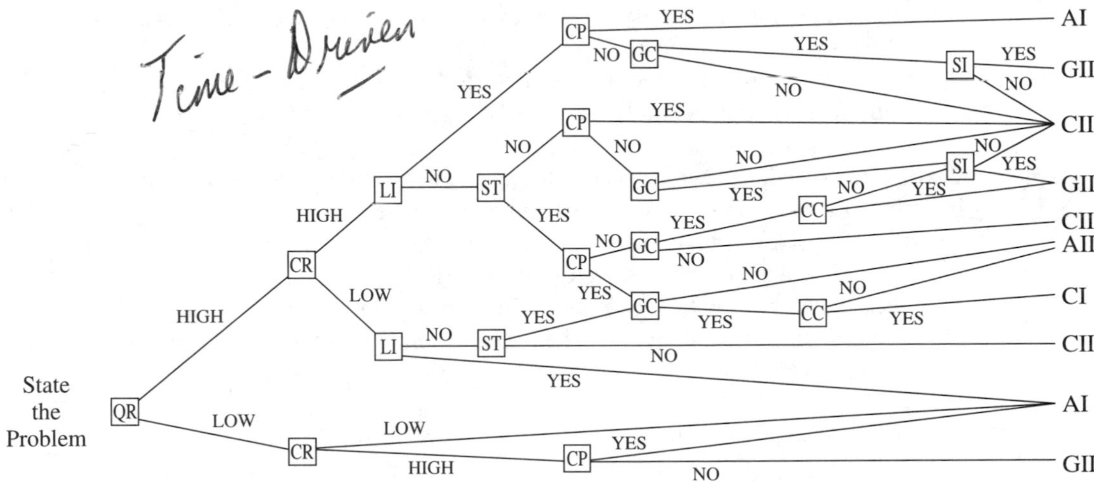

FIGURE 3.4 Vroom-Jago Time-Driven Decision Tree: Group Problems

Source: Reprinted from *The New Leadership: Managing Participation in Organizations* by Victor H. Vroom and Arthur G. Jago, 1988, Englewood Cliffs, NJ: Prentice-Hall. Copyright 1987 by V. H. Vroom and A. G. Jago. Used with permission of the authors.

Your Turn

You are the principal of a 1,200-student middle school and are confronted with the following situation. Analyze the situation. At the conclusion of the case, you will apply the Vroom-Jago tree.

CASE STUDY

The school houses grades 6 through 9. There is need to review the social studies series currently in use. Because your own teaching field is social studies, you have more than a casual interest in and knowledge about the situation. You also have a strong opinion that the current series does not adequately depict the contributions made by minorities.

The social studies department seems split on the issue, containing two teachers who do not want to use any text at all; several teachers who are very satisfied with the current text; and three or four others who favor at least two other series. (Board of education policy requires one adopted text series but does permit supplemental works when it can be shown that there is good reason to do so.)

The chairperson of the department is undecided on the matter and requests that you "do something." A review of staff evaluations reveals that one of the teachers who wants no text at all is among the top rated in the school. She is unhappy with the more conservative posture of many other colleagues and has indicated that unless a more positive stand on the multicultural nature of society is taken by the department, she will go elsewhere A *cause célèbre* looms.

Your task is to decide what decision process will lead you to the maximum feasible decision by applying the Vroom-Jago model.

Using the Decision Tree. To use the Vroom-Jago tree, first clearly state what you believe to be the problem. Then assume you are development driven and, using Figure 3.3, begin at the left side of the model with question "QR." If your response to this question is "high," then you proceed to question "CR," and so on.

For each answer, take a moment to justify your response. Proceed through the decision tree until a terminal is reached. The terminal will indicate the maximum feasible decision procedure.

Authors' Analysis of the Case. Using the tree, the maximum feasible process appears to us to be CII. At issue is the selection of the social science series, and this is what we see as the problem to be solved. So stating, the tree is entered and question QR receives a "high." (There is clearly a quality requirement; the issue is a high priority and there are "unequal" solutions.)

The next question asks about the importance of subordinate commitment to the decision. We believe there is a need for "high" commitment. Little commitment would seem to mean the text would not be used or would be misused. We are now at the leader information question and our answer to that is that the leader (us) does not have enough information. Nor do we believe the problem is "structured"—the answer to this particular issue would not seem to be "programmable." We are now at "CP." Do we think that subordinates will commit to a unilateral decision made by us? Perhaps; you'd really have to be there to know, but given the nature of the problem and the presumed intensity of feelings, our answer is "no." And how about "goal congruence"? It wouldn't seem that you could count on this given the information about the range of beliefs on the staff, so we said "no" and the terminal we are taken to is CII. Had the response to the goal congruence question been "yes," we would have had to address the conflict question. Depending on the answer to that—and a "yes" there would seem the likely response—we could have ended up at GII.

In either instance—and good judgment must be present for good decision processing—you are taken to the process that will most likely achieve the best result.

THE WORK GROUP AS A PROBLEM-SOLVING UNIT

The school executive is looking for the best solutions to problems—routine and non-routine. Such solutions will not occur in an organization of interacting humans unless processes are employed that make appropriate use of the collective intelligence of these humans. Thus, effective principals deliberately and frequently engage their staff in problem-solving activities.

Productive relationships develop as a result of engaging in important activities together. It is then possible for the strengths and weaknesses of fellow members to be known, revealing who can be counted on for what kinds of expertise. Knowing where certain kinds of expertise exist permits the principal to create effective teams to focus on troubling schoolwide issues, existent or anticipated. Thus, effort spent to help a work group develop problem-solving skills will pay rich dividends.

Setting Realistic Decision-Making Limits

Irrespective of the maturity of the staff, few problem-solving groups can be permitted to operate completely unfettered. Real-world constraints must always be contended with. Any group charged with helping to resolve an issue needs to know the "rules of the game" if the expectation is a decision that can be implemented. The following considerations provide a solid basis for maximum effective use of problem-solving groups:

1. Decide if the task force is to be advisory in nature. That is, is it a CII or is it a GII? Are decisions to be suggestions only, or is the group to be charged with coming up with final decisions?
2. Cooperatively set a realistic time line. This would include further data collection periods, preparation of final reports, generation of new program alternatives, and the anticipated implementation date, among other milestones.
3. Establish a tentative budget for the project phases. Possible line items include released time costs, materials costs, transportation, and meals.
4. Review any districtwide policies or state laws that might impinge on the nature of any resolution scheme. For example, is there a systemwide or statewide adopted basal reading series that must be lived with no matter what? Does the state provide for experimental programs?
5. Establish the "essential conditions" that any decision must fit in order to be acceptable.
6. Set up regular interaction sessions about progress and findings.

Levels of Decision Making and Participation

Who should be involved in decision processing? Who makes the final decision? Does participatory management mean committees for everything? How will anything get done? Good decisions require good information and a willingness on the part of those affected to implement the decision. But that does not translate to mean the same approach to every problem-solving activity, nor does it mean the executive never takes action without some kind of agonizing consensus session.

The persons to be involved in decision processing *and the nature of that involvement* of necessity will differ, depending on the issue to be resolved, if the product is to be the maximim feasible decision. The work of Lancto provides much help in the consideration of who needs to be involved in what and to what end.[9]

Lancto proposed five levels of participation in decision making in the school and submitted that the kinds of decisions to be made vary by level. Sometimes the participation is at the advisory level; sometimes it will result in final decisions. In shared decision making, the staff works with the principal in two ways: (1) giving advice before the principal makes certain decisions and (2) making decisions in predetermined domains. Figure 3.5 illustrates the decision levels and provides examples of the kinds of decisions to be made at the different levels.

FIGURE 3.5 School-Based Decision-Making Levels

Levels of Participation

1. Decisions made by individual teachers
2. Decisions made collectively by teachers (may also involve students and parents in an advisory role)
3. Decisions made collectively by teachers, principals, and other auxillary administrators (parent and student participation where appropriate)
4. Decisions made by administrators, department heads, and building supervisors after consultation with staff (schoolwide advisory councils are often a good mechanism for this)
5. Decisions made solely by the principal or other designated administrator

Typical Kinds of Decisions to Be Made at Each Level

Level 1: Classroom teaching strategies; enrichment; remediation

Level 2: Selection of instructional materials and texts; use of time and allocation of resources within a grade level or department—including staffing patterns

Level 3: Curriculum decisions involving more than one group or instructional unit; scheduling; scoping and sequencing across subjects and grade levels; sequential texts, materials, and other instructional protocols involving two or more instructional, support, or administrative units; any other decisional matters affecting more than one unit

Level 4: Schoolwide scheduling; budget recommendations to the central office; balancing resources/resolving conflicts; appraisal and evaluation strategies; development of school effectiveness reports to district offices and state agencies

Level 5: Legal issues such as teacher remands; official recommendations to superintendent on the reemployment of staff and tenure; final decisions on the general use of the building and other physical facilities; allocation of resources for the school plant in general; selection and assignment of support staff

The model is useful because it clearly sets forth varying degrees of participation in school-based decision making. It helps avoid misunderstandings about roles, responsibilities, and authority to act.

Site-Based Management: Enlightened Suzerainty

Historically, *suzerainty* meant that there was one nation that controlled another nation in international affairs but otherwise permitted domestic sovereignty. The term was originally used to describe a feudal lord to whom fealty was due because the lord provided protection and sustenance in time of need. In matters domestic and in the usual course of events, the local unit (family or town) operated in an independent manner; in relations with the outside world (foreign affairs), the lord would prevail.

If the negative feudal connotations are removed, one has an appropriate conceptual model for the organization of schools and school systems. Suzerainty does provide local autonomy. Individual school units (buildings, departments, and teachers) should be imbued with autonomy when it comes to operating within the local sphere.

The school is a unique, complex unit with its own culture, norms, and relationships. An already effective school may have achieved its stature through innovative, unorthodox strategies and structures that the imposition of stringent standards and policies from the central office might destroy.

The prescription, therefore, is for a strategic independence, but not total freedom from control from the central office. What this means is that system policymakers should continue to be expected to set standards for student achievement and other desired outcomes for the school system as a whole, but they should avoid specifying the means by which these ends are to be achieved in any particular school.

Complex school systems can neither be organized as confederations nor should they be organized as highly centralized bureaucracies. Individual school units need to be free to grapple independently with and solve problems indigenous to the unit. However, some problems are best dealt with at levels above the individual school unit, or are problems that are shared with a number of other schools. Such problems require a different kind of problem-solving mechanism and less local autonomy, but much engagement of these appeared.

There are any number of ways to engage others in problem-solving activities. Simply being asked for an opinion is a degree of involvement. More formalized mechanisms may be appropriate, however, to be employed for specific purposes. Of particular interest to the principal may be independent problem-solving groups.

PROBLEM-SOLVING WORK GROUPS

Many problems are better addressed and solved at the operational level without interference from a superordinate structure. In such instances, the superordinate structure serves as a support unit, providing such resources as might be needed and performing in an oversight role only.

The argument in favor of such a practice is that autonomy is placed appropriately, permitting maximum latitude in decision making at the lowest possible operating level. The problem-solving work group (PSWG) is an action group. It resolves problems rather than simply identifying them.

A PSWG is a small group of workers with similar responsibilities who voluntarily meet for an hour or more each week to discuss school-related problems, investigate causes, recommend solutions, and take corrective action. It is organized horizontally rather than vertically. No structural changes are required in the organization; it fits into any existing structure. Distinguishing features are:

- The PSWG consists primarily of a regular work group (e.g., department, grade-level, or cross-level group of teachers, counselors, and and so on; such a group is not limited to the professional staff).
- Membership is voluntary.
- The group meets regularly once a week.
- The group solves problems rather than identifying problems for the principal or others to solve.
- PSWGs are imbued with appropriate authority and a modest budget.

The PSWG requires administrative support, which may take the form of providing a meeting place and time off from instructional duties to meet. The principal may or may not be a member of the PSWG but someone who is a part of the school's administrative team is a member. The role of the participating administrator is that of convenor and facilitator. Having an administrator in the group ensures upward communication.

THE GARBAGE CAN MODEL OF DECISION MAKING

The garbage can model inverts the problem-solving process from a focus on finding solutions to problems to a focus on identifying a problem for which the principal or the work group has a solution. What we have in the garbage can are solutions in search of a problem. Hoy and Tartar wrote, "The garbage-can model explains why solutions are proposed to problems that do not exist, why choices are made that do not solve problems, why problems persist in spite of solutions, and why so few problems are solved."[10]

Now, it is true that not everything in and about the organization proceeds on a rational basis at all times. In the first chapter, we wrote about the informal dimension of organizations and the mighty impact this dimension has on the direction organizations take. Moreover, principals have their own notions and preferences of what it is they would like to see solved or what solutions they would like to try out, whether there is a real problem or not. Principals have hunches about what might be getting in the way of the school being more effective. Good, we say; principals ought to be thinking about such things.

However, locking in on a hunch or presenting a solution to a nonexistent problem simply because one is intrigued by the solution takes one to the garbage can. The garbage can contains unfocused solutions and activities, pet ideas and political exigencies, as well as time limitations, budget constraints, and inadequate information. "Don't just stand there, do something" often becomes the driving force. Activity replaces productivity.

Even if nonrational behavior, or even apparently irrational behavior, can be explained by the garbage-can model, better ways are at the disposal of the principal who wants the school to be a high-performing organization. The way to stay out of the garbage can is through systematic problem analysis and avoidance of solutions that do not really address what is getting in the way of the school becoming maximally productive.

The school did not become what it is overnight and it won't become better overnight and it won't become better *ever* unless problems are correctly identified, issues defined, and solutions generated that focus on what it is that is getting in the way. Rational processes are required. This in no way diminishes the effectiveness of intuitive leaps nor does it diminish the importance of "hypothesis testing." It simply suggests that until the problem is thoroughly analyzed, intuition is restricted and bad hypotheses are stated. (We devote much attention in Chapter 4 to the manner in which problems can be analyzed and solutions generated that take the work group to resolution or at least to problem mitigation.)

To be sure, certain political realities and certain other extra- and intraorganizational forces must be contended with, but these too can best be attended to by more rational decision-making approaches. Political exigencies, budget realities, limitations of time, and insufficient information can be—and must be—factored into rational decision processes. But the garbage can contains unrelated collections of unfocused thoughts and conditions. Stay out of the garbage can. How? Figure 3.6 offers hope. It is a flowchart designed to remove clutter from decision processing and decision making. It takes into account the social and political realities of the milieu within which the school operates. The model is appropriate for problem solving at any level and with any group.

SUMMARY

The essential executive act is decision making. Decision making is problem solving—or it ought to be. But decisions are not made very well in a vacuum. Moreover, there are few decisions that are made in the organization that do not affect the lives of others and require others to behave differently tomorrow than they did today.

Thus, the final act—the decision—must be subject to an intellectual process. The first step is to discover what the problem is. Subsequent steps (the decision-making process) may require creative approaches and the wisdom of others in the work group.

Much research about decision processing has been conducted over the years. One of the most useful applications of this research has been the Vroom-Jago model. In this approach, various conditions existing in a problem situation are subjected to analysis and the decision maker is led to a decision process that is most likely to result in a maximum feasible decision.

It is important that decisions be made and problems solved at the appropriate level. Staff at the building levels, operating under the concept of enlightened suzerainty, can be expected to develop good solutions to troubling issues. And stay out of the garbage can!

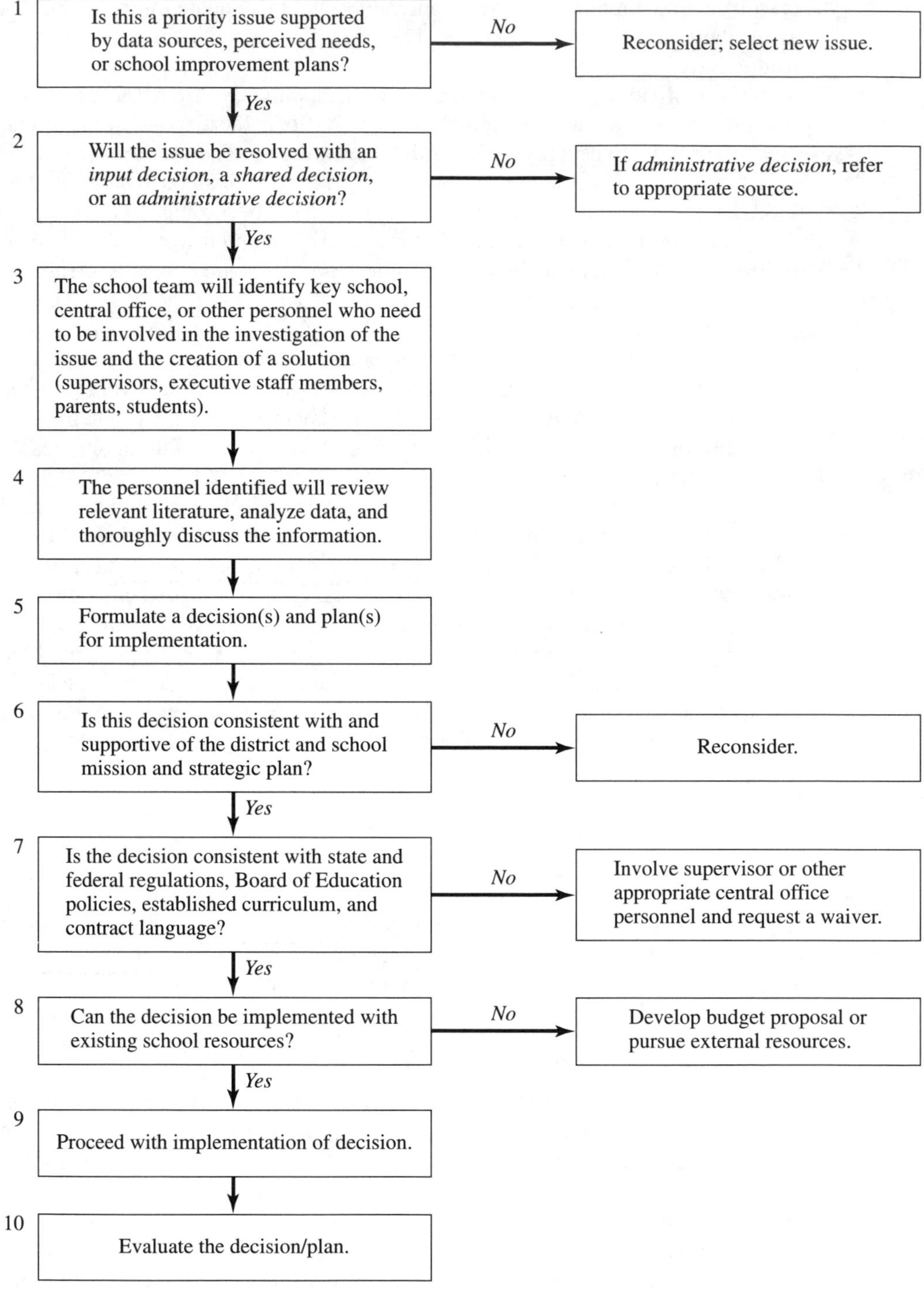

FIGURE 3.6 Decision-Making Flowchart

ACTIVITIES

1. Reflect on the Maier model. Identify problems or issues that in your own experience would have fallen into each of the quadrants. What actually occurred in each of these incidents? How might the incident have been handled?

2. Review Case Studies 2 and 5 at the end of this book. Apply the Vroom-Jago decision tree. Use both the development-driven and the time-driven tree. Pay particular attention to your statement of the problem. Discuss your approach with a small group of colleagues. Try to achieve consensus on both the nature of the problem and the maximum feasible decision process.

3. Turn to the ISLLC Standards found in Appendix B. Review the performances listed with Standard One. Describe which decision processes you would use to implement the fourth performance on the list: "the vision is developed with and among stakeholders." How would you carry it out?

ENDNOTES

1. Mark A. Smythe and Jean Brownlee-Conyers, "Teacher Leaders and Their Principals: Exploring the Development of New Working Relationships," *Educational Administration Quarterly 28,* no. 2 (May 1992): 150.

2. Larry W. Hughes and Gerald C. Ubben, *The Elementary Principal's Handbook: A Guide to Effective Action,* 4th ed. (Boston: Allyn and Bacon, 1994).

3. Norman R. F. Maier and Gertrude C. Verser, *Psychology in Industrial Organizations,* 5th ed. (Boston: Houghton Mifflin, 1982), p. 173.

4. Victor H. Vroom and Philip W. Yetton, *Leadership and Decision-Making* (Pittsburgh: University of Pittsburgh Press, 1973).

5. Victor H. Vroom and Arthur G. Jago, *The New Leadership: Managing Participation in Organizations* (Englewood Cliffs, NJ: Prentice-Hall, 1988).

6. Maier's work and the work of Vroom and Yetton as well as Vroom and Jago are based on earlier concepts advanced by Simon. Simon's "Zone of Acceptance" model was based on two questions: "Is the issue relevant to others in this organization?" and "Do others in the organization have the expertise to deal with the issue?" If the answer to both of these questions was no, then whatever decision was made was likely to fall within the subordinates' zone of acceptance. Thus, little or no involvement in the decisional process would seem necessary. If the answer to both questions was yes, then Simon wrote there was a need to engage others in an examination of alternatives or, at least, in the collection of additional information. Herbert A. Simon, *Administrative Behavior* (New York: Macmillan, 1947).

7. Vroom and Yetton, *Leadership and Decision-Making.*

8. A "structured" problem is one in which the decision maker knows three components of the problem: the current state (what "is"), the desired state ("outcome"), and the mechanisms needed to get from one state to the other. The problem, in effect, is programmable; creative solutions are not needed. The more structured a problem is, the less likely great participation in its solution will be required.

9. Robert M. Lancto, "An Inquiry: Shared Decision-Making," *The Journal of SAANYS 18,* no. 3 (Winter 1987–88): 13–17.

10. Wayne K. Hoy and C. John Tartar, *Administrators Solving the Problems of Practice* (Boston: Allyn and Bacon, 1994), p. 61.

SELECTED READINGS

Fisher, B., and D. Ellis. *Small Group Decisionmaking,* 3rd ed. (New York: McGraw-Hill, 1990).

Greer, John T., and Paula M. Short. "Restructuring Schools," in *The Principal as Leader,* 2nd ed., ed. Larry W. Hughes (Upper Saddle River, NJ: Prentice-Hall, 1999).

Hallinger, Philip, and Don Richardson. "Models of Shared Leadership: Evolving Structures and Relationships," *The Urban Review 20,* no. 4 (December 1986): 229–245.

Hughes, Larry W. *The Principal as Leader,* 2nd ed. (Upper Saddle River, NJ: Prentice-Hall, 1999).

Kamlesh, Mathur, and Daniel Solow. *Management Science: The Art of Decision Making* (Englewood Cliffs, NJ: Prentice-Hall, 1994).

Keith, Sherry, and Robert H. Girling. *Education, Management, and Participation* (Boston: Allyn and Bacon, 1991).

Shapiro, Joan P., and Jacqueline Stefkovich. *Ethical Leadership and Decision Making in Education* (Mahwah, NJ: Erlbaum, 2000).

CHAPTER FOUR

SCHOOL IMPROVEMENT THROUGH SYSTEMATIC PLANNING

If you don't know where you are going,
It doesn't much matter what you do.
—*Alice in Wonderland*[1]

This chapter describes a process of organizing for school improvement through a systematic plan of action. It also describes a number of tools that may be used to aid in systematic planning.

The principal's role in instructional leadership discussed in Chapter 2 pointed out the importance of beliefs and values in establishing a vision for the school. Out of the vision and the underlying values one holds about education, one should develop expectations for one's schools. Expectations may begin from one's own individual values or may start from ideas suggested or mandated by others, but eventually, they must grow to the collective expectation of a larger set of stakeholders of the school. Plans for improvement should grow out of these expectations.

Efforts to bring about change or initiate something new for one's school should usually begin with a plan. Good local school planning involves the translation of concepts, ideas, beliefs, and values into a vision of what a good school should be, as well as a clarification of the general mission for the school.

Recognizing that most often the plan is for the improvement of an existing ongoing school, one begins with gathering and analyzing information about the existing school program and the community and students it serves. The planning continues with the review or development of the stated school mission and beliefs one holds about education. The third task is to determine goals and expectations for student learning and how one proposes to measure them. Analysis then turns inward to a comparison of current instructional and organizational practices to research based indicators of high-performing systems. Analysis of data generated from these steps provides the basis for the development of an action plan for school improvement. The final step is the implementation of the plan and the recording of the results.

THE PRINCIPAL'S ROLE

Schools really can make a difference in the achievement levels of students, but a school is most often only as good or bad, as creative or sterile, as the person who serves as the head of that school. The research on effective schools highlights the role of the principal in establishing goals and objectives for the school.

What do effective principals do?

> Principals of effective schools are strong instructional leaders who know how to manage time and money effectively...they concentrate on priority goals...they set as their main goal the acquisition of basic skills...effective principals have high expectations for all students and they will enlist the support of others in meeting common goals.[2]

The principal is the one person in a school who can oversee the entire program because of his or her interest in the success of the entire school and all of its parts. Therefore, the principal is in the best position to provide the necessary sense of direction to the various aspects of a school. Research has shown that the most effective principals have a clear sense of purpose and priorities and are able to enlist the support of others toward these ends.

Many of the problems of direction within a school organization are very subtle, will be difficult to solve, and require great conceptual and technical knowledge of curriculum, instruction, and learning. The principal must have the necessary understanding to find proper and just solutions to these problems and many others like them.

Above all, it is absolutely necessary to involve others. The success of any school improvement rests with the active involvement of all stakeholders in the school. From the collective gathering of baseline data, through the hammering out of the collective beliefs and goals, to the review of expectations for student learning, to the ultimate decisions of how to improve the school, a wide variety of people must be involved for their ideas and for their ultimate ownership.

GATHERING BASELINE DATA

Data-driven decision making is a major theme of the previous chapter and clearly illustrated by the flowchart in Figure 3.6. What kinds of data are available about one's school? How might these data be organized to help one make wiser decisions? What data should be gathered to help one better profile the school?

Demographic Data

Basically, principals are looking for descriptive or demographic information about their students, staff, and parent and community involvement with their schools. A list[3] of what one might gather is as follows:

STUDENT DATA

1. Enrollment history (length of time in current school and previous school)
2. Attendance, tardiness (percent)
3. Living in single-parent or two-parent household
4. Ethnicity, gender
5. Parental education level
6. Free/Reduced price lunch (percent and number)
7. Academic Assistance Program enrollments (percent and number) (special education, bilingual, ESL, gifted, etc.)
8. Program or course enrollments (percent and number) (regular academic, vocational, advanced placement, etc.)
9. Number of retentions
10. Office discipline records
11. In-school and out-of-school suspensions (with reasons)
12. Expulsions (with reasons)
13. Drop-outs (percent and number)
14. Postgraduation activities (college, military, employment)

COMMUNITY DATA

1. Description of community residents by age, level of education, race, marital status, income, education, etc.
2. Economic and social conditions of the community
3. Measures of the extent of involvement of the community in the school
4. Residents with school age-children (percent and number)
5. Other youth serving organizations in the community and services available

STAFF DATA

1. Size and deployment of staff
2. Summary of staff qualifications (degrees and institution, certifications, years of experience)
3. Staff absenteeism (number of days, sequence of days, days of week, reason, etc.)
4. Outside interests (hobbies, travel, businesses, etc.)

Outcome Data

Each year, assessment or achievement information is gathered from students to determine each child's individual academic progress. Many of these same data can be used in a collective way to assess the performance of the school and its various programs. These data are usually of most value for analysis when they are recorded in such a way as to allow trend analysis across three or more years, as shown in Figure 4.1. These data are particularly useful when they can be disaggregated by logical demographic categories such as those listed in the student and staff data sections just shown. This means that each item of data carries the identifying number of the student that generated it. In this manner, trend information can be calculated across years. Some of these data are easily quantifiable, allowing for statistical analysis, whereas others are more qualitative in

Subject Area	1997	1998	1999	2000	2001
Reading	54	55	56	57	56
Language	53	52	53	54	53
Math	51	53	54	55	54
Science	56	54	53	54	52
Social Studies	53	53	54	53	52

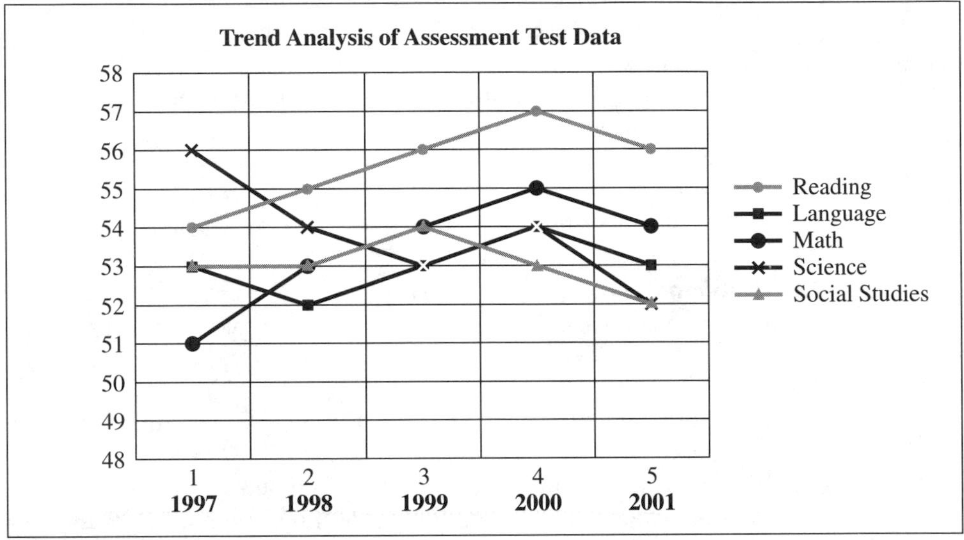

FIGURE 4.1 Ubben Elementary School Trend Analysis of Assessment Test Data

nature, allowing only for classification by demographic category. Assessment data commonly gathered by schools include:

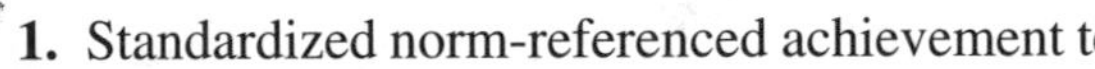

1. Standardized norm-referenced achievement tests
2. Writing assessments
3. Competency tests (criterion referenced—measured against predetermined curriculum standards)
4. End-of-course assessments
5. Gateway tests (required for passage to higher grade or graduation)
6. SAT/ACT
7. Early childhood assessments (readiness tests)
8. Authentic assessment artifacts (portfolios, performances, projects, products, etc.)

Stakeholder Survey Data

Another very important data source to help profile a school can be found in the opinions and attitudes of the school's stakeholders. Stakeholders are those individuals that have some reason to believe they are part of the school community. Included are students, parents, community members and local business employees, school faculty and all other staff members, administrators in the building as well as those in a district office, and others. Much valuable information can be gathered from stakeholders through informal contacts, but carefully prepared surveys sent to representative samples of the stakeholder groups often allows for easier data analysis and reporting.

Many survey forms for stakeholders are available from various educational organizations such as the NSSE Opinion Inventories.[4] For example, the NSSE inventories include separate survey forms for each stakeholder group and include questions about quality, strengths, and limitations of the school as well as quality changes over time. The results for each school are compared with a national sample.

In many cases, it is better for the principal to develop his or her own survey materials when specific program areas or problems are to be targeted. A needs assessment instrument can be created by using the belief statements as a base. A series of items that can be rated on a five-point Likert-type rating scale, ranging from strongly disagree to strongly agree, are developed for each belief statement. An illustration of a needs assessment statement is as follows:

SA	**A**	**N**	**DA**	**SD**	
1	2	3	4	5	Programs and varied instructional techniques are provided in order to respond to each child's individual needs and differences.

Statements can be grouped into logical categories, weighted, and scored. For example, if belief statements are organized around concepts from the effective schools research, including time, climate, basic commitment, staff, curriculum, leadership, and evaluation, several assessment items could be written for each of the categories. Responses can be divided by the number of items in the category in order to be viewed equally. This will allow comparison between categories for later priority determination. Figure 4.2 gives a complete illustration of a needs assessment instrument, including a weighted scoring sheet that is organized around effective schools concepts.

FIGURE 4.2 Needs Assessment

School Excellence Inventory

Directions: Rate the following Items on a scale of 1 to 5 to reflect your opinion of your school. (1 = Low…5 = High)

	(Low)				*(High)*
1. Students have favorable attitudes toward school and learning.	1	2	3	4	5
2. Students' learning is frequently evaluated using curriculum-referenced materials.	1	2	3	4	5
3. The staff has high expectations for the students and adults with whom they work.	1	2	3	4	5

(continued)

FIGURE 4.2 Continued

4. Students' time on-task behavior is maintained at a high level because:
- **a.** A climate of order and discipline has been established. 1 2 3 4 5
- **b.** Limited time is used in maintaining order. 1 2 3 4 5
- **c.** Classroom management tasks have been "routinized" to maximize available instructional time. 1 2 3 4 5
- **d.** The school staff has made a commitment to maximize learning time by reducing impediments to learning and interruptions of the school day. 1 2 3 4 5

5. Each student and parents receive regular feedback regarding the student's progress. 1 2 3 4 5

6. Student attendance rates are high. 1 2 3 4 5

7. There is a clear understanding of what the school believes in and stands for, which includes:
- **a.** An academic focus. 1 2 3 4 5
- **b.** A belief that all students have the ability to learn. 1 2 3 4 5
- **c.** An expectation that each student will learn. 1 2 3 4 5
- **d.** High expectations for each student. 1 2 3 4 5

8. Teachers regularly utilize techniques to assure that all students are learning. 1 2 3 4 5

9. Staff members are evaluated regularly. 1 2 3 4 5

10. Programs and varied instructional techniques are provided in order to respond to each child's individual needs and differences. 1 2 3 4 5

11. Students feel valued and successful. 1 2 3 4 5

12. Individual help is provided to students when needed. 1 2 3 4 5

13. School staff members exhibit a high degree of concern and commitment for the achievement and well-being of each student. 1 2 3 4 5

14. The principal is effective because:
- **a.** He or she understands the process of instruction, and accepts the responsibility for being an instructional leader. 1 2 3 4 5
- **b.** He or she is an able manager. 1 2 3 4 5
- **c.** He or she has high attainable expectations for the students and adults with whom he or she works. 1 2 3 4 5
- **d.** He or she has goal clarity (a clear sense of purpose and priorities) and is able to enlist the support of others in understanding, accepting, and accomplishing those ends. 1 2 3 4 5
- **e.** He or she recognizes the importance of (and actively involves) the people who work in and who are served by the school. 1 2 3 4 5
- **f.** He or she assists the school staff in implementing sound instructional practices. 1 2 3 4 5

15. Students receive prompt feedback on their work. 1 2 3 4 5

16. A high level of staff and student morale exists. 1 2 3 4 5

17. Members of the school staff are cooperative and supportive of each other. 1 2 3 4 5

18. The curriculum:
- **a.** Emphasizes mastery of basic skills. 1 2 3 4 5
- **b.** Is well defined. 1 2 3 4 5

FIGURE 4.2 Continued

	c. Is appropriately sequenced and articulated from grade to grade and from subject to subject.	1	2	3	4	5
	d. Includes clearly defined learner goals.	1	2	3	4	5
	e. Is regularly evaluated.	1	2	3	4	5
19.	Techniques are used to pinpoint individual student's strengths and weaknesses.	1	2	3	4	5
20.	The staff is competent and continues to grow and learn.	1	2	3	4	5
21.	The school is open to and encourages participation and involvement by parents and other citizens.		1	2	3	4
22.	Parents, students, and staff place a high priority on learning.	1	2	3	4	5
23.	Students are instructed at the appropriate level of difficulty.	1	2	3	4	5

SUMMARY SHEET
SCHOOL EXCELLENCE INVENTORY

TIME	CLIMATE	BASIC COMMITMENT	STAFF	CURRICULUM	LEADERSHIP	EVALUATION
#4a = ___	#1 = ___	#7a = ___	#3 = ___	#10 = ___	#14a = ___	#2 = ___
#4b = ___	#6 = ___	#7b = ___	#9 = ___	#18a = ___	#14b = ___	#5 = ___
#4c = ___	#11 = ___	#7c = ___	#13 = ___	#18b = ___	#14c = ___	#8 = ___
#4d = ___	#16 = ___	#7d = ___	#17 = ___	#18c = ___	#14d = ___	#12 = ___
Total = ___	#21 = ___	#22 = ___	#20 = ___	#18d = ___	#14e = ___	#15 = ___
+4 = ___	Total = ___	Total = ___	Total = ___	#18e = ___	#14f = ___	#19 = ___
	+ 5 = ___	+ 5 = ___	+ 5 = ___	Total = ___	Total = ___	#23 = ___
				+ 6 = ___	+ 6 = ___	Total = ___
						+7 = ___

DETERMINING VISION AND MISSION

Every school today must strive for quality. When improvement is seen in a school's quality, it is usually because the school has a vision of what quality represents and a sense of direction toward creating a quality program. The sense of direction can be developed for a school through the creation of a statement of beliefs (vision), a set of goals (mission), and specific objectives to be achieved (outcomes). Each of these three levels—beliefs, goals, and objectives—has a specific purpose in the planning process and each contributes in determining direction and showing interrelationships (see Figure 4.3).

A *statement of beliefs* can be thought of as a foundation or a philosophy for the school and should represent the collective thinking of the staff and community repre-

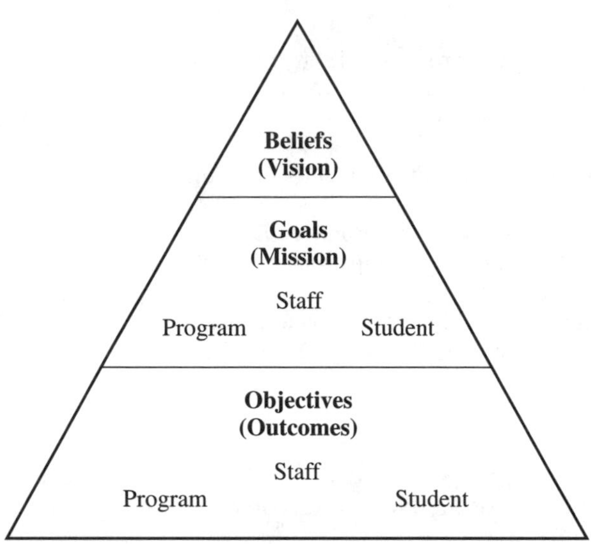

FIGURE 4.3 Determining Direction and Purpose for the School

sentatives. For example, the statement "Every child can learn and achieve mastery" is a statement of belief. It is part of one's philosophy of education.

A *goal statement* is a statement of intended direction (mission) relative to a belief statement (vision). For example, a school goal could be "Successful learning experiences will be provided for every child each day." This is a specific statement of intent. A goal, however, is often something that a school strives toward but may never totally achieve.

Just as goals should be an outgrowth of a philosophy or belief, *objectives* should be extensions of goals. Objectives are more specific than goals and should be obtainable, often within a stated period of time. An illustration of a program objective is "Instructional objectives will be developed by the staff for the reading and math curricula this year."

Total Quality Management (TQM) speaks of performance goals and process goals. These suggest that some goals or objectives will be stated in such a manner that they are measurable in some meaningful way. An example might be "Unit test scores, when charted over time, will show overall class improvement." However, Deming, in laying out the principles of TQM, cautions against setting work standards that prescribe numerical quotas.

Framework for Establishing Beliefs or Vision Statements

The vision, beliefs, and philosophy for a school should relate to societal expectations, wants and needs of the community, and the individual differences of children. Such a list can best be organized with an outline or framework of concepts and ideas to be included. There are many different ways such a framework can be organized. Three different frameworks or structures are included in this chapter for consideration.

Evaluative Criteria Framework

A second perspective of what approach should be used in developing a vision statement of philosophy or beliefs is drawn from the *evaluative criteria* guidelines of the national accrediting associations. They suggest considerations should be given to the following:

1. Relevance of the statement of philosophy to the larger purpose of the American democratic commitment.
2. Attention to intellectual, democratic, moral, and social values, basic to satisfying the needs of the individual and his culture.
3. Recognition of individual differences.
4. The special characteristics and unique needs of elementary school children.
5. Concern for the nature of knowledge and for the nature of the learning process as they apply to learners and their total development.
6. Consistency of philosophy with actual practice.
7. Identification of the roles and relationships expected of the community, the student, the teacher, and the administration in the educational process of the school.
8. The role of the elementary school program of the school district and the importance of the articulation with other elements of the overall educational program.
9. The responsibility for making a determination as to a desirable balance among activities designed to develop cognitive, affective, and psychomotor demands.
10. The relationship of the school and all other educational learning centers.
11. The responsibility of the school toward social and economic change.
12. The accountability of the school to the community it serves.[5]

Effective Schools Framework

The research on effective schools also suggest specific areas that might be considered for inclusion in a beliefs and goals listing. A summary of major areas includes the following:

1. Schoolwide measurement and recognition of academic success
2. A positive student climate emphasizing an orderly and studious school environment
3. A high emphasis on curriculum articulation
4. High support for good methodology
5. High expectations and clear goals for performance of students
6. Parental support for the education of students

These three frameworks for identifying beliefs statements obviously have some degree of overlap. But each also has a certain rationale for its own structure. The school might elect to use one of the three frameworks or create its own structure from a combination of them. One or more belief statements can be written for each of the areas on the outline.

Vision and Mission Development Process

The process of establishing a sense of direction in a school must be a dynamic one involving teachers, community members, and, in some cases, students. In reality, the interaction and debate of the processes in determining what the document is to include is more important than the product itself in that the vision and mission are important only if they are alive. Beliefs must be kept alive in the minds of staff and community, and those people must feel that the goals and objectives relative to those beliefs are appropriate.

Staff/Community Consensus. The initial formulation as well as the regular reviews and updates of the belief statements should be done using a staff/community/student consensus model. The participants are divided into writing teams consisting of three to five members, including all members of the faculty. Each writing team should be structured to create maximum internal variability. This means that each team should have teachers from different grade levels, subject areas, and experience background. If community members and students (secondary) are participating, one or more should be assigned to each writing team.

Each writing team should be given a complete list of belief topic areas. The team's task will be to write one or more statements regarding what it believes for each of the topics. For example, if one of the topic areas asks the team to list its beliefs regarding curriculum, the members might ultimately write a statement such as "We believe that the school staff should collectively review the basic objectives and strategies for teaching and learning and periodically reexamine and reconstruct objectives in view of current curricular priorities."

Each writing team should develop statements for each aspect of the belief framework. This may require 6 to 12 or more statements from each writing team. Upon the completion of the initial writing task, each writing team is asked to select one representative member from the group to meet with a similar member from each of the other teams to form a consensus team to discuss the statements written down by each team on the first topic. A second representative should be identified for the second topic as well as a third and fourth until all writing team members are representing their team to a consensus team consisting of one member from each of the other writing groups. Figure 4.4 illustrates the writing team–consensus team structure.

These newly formulated consensus teams review the written statements on the assigned topic from each of the writing teams and select, combine, and rewrite the submitted statements until they have developed a series of statements on the assigned topic that their group accepts. Each team representative then takes the newly combined set of statements on the team's topic back to his or her original writing team for discussion, additional modification, or ratification.

If the original writing team feels that the rewrite of the consensus team does not reflect the original team's beliefs, team members should modify the consensus team's work. The consensus team would then be reconvened to consider the recommended modifications. If necessary, the statements may go back and forth several times. The

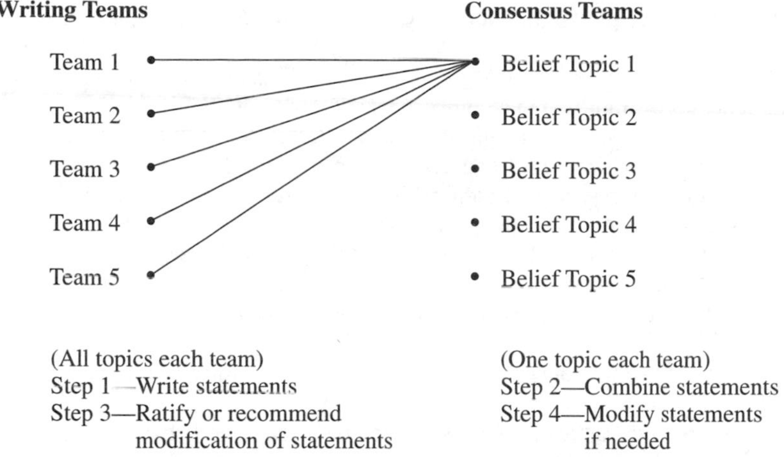

FIGURE 4.4 Writing Team—Consensus Team Structure

other consensus teams are carrying out the same procedures for their topics. The final set of belief statements developed by a school using this process is shown in Figure 4.5.

CLARIFYING EXPECTATIONS FOR STUDENT LEARNING

What should be the expected outcomes for students? What does the principal want his or her students to know and be able to do? What values does the principal wish his or her students to hold? The goal of this phase of the school improvement is to gain clarification through the development of a shared set of expectations for student learning and achievement. Most important is the need for all those who have a stake in the success of the school to agree on the broad areas of knowledge, skill, and abilities that students should be able to demonstrate when they exit from the highest grade in the school. This shared consensus of student-desired outcomes can provide the stakeholders of the school—students, parents, staff, and community—with a clear sense of direction and purpose for the education of children in the school. Student performance is the real purpose for efforts at improvement and the reason behind any school improvement planning process.

Process

Once again, the process of developing a shared vision of student expectations is critical to the success of any plan developed. A committee process with all stakeholder groups participating is extremely important. A shared vision is the desired outcome.

The process of developing a shared vision should begin with a review of the documents previously developed as part of the improvement planning. These include the

FIGURE 4.5 Sample High School Vision and Mission Statement

Vision: We believe that Manor High School is a unique educational environment. Its uniqueness is exemplified in certain aspects of its design. It is designed to meet the individual needs of a larger percentage of students than is possible in the traditional system; to avoid a mass-produced, molding effect; to provide a distinctly pleasant atmosphere for learning; to foster respectful relationships; and to serve the community.

We believe that all students have needs that must be fulfilled. We believe that all students are unique as individuals—that they develop at different rates and in different manners. We believe that students have a natural desire to learn independence, responsibility, self-assertion, democratic ideas, and the skills necessary to solve present and future problems.

We believe the role of the student is to involve himself or herself responsibly in the learning experience.

We believe that learning is evidenced by a behavioral change. It is a continuous process that takes place in the home, community, and school.

We believe that the role of the teacher is (1) to design learning opportunities and (2) to provide each student for whom he or she is responsible the freedom to learn what the student needs to take a productive and rewarding part in society. The teacher is an advisor and sharer.

We believe that teaching and learning can best be accomplished through interaction and involvement of students, staff, administration, and community.

We believe that the administration is responsible for supplying and maintaining all the physical accouterments of the school. The principal is to be an instructional leader but shares with students, teachers, and community the task of facilitating and coordinating learning. His or her leadership should be participatory and not authoritarian.

Mission: The mission of Manor High School is to establish a student and community learning center with high expectations for student performance designed to facilitate stimulating learning experiences and harmonious social interactions in which each individual has the opportunity to realize his or her full potential.

It is our endeavor to develop the following qualities to a high degree through conscientious and dedicated guidance and instruction. These qualities are:

1. The self-evaluative ability of the individual
2. The positive attitude of the individual toward himself or herself and others
3. The independence and responsibility in the individual
4. The creativity in the individual
5. The ability to be self-assertive
6. The acquiring of knowledge relative to both the mental and physical needs and abilities of the individual
7. The critical thinking and decision-making ability of the individual
8. The ability of the individual to contribute to and to make his or her way in our society

beliefs (vision) and goals (mission) statement and a review of the data gathered for the school profile. The analysis of these documents will help to identify stakeholder expectations, and the assessment and evaluation results will help identify the current learning levels. The statements of expectations for student learning to be developed, when finished, should reflect the beliefs and goals identified in the vision and mission statement.

The next step by the student outcomes committee should consist of two reviews of current practice and thought. The first should be a review of current research and theory of instruction methods and learning. Chapter 7 provides a basis for this type review. The second review should be of current school, district, state, and national goals for student learning. Several different frameworks or approaches to curriculum design are discussed in Chapter 6. Most of the national curriculum organizations (e.g., National Council of Teachers of Mathematics, National Council for Social Studies, National Council of Teachers of English, etc.) have published goals and standards in their respective program areas. The NSSE has several support documents to help local schools with developing goals for student learning.[6]

Based on the reviews of vision and mission, the previously developed school profile, and current practices in learning and standards for curriculum, the next step is to develop a statement of desired results for student learning. The statements should include the desired knowledge, skills, and abilities that a well-educated child should be able to demonstrate. They should be stated clearly to show what the student should know or be able to do.

If these tasks of identifying desired results of student learning are done thoroughly for all curriculum areas, it becomes a monumental task. In fact, it becomes a major component of the curriculum audit process. The entire process must be seen as a multiyear, multicycle process and part of a larger five-year strategic plan for the school, with only small parts of the entire process becoming the focus each year. For this reason, it is suggested that only a manageable number of schoolwide goals be identified for immediate attention.

A review of student learning needs should become the basis for the identification of goals to be initially targeted for action. Once again, a review of the data gathered in the school profile, along with the desired outcomes for the students, should be the basis for the needs assessment. Be careful to base the assessment on a broad review of student achievement. Do not get caught in the trap of looking at standardized achievement data only because this is easiest to use or because others are emphasizing it. But rather, make an effort to look at a broad base of student performance data. For example, portfolios of student work, essays or writing projects, oral presentations, group projects, open-ended problem-solving situations, self-assessment, peer assessment, term projects or research projects, or performance activities often are more valid measures of student performance.

A tentative list of 5 to 10 goals should be identified for initial consideration with 2 or 3 goals becoming the major focus. Others can be added later when success is observed with the first set. If too many goals are initiated, focus is lost and positive results harder to achieve. Be sure to continue to review all goals, recommendations, and decisions with the stakeholder committee for their consideration and acceptance.

ANALYSIS OF INSTRUCTIONAL AND ORGANIZATIONAL EFFECTIVENESS

The purpose of this analysis is to examine the quality of the work of the school on behalf of student learning. If schools look only at the desired results of student learning and pay no attention to the processes whereby the learning can take place, little will be accomplished.

A dual focus on the quality of the work of students and on the quality of the work of the school is required for school improvement to take place. The school's strengths and weaknesses should be identified. This can be done through a review of the literature on school organization as well as by observing quality practices in other schools through out the nation.

It is important to think of the school structural framework as an integrated system with each of the several organizational components closely related to one another. Systems theory requires that specific thought be given to each of several organizational components of the program: (1) curricular organization, (2) instructional processes, (3) student grouping practices, (4) staff organization, (5) the scheduling of learning time, and (6) facility utilization and design. Although the six components can be separated for discussion purposes, the program that results for any particular school must give detailed attention both to the contribution that each component makes to the achievement of the goals and objectives of the school and the development of each component in such a way that it is compatible with the other five components. For example, a belief statement may speak to the importance of meeting the individual needs of each child. From this belief statement a goal of individualizing instruction might be selected. This instructional format must then be supported with a student grouping plan, staffing plan, and schedule. In turn, if the staffing selection proposes team teaching, the facility utilization design should provide appropriate work spaces for teaching teams.

The organizational components are not equally important and should not be considered as equals, nor are they independent entities. Decisions regarding the organization of the curriculum and instructional program should be made first. These must logically be based on the beliefs and goals for the school. The other four components serve the first two.

The first step should be the review of *best practice* for effective schools as described in current educational research. Chapters 6, 7, 11, and 12 provide excellent reviews of current literature and ideas on each of these instructional organization components designed to bring about maximum student achievement and learning. These topics should be reviewed in conjunction with the vision, beliefs, mission, and goal process started earlier in the improvement process.[7]

Several other areas should be considered in the review of organizational effectiveness that are less directly connected to the instructional systems but are nevertheless critical to the overall effectiveness of the school. These include:

- *Practices of Leadership in the School.* Do the leaders support teaching and learning, develop schoolwide plans for improvement, make decisions that are research based, make decisions using collaborative techniques, monitor instruction, and manage the organization for safe operation and an efficient learning environment?

- *Learning Community Building.* Is there evidence of a good working climate in the school, with the staff functioning as a energized supporting learning organization? Is there a good working relationship in the school that engages parents and families as partners in the learning process? Is there a collaborative network with community members and groups, youth serving agencies, clergy and government leaders, and leaders in higher education and business?
- *Use of Technology.* Is there evidence that newer technologies of modern communication and computing are being integrated into the management of the school and the instructional programs of the school, providing students with a variety of skills and opportunities for expanded learning?

Documenting current practice in the school is the second step in the process of investigating the instructional and organizational effectiveness. This should be done using several approaches:

- *Document Review.* Instructional organization in schools is supposed to be well documented. Curriculum frameworks, lesson plans, teacher assignments, student schedules, minutes from faculty meetings and team meetings, and daily bulletins all provide insight into the reality of how instruction is currently organized and managed. These documents should provide a basis for analysis. On the other hand, if these documents do not exist or are very sketchy in the information they provide, this probably also delivers a message about what may be a lack of instructional organization.
- *Faculty Survey.* Survey the faculty regarding instructional practices currently being used. The School Excellence Inventory shown in Figure 4.2 focuses on instructional practices. The NSSE Survey of Instructional and Organizational Effectiveness[8] covers many of the identified topics, or the principal may wish to develop his or her own instrument tailored to specific questions and needs.
- *Observation and Interview.* An interview and observation schedule may be developed to gather information about instructional and organizational practices in the school. Although these data are often more difficult to summarize and illustrate in graphic form, they offer an opportunity for greater depth of analysis with reasons why certain things are as they are.

Summarize the findings of the investigation into instructional and organizational practices in the school and compare them to what was found in the literature regarding "best practices." From this analysis, identify school priorities for building and strengthening the instructional and organizational program of the school. Be sure to remember the "systems" nature of many of these organizational structures and that they need to be considered collectively when contemplating change.

Finally, return to the stakeholders, particularly the school faculty, for consensus. Select, with faculty involvement, from the priority list those instructional and organizational components that best support desired learning goals from the earlier analysis that clarified expectations for student learning and set priorities and targets for improvement.

By this time, the School Improvement Committee and school stakeholders have completed a school profile with a heavy emphasis on data; constructed a vision, mission, beliefs, objectives document with the involvement of each stakeholder group; identified appropriate learner outcomes for the school with targeted areas for improvement; and completed an analysis of the instructional and organizational structures of the school with priorities identified that complement those selected in the learner outcome section. The next task will be to build a plan of action.

ACTION PLANNING/PROJECT MANAGEMENT

Action planning is what professional planners label *programming an objective,* and that label is descriptive. The action plan contains the following:

- A description of the several activities necessary to achieve an objective
- The relationship of these activities to each other
- The assignment of specific responsibilities to individuals who will see to the implementation of the activities
- A time frame and chronology of activities and events
- An evaluation process

There are no guarantees that the plan will succeed in solving the existing problem, of course, and that is why the last element of the plan provides for an evaluation. The activities in the plan may be best thought of as "hypotheses"—more than a hunch, perhaps, certainly more than a hope, but nevertheless, not certainties. Therefore, it is necessary to evaluate the efficacy carefully, not only of the total project but also of the specific activities comprising the project.

Once the action plan is developed, project management is in great part a monitoring process. The project manager may be the principal but not necessarily so. Any person on the staff with good administrative skills and an interest in the project may be a likely candidate to become the manager.

This becomes an excellent way for the principal to develop and capitalize on the leadership skills of staff members, including assistant principals, faculty, and resource or support personnel. It is important that adequate resources be provided to the person put in charge of managing a project. This may include released time and secretarial service, as well as a budget.

Problem Analysis

Care must always be taken that the presumed problem is adequately analyzed before moving into an elaborate action plan. It is at the problem analysis point that a force field analysis proves helpful.

Force Field Analysis. Kurt Lewin, applying certain physical laws to the organizational setting, concluded that things stay the way they are in organizations because a field of opposing forces is in balance. One way to think about a problem situation is to regard the situation as being as it is because of positive ("driving") and negative ("restraining") forces that are equal in strength. The driving forces are current conditions and actions present in the organizational environment (or in the community, or even in society as a whole) which are such that change is encouraged. Restraining forces are conditions or actions which are such that change is discouraged or inhibited. These can be thought of as negative, or "minus," forces in the developing equation.

The force field concept issues from the physical law that a body at rest (in equilibrium) will remain at rest when the sum of all the forces operating on it is equal to zero. The body will move only when the sum is not zero, *and it will move only in the direction of the unbalancing force.*

It is not difficult to observe this phenomenon in organizations. The productivity of a school staff, the state of the school-community relations program, the success level of the intramural program, among any number of other observable situations are all subject to explanation (and change) by force field analysis. A thing is where it is because the sum of the *power* of the counterbalancing plus and minus forces is equal to zero—and the situation is "frozen."

Power is a key word here because equilibrium is not achieved by a simple equal *number* of forces. It is the strength of the force that is important. One overwhelming positive force (e.g., the infusion of huge amounts of federal or state dollars) may be quite sufficient to change dramatically the nature of a science program that had suffered from lack of equipment, inadequately prepared teachers, and lack of community concern. Similarly, a large, vocal, and interested religious group might impact mightily on the nature of a science curriculum in any particular community, despite research evidence about inquiry methods, adequate budget, well-trained teachers, or bright students, among any number of other forces that would otherwise be generative of good programming.

Movement (that is, change) will take place only when an imbalance is created. An imbalance will occur by eliminating forces, by developing new forces, or by affecting the power of existing forces. The imbalance "unfreezes" the current situation and the situation will change and a new state of equilibrium achieved. To recapitulate, an imbalance may be created by:

- The addition of a new force(s)
- The deletion of a force(s)
- A change in the magnitude or strength of any of the forces

Any plan that is developed after the force field analysis is conducted will probably make use of all three ways of creating an imbalance.

There is evidence, however, that attempting to increase only positive forces creates much tension in the system, and often the intensity of the restraining forces correspondingly increases. This leaves the organization no better off, and sometimes worse off, because of new tensions. The best results occur when the first effort is directed to reducing the intensity of the restraining forces. Also, there may be little or nothing that can be done about some of the forces—a few may be imponderables, others simply may be outside of the control of organization members.

Engaging in force field analysis focuses thinking and may result in a restatement of the problem. Often, what appeared to be the problem is really a symptom; one of the identified "restraining forces" is actually the problem that requires attention. Thus, a principal, project manager, and staff must have open minds at the early stages in order that energies are ultimately focused on the right issues and not dissipated on things that are only symptomatic.

CASE STUDY

You are the principal of a middle school with an enrollment of 800 students. The composition of the student body is racially and ethnically heterogeneous, with perhaps few more children from families at the lower end of the community's economic continuum.

During the gathering of data for your School Improvement Plan, you become aware that all might not be well with the reading program in your school. The students in grades 7 and 8 do not seem to be reading as well as might be expected. There are a number troubling indicators.

As you review scores on standardized tests, the Iowa Test of Basic Skills among these, you observe that your students, in the main, are well below norms for the system as a whole and for the nation. Several of your teachers have also expressed concern about the reading skills of their students. The librarian has commented about a low circulation rate even among the usually more popular children's books. Senior high school principal colleagues have remarked to you that the incoming students from your school seem to have less well-developed reading skills.

As you examine the situation, you reach the conclusion that something is functionally wrong with the reading program, and the anticipated outcome—adequately skilled readers—is not being realized. You decide your reading program should become one of the targeted areas for your School Improvement Plan.

An example of a partial force field analysis of this problem appears in Figure 4.6. In any given real situation, many forces beyond those suggested in the example could exist. When conducting such an analysis, it is important to focus only on *what is,* not on *what might be* or on what one wishes were so. The purpose of the force field analysis is to get the problem under an analytical lens, so that a feasible solution (action plan) can be developed either to solve or ameliorate the problem.

Generating Action Plans

Once the force field analysis has been completed, it is time to generate ideas for activities that, if accomplished, could be assumed to help solve the problem. Creative thought is what is sought. To do this, a principal could lead the staff in any of the three tech-

FIGURE 4.6 Example of a Force Field Analysis

Problem: The pupils in Hughes Middle School are not developing good reading skills.

FACILITATING FORCES (+)	RESTRAINING FORCES (−)
Instructional Materials Center	Student transiency (over district average)
Full-time librarian	Bilingual population
Budgeted for 3 aides	Bimodal distribution of teachers (many first year)
Funded ESL program	New reading series program; no in-service
New reading series	Parental involvement in school activities slight
Assistant principal is a reading specialist	Little study room in homes—high number of apartment and project dwellers
State mandated and funded tutorial program	Teacher turnover above district average
Most children walk to school (no bus students)	Single-parent and two-wage earner homes (people not readily available)
Expressed teacher concerns	No role models
Flexible schedule	Staff overload

niques for "unstructured" problem solving described in Chapter 3. Brainstorming or the nominal group techniques most easily lend themselves to this. There is one caveat: If the solutions generated do not relate in any way to the pluses and minuses in the force field analysis, they probably should be discarded. Unless the activity is such that it would seem to reduce a negative or strengthen a positive, then that activity cannot be expected to help solve the problem. All project activities must be related to the force field. Figure 4.7 illustrates this.

The Project Planning Document

Complex problems require the use of a planning document. The resolution of simple problems may not require an involved procedure, but the logic and steps in the project planning document are nevertheless applicable and should at least be a mental process. The document is the project manager's guide, and serves also as a monitoring device.

Figure 4.7 illustrates a comprehensive problem resolution document. Using the previous case as an example, the project goal is stated, activities are delineated, target dates are established, and specific persons are identified who have assigned responsibilities for the implementation of the activities.

In many instances, a specific activity may be especially complex and composed of several components to be carried out before the activity is accomplished. The responsible person would develop a similar document for use with his or her team and the project would be desegregated to another level. The point is, with such a document,

FIGURE 4.7 **Action Planning: The Problem Resolution Document**

Project: Improving the reading skills of seventh- and eighth-grade students at Hughes Middle School

Project Manager: Kay Weise, Assistant Principal
Completion Date: June 1*
Start Date: August 15

ACTIONS	START/ COMPLETE	RELATION TO FORCE FIELD (WHAT +/–)	COORDINATOR
Volunteers Program	10/1-cont.	#5(–)	Holland
After-school study program	11/1-cont.	#6(–)	Norris
"Why I Read" speakers	11/1–6/1	#9(–)	Carspecken
New teacher in-service program: Reading in subject areas	8/15–2/15	#6(+) #9(+) #3(–)	Craig
Reader of the Month Award	9/15–6/1	#1(+) #2(+)	Tanner
"Here's an Author"	2/1–3/1	#9(–)	Strahan
Story-Telling Time	10/5–5/15	#2(+) #3(+) #10(+)	Miller

*Actions #1 and #2 continue beyond June.

tasks are clearly spelled out and all are made aware of precisely what it is that is being attempted, how, who is responsible, when, and for what.

Putting the Plan into Operation

The project has now been separated into a series of activities. Complex activities have been subdivided into elements or events, the completion of which will conclude the activity, and responsibilities have been assigned and accepted. Before proceeding, there is need to establish realistic target dates, develop the project calendar, and put into place a monitoring and evaluation process. Project planning computer software is of great assistance in organizing and managing large projects.[9] Each of the activities and documents listed in this section can be efficiently developed with a good computer planning package.

Establishing Target Dates

Establishing precise starting and completion times for the project as a whole, as well as for each of the separate project activities, is critical.[10] In order to establish realistic completion dates, it is essential that those involved in the project understand (1) the nuances of the problem; (2) certain organizational realities, including, for example, requisitioning and purchasing procedures and time lines; and (3) the capabilities of the staff. If these conditions are met, then it is possible to set realistic target dates. To do this, the project team raises two questions: "If unanticipated problems arose—strikes, floods, a championship basketball team—what is the most pessimistic date by which this project could be completed?" Then the question is asked: "If all went well—no one became ill, adequate resources were available, the purchasing department finally got its act together—what is the most optimistic date by which this project could be completed?" The realistic target date is a point midway between the pessimistic and optimistic dates.

THE PROJECT CALENDAR: GANTT CHARTING

Once the activities and tasks have been delineated, the specific elements of the more complex activities detailed, and responsibilities assigned, the master schedule needs to be developed and posted. This is developed in the form of a *Gantt chart*. Figure 4.8 depicts a Gantt chart for the case study presented earlier. In the Gantt chart, each project activity is listed, along with the elements or tasks composing each activity and an indication of the targeted starting and completion dates of every entry.

The Master Project Document

The preparation of a master project document is an important responsibility of the project manager. The document may simply be a loose-leaf binder within which is placed the comprehensive problem resolution document, key personnel checklist, Gantt chart, minutes of team meetings, and any diary entries or other notes that might help future project managers. Such a document is of great assistance in the monitoring and evaluation process.

Monitoring and Evaluating the Project

The project manager's responsibility is to help the project team stay on schedule. This does not mean daily, or even weekly, supervision; it does mean frequent conversations with individual activity coordinators and regular team meetings for the purpose of information sharing and "midpoint corrections."

Other monitoring devices are available to the principal or project manager to help keep the project on target or to adapt to changes in the environment. Prominent posting of the Gantt chart will serve as both advertisement and stimulator.

Summative Evaluation

If regular monitoring has been occurring, then formative evaluation has been taking place. What remains to be developed is the summative evaluation. That is, how will the principal know if the project resulted in the desired outcome? Are things better? What worked? What did not work? What should be continued? What should not be continued?

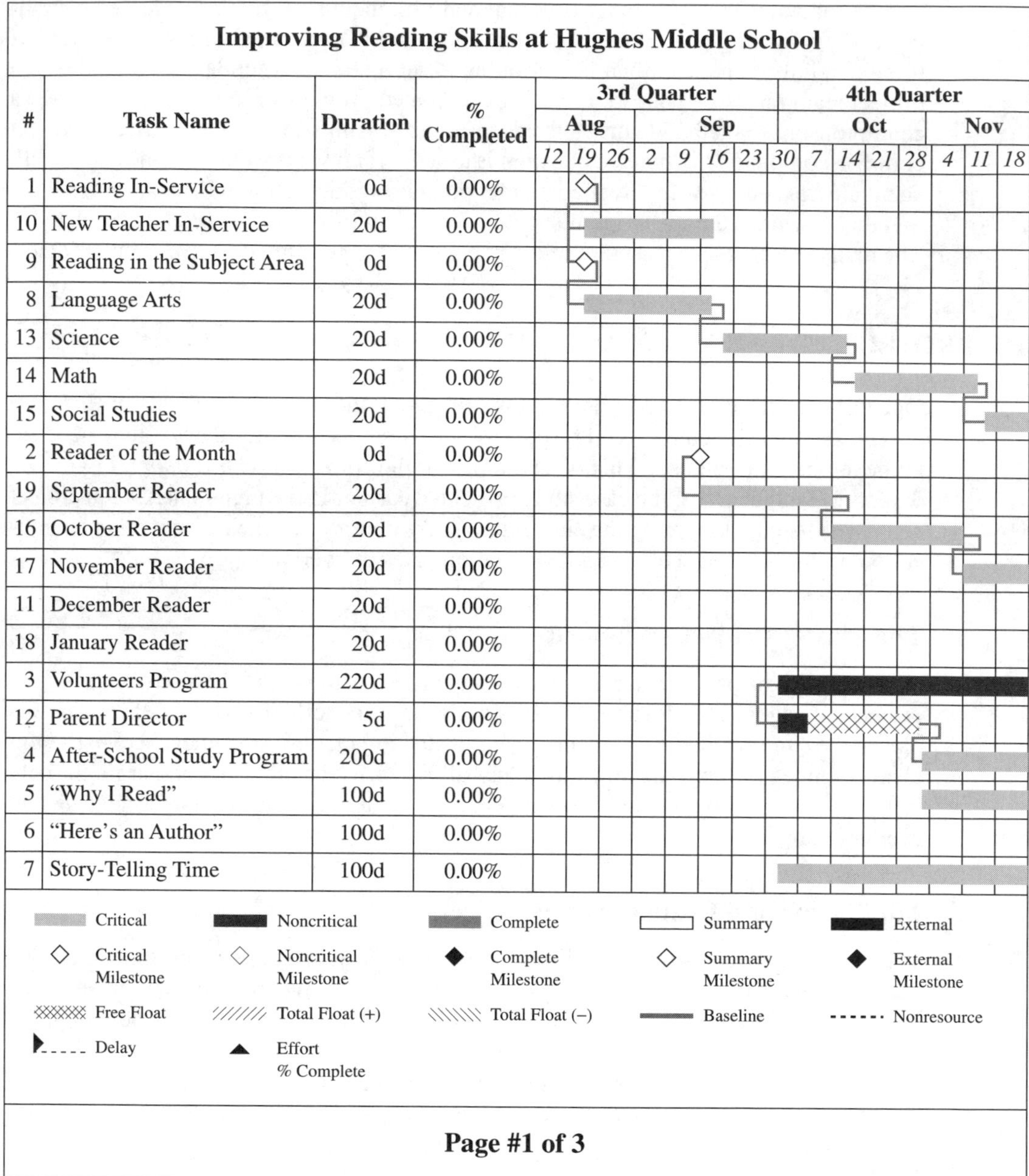

Improving Reading Skills at Hughes Middle School

#	Task Name	Duration	% Completed
1	Reading In-Service	0d	0.00%
10	New Teacher In-Service	20d	0.00%
9	Reading in the Subject Area	0d	0.00%
8	Language Arts	20d	0.00%
13	Science	20d	0.00%
14	Math	20d	0.00%
15	Social Studies	20d	0.00%
2	Reader of the Month	0d	0.00%
19	September Reader	20d	0.00%
16	October Reader	20d	0.00%
17	November Reader	20d	0.00%
11	December Reader	20d	0.00%
18	January Reader	20d	0.00%
3	Volunteers Program	220d	0.00%
12	Parent Director	5d	0.00%
4	After-School Study Program	200d	0.00%
5	"Why I Read"	100d	0.00%
6	"Here's an Author"	100d	0.00%
7	Story-Telling Time	100d	0.00%

FIGURE 4.8 The Project Calendar: Task List and Gantt Chart

To lend specificity, clarity, and form to the evaluation process, it is useful to think of the several activities as "hypotheses." In the case study, it was believed that if certain activities were carried out, students would evidence better reading skills. These hypotheses must be tested, for it is pointless to engage in a series of activities if there are no provisions to determine whether the results were sufficient to justify continued expenditure of resources.

At the beginning of any project it is important to state the indicators of achievement that the project staff is willing to accept as evidence of movement in the direction of the desired outcome. These indicators best come from restatements of the symptoms of the problem as originally stated. In the case study, some of those symptoms were

1. Standardized test scores were below system norms.
2. The circulation rates of library books was low.
3. Caustic comments were received from senior high school principals.
4. Teachers in the building expressed concerns.
5. There is high teacher turnover.

Changes in these conditions provide a basis for evaluating the effectiveness of the project. A review of test data, surveys of teachers and administrators, circulation rates, and formal and informal feedback from students and parents are all available tools for determining whether the project was successful. Moreover, it may be that certain of the activities were more productive than others. This, too, needs to be investigated and any changes made so that energies and other resources are focused for maximum benefit.

SUMMARY

The subject of this chapter has been goal setting and systematic problem identification and resolution using the School Improvement Process as the vehicle for change. Schools exist in an environment of change. The productivity of any particular school organization will depend in great part on the ability of leaders to analyze current conditions and future challenges, develop goals, and implement strategies for attaining the goals.

Instituting a process for identifying needs, and developing a plan to resolve these needs in a manner consistent with system needs is critical to effective building level leadership. Action planning and project management are fundamental skills that must be employed to meet this challenge satisfactorily.

ACTIVITIES

1. Review Case Studies 1, 2, and 5 at the end of this book. Apply the goal setting and strategic planning concepts expressed in this chapter. How might you proceed in addressing the problems cited in these cases? Set forth a strategy to overcome the problem.
2. Review the activities at the end of Chapters 9 and 14 for further planning activities.
3. Turn to the ISLLC Standards found in Appendix B. Review the performances listed with Standard One. Review the vision, mission, and belief statement for your school. Do the actions of your school staff reflect these statements? Are they posted or distributed to your stakeholders?
4. Does your school have a written School Improvement Plan? If so, review the plan. How is it being implemented? How long has it been in place? What results can be seen? How is the community involved?

ENDNOTES

1. Comments of the Cheshire cat to Alice *(Alice in Wonderland)* upon her request for directions after admitting she didn't know where she wanted to go.

2. *Good Schools: What Makes Them Work* (Washington, DC: National School Public Relations Association, 1980).

3. It is best if these data can be maintained in a database by child along with achievement data and grades. The data can then be tallied for demographic descriptions but can also be used to divide student into demographic groups for achievement comparisons. For example, How do the grades of children who come from single-parent homes compare with those from two-parent homes?

4. The NSSE Opinion Inventories are designed for teachers, students, parents, and community members to address a series of issues of concern to most schools. The survey forms are available from the National Study of School Evaluation, 1699 East Woodfield Road, Suite 406, Schaumburg IL 60173.

5. *Elementary School Evaluative Criteria* (Arlington, VA: National Study of School Evaluation, A Guide for School Improvement, 1973), pp. 39–40.

6. NSSE Indicators of Schools of Quality published in collaboration with the Alliance for Curriculum Reform provides a broad review of both school wide goals for student learning as well as specific instructional area goals.

7. It should be noted that although the Improvement Planning Process discussed in this planning chapter appears to be a step-by-step linear process, it is best done as an interactive process with each section influencing and being influenced by the other components. In other words, an idea discovered while developing this section of the analysis of instructional and organizational structure may cause a committee to modify a belief or change the wording in a vision statement or somewhere else in the plan.

8. The NSSE Survey of Instructional and Organizational Effectiveness is available from the National Study of School Evaluation, 1699 East Woodfield Road, Suite 406, Schaumburg IL 60173.

9. The Gantt chart illustration (Figure 4.8) uses *Project Scheduler 6 for Windows* by Scitor Corporation. There are many other good planning programs on the market, such as *Microsoft Project*.

10. In not all cases will the completion of one activity, or one component, depend on another, but sometimes this will be so. Even when this is not so, it is nonetheless vital that activities be completed on time. When a project is very complex and has many interrelated parts, it may be necessary to institute the Program Evaluation Review Technique (PERT). PERT will depict the order in which each of the activities and any subactivities must occur, as well as the relationship of one activity, event, or element to another.

SELECTED READINGS

Arterbury, Elvis, and Shirley M. Hord. "Site-Based Decision Making: Its Potential for Enhancing Learner Outcomes." *Issues . . . about Change 1,* no. 4 [on-line] < www.sedl.org >.

Barker, Joel A. *Future Edge: Discovering the New Paradigms of Success* (New York: William Morrow, 1992).

Brandt, R. "Coping with Change." *Educational Leadership 48,* no. 7 (1991): 3.

Buell, Nancy A. "Building a Shared Vision—The Principal's Leadership Challenge." *NASSP Bulletin 76,* no. 542 (March 1992): 88–92.

Carlson, Robert V., and Gary Awkerman (Eds.). *Education Planning: Concepts, Strategies and Practices* (New York: Longman, 1990).

Carnine, D. *Will Mandating Instructional Approaches Help Teachers of Diverse Learners? Forebodings from California* (Eugene, OR: National Center to Improve the Tools of Educators, University of Oregon, 1994).

Clarke, John H. "Growing High School Reform: Planting the Seeds of Systemic Change." *NASSP Bulletin 83* (April 1999): 109.

DuFour, Richard P. "Help Wanted: Principals Who Can Lead Professional Learning Communities." *NASSP Bulletin 83* (1999): 12–17.

Ellison, Linda, and Brent Davies. "Strategic Planning in Schools: An Oxymoron?" *School Leadership and Management 18,* no. 4 (November 1998): 461–473.

Fullan, Michael G. "Turning Systemic Thinking on Its Head." *Phi Delta Kappan 77,* no. 6 (1996): 420–423.

Fullan, Michael G. *Change Forces: Probing the Depth of Educational Reform* (London: Falmer Press, 1993).

Gardner, Howard. *Multiple Intelligences: The Theory in Practice* (New York: Basic Books, 1993).

Gaynor, Alan K., and Jane L. Evanson. *Project Planning: A Guide for Practitioners* (Boston: Allyn and Bacon, 1992).

Glasser, William. *The Quality School* (New York: HarperCollins, 1992).

Glickman, C. D. *Renewing America's Schools* (San Francisco: Jossey-Bass, 1993).

Goodlad, J. I. *A Place Called School: Prospects for the Future* (New York: McGraw-Hill, 1984).

Hedges, L. V., Laine, R. D., and Greenwald, R. "Does Money Matter? A Meta-Analysis of Studies of the Effects of Differential Inputs on Student Outcomes," *Educational Researcher* (April 1994): 5–14.

Holt, Maurice. "The Educational Consequences of W. Edwards Deming." *Phi Delta Kappan 74,* no. 5 (January 1993): 382–388.

Hord, Shirley M. "Realizing School Improvement through Understanding the Change Process." *Issues . . . about Change 1,* no. 1 [on-line] < www.sedl.org >.

Hughes, Larry W. "Organizing and Managing Time," in *Developing Skills for Instructional Supervision,* ed. James Cooper (New York: Longman, 1984), Chapter 3.

Hughes, Larry W., and Gerald C. Ubben. *The Elementary Principal's Handbook: A Guide to Effective Action,* 4th ed. (Boston: Allyn and Bacon, 1994). Especially see Chapters 5 and 21.

Jacobs, Heidi Hayes (Ed.). *Interdisciplinary Curriculum: Design and Implementation* (Alexandria, VA: Association for Curriculum and Supervision Development, 1989).

Johnson, William, and Johnson, Annabel M. "World-Class Schools in the 21st Century." *NASSP Bulletin 83* (April 1999): 606.

Kazis, Richard. *Improving the Transition from School to Work in the United States* (Washington, DC: American Youth Policy Forum, Competitiveness Policy Council, and Jobs for the Future, 1993).

Little, Judith Warren. "Teachers' Professional Development in a Climate of Educational Reform." *Educational Evaluation and Policy Analysis 15* (1993): 129–151.

Marzano, R., Pickering, D., and J. McTighe. *Assessing Student Outcomes* (Alexandria, VA: Association for Supervision and Curriculum Development, 1993).

McLaughlin, Milbrey W. "Fostering Teacher Professionalism in Schools," in *Restructuring Schools: The Next Generation of Educational Reform,* ed. Richard F. Elmore and Associates (San Francisco: Jossey-Bass, 1990), pp. 59–96.

Murphy, John, and Jeffery Schiller. *Transforming America's Schools* (LaSalle, IL: Open Court, 1992).

National Forum on Assessment. *Principles and Indicators for Assessment Systems* (Cambridge, MA: Fair Test, 1995).

Pawlas, George E. "Vision and School Culture." *NASSP Bulletin 81* (March 1997): 587.

Preuss, Paul. "Converting Goals to Achievements." *Multimedia Schools 6* (May/June 1999): 3.

Purkey, Stewart, and Marshall S. Smith. "Effective Schools: A Review." *Elementary School Journal 83,* no. 4 (1983): 427–452.

Schlechty, Philip C. *Schools of the 21st Century: Leadership Imperatives for Educational Reform* (San Francisco: Jossey-Bass, 1991).

Sergiovanni, Thomas J. *The Lifeworld of Leadership: Creating Culture, Community and Personal Meaning in Our Schools* (San Francisco: Jossey-Bass, 2000).

Sizer, Theodore R. *Horace's School* (Boston: Houghton-Mifflin, 1992).

Solkov-Brecher, Janice I. "A Successful Model for School Based Planning," *Educational Leadership 50,* no. 1 (September 1992): 52–54.

Sparks, Dennis. "A Paradigm Shift in Staff Development." *Education Week 42* (March 1994).

Stevenson, Harold, and James W. Style. *The Learning Gap* (New York: Summitt, 1992).

Stufflebeam, D. L., McCormick, C. M., Brinkerhoff, R. O., and Nelson, C. O. *Conducting Educational Needs Assessment* (Boston: Kluwer-Nijhoff, 1985).

Sybouts, W. *Planning in School Administration: A Handbook* (New York: Greenwood Press, 1992).

Valentine, Evelyn Pasteur. *Strategic Management in Education: A Focus on Strategic Planning* (Boston: Allyn and Bacon, 1991).

Vann, Allan S. "Setting Specific Annual School Goals." *Principal 69,* no. 5 (May 1990): 43–45.

Walberg, H. "Generic Practices," in *Handbook of Research on Improving Student Achievement,* ed. G. Cawelti (Arlington, VA: Educational Research Service, 1995).

Wiggins, G. "A True Test: Toward More Authentic and Equitable Assessment." *Phi Delta Kappan 70,* (1989): 703–713.

Wiggins, G. P. *Assessing Student Performance: Exploring the Purpose and Limits of Testing* (San Francisco: Jossey-Bass, 1993).

Wilson, Richard B., and Mike Schmoker. "Quest for Quality." *The Executive Educator* (January 1992): 18–22.

PART II

DEVELOPING A POSITIVE SCHOOL CULTURE

The school leaders of the twenty-first century must have knowledge and understanding of student growth and development; applied learning theories; applied motivational theories; curriculum design, implementation, evaluation, and refinement; principles of effective instruction; measurement, evaluation, and assessment strategies; diversity and its meaning for educational programs; adult learning and professional development models; the change process for systems, organizations, and individuals; the role of technology in promoting student learning and professional growth; and school cultures. They should also believe in, value, and be committed to student learning as a fundamental purpose of schooling; the proposition that all students can learn; the variety of ways in which students can learn; life-long learning for self and others; professional development as an integral part of school improvement; the benefits that diversity brings to the school community; a safe and supportive learning environment; and preparing students to be contributing members of society. ISLLC Standard Two supports these standards.

> **Standard 2: A school administrator is an educational leader who promotes the success of all students by advocating, nurturing, and sustaining a school culture and instructional program conducive to student learning and professional growth.**

Part II addresses this standard and the knowledge, dispositions, and performances that accompanies it.

CHAPTER FIVE

CREATING A POSITIVE LEARNING CLIMATE

Just as the teacher establishes the climate for the classroom, the school principal plays a significant role in establishing the climate for the school. How teachers perceive and interpret the actions of the principal leads to the construction of the culture of the school and, in part, each teacher's classroom culture.

—Gene Hall and Archie George[1]

Good schools are characterized by high standards, high expectations, and a caring environment. Good schools are also invariably orderly places. Misbehavior is dealt with quickly, fairly, openly, and without recrimination. Importantly, in good schools, the entire school community knows what the expectations are, supports these expectations, and understands and supports the rules that are designed to ensure a positive learning climate. Faculty and students seem to care about each other.

Analyses of leadership styles and support behaviors reveal that principals in high-performance schools are assertive and task and academically oriented. In effective schools, the discipline code is clear and the principal is viewed as "firm and friendly" but not as a "pal." Good principals are mobile and highly visible in the halls, classrooms, and cafeteria. They spend much time monitoring behavior, troubleshooting and conferring with teachers.

IT'S NO SECRET

Study after study and myriad reports from practicing principals reveal four essential ingredients of the maximally productive environment for learning and positive student control:

1. Clear, firm, and high teacher and administrator expectations
2. Consistent rules and consequences that directly relate to breaking these rules
3. A decided and well-implemented emphasis on the self-esteem of all students

4. Public and private acknowledgment and rewarding of positive behavior by students

THE SCHOOL AS A CULTURE

Schools have a complex student society, and many things go on in a school that seemingly have little relationship to the curriculum. All of these "things," including the curriculum, have a mighty impact on the learning climate of the school. Creating a positive learning climate requires a great understanding of the needs of learners. The needs of learners are varied and only partly addressed by a formalized set of classroom and cocurricular activities.

The real or perceived normative behavior of a student body will determine reward or punishment practices, teacher and administrator attitudes and behaviors, and even teacher and administrator attrition rates. Some schools in a community may be classified as "tough" schools; others as "good places to work"; most often, these references reflect normative student behavior patterns. But normative behaviors and mass actions to the contrary, a student body is composed of many bodies and, although certain groups may determine in great part the "accepted" behavior, the student who walks through the door of the principal's office is an individual complex of forces that may or may not epitomize the student body.

The focus of this chapter is on student behavior and positive student control mechanisms to help students be successful. The chapter is organized into three parts. The first part contains a discussion of principles for achieving positive student control. Included are suggestions for the development of sensible rules and regulations. We conclude the section with an examination of gangs and violence. The second and third parts of the chapter include discussions about student counseling programs and other student services.

POSITIVE STUDENT CONTROL

For more years than we care to think about, we have been actively engaged in working with principals and school faculties throughout the United States and other nations. Few things are universally true in this world but we have *never* been in a school that had a productive learning environment that was not also orderly. The schools were not always quiet, but they were always orderly. Students and teachers were going about the business of learning in an efficient, effective, and caring way.

People (staff, students, and parents) knew what the rules were and worked hard to see that they were abided by. Transgressions were dealt with quickly, fairly, and without lingering resentments. In these schools it was the uniform practice to follow the principles of substantive and procedural due process in spirit and in practice.

Five Premises about the School Environment and Students

Our discussion about schooling and student behavior is based on five premises:

1. Schooling occurs in a group context. Therefore, the behavior of any individual student will instantaneously have an impact on the behavior of other students.
2. Learning occurs best in an orderly environment.
3. An orderly environment can be best achieved by policies and strategies that promote self-regulation of behavior (internal control) rather than policies and strategies that try to force compliance with elaborate control mechanisms and overuse punishment (external control).
4. The environment is enhanced when the staff behaves in an orderly and internally controlled way.
5. The rules to guide behavior should be simple, well known, and continuously reinforced.

The Development of a Positive Program

The principal of a school has a particular responsibility to lead the staff in developing school policies to control student behavior. This is not to suggest that the principal personally should write the policy, but it is the principal who must develop the procedures by which the staff can establish a behavior philosophy, disciplinary procedures to be followed, and techniques for corrective action.

Fundamental to an orderly learning climate are well-understood, appropriate, and consistently applied rules and procedures. Once the rules are in place, there are two equally important conditions that must be met: The rules must be promulgated in a manner that ensures understanding by all affected, and there must be regular and systematic evaluation of the need for and efficacy of existing rules. Times change, needs change, and appropriate response patterns change. It is important that rules be examined routinely in view of whether they continue to serve the intended purpose in an effective and efficient manner.

It All Starts in the Classroom

Professor Wilford Weber at the University of Houston has developed a classroom climate instrument that can be easily employed by a principal for use in giving behavioral feedback to teachers about their interactions with students during a class period or learning event. Figure 5.1 depicts behavioral statements and an observation instrument based on these behavioral statements. Basic to the process are three assumptions:

1. Instruction and learning take place best in a positive social and emotional environment
2. The social and emotional environment is largely a function of teacher-student interpersonal relationships

FIGURE 5.1 Classroom Climate Indicator

1. The teacher establishes clear expectations as evidenced by:
   - ■ ______________________
   - ■ ______________________
2. The teacher establishes and enforces reasonable rules as evidenced by:
   - ■ ______________________
   - ■ ______________________
3. The teacher communicates respect for students as evidenced by:
   - ■ ______________________
   - ■ ______________________
4. The teacher communicates genuineness (integrity) as evidenced by:
   - ■ ______________________
   - ■ ______________________
5. The teacher communicates empathy as evidenced by:
   - ■ ______________________
   - ■ ______________________
6. The teacher communicates unconditional positive regard for students as evidenced by:
   - ■ ______________________
   - ■ ______________________
7. The teacher uses positive reinforcement as evidenced by:
   - ■ ______________________
   - ■ ______________________
8. The teacher uses mild desists as evidenced by:
   - ■ ______________________
   - ■ ______________________
9. The teacher applies appropriate negative consequences for "out-of-line" behavior as evidenced by:
   - ■ ______________________
   - ■ ______________________

FIGURE 5.1 Continued

10. The teacher fosters group cohesiveness as evidenced by:

- ______________________________
- ______________________________

11. The teacher establishes and maintains productive group norms as evidenced by:

- ______________________________
- ______________________________

12. The teacher demonstrates an understanding of "what it's like to be a kid" as evidenced by:

- ______________________________
- ______________________________

Courtesy of Dr. Wilford A. Weber, Professor of Curriculum and Instruction, University of Houston.

3. The teacher—*not the student*—is the major determiner of the nature of those interpersonal relationships.

Twelve teacher behaviors comprise the conditions that foster and maintain a positive classroom atmosphere. These behaviors appear in Figure 5.1 as a part of the instrument, which requires that there be specific examples of the behavior being demonstrated during the lesson observed. It is from this instrument that a postobservation conference can be based and suggestions or a growth plan developed. (See Chapters 7 and 9 for a discussion of clinical supervision and growth plans.)

The Classroom Climate Indicator displays important aspects of a positive classroom climate and how to achieve these. Clearly, not all of these would necessarily be evidenced in a single classroom observation, but over time—and over a school day—all ought to be observable. At the least, a basis for a principal working productively with teachers in the improvement of classroom conditions is provided.

Developing Good Rules. It is axiomatic that if staff and students are to be held accountable for certain standards, these expectations must be established and promulgated *ahead of their application* in a manner that makes them easily disseminated, learned, and understood. A principal has the responsibility to prescribe reasonable controls for the efficient day-to-day operation of the schools.

What is "reasonable"? A rule of thumb applied most frequently by the court is: "Does the regulation enhance the education of the children, promote their interest and welfare, and is it for the common good of education?" It is implicit that the regulations be within the legal authority of the school district. Regulations beyond the province of the school board are not enforceable. A long-standing decision has held that "boards are not at liberty to adopt according to their humor regulations which have no relevance to the schools' purposes.[2] This would be no less true in the matter of rules and regulations prescribed by the principal.

Moreover, while it is sound practice to develop procedures and guidelines that provide for consistency of school operation, conscious parsimony will serve best. Developing long lists of dos and don'ts in an attempt to cover every contingency can create a school climate in which the name of the game becomes beating the system—a climate in which staff and students derive a perverse joy from testing the limits.

Neither the extreme of rules for every occasion nor its opposite, no rule at all, is sensible. Principals within the school and teachers within the classroom have the right *and the obligation* to determine reasonable policies governing the conduct of their charges, not only to maintain a proper educational climate but also for safety.

Other Factors Influencing Behavior

There are other conditions well within the control of the school administrator and staff that contribute much to the learning climate. Disorder and lack of control in schools are frequently a result of the existence of large, impersonal masses of students. Students' feelings of alienation and teachers' feelings of helplessness must be recognized and can be addressed by the reorganization of schools into smaller learning communities. The "school within a school" concept *is* relevant.

It is also true that most of the severe disciplinary problems are caused by a very small percentage of the students. Special facilities and methods are needed to handle the more severely disruptive children if these cannot be handled effectively in the classroom. Crisis intervention centers, "adaptive behavior classes," and in-school suspensions, among a number of other common practices, respond to this problem.

The principal's own behavior and activities will help set the tone. A principal who helps teachers develop good disciplinary practices, a principal who maintains direct contact with students, and a principal who is visible and active in the hall, cafeteria, and library is critical to a good learning climate.

ACTIVELY ENCOURAGING A POSITIVE LEARNING ENVIRONMENT

> We have to assure these children that while they are with us they are safe and will be treated well. For some that may be all we can do but we must do that. We may not be able to control what goes on in any child's life before or after school. But here they will not be abused and they will be treated fairly. And they will be protected and they will be respected. And we're going to help them learn how life can be.[3]

A Promising Model

DuSable High School in Chicago is a good example of how one principal restructured his high school to address the impact that alienation and an inadequate social response system have on student behavior and the increasing incidence of violence in schools. DuSable serves an inner-city neighborhood that, at best, has been called "mean." It is not a huge high school—on any given day the number of students in attendance will be about 1,000—but the organizational framework at DuSable would work in any school, larger or smaller. With a combination of well-trained teachers and an organization characterized by a "house plan," serious discipline problems are significantly down and attendance is up.

The school is organized into 11 houses that operate under the philosophy of Theodore Sizer's Coalition of Essential Schools. DuSable is a member of the Coalition. The philosophic base is that anonymity and intellectual chaos are a concomitant of large schools—unless there are structural and instructional changes beyond simply adding more teachers, more sections of classes, and increasing the number of security personnel.

According to Sizer, large schools need to create cadres of students and teachers Sizer has referred these cadres as "clutches." The large school should be characterized by "a clutch of kids with a clutch of teachers. That's important because it's hard for any one of us to size up any kid well. If teachers have time to discuss these kids, they're liable to get a pretty good fix on them. They know them when they get into trouble. . . . At the same time, the students know they are cared for."[4]

At DuSable, each of the 11 houses has 8 to 10 teachers. Each of these teachers has undergone intensive and extensive training in curriculum planning, team building, and ways to assess student progress well beyond the usual standardized achievement tests. A learning community is created that at once contains the intimacy required to diminish alienation. The key ingredients are well-trained teachers, a restructured curriculum, block scheduling, and learners and teachers as teams.

Personalizing the School

The DuSable example has much relevance to creating an inviting school environment—an environment within which students take ownership of their school and behave in ways that are socially responsible.

Sizer stated, "Personalization is the single most important factor that keeps kids in school."[5] And, no surprise here—staying in school is the single most important factor in student learning. In a study that examined data from all 50 states and the District of Columbia and focused on student outcomes, fiscal issues, and student persistence in schools (that is, not dropping out). Hashway reached the conclusion that "the most influential factor upon school persistence is school achievement." Very important and pertinent to our discussion here, Hashway went on to write, "Students who view themselves as successful will stay in school."[6] To this same point, Achilles and Smith wrote, "Educators know that those who do best in school, who are rewarded by school participation, and who like school are also those who are most often not absent and not dropouts."[7]

Positive learning environments are characterized by outward and readily recognized mutual expressions of appreciation and respect—from student to student, teacher to student, teacher to teacher, teacher to administrator, administrator to student—

honestly given and graciously received. Positive learning environments are also characterized by mechanisms for the early identification of students who are drifting from the central purpose of formal schooling. Finally, positive learning climates are characterized by orderliness and a compassionate concern for the security of all members of the school family. Action-oriented programs are required to create the positive learning environment.

"Hoopla." The efficacy of public rewards for achievement cannot be underestimated. "Hoopla" is not hokey; the most productive organizations—in private and public sectors—make much of measured progress toward goals and of individual accomplishment. Acknowledgment of achievement shouldn't be limited to only students; the entire school family, custodians, bus drivers, teachers, counselors, and all the rest, deserve public recognition for jobs well done.

Effective methods of acknowledgment abound: T-shirts, public ceremonies, special parking privileges, positive time-out, bulletin board exhibits, standing ovations at assemblies, stars and stickers, "Number One" clubs, prizes, badges, friendly taps on the shoulder, and the list could go on. The point is that praise, sincerely given, works.

"Hoopla" is also important to help individuals recognize their own achievements without benefit of others' approval. Self-approval is sustaining. Teachers can help students in this by asking them to share a personal accomplishment that they are proud of but that others may not know about. Principals can do the same with the staff.

Adult Visibility. Community volunteer programs that have increasing numbers of parents and other citizens in the schools are a great help in reducing the incidence of violence and gang activity. We are not referring here simply to "parent patrols" in the halls and the like, although this is one type of activity that has been used that has shown some success. Any of a variety of volunteer programs that increase the conspicuous visibility of adults—and particularly parents—in the schools will help. Children report feeling safer when adults are around.

Gangs. Policies and procedures that decrease gang activity may be best developed locally to meet local needs. Some general considerations can be found in the research and literature, however. Figure 5.2 identifies some steps a school staff can take if there is evidence of gang activity on the campus.

Achilles and Smith have summed the principal's responsibility:

> The principal *must* ensure a safe environment that encourages learning. Pupils need to feel safe so they can attend to the school's learning goals; pupils who are trying to learn must be free from harassment, violence and external diversions that distract them from the tasks of learning. Teachers should be free to work at teaching rather than at order and control."[8]

Gangs are *not* loose social networks, however, and even though the attraction may be protection and friendship, *the goal of a gang is control and social intimidation.* Gangs operate outside of the civilized social fabric and in lawless ways.

FIGURE 5.2 There Is a Gang in the House

Steps to Be Taken if Gang Activity Is Suspected

School administrators should:

- Establish the school as neutral ground and adopt a "no-tolerance" policy for gang activity.
- Distinguish between youthful misbehavior and delinquent or criminal acts.
- Cooperate with other social agencies, including the police or sheriff's department, to train school personnel in how to identify and handle gang members.
- Create a mechanism for mediating student conflicts, including consideration of peer mediation.

Teachers should:

- Treat all students fairly and consistently.
- Incorporate gang issues into class lessons; address rights and responsibilities of citizens, decision making, and problem-solving skills.
- Establish good lines of communication with parents.
- Be aware of community resources that are available.

Generally speaking, a gang is a group who meets the following criteria:

- The group has a name and an identifiable leader or leadership structure.
- The group maintains a geographic, economic, or criminal activity "turf."
- Members associate on a regular and continuous basis in school and out of school.
- The group has visual symbols—insignia, greeting patterns, distinguishing dress, and so on—that readily identify one as either a member or nonmember.
- The group engages in delinquent or criminal activity. Delinquent and/or criminal activity is what differentiates a gang from organizations that often are otherwise visually consistent with stereotypic images of a gang.

School personnel need to become familiar with the symbols, terms, phrases, and other identifiers of gang presence. Figure 5.3 describes telltale signs suggesting the presence of gangs in the school.

The School as a Safe Haven

Schools should be safe places irrespective of the nature of the neighborhood from which the students come. This means a zero-tolerance policy for major transgressions. No weapons, no controlled substances, no graffiti—this must be the policy of the school, and all personnel and all students need to be advised of this and what to do when these are discovered. What should be done if this policy is violated? Report it, immediately. The principal's responsibility is to get the transgressor out of contact with the rest of the student body—immediately. If it is a criminal act, then other agencies need to get involved as well.

FIGURE 5.3 There May Be Gangs

There May Be Gangs if . . .

Graffiti: Unusual or indecipherable signs, symbols, alphabets, and nicknames on walls, notebooks, papers, and clothing might be signals of gang presence.

Colors: Members of gangs often reveal a subtle or obvious choice of clothing or color of clothing, or wear specific brands or styles of clothing, hats, shoes, jewelry, or haircuts, or may wear their clothing in distinctive ways, such as one jean leg rolled up.

Handsigns, Handshakes, or Unusual Language: Members often have unusual ways of greeting or signaling each other.

Initiations: Otherwise unexplainable wounds, skin carvings, tattoos, bruises, or injuries may be the result of gang initiation ceremonies.

Behavior Changes: Sudden changes of moods or behavior, as well as unexplainable poor grades can signal gang involvement.

Interagency Cooperation. The school is not the only agency that has a stake in an orderly and safe environment. Large and small communities are depending more and more on an interagency approach. On any principal's phone list ought to be the numbers of the police juvenile division, Child Protective Services officers, juvenile court officials, Crime Stoppers organizations, and any departments of youth development, whatever they might be entitled. Additionally, the school records office needs to have the number and name of the responsible adult in the youth's home. Some success has been achieved in such cities as Chicago, Baltimore, and Knoxville, among many others where schools and mayors' offices have moved to develop formal councils and networks to provide for interagency cooperation.[9]

THE COUNSELING PROGRAM

Counseling programs are too often thought of as an array of activities extended to the classroom by a designated person called a guidance counselor. Our position is that this is totally inadequate and at times counterproductive to the needs of students. A good counseling program needs to include teachers in a direct and organized way and avoid overreliance on guidance counselors.

Guidance counselors often suffer from highly unrealistic expectations of their colleagues. In these days of troubling anonymity in large school units, of drop-ins and spiritual drop-outs, an approach different from that which locates all counseling responsibilities in one office is required. The need is for a total school commitment to the counseling function.

A different mode of organizing counseling services in the schools is needed—not because trained guidance counselors aren't important, but because as presently organized in most schools, their skills are not being used maximally. The function of counseling is so critical to the development of students that a better approach must be employed.

Student advisement and guidance in the elementary and middle schools especially should remain the function of the classroom teacher, and a continued effort should be made to include teachers as part of a counseling team in the secondary schools as well. The main problem the classroom teacher faces in organizing an effective student advisement program is usually one of time. There are ways to gain time for student counseling however. Organizing activities and dividing some of the responsibilities with other appropriate personnel will assist teachers in this endeavor.

Nevertheless, the basic advisement and guidance functions to be performed for a particular student need to be in the hands of a single professional—someone who has a picture of the whole student. A person designated as school guidance counselor with the usually recommended student-counselor rates of 300 to 1 cannot be expected to develop very many such relationships; only perfunctory interpersonal encounters are probable. It is absurd to think otherwise.

Advisor-Advisee Systems

A teacher-student advisement system can result in better student counseling. In one such system, each teacher assumes responsibility for the curricular decisions and learning goals for a particular group of students. The ratio of students to advisor is based on the total student-staff ratio in the school. Many schools involve every professional staff member in the school, including the principal, librarian, and specialists. Involving everyone reduces the ratio and also provides every staff member with direct student contact on an individual basis. Advisors become mentors.

In this approach, a school is divided into clusters, with a counselor and a principal or assistant principal acting as administrative head. The counselor serves as a "Master-Advisor" for 15 to 20 teacher-advisors. The teacher-advisor has no more than 20 students for whom counseling is performed.

The teacher-advisor's primary role is to work individually with students in much the same way that formerly was expected of the guidance counselor. The guidance counselor's role is that of expert-consultant to groups of teachers. The teacher-advisor is both friend and advocate and strives to know the student in ways well beyond what a teacher can with the usual classroom loads. He or she is a person to whom the student can talk freely about school problems and work through solutions.

Not all teachers are personally disposed nor equally able in such a role. Care needs to be taken to adequately prepare the staff for the role. In-service skill sessions will need to be developed and a good monitoring system maintained if the approach is to work well.

Among the many positive outcomes of such a system is the reduction of anonymity felt by many students in schools, both large and small. Shyness, transience, previous bad experiences with schooling, poverty among other symptoms of at-risk students and the simple human need of all of us for an anchoring friendship in times of need can be dealt with effectively with a teacher-advisor system.

Organizing Counseling Activities

Three basic counseling activities need to be carried out: group counseling, individual student counseling, and parent conferences.

Group Counseling. Group guidance activities can be of a variety of types, but the underlying concept is the advisor's responsibility to aid the students in developing good peer relationships, good personal problem-solving skills, and good attitudes about learning.

Individual Counseling. Individual counseling has two purposes. First, it provides the opportunity for each student to interact with his or her advisor as a friend and confidant. Second, it provides for frequent program planning and evaluation conferences. At least biweekly conferences are suggested, and these should function as the main stage for academic planning. The following comments of a teacher describing the preparation for and conduct of counseling sessions are illustrative:

> For each of my students, I have a file folder in a box next to my desk. Every paper completed by that student is placed in that folder after it has been appropriately graded or reviewed. It remains there until the night before our scheduled appointment. Each night I take home the folders of the three students I am to see the next day and regroup and review their papers according to subjects. I also review my notes from earlier conferences with each student and look at the goals we established in previous weeks. I then write down tentative goals that I have in mind for the student for the next two-week period. The next day when that student comes to my desk for his conference, I review with him his schedule of activities and the amount of time that he has spent in each subject area. We then go over his papers and l ask if he is having any particular problems. I will note for him problems I have identified from my review. Next, we look to see whether previously set goals have been achieved and begin our discussion of which goals and learning activities should come next. I prefer that each of my students set goals for themselves rather than for me to always have to suggest them. We each write down the goals agreed upon and identify some of the activities to be done toward each. As might be expected, most are continuations of previously laid plans but if new interests or needs have developed, these are to be included. Finally, a cover letter is stapled to the entire collection of papers to be taken home to the parent.

Some teachers prefer to develop systems and forms with which to set and record goals. These can also be shared with parents and made a part of the student's yearly diagnostic file. An example of such a form is shown in Figure 5.4. Such record development and record keeping are greatly facilitated by only a modest use of any of a number of readily available data-based software programs formatted for the kind of microcomputers that the school owns.

Parent Conferences. Regular conferences with parents or guardians contribute to the development of a positive learning climate. In addition to as-needed "crisis" conferences, direct relationships between teacher and home should occur in the form of

FIGURE 5.4 Setting and Recording Student Goals

Advisement Conference Report

______________________	______________________
Student Name	Term
______________________	______________________
Advisor	Date

A. Goals set by student and teacher:

B. Adjustments/accomplishments toward previously set goals:

C. Additional teacher comments:

D. Additional student comments:

E. Next conference date: ______________________

schoolwide planned parent-teacher conferences two or three times a year. These must be carefully organized and scheduled, however.

Numerous factors must be taken into consideration for these schoolwide programs to be successful. For example, two working parents in a home might preclude attendance at parent-teacher conferences scheduled during the normal school day. Similarly, single-parent homes present scheduling problems. Transportation may be a factor, too, especially if schools are organized on something other than a neighborhood basis. Magnet school programs, for example, present special problems. These and other constraints can be overcome if there is a sincere desire on the part of teachers and other school personnel to do so.

Organizing the conferences can be made a task of a joint community-teachers' group, perhaps the responsibility of a PTO task force. Again, one must be sure that the group that is assigned the task of organizing the effort is generally representative of the neighborhood or community that the local school serves. Also, the bilingual, multicultural norms of school-community members must also be considered.

Establishing a Good Advisement Program

Maximum flexibility in advisor assignments can be achieved by the expanded team concept. This will help keep the advisor-student ratio reasonable. Advisors should schedule meetings regularly with advisees, both on a group basis and individual basis. The total weekly commitment to advisor-guidance functions of an individual nature is approximately four hours per week during the school day while students are available and two hours after school, or when parents are available. Group guidance activities can be built into the regular school schedule, setting aside approximately 30 minutes each day, for a total of 2½ hours each week.

A regular appointment calendar on a two-week rotation should be established, with each student aware of the designated time well in advance of the conference. Figure 5.5 is an example of such a schedule.

Providing adequate time for teacher student or teacher-parent conferences is of top priority. The more flexible the school program, the easier it is to schedule conferences during the school day. An effective way to provide more conference time is to lengthen the school lunch period an additional 15 or 20 minutes. The provision of an expanded noon activities program, and opening the study and instructional media areas, will provide for those students who are not having conferences.

Selecting the Advisor. The advisor must be able to communicate with each student on a friendly, personal basis. In order for this to be accomplished, a good personality match between advisor and student is essential. This is best achieved if several choices for advisor assignment are available. Alternatives for advisor assignment for each student exist when the guidance program is operating on a team or expanded team basis. After staff and students have become acquainted in the fall term, each member is

FIGURE 5.5 Student Advisement Schedule (week 1 in a two-week cycle; 15 minutes each conference)

	Monday	**Tuesday**	**Wednesday**	**Thursday**	**Friday**
8:00 **Early bus arrivals**	David Thomas	Betty Baitland	Bart Herrscher	Cynthia Norris	Makeup
	Classes begin				
11:45	Lunch				Makeup
12:15	Douglas Edward	Patricia Holland	Anne Venditti	Kevin Arthur	
3:00	Classes end				
3:10 **Late bus departing**	Phyllis Selter	Lupe Hernandez	Will Weber	Howard Jones	Makeup

assigned an appropriate number of advisees, keeping in mind the needs of each individual student and which team member might best meet those needs.

A school organizational structure that greatly enhances the effectiveness of the advisement program is multiage grouping. This approach places students with a particular team for two or three years, each student keeping the same advisor during that entire period.

The Role of the Guidance Counselor

The guidance counselor has a particularly important function. In the system just described, the guidance counselor must assume six responsibilities:

1. Become attached to a team and assume an advisor responsibility in order to keep in close touch with the program and with the other specialists within the school.
2. Function as a school referral agent for problems identified by the advisor and faculty.
3. Conduct diagnostic work beyond that possible for teachers to do.
4. Administer and supervise the advisement program. The level of advisement activities proposed in this chapter far exceeds that typically carried out in school. In order for it to operate well, a good advisement program requires constant attention, encouragement, and coordination.
5. Provide and direct staff development activities in the techniques of advisement, including teacher training for both group guidance functions as well as individual student academic diagnostic work and techniques for personal counseling. A major portion of the guidance counselor's role should be spent directly in staff development activities.
6. Assist the teachers in establishing and maintaining a good in-class student personnel record system. These are the records maintained by the teacher for day-by-day counseling and academic prescriptions.

STUDENT SERVICES

Student services include all of those special support functions outside of the curricular and cocurricular offerings at the building level that impinge on the development of the student. The array of services offered by a school district adds a necessary quality to the individual school operation. The student services professional provides technical services and additional professional insight in the diagnosis, prescription, and treatment of individual learner difficulties as well as balanced programs for all learners. The principal's role in this is crucial. It is the principal who must provide for the organization, coordination, and articulation of such services at the building level.

Student Referral System

Most school systems have a number of specialists available to the student to meet needs beyond those that can be met by the regular school staff. Each school should have someone designated to coordinate the special services needs for the school. The guidance counselor is an appropriate referral agent to determine needs for services, as well as for identifying the proper source for those services.

It is good practice for principals to prepare and disseminate a list of available services, and people to contact for those services, so that teachers, parents, and other community members will know to whom they can turn for help with particular problems. Included on such a list would be counselors, including guidance, special education, and attendance; school psychologists; special education resource teachers; pathologists; home-bound teachers; reading specialists; diagnosticians: and other special personnel provided by the district.

Principal's Role in Coordination and Articulation

With respect to the delivery of pupil personnel services, the principal is truly the person in the middle—not as a gatekeeper but as a facilitator. Referrals, if not routed directly through the principal, should at least be made with an information copy to the principal. Why? *Everything that goes on in and around the school is the responsibility of the principal*—and that includes the proper delivery of support services. The reason for centralizing many student personnel services is because of the systemwide impact of these services and because individual school needs vary widely enough to make it more efficient to centrally house some services to provide maximum access in time of need. Such a model works well, provided the principal recognizes a responsibility to continually be aware of student and teacher needs in the building, and to investigate whether their needs are being met in a timely and efficient manner by the student personnel services division.

SUMMARY

For many children and youth, the school is the only stable thing in their lives. For some, it is the only place they can get a decent meal. For these and still others, it may be the only place they are safe from an otherwise marauding, hazardous, and unstable world. And for these and others, it may be the only place where they may be rewarded for behaving and succeeding in socially acceptable ways. School should be a place where every student can learn what a civilized world there can be. We like the words of Barbara Ries Wager: "We . . . faced the fact that we had forgotten what our forbearers of 50 years ago knew so well: that one of our most crucial missions is the civilizing process itself, that this historic professional mission had been eliminated from our intellectual repertoire."[10] At Ries Wager's school, that mission is being preserved.

And so we return to the thoughts of principal Karon Rilling: "And they will be protected and they will be respected. And we're going to help them learn how life can be." That is what this chapter has been all about.

ACTIVITIES

1. Review Case Studies 4, 11, and 23 at the back of this book. Assume data provided relate to a school for which you are principal. Respond to all of the situations. Given the information provided, any reasonable assumptions, and the concepts presented in this chapter, address the issues.

2. Review Case Studies 12 and 24. Both of these incidents have occurred in the school for which you are principal. Your school is traditionally organized into the standard grade levels and teaching assignments. What approach will you take in each instance to resolve the issues?

3. Review Case 21. Role-play a counseling session with Timmy.

4. Turn to the ISLLC Standards found in Appendix B. Review the performances listed with Standard Two. Reflect on which of the standard items relate directly to the material presented in this chapter. Identify one knowledge area, one disposition, and one performance to link directly to a concept or idea discussed in Chapter 5.

ENDNOTES

1. Gene E. Hall and Archie A. George, in H. Jerome Freiberg, *School Climate: Measuring, Improving and Sustaining Healthy Learning Environments* (Philadelphia: Falmer, 1999), p. 165.

2. *State* v. *Fond du lac Board of Education,* 63 Wis. 234, 23 NW 102, 53 Am. Rep. 282 (1985).

3. Karon Rilling, Ed.D., Principal of Humble Middle School, Humble (Texas) Independent School District to a graduate class of aspiring school principals at the University of Houston.

4. Reported in Maribeth Vander Weele, "Chicago Hope," *The Executive Educator 17,* no. 2 (February 1995): 23.

5. Reported in Roberta Shore, "How One High School Improved School Climate," *Educational Leadership 52,* no. 5 (February 1995): 76.

6. R. A. Hashway, "Does Money Make a Difference? An Econometric Analysis of School Outcomes," *National Forum of Applied Educational Research Journal 2,* no. 2 (1989–90): 59.

7. Charles M. Achilles and Penelope Smith, "Stimulating the Academic Performance of Pupils," in *The Principal as Leader*, ed. Larry W. Hughes (New York: Macmillan, 1994), p. 256.

8. Ibid., p. 259.

9. See, for example, Elizabeth Crouch and Debra Williams, "What Cities are Doing to Protect Children," *Educational Leadership 52,* no. 5 (February 1995): 60–62.

10. Barbara Ries Wager, "No More Suspension: Creating a Shared Ethical Culture," *Educational Leadership 50,* no. 4 (December 1992/January 1993): 37. Wager is Principal of an inner-city school in Rochester, New York, and was writing about how her school moved from "chaos to harmony" once disciplinary goals and processes were clarified and an "ethical culture" created.

SELECTED READINGS

Armstrong, Coleen. "How About Some Creative Discipline." *Principal 74,* no. 33 (January 1995): 51–52.

Books, Sue (Ed.). *Invisible Children in The Society and its Schools* (Mahwah, NJ: Erlbaum, 1998).

Cantrell, Robert P., and Mary Lynn Cantrell. "Countering Gang Violence in American Schools." *Principal 73,* no. 2 (November 1993): 6–9.

Freiberg, H. Jerome (Ed.). *School Climate: Measuring, Improving and Substaining Healthy Learning*

Environments (Philadelphia: Falmer Press, 1999). See Chapters 1, 5, and 9, especially.

Hughes, Larry W. (Ed.). *The Principal as Leader* (New York: Macmillan, 1994). See Chapter 10, especially.

Schreiber, Vicky D., and Martin Haberman. "Building a Gentler School." *Educational Leadership 52,* no. 5 (February 1995): 69–71.

Shore, Rebecca. "How One High School Improved School Climate." *Educational Leadership 52,* no. 5 (February 1995): 76–78.

Sullivan, Judy S. "Elements of a Successful In-School Suspension Program." *NASSP Bulletin 73,* no. 516 (April 1989): 32–38.

Vander Weele, Maribeth. "Chicago Hope." *Executive Educator 17*, no. 2 (February 1995): 22–24.

Wager, Barbara Ries. "No More Suspension: Creating a Shared Ethical Culture." *Educational Leadership 50,* no. 4 (December 1992/January 1993): 34–37.

CHAPTER SIX

THE SCHOOL CURRICULUM

The purpose of school is not merely to help students achieve academically in school, but to prepare them to lead fulfilling lives.

—Elliott Eisner[1]

Leadership involves both conservation and innovation. Nowhere is this truer than in the realm of curriculum administration. School principals, if they desire to be strong instructional leaders, must maintain a careful balance between these two purposes. To lean too far in either direction runs the risk that the instructional program will either become outdated and obsolete or will not be grounded in past traditions and accomplishments.

Leaders who provide clear vision and curricular leadership have a thorough knowledge of curriculum theory and philosophy. They understand how these varied theoretical frameworks are exhibited in the present curriculum, they have an awareness of the school clientele and their unique learning needs, and they possess an appreciation for what can be accomplished through curriculum change. An effective curriculum leader also demonstrates a clear, systemic view of the organization and its purpose and goals and ensures that the curriculum is consistent with the school's purpose. This chapter will explore curriculum leadership and the various tasks and dimensions of that responsibility. In addition, the chapter will provide an overview of various curriculum orientations and their implications for enriching the standard curriculum. We begin with an overview of the principal's role in the administration of curriculum.

THE PRINCIPAL'S ROLE IN CURRICULUM ADMINISTRATION

The pressures on the curriculum are many. The principal must take a proactive role in dealing with these issues or be overwhelmed by the demands of others. Many curriculum tasks to be performed in the school require the involvement of the principal. He or she must be a major player and decision maker for many of these tasks and certainly must provide initiative and leadership for all of them. In Chapter 2, we discussed the important role that the principal plays in fostering the empowerment of teachers and in providing the structures that promote "substitutes for leadership."[2] Although this does enable teacher leadership to emerge, the principal's role as facilitator of that development has everything to do with curriculum leadership. Allowing teachers to take ownership for their own classrooms places the role of the principal far more solidly into the transformational leadership arena than in the transactional one. Providing oversight and leadership from an influential power base rather than from authoritative control allows curriculum-related tasks to be accomplished through shared responsibility. These curriculum-related tasks could include:

- Analyzing what subjects, topics, knowledge areas, skills, and abilities should be taught in the school

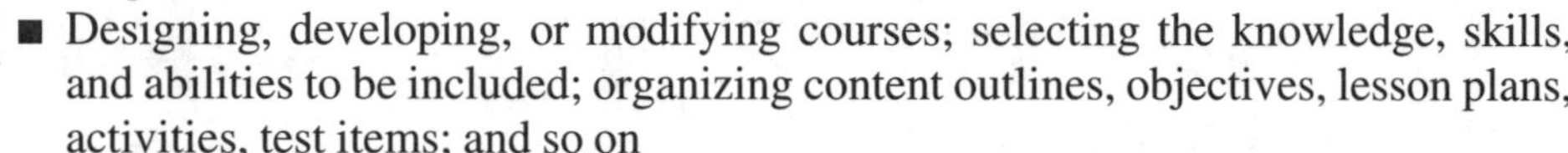

- Designing, developing, or modifying courses; selecting the knowledge, skills, and abilities to be included; organizing content outlines, objectives, lesson plans, activities, test items; and so on

- Delivering the curriculum; determining the array of available courses; sequencing courses or units; scheduling courses with concern for balance, flexibility, availability; and the like

- Evaluating curriculum by determining the congruence among course objectives, content taught and student evaluation, as well as a review of the relevance of the curriculum for the students and community served

Obviously, the major participants in many of these tasks will be teachers and possibly subject area supervisors. On the other hand, as the field continues to move more toward site-based management, coupled with the concepts of magnet schools and schools of choice, the principal will need to take the major oversight responsibility for the restructuring of the curriculum for the local school. Understanding curriculum orientations is a beginning point.

Understanding Curriculum Theory

Curriculum administration is a dynamic rather than static process. It is crucial that the principal and all others who lead in the design and adoption of the school curriculum have an understanding of the philosophical frameworks that help shape curriculum. This knowledge is important, not only for understanding more completely the nature of the presented curriculum (the conservator's role) but also in being prepared to more effectively restructure that curriculum in response to the emerging needs of those being served (the innovator's role).[3] Viewing the organization from a systemic perspective, the leader provides direction as a conservator of curriculum content and delivery, as well as an innovator and advocate for necessary change.

McNeil[4] presented four basic threads of curriculum theory: humanistic, social reconstuctionist, technological, and academic. He provided a frame for understanding these four varied philosophical orientations to curriculum by considering their respective purposes, how they view the roles of teacher and learner, and the advantages and disadvantages of each orientation. The four orientations that will be addressed are the humanistic approach, the sociological approach, the technological approach, and the academic approach.

The first two, humanistic theory and social reconstructionism, are cast in the realm of contemporary philosophy stemming from the philosophies of progressivism and reconstructionism[5] and promote the following as their basic instructional objectives:

- To promote democratic social living
- To improve and reconstruct society; education for change and social reform[6]

The last two, technological and academic curriculum theory, are cast in the realm of traditional philosophy stemming from perennialism and essentialism.[7] These philosophies promote the following objectives:

- To educate the rational person; to cultivate the intellect
- To promote the intellectual growth of the individual; to educate the competent person[8]

Each of the four curriculum orientations will be discussed in detail in the following sections.

The Humanistic Perspective

Purpose. The humanistic perspective centers on the individual. Focus is on maximizing the potential of the individual in all areas: cognitive, affective, and psychomotor. It is a holistic approach to learning where educating the whole child takes precedent over mere academic achievement. Humanistic curriculum is aimed toward the concepts of individual meaning, freedom, integrity, and autonomy. Based on the theories of such humanists as Abraham Maslow[9] and Carl Rogers,[10] the notions of self-actualization and personal meaning are emphasized. A premium is placed on the "joy of learning" with attention being given to the development of "peak experiences" where cognitive and affective learning take place simultaneously.

Affective development is an integral part of the humanistic curriculum. The focus is on self-awareness and on forming moral and ethical principles for oneself rather than on "teaching" values as is advocated in many character education programs currently in vogue. Values clarification[11] techniques are often part of the curriculum that stresses the development of intrapersonal and interpersonal intelligence, referred to by Goleman[12] as emotional intelligence. Goleman compared his work with the writings and research of several others, such as Salovey,[13] Gardner,[14] and Sternberg,[15] and concluded that the following domains of emotional intelligence listed by Salovey seem most important to frame his work:

1. Knowing one's emotions
2. Managing emotions
3. Motivating oneself
4. Recognizing emotions in others
5. Handling relationships[16]

The Principal's Role. The principal's influence is a necessary ingredient for successfully integrating this curriculum approach into the school setting. The principal serves as a role model for the important values and behaviors necessary for shaping this curriculum orientation. Human respect forms the cornerstone of humanistic education and it is the principal who sets the tone and serves as a model for the human relationships necessary for this approach to be implemented.

The Teacher's Role. Central to the humanistic curriculum is the emotional relationship established between the teacher and the student. Trust, acceptance, and mutual understanding form the cornerstones of this relationship. The teacher seeks to establish an atmosphere for learning that enables and calls forth the potential often not recognized by the student alone. The climate of acceptance allows for risk, experimentation, and growth as the teacher serves as facilitator of the learning experience. Rogers expressed these qualities in his book, *Freedom to Learn.*[17] The research on effective schools[18] also presents many humanistic characteristics as necessary conditions for the climate that should surround learning. It is interesting to note that even in the midst of an emphasis on the basics, these conditions are deemed necessary and supportive to student learning.

The Student's Role. In this approach, the student takes personal responsibility for learning and behavior. Self-direction is encouraged both cognitively as well as affectively. Students learn to accept and deal with the responsibilities associated with their own behavior as well as learn to form their own opinions and to think creatively. The emphasis is placed on personal independence and autonomy that carries with it the responsibility for one's own actions. It is an intrinsic process designed to foster mature thinking and behavior.

Approaches to Humanistic Education. The affective dimensions of learning have been emphasized for some time in schools, but generally in the field of counseling. Rogers is a major contributor in shaping the concepts and applications of this approach to the classroom. His book, *Freedom to Learn,* as well as by his emphasis on counseling have been important contributions to this view of curriculum.[19] Glasser has had a similar impact with his work concerning *Reality Therapy*[20] and the group process approaches to learning that he classifies as *thinking meetings*.[21] Self-awareness and self-discipline are the primary goals in the work of both these researchers rather than an emphasis on the external controls often emphasized in formal discipline plans. The student is encouraged to think for himself or herself, and to form opinions and make judgments based on rational consideration of self and others. The student is taught to take responsibility for his or her own learning and behavior through the application of natural consequences.

An emerging interest in humanistic education is also reflected in the current concept known as *confluent education.* In this curriculum model, the emphasis is on integration of the affective domain with the cognitive domain in the development of lesson materials. It is often referred to as an "add-on" approach, since emotional domains, attitudes, and values are included with the traditional subject matter. This is done in order that the student may experience personal significance in what they are learning. In a confluent lesson, there would be the following:

- Participation of all in a democratic learning experience
- Integration of thinking, feeling, and responding
- Relevant subject matter that touches the needs and lives of students
- Focus on self as the center of the learning experience
- Aim . . . [is] toward development of the total person within a human society[22]

In all aspects of the humanistic curriculum there is an emphasis on the holistic nature of learning, or the Gestalt, which is the greatest advantage of this curriculum model. Its integrative nature encourages students to make connections, develop critical awareness, and respond in meaningful personal ways to their learning experiences.

A Critique. Major critics point to the difficulty in providing a sequential presentation of concepts and skills with this approach and to its overemphasis on the individual rather than the group. Others see the development of the individual as a necessary precursor to development of the group[23] and view the humanistic curriculum as an approach that encourages civic responsibility and service to others.

Social Reconstructionism

Purpose. Those who advocate this approach view the curriculum as the agent of social change. Curriculum is considered the vehicle for bringing about needed changes in the social order and is designed to help individuals and groups elevate their oppressed conditions, thereby improving their opportunities to participate fully in a democratic society.

Social responsibility involves finding ways to become an integral part of the group and to come to consensus on important social matters. In this curriculum approach, major emphasis is on developing a strong values base from which to respond and take action relative to the many problems facing society.

Social reconstructionists view an effective curriculum as having three major cornerstones: "It must be *real,* it must require *action,* and it must teach *values.*"[24] Major emphasis is on learning that is relevant to the learner and that is central to the issues students face in their daily lives. No real learning occurs until action is taken on that learning. Social responsibility is central to the purpose of knowledge acquisition.

Social reconstructionists, such as Michael Apple,[25] Henry Giroux,[26] and Jeannie Oakes,[27] consider current public education to be "reproducing" a social order that is not always consistent with democratic principles and one that continues to maintain a stratified social order. They advocate the critical examination of current situations within schools and the use of curriculum as a means of liberating all students to an equal access to a meaningful education. It is their belief that such practices as ability grouping and pullout programs tend to perpetuate this tendency.

Closely aligned with the ideas of the reconstructionists are the curriculum futurologists who advocate studying emerging trends and taking action to prevent "bad" futures. Leading proponents of this approach[28] advocate building curriculum by planning the future. These writers do not suggest that students be assisted in *adapting* to a future imposed on them, but that they *take action to prevent* those things that loom as destructive tendencies. Critical theory, or consciousness, separates social reconstruction from social adaptation. Social adaptation is based on an analysis of society but is aimed at helping students adapt to an impending future rather than to question it and take responsible action to prevent it.

The Principal's Role. The principal's role is leadership oriented. It calls for a continual examination of current practices and the effects of current curriculum on the lives of students. Principals must serve as values consciousness raisers,[29] problem finders, and visionary leaders who can enable all constituents to be actively engaged in the learning process. In Chapter 1 we discussed the moral and ethical responsibilities that are central to principal leadership in this curriculum orientation. Principals must take special note of situations in which the "hidden curriculum"[30] is creating oppressive situations for certain groups of students and take action to prevent unfair or undemocratic practices from taking place.

The Teacher's Role. The teacher serves as a facilitator of the learning process. It is the teacher's task to assist students in identifying their interests and connecting those interests to a national and world perspective.[31] In many cases, the teacher serves as a bridge between the community and the student in regard to the special interests that the student might have. Gaining the cooperation and collaboration of outside agencies in establishing service projects and other community-related partnerships are also a part of the teacher's role.

It is important within the classroom setting for the teacher to be skilled in establishing and working with groups and in promoting opportunities for collaboration among students. Social reconstructionism is a natural curriculum orientation for reinforcing the notions of learning communities (dealt with in Chapter 2).

Approaches to Social Reconstructionism. Two current examples of this curriculum have become very prevalent in today's schools: problem-based learning[32] and action learning. Both of these have implications for student learning as well as teacher learning. In Chapter 13, we discuss five models of staff development for teachers. Two of the models (inquiry and school improvement process) relate to this concept. The social reconstruction orientation to curriculum is also closely related to the current notions of inclusion, cooperative learning groups, teaming, and cohorts, all of which have been discussed in other chapters. We will spend some time in this discussion on a current application of this curriculum orientation: action learning.

Action Learning. Some 400 seniors in a midwestern high school performed tasks in the community as part of their twelfth-grade social studies class. More than 90 percent of the senior class chose to do community service instead of writing a research paper. The students worked in a variety of endeavors, including political campaigns, voter registration drives, elementary and junior high schools, daycare centers, nursing homes, county recreation departments, and other places where they were needed. The only criterion for selecting placements was that the students work with people, not in clerical jobs. Finding placements for such a large number of students was facilitated by holding a community fair each fall. Those community agencies that desired student assistance set up tables or booths and the students shopped around for a volunteer opportunity that interested them and met their time and transportation limits. Students did their volunteer work during unscheduled time during the school day or after school.

Action learning is based on the concept of young people learning by doing and tying this concept into the idea of learning by serving. It is learning through a combination of direct experiences and associated instruction or reflection. The purposes that action learning can serve and the student experiences it can offer vary greatly from school to school. The emphasis can be on "service learning," which connotes activities focused on self-development. All the varied approaches, however, put the emphasis on the personal involvement of young people in the wider community and recognition that learning does and should take place outside the classroom. Actual learning situations can include volunteer services, internships, community surveys and studies, social and political action, shadowing a person to explore a career role, living in another culture, and work experience. Of course, many of these activities are very common to some vocational programs, but in fields such as math, English, health, history, and government, the practice to go along with the theory is less common.

Schools that offer action learning identify a variety of objectives for their program, including:

1. Contribution to a young person's social development and his or her sense of responsibility for the welfare of others
2. Intellectual development—academic subjects take on added significance when students can apply their classroom knowledge to real problems
3. Career education—being able to see firsthand and participate in a variety of possible job roles
4. Benefits to the school—breaking down the barriers between the school and the wider community
5. Benefits to the community—the ability to provide many community services that would not have been possible without student volunteer help

Organizing for Action Learning. Many different action learning programs have been implemented, each with its own unique characteristics. Analyses of these different programs show five basic types of action learning situations, ranging from the minimum integration with the school program to almost total involvement. From least involvement to most, the action learning programs are described here.

A Volunteer Bureau. The school or the student identifies volunteer activities. The work is done during unscheduled time, study hall time, or before or after school. In some cases, arrangements are made for half-day release of all students participating in the volunteer program on a particular day of the week. The staff coordinator of volunteer programs is valuable in providing coordination to the program by identifying and placing students, following up, and reviewing the student's work. The student usually has the prime responsibility for initiating his or her community experience, with the school providing a coordinating function.

Community Service for Credit. The same basic plan arranged as a volunteer bureau can be carried out, adding to it some form of academic credit for student participation. The school may actively promote the program or the student may possibly still be the initiating agent.

Laboratory for Existing Course. Projects organized in conjunction with regular courses are used often in lieu of research papers or other assignments. Students may engage in community activity during school hours or after school, depending on their schedules. Often, as the students become more involved in community projects, course content begins to be altered toward the more practical useful information, emphasizing teaching systematic observation, data gathering, and community involvement.

Community Involvement Course. A formalized course in community involvement draws on the major features of the laboratory idea (from the previous model) along with the service for course credit concept. The course, though, has its entire structure organized around community involvement and draws all of its data for the course directly from the community. A course title such as Student Community Involvement might be appropriate.

The Action Learning Center. The center carries the students and teachers into the community, where they gain their total experience. This type of course is often interdisciplinary in nature and may be staffed by specialists who repeat the experience several times each year for different groups. Projects such as mountain camp-outs, canoe trips, rebuilding deteriorated homes, and other forms of community action are illustrative of this idea.

Action Learning Guidelines. Guidelines for directing action learning programs have been proposed by the National Association of Secondary School Principals:

1. The program must fill genuine needs of adolescents and of society in involving youth in tasks that are recognized as important by both young people and adults.
2. It must provide a real challenge to students, offering them an opportunity to extend their skills and their knowledge.
3. An opportunity for guided reflection on the service experience is necessary and this opportunity should be continued during the period of service.

4. Successful programs provide participants with the sense of community, that special feeling that comes from sharing a goal and working toward it with others.
5. A learning-by-serving experience should contribute to the knowledge that adolescents need regarding career options open to them in the adult world and offer some opportunities to work cooperatively with competent adults who are models for these options.
6. In format, the program must be both structured and flexible. Many projects have failed because they were too rigid to respond to changing conditions, and others have been unsatisfactory because they were too loosely structured to bring out a clear and continued sense of direction.
7. The program must promote a genuine maturity by allowing young people to exercise adult responsibility and be held accountable for their actions. This means, among other things, that students should actively participate in decision making and governance of the project in which they are learning by serving.
8. The stimulus for a worthwhile project or program can come from innumerable sources, so keep your eyes and minds open for leads as to needs, people, and places. Be particularly alert to hints that young people themselves may drop. They often are closer to the subtle but serious needs of the community than are school teachers and administrators.
9. Try to determine the optimal life span for a given learning-by-serving project and make this an element in planning and administration of the program. Probably more than most other aspects of secondary school curriculum, learning-by-serving programs have a constant need for new blood.

Critique. One of the major criticisms of the social reconstruction curriculum is that few agree on what is best for the future or present society. As McNeil suggested, "We can expect accelerated curriculum development along reconstructionist lines whenever there is a need to resolve a conflict in values. Such a need often exists in multi-cultural neighborhoods."[33] Within these communities there are certainly differing values, customs, and languages, which can create disagreements about just what the nature of the curriculum should be. As parents become more involved with the schools and schools with the community, there will likely be more opportunities for conflict between the groups as to *what should be taught* and *how it should be taught*.

Technological Curriculum

Purpose. Often referred to as the *measured curriculum,* this conception of curriculum contains such elements as "behavioral objectives, time on task, sequential learning, positive reinforcement, direct instruction, achievement testing, mastery in skills and content, and teacher accountability."[34] This curriculum orientation is based on general systems philosophy that emphasizes specification of instructional objectives, precisely controlled learning activities designed to achieve those objectives, and criteria for determining mastery of the objectives stated. The curriculum is highly skill based and operates heavily at the lower levels of knowledge acquisition (i.e., knowledge, comprehension, and application). Its purpose is to systematize learning and make it more predictable, reliable, and measurable.

The Principal's Role. Certainly, the principal functions as a manager in this orientation, although challenging organizational members toward goal accomplishment is a leadership activity. It is the job of the principal to see that things are being taught as they have been designed, to monitor and keep track of progress, to challenge through high expectations, and to ensure that teachers produce high gains in student productivity. In this orientation there is a high degree of authority and oversight to see that what is expected to be accomplished is being accomplished. The principal operates very much in the context of the machine metaphor in the technological orientation with more of an emphasis on a transactional approach than a transformational one.[35]

The Teacher's Role. The teacher's task is to manage the curriculum that has already been established and to teach according to the "how to" that has been determined. In that sense, the teacher functions almost like a laborer or craftsperson rather than a professional or artist.[36] The teacher must closely monitor students' progress and take responsibility for their success or lack of it.

Approaches to Technological Curriculum. The technological curriculum is very much present in the form of basic skills acquisition, mastery learning, time on task, curricular alignment, directive teaching models, and other models of sequential curriculum delivery. (Many of these are discussed in Chapter 10.) In a later section of this chapter we will discuss curricular alignment and planning. For these reasons, little attention is given to the application of this curriculum orientation at this time.

Critique. One of the major criticisms of this orientation is its limitation for concept teaching and learning. With its primary focus on basic mastery and lower levels of thinking, it does little to inspire higher-order thinking processes such as analysis, synthesis, and evaluation of concepts. Although more straightforward tasks might be taught more readily by a sequential approach, some believe that the technological approach "is a limited tool for nonprocedural tasks and may even hinder proficiency."[37] Related to this limitation is its almost exclusive focus on subject matter, or cognitive development, to the exclusion of the person, or affective dimension. In defense of this measured curriculum, however, there are some benefits that structure, sequence, and accountability have brought about. As Klein suggested,

> It is compatible with some of the major educational outcomes valued by society-a store of knowledge about the world, command of the basic processes of communication, and exposure to new content arenas. But this conception and design of curriculum cannot accomplish everything students are expected to learn.[38]

Academic Curriculum

Purpose. The purposes of the academic curriculum are to train minds and to teach students to do research.[39] This orientation to curriculum is based on the idea of a "storehouse of knowledge" that has been handed down from the past and that contains a "body of truths" that is fixed and absolute. In this approach, there is a core of knowledge that every student should possess, and learning is acquiring knowledge through the disciplines. The emphasis is on cognitive development with particular stress on critical thinking based on a rational consideration of "truths." Truths are contained in the "three Rs, as well as liberal studies or essential academic subjects."[40]

Much emphasis in this orientation is placed on excellence and maximizing one's potential in the academic realm. Subject matter is important for its own sake and greater degrees of importance are place on some subjects than others. The forms and structure of knowledge are as important as the content itself. More recently, however, applications of this curriculum approach have emphasized integrated studies rather than the isolated content previously emphasized.

The Principal's Role. Certainly, the principal must model and encourage excellence! A model of high motivation to achieve must be exemplified. Life-long learning should be celebrated throughout the school and the principal should assume a major responsibility to ensure the competence of teachers through high standards and supervision.

The Teacher's Role. The teacher is a disseminator of knowledge or a "sage on the stage." Since teachers serve as authorities relative to their subject areas, they plan and direct the learning activities with less input from students. The mode is typically direct instruction, with little attention devoted to group involvement or creative thinking activities.

Approaches to Academic Curriculum. Some of the more current applications of the academic curriculum include a renewed interest in a "core curriculum" in both the university and public school arenas. The back-to-basics movement and the idea of a national curriculum advocated by writers such as Hirsch[41] and others tend to reinforce this idea. A particularly popular application of the academic model is the *Paideia Proposal*, which emphasizes a uniform educational system based on a course of study including such offerings as philosophy, literature, history, mathematics, natural science, and fine arts. It includes an emphasis on critical thinking and moral judgment and eliminates such "frills" as vocational education.

A second approach to the academic curriculum can be found in the concept of integrated studies. This movement is particularly popular in the middle school movement and is facilitated through the use of teams. Chapter 7 of this text addresses ways in which schools can be structured for maximum utilization of this approach.

Critique. This approach has been criticized by some for being too "adult focused" and uninspiring to students. There appears to be too much emphasis on content and not enough on process. In addition, there is little emphasis on the application of knowledge, which makes relevance even more difficult to establish.

Each of the orientations presented is important to consider as a "piece" of the total curriculum available to students. Certainly no single model has all that is needed to produce a balanced curriculum for students. The most effective curriculum is one in which there is a blend of several approaches. We turn our attention now away from *why we teach what we do* to *what we teach and how it should be taught.*

CURRICULUM ANALYSIS

The introductory section of this chapter points out the pressures faced by every school in determining what is to be the curriculum of the school. The school staff must have an orderly logical way of going about the task of making these curriculum decisions. The first step is often one of determining if the curriculum decision is theirs to make. Many states have curriculum requirements imposed by their legislatures or state departments of education. In other cases, local boards of education determine what subjects are to be taught. In reality, few, if any, decisions on course offerings or the number of hours of instruction in a certain subject are left to the local school.

The local school's role in curriculum analysis generally has two domains. One is to select a few elective offerings for the schools curriculum; for most schools, this is a relative minor part of the overall curriculum. The more significant task is the responsibility to determine the content to be taught in almost every course in the school. Policymakers may determine course offerings by title, but rarely do they dictate the detail of the knowledge, skills, and abilities (KSAs) to be included within the courses. States often provide curriculum guides and some local school districts will provide prescribed content outlines, but usually the detail of what is to be taught is left up to the local school.

The responsibility for determining the detail of curriculum content for the school needs to be assumed by the professional staff of the school under the leadership of the principal. If the staff does not act collectively, it will go by default to the individual teacher or the author of the selected textbook.

The determination of the content (KSAs) of virtually every course and subject offered by the school should be as the result of a joint effort by two or more faculty members. Curriculum requests, such as the ones mentioned at the beginning of this chapter, should be submitted to the appropriate faculty curriculum team for consideration.

Curriculum committees can be organized around either a grade level or subject matter. Grade-level committees develop the content for the entire curriculum for a particular grade. This is a common elementary school approach, but it is becoming popular as a way to review middle school and high school curriculum as well. This approach emphasizes the *horizontal* dimension of the curriculum, which usually includes all the subjects available to a student at a given time. When a student participates daily or weekly in social studies, English, science, mathematics, health, art, music, and physical education, one is describing the horizontal dimension of the curriculum. The horizontal structure of most U.S. schools is relatively uniform, and curricular areas are almost standard among schools and among grade levels. The horizontal balance remains about the same from year to year, providing students with equal amounts of time in each subject area.

Schools that are departmentalized, such as some upper elementary and junior high schools, have an additional problem with horizontal organization. The departmentalization creates *compartmentalization*, and the several disciplines taught are often not well coordinated or integrated for the students but taught as separate and unrelated bodies of knowledge.

An interdisciplinary curriculum using combinations of subjects offers ways to reestablish the integration of school subjects. In the lower elementary grades, this is best represented with so-called whole-language programs. There is a pedagogical movement away from discrete skills sequencing in the teaching of reading, for example. This approach integrates listening, speaking, reading, writing, and critical thinking. The whole-language approach is literature and subject matter based and is heavily student-experience based rather than issuing from teacher-prepared worksheets and other didactic materials.

Thematic units, also often literature based, offer interdisciplinary studies. Figure 6.1 is an illustration of an elementary school thematic unit outline. Note that it includes skill areas to be taught in reading, language, mathematics, research, and higher-order thinking. Applications to social studies, science, and art are part of the unit as well. The entire unit is organized around a book about Benjamin Franklin.

Subject matter curriculum committees develop the content for a particular subject area such as social studies. This group will review and plan social studies content for all courses within one discipline for combination of grades such as K–5, 6–8, or 9–12. This subject matter approach is effective in providing good vertical articulation for the curriculum.

The sequence of the skills or topics taught within a particular course of study overtime—week by week, semester to semester, or year to year—represents the *vertical* dimension of the curriculum. Many resources are available to provide suggestions to the school or system's staff in the development of curriculum guides, including objectives and test items for vertical organization.

The voluntary National Curriculum Standards developed by the U.S. Department of Education represent a major national resource for curriculum guides. National professional associations for the various disciplines—such as the International Reading Association (IRA), the National Council of Teachers of English (NCTE), and the National Council for the Social Studies (NCSS), as well as many others—have curriculum outlines available. Many state departments of education also have developed curriculum guides for their own state schools and will sell them to schools in other states upon request. For example, California completed model curriculum standards for grades 9–12 in English/language arts, foreign 1anguage, history/social science, mathematics, science, and visual and performing arts[41] (see Figure 6.2). Textbook publishers often provide curricular management systems, including skills continua, mastery tests, and tracking systems to support their materials. A number of local schools developed federally supported projects promoted through the National Diffusion Network and listed in the catalog entitled *Educational Programs That Work* which also includes curriculum guides.[42] Finally, the Instructional Objectives Exchange (IOX) has compiled lists of objectives and test items organized by subject area and difficulty level that pro-

FIGURE 6.1 Sample Interdisciplinary Unit

What's the Big Idea, Ben Franklin?
Novel Study
and
Integrated Unit for Grade 3
by Judy Rehder and Kaye Williams
Knox County Schools

Content and Skills Covered in This Unit

Social Studies/History

1. Reading and using maps—legends, distance scales, locating places, and tracing routes, latitude equator
2. Understanding of the duties of an ambassador
3. Understanding of the causes of the American Revolution and what it was
4. Understanding of the Declaration of Independence and the Constitution of the United States
5. Cities—organization, fire departments, libraries—how people work together
6. Understanding of occupations and apprenticeships then and now
7. Understanding of how cities grow based sometimes on physical location
8. Understanding of how latitude affects climate
9. Understanding of how water and warm water currents affect climate
10. Understanding of the printing process and newspapers—understanding the effect of newspapers, etc. on people
11. Learning to work together on group projects

Science

1. Understanding what electricity is
2. Understanding how electric currents work
3. Understanding what will conduct electricity
4. Understanding dangers and safety measures related to lightning and electricity
5. Understanding how electricity has affected life
6. Understanding of seasons and earth/sun relationships
7. Scientific method
8. Inventions and Inventors
9. Understanding how soap is made

Art

1. Printmaking—vegetable prints
2. Drawing illustrations for a how-to book
3. Looking at famous American artists of this period
4. Making candles

Reading

1. Main idea, sequencing, details, inference, cause/effect
2. Reading to learning how to do things
3. Reading to learning information

FIGURE 6.1 *Continued*

Language Skills

1. Letter writing
2. Report writing
3. Writing poetry and prose and understanding the difference between
4. Using capital letters in place of names and titles
5. Underlining titles of books
6. Use of the comma—series and dates
7. Use of a dash
8. Forming plurals
9. Forming possessives
10. Dividing words into syllables at the end of a line
11. Suffixes and prefixes
12. Oral communication skills

Math

1. Magic squares
2. Figure distances on a map
3. Figure ages and differences in time

Research Skills

1. Encyclopedia
2. Almanac
3. Maps
4. Other books
5. Gathering information
6. Organizing information
7. Utilizing information
8. Sharing information

Higher Levels of Thinking and Working

1. Comparing and contrasting
2. Cause/effect
3. Productive thinking
4. Analysis
5. Synthesis
6. Evaluation—decision making
7. Drawing inferences/conclusions
8. Application
9. Working together in a constructive manner in small groups
10. Self-discipline and management skills for independent work

Related Mini-Courses

1. WHAT A SHOCK!!!—Experiments and experiences with electricity
2. WEATHER OR NOT!—Observing, recording, and forecasting weather
3. BRIGHT IDEAS!!!—A look at inventions and inventors—becoming inventors

Source: Reprinted by permission of Judith J. Rehder, Kaye Williams, Chilhowee School.

FIGURE 6.2 High School Economics Model Curriculum

High-School Economics Course

In order to achieve this basic understanding, students should master the fundamental economic concepts, appreciate how the principal concepts of economics relate to each other, and understand the structure of economic systems.

The model curriculum standards are enclosed in boxes. The terms below them are useful in understanding the standards, and the activities are offered to assist the teacher in developing these terms and concepts in the classroom.

Philosophy and Prerequisites for Economics

Students should have:

- An ability to read and understand charts and graphs
- A capacity to understand the nature of resources and the human interest in acquisition of goods and services
- A basic familiarity with institutions of our economic system

MODEL CURRICULUM STANDARDS FOR ECONOMICS

1. A course should demonstrate that the study of economics requires the understanding of certain fundamental concepts and terms. Among these are the terms with definitions that appear in the Glossary at the end of this section.

2. A course should include a study of the tools of analysis, such as charts, graphs, statistics, and marginal analysis.

3. A course should show that economists measure economic performance by using certain economic indicators.

- National Income Accounting
- Gross National Product (G.N.P.)
- Consumer Price Indexing
- Inflation
- Measurements of unemployment

Activities:

- Discuss unemployment and how it differs between population groups, depending on age, sex, and race.
- Analyze the history of inflation in the United States since 1973.
- Compare the inflation rates among countries, i.e., Mexico, Switzerland, Brazil, Japan, and the United States; and discuss the impact of these rates on the domestic economies and world trade.
- Show how changes in the Gross National Product (G.N.P.) measure changes in production.

FIGURE 6.2 *Continued*

4. A course should make it clear that the basic economic problem facing society is the condition of scarcity, or limitation on productive resources relative to human wants. As a result of this scarcity, choices must be made, taking account of the opportunity costs of each choice.

- Scarcity
- Trade-offs
- Economic choices
- Opportunity costs
- Wants
- Productive resources

Activities:

- Discuss the trade-off between producing more consumer goods and more investment goods.
- Review the economic history of the United States with regard to the growth in our productive resources.
- Consider the opportunity costs of completing high school, taking a part-time job after school, or going to the movies instead of doing required homework.

5. A course should demonstrate that all societies have economic systems that enable them to make choices on what to produce, how to produce it, and for whom to produce it. The economic system of the United States relies primarily on the market to make these choices.

- Economic systems
- Market
- Market economy
- Traditional economy
- Command economy
- Role of government
- Income distribution
- Supply and demand

Activities:

- Compare the economic system of the United States with one or more other economic systems with regard to how choices are made on what to produce, how to produce, and for whom to produce
- Discuss the role of the government in the largely market economy of the United States. In particular, when does the government interfere in private choices as to what to produce and for whom to produce it?
- Compare and contrast the economy of the Rancho system operated by the Californios with that which the Anglo-Europeans brought to California after 1850.

Source: Reprinted, by permission, from *Model Curriculum Standards: Grades Nine Through Twelve,* © 1985, California State Department of Education, Sacramento, pp. HS-52 and 53.

vide an excellent resource for curriculum planners in the selection of objectives in matching test items.[43] The test items, many of which are classified according to Bloom's Taxonomy, make excellent contributions to test item banks.

CURRICULUM DESIGN AND DEVELOPMENT

Each school serves a unique community. Therefore, each school must ultimately take responsibility for the design and development of its own curriculum. The principal provides the leadership for these tasks working through the faculty. The faculty curriculum committees used for curriculum analysis can build on their earlier curriculum analysis efforts and continue with the design and development tasks.

Effective schools research identified the importance of a well-designed curriculum structure to the development of effective schools. The recommended structure included for each subject or course a list of knowledge, skills, and abilities; specific student outcomes to be accomplished; well-designed lesson plans with instructional strategies, activities, and resources identified and matched to expected outcomes; and evaluation items created for each objective with a recommended mastery level for the evaluation. Each of these components is coordinated to achieve congruence throughout the curriculum, as shown in Figure 6.3.

Objectives and test items developed for the various course structures should be analyzed for the depth of learning they require. A classification system such as Bloom's Taxonomy[44] provides a method to determine the level of learning being expected of students. Bloom's Taxonomy of Cognitive Objectives, which includes the domains of knowledge, comprehension, application, analysis, synthesis, and evaluation, is valuable in ensuring high-order skills are developed within the various disciplines.

The course outlines, objectives, and tests should be used by all the teachers in the school who might be teaching that particular subject at that grade level. These curriculum structures, in some cases, may be based on a state-approved curriculum, may be organized around a particular text series developed by a districtwide curriculum committee, or may be constructed by the teacher or teachers in an individual building. The

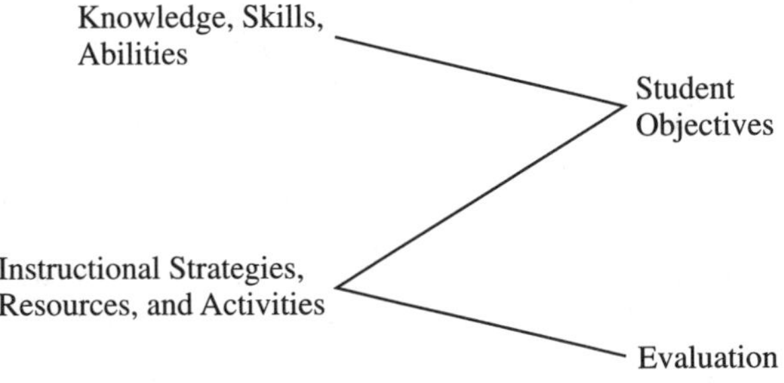

FIGURE 6.3 Curriculum Structure

prescribed curriculum should be at least the work of two or more professionals and determined in concert by their joint effort.

Any discussion of curriculum must pay heed to the effects of maturation on changes in student interests and needs. Several notions in particular are significant when considering the organization of a school. The first is that all children do not mature at the same rate and thus all are not ready for the same curriculum at the same time. The difference in maturation of boys and girls is quite obvious, both physically and mentally. The same variation in size, mental capacity, interests, and needs also exists within children of the same sex at a given age, only to be in a different balance or relationship after several more years of maturation. These differences should have a bearing on both instructional techniques and curriculum offerings, as well as on ways of grouping students.

CURRICULUM DELIVERY

Although curriculum delivery may seem to be largely the responsibility of the teaching staff, there are many major delivery tasks that encompass the entire school, thus requiring the leadership of the principal. These include determining which courses are to be offered, sequencing courses and/or units, and scheduling courses with concern for curriculum balance, continuity, flexibility, and availability. In addition, materials and equipment must be made available for quality instruction in today's world of changing technology.

An important aspect of curricular organization from the effective schools research is the concept of *curricular alignment*.[45] Once a structured curriculum has been adopted and supposedly implemented for each subject area, the questions become: "Are the teachers following it?" "Is the content presented to the students the same as indicated by the stated curriculum?" The teacher who takes the student only two-thirds of the way through the prescribed topics for the year is out of alignment with the planned curriculum. The classroom teacher who spends an inordinately large amount of time on his or her favorite topic and slights or ignores the prescribed topics is out of alignment with the agreed-upon curriculum.

The concept of curricular alignment is particularly significant when accountability for learning is important. If the school's evaluation system of either standardized achievement tests or criterion-referenced tests is matched to the anticipated curriculum, a serious curricular alignment problem could lower test scores significantly for children who were never given the opportunity to master the content measured by the tests. Curricular alignment includes, therefore, the alignment or coordination of what is taught with what is to be measured.

Curricular alignment, however, is more global than just the match between what is taught and what is measured. It also encompasses the articulation and coordination of the school's philosophy to goals, goals to objectives, objectives to instruction, and instruction to evaluation. For example, if the school's philosophy includes the statement "We believe critical thinking and decision making skills are important for every student to develop," then a goal should exist such as "to provide courses that help students develop critical thinking skills." Objectives also need to exist that speak to developing critical thinking skills. To illustrate, "a student will be able to demonstrate critical thinking skills by (1) defining a problem, (2) identifying and judging information relative to the problem, and (3) solving the problem and drawing conclusions." Instructional activities at a variety of levels of sophistication need to be incorporated into the several different courses and, finally, test items need to be utilized that are designed to measure critical thinking skills. The lack of any of these items may result in curricular misalignment.

If good teaching is an art, should classroom teachers have the freedom to change, adapt, and take advantage of unique opportunities for learning as they evolve? Freedom in the classroom certainly is desirable, but it can be thought of primarily as a problem of teaching technique or strategy and should not necessarily be a problem of content or curriculum unless a teacher drifts too far from a prescribed curriculum. If that occurs, then maybe it is time to evaluate the approved curriculum or otherwise indicate to teachers that they are expected to follow the agreed-upon plans.

CURRICULUM FLEXIBILITY

It is important to give adequate attention to individual differences and varying maturity rates and levels and to recognize that student interests and needs are broadly based. The organization of a school program must account for these needs, interests, and capabilities in all their diversity and provide learning experiences that will motivate all students.

If individual differences are to be recognized, both the vertical and horizontal dimensions of the curriculum require flexibility. Figure 6.4 illustrates the three different rates of learning. Since most children vary from the norm, the curriculum needs to be organized to allow each child to progress individually, as shown by lines A, B, and C.

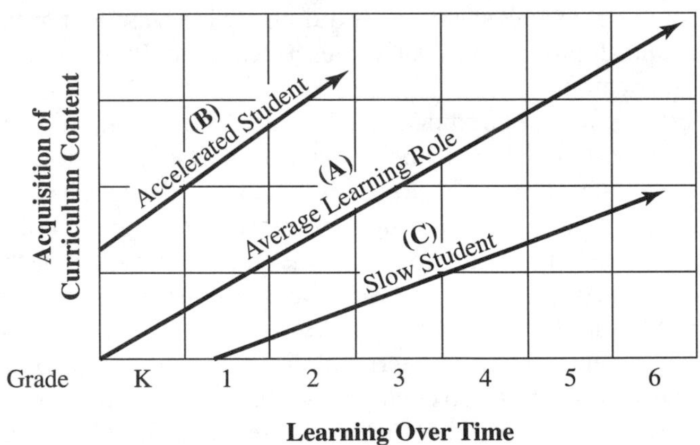

FIGURE 6.4 Impact of Individual Differences and Rates of Learning on Curriculum Needs

The organization must allow both child B and child C access to appropriate information as it is sequenced according to the difficulty of concepts and materials. The achievement of the student overtime will depend, therefore, on the capability of the student to learn and the time committed to that subject.

In subjects such as reading and mathematics, where one has traditionally assumed that all basic skills are taught in the elementary school, it is important to recognize that, because of their slow maturation rates, a large portion of children in fact have not learned these basic skills at a satisfactory level in each grade. Therefore, these subjects must be continued through the middle school years and on into high school.

CURRICULUM CONTINUITY

How much freedom should a student have to pursue needs and interests when curriculum selection is determined? Should a student have unlimited choice or should he or she be guided according to some plan? Should the student have few curricular choices and be expected to take all required subjects? How can the school arrange curricular opportunities for the student who can move rapidly up a vertical skill sequence ladder, for the student who progresses at a slower rate, for the student who wants or needs an extremely broad range of content areas, and for the student who must concentrate on basic skills? In the past, educators have not differentiated for individual students but have provided a very basic curriculum for everyone, allowing for little variation. This traditional curriculum included the same basic subjects in each year of a child's education.

CURRICULUM BALANCE

The school is under frequent pressure to expand its curricular offerings. However, the time available for instruction has remained relatively constant, although there is increasing interest in extending the length of the school year. However, only a limited number of hours each day are available for instruction. Difficult and sensitive decisions must be made to determine what alterations in the curriculum offer the best promise of an enhanced learning environment. Frequently, too, many aspects of the curriculum and the time allotted are mandated by state rules and regulations. But there are many aspects of the curriculum that are at the discretion of local boards of education and schools.

Each school should have guidelines to use in making good decisions about these discretionary aspects and to provide a balanced curriculum free from momentary fads or the wishes of this or that special-interest group. John Goodlad, in his book *A Place Called School,*[46] suggests that adequate attention be paid to each of the "five fingers" of the curriculum each year. His five fingers come from the Harvard report published in *General Education in a Free Society*.[47] The fingers are mathematics and science, literature and language, society and social studies, the arts, and vocational programs. Goodlad goes on to indicate that he feels elementary programs are too heavily directed toward language arts and mathematics.

Goodlad recommends that for high schools, literature and language and mathematics and science each be 18 percent of a student's program, with the other fingers comprising 15 percent each. Physical education, he believes should receive up to 10 percent attention, with the remaining time to be spent on guided individual choices.

J. Lloyd Trump,[48] in a much earlier work, suggested that all students receive at least some exposure to each discipline on a continuing basis each year they are in school, even though they may not at the time be taking a course in that discipline.

CURRICULUM CLASSIFICATION SYSTEM

A curriculum materials classification system is also a desired curricular feature for all schools. School resources—the materials, books, pamphlets, worksheets, filmstrips, tapes, kits, software, and so on—that fit the curriculum structure of the school are many and vary significantly from school to school, even in the same district. The average school has over 20,000 curricular items in its holdings. Teachers seldom are aware of all the curriculum resources for particular topics or objectives they plan to teach and seldom are they able to remember the difficulty level or instructional format of these many resources.

As part of the overall effort to provide structure to the curriculum, concern must be given to organize curriculum resources through some type of materials classification system that matches the school's adopted curriculum and its instructional objectives. An excellent prototype to consider is the Annehurst Curriculum Classification System.[49] This system classifies materials on the basis of subject matter and appropriate student characteristics, such as age level, perception type, and so forth. A retrieval system is available for manual or computerized searches to match all available materials to particular courses, topics, and students. Most of the computerized library retrieval systems that provide for bar code identification of materials can incorporate the schools instructional materials as well. Using these systems places all school materials under one cataloging system, usually under the direction of the school media program.[50]

Test Item Bank

The secret of good curricular alignment often lies with the school's ability to monitor its progress through evaluation. The development of a test item bank or collection of test items that reflect the prescribed content of the curriculum guides to be used by the staff becomes a way of providing some of this monitoring ability. The bank consists of a minimum of three or four test items for each of the stated objectives for the course. Tests are then compiled to measure the mastery of students on each objective in the curriculum outline by including one or more test items for each objective at appropriate levels of difficulty. Test item profiles reflecting the percentage of items from each of the levels of Bloom's Taxonomy can also be prescribed for each test.

Teachers, having contributed the test items to the bank and knowing their students will be evaluated in all aspects of the content assigned to their particular course study, are motivated to maintain a high degree of curricular alignment with the prescribed course of study. By having multiple items in the test bank and drawing on them randomly for particular test administrations, reduction in the opportunity to "teach the test" can also be accomplished. The major change in the system is one of making the staff collectively responsible for curriculum and evaluation instead of allowing each individual teacher to function as an autonomous agent for those responsibilities.

A CURRICULUM MODEL

Consideration of the needs and interests of students throughout the curriculum should accommodate different maturity levels. Furthermore, curriculum must be divided into priorities with different weightings for each subject. Equal emphasis on all curricular areas is not necessarily appropriate for each year. For example, basic skills in language and computation are obviously needed in the early years of education. As a child matures and as interests broaden, the curriculum of the school should expand along with the child. By the middle of the elementary school years, the curiosity of most children is very broad in scope, and a child may participate in a great variety of different elective explanatory curriculum areas over the course of the year. Obviously, if the child participates in many different activities, covering most in depth is unlikely.

The pattern of elective curricular choices may need to be somewhat different for each child. For example, during one quarter, a particular child may select sewing, leisure reading, entomology (the study of insects), music appreciation, spelling skills, and math games. A second child may select topics on the basis of what friends select because of a real need to belong to a specific group. The following quarter the pattern for both children might be different This normal variation of curricular interests among children raises the important question of what areas of learning are common to all children.

Organizing curriculum around areas of importance rather than considering all curricular areas equally offers one solution. In this way, varying emphasis can be placed on different areas as appropriate during each segment of a student's school career. One well-accepted model clusters curriculum into four major areas:

1. Basic skills
2. Common learning
3. Exploratory areas
4. Specialization

Figure 6.5 shows the type of subjects to be included in each area.

Time-on-task studies demonstrate that the amount of engaged time a student spends in a particular discipline has a direct effect on the student achievement in that subject.[51] These studies on academic learning time (ALT) usually emphasize the importance of the efficient and effective use of time. However, the total amount of allocated time is probably an equally important factor. The most effective way to improve a stu-

FIGURE 6.5 Major Curriculum Clusters

Basic Skills	**Common Learning**
Reading	Health
Arithmetic	Social studies
Psychomotor skills	Science
	Language
Exploratory Areas	**Specialization**
Social sciences	College prep
Science	Computer science
Art	Drafting
Music	Commercial foods
Mathematics	Distributive education
Typing	Horticulture
etc.	etc.

dent's achievement in any particular subject is simply to increase the amount of allocated time for the subject, recognizing of course that a corresponding decrease in other subjects must occur unless the school day is lengthened. In other words, if school officials are under tremendous pressure to improve reading and math achievement scores, increasing the number of minutes spent each day in those subjects will generally result in improved achievement, assuming the quality of instruction is constant.

Society demands that children learn certain basic skills, which include skills in communication and computation and a knowledge of basic health care and physical education. U.S. society also requires basic familiarity with other more general areas, such as the knowledge of democracy and the way it works. A school can provide this information in many different ways. A real danger exists in curricular organization in regard to what to include as required common learning. It is easy to include so many topics that all of the available school time is utilized to teach this information and no discretionary time remains for exploratory and student-selected curriculum. Thus, areas of common learning must be kept to a bare minimum if other concepts are to have room in the program. The interrelationship of basic skills, common learnings, and exploratory or student-selected activities can be diagrammed as in Figure 6.6.

Initially, schools concentrate on basic skills development. This work consumes most of a child's time during the early years of school, gradually diminishing as a percentage of the total time spent on learning as other things are added to the program. Common learning curriculum may begin in small amounts during the child's early mastery of basic skills and increase as skills are learned. The exploratory or student-selected aspect of the curriculum should continue to broaden as a child matures. The curriculum will reach its greatest breadth at a point approximately midway through the school career when it is made up of many varied and diverse parts, including courses of the student's own choosing.

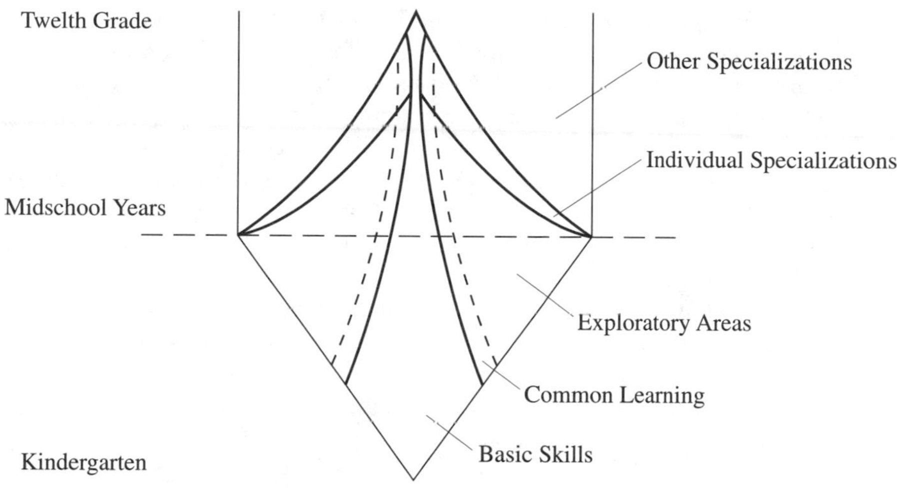

FIGURE 6.6 Curriculum Model

The time involvement of the child in the several parts of the curriculum varies, but the school year contains only a predetermined amount of time. In the early years, the curriculum has depth or concentration only in basic skills, with a relatively narrow scope of courses. By the time the child has reached the midschool point, time can be spent on more curricular areas. In other words, with so many curricular selections available during those middle years, students will spend less time on a particular subject. A child will be expected to learn some about many things rather than a lot about a few things.

By considering the natural motivation of the child, this expanding curricular organization better meets his or her growing curiosity during the elementary and middle school or junior high school days. In high school, the needs and interest of students begin to change. They begin to make tentative decisions relating to life as an adult. Puberty brings about emotional and psychological changes. The organization of the school system should take this into account. These changes have particular implications for curricular organization.

The interests and needs of children collectively continue to remain very broad and diverse, requiring a continued wide range of curricular offerings. On the other hand, the interests and needs of a particular child usually narrow as future life goals are sorted out. The curriculum of the school must allow students to begin to narrow their own curriculum into a specialization when they reach a maturity level that calls for it. The implications here for a flexible and active guidance program are also apparent.

During high school, the individual child begins to devote more and more time to an area of *individual specialization,* as shown in Figure 6.6. Specialization gradually replaces the exploratory phase of a student's curriculum. This individual specialization may entail a specific vocational program of one type or another. It may mean preparation for a particular vocation requiring continuation into a specific college program, or it may simply mean a decision to go to college.

For example, if a particular child is not progressing in reading skill development at a rate comparable to the majority of children that age, the child should probably spend a greater proportion of time in basic skills. The question then is what should give way? The choices probably rest between common learning and exploratory activities.

At first glance, it would seem that exploratory activities should probably give way to common learnings. But should they? Many children need strong motivation during the middle elementary years to keep up their interest in school. If exploratory activities are diminished for an increased skills emphasis, all interest in school on the part of the student may be lost. On the other hand, if the common learning areas are reduced instead, the interest in the exploratory areas might save the day (or the year), allowing a return to common learning later. One might even consider the content of the common learning areas as appropriate material for instruction in basic skills, providing a double-barreled program with the emphasis on the skills rather than on the common learning content.

OFFERING CURRICULAR BREADTH

Special Programs for Special Students

Students Who Are Gifted. Exploratory areas are one of the best opportunities to provide supplementary activities to gifted students and still have them participate with all children in the majority of curricular areas. Special programs in natural science, technology, mathematics, and other areas can be made available on an interest basis or on a selective-qualification basis while still providing other programs for all children.

Students Who Are Disabled. In a similar fashion, students with one or more disabilities also need the opportunity for exploratory opportunities. Often, when these students have difficulty acquiring basic skills, opportunity for exploration gets a low priority and is replaced by additional basic skill activities. This presents a real dilemma in that well-taught exploratory activities often are a child's major motivator for the entire school program. Thus, the reduction in exploratory activities reduces the motivation that is so desperately needed for learning the basic skills.

Mini-Courses

Curricular breadth at the secondary level is also possible. A number of techniques are available. A *mini-course* is a short course usually offered for one marking period of six to nine weeks; it is frequently nontraditional in its content and organization. Mini-courses are a functional method of creating desired variety, flexibility, and open access to content within a high school curriculum.

The concept of the mini-course is to offer to students a learning experience either within one of the given disciplines or from a multidisciplinary approach in an effort to better meet their needs and interests. When a great variety of mini-courses are offered, the curriculum is broadened. When mini-courses are available on a nonsequenced basis, maximum access to the curriculum is obtained. When necessary, some sequencing can be accomplished through the use of an introductory course within a particular discipline, followed by a series of mini-course options. But in many cases, sequencing to meet individual student needs is carried out internal to course structures.

Honors Courses and Advanced-Placement Courses

Creating special courses for highly motivated or high-achieving students offers ways to meet special needs. Honors courses are generally restricted to students who have a grade-point average or achievement test score above a predetermined level. Often, too, students must maintain a grade of B or better to remain in the course. Assignment to a particular honors course neither precludes assignment to another such course, nor does it result in assignment to all other honors courses.

Advanced-placement courses are similar to honors courses but are available to juniors and seniors only. Successful completion of such courses, if they have been approved by the College Board, may result in college credit.[52]

Caution should be exercised in the use of advanced classes to not create a totally separate curriculum for academically talented students. It is important that heterogeneity also mark the student population of some classes. High-achieving students serve as good examples for lower-achieving students. Moreover, high-achieving students profit from working with all levels of the school population, socially and intellectually. The use of techniques for cooperative learning, discussed in the next chapter, work well when a range of student abilities are included in a class.

SUMMARY

In this chapter we have discussed the role of the school principal in curriculum design and administration. We have explored various curriculum orientations as a foundation for determining not only *what* is being taught, but what *should be* taught and *why.* We have stressed the importance of curriculum design being a joint responsibility between principal and teachers, and we have presented a foundation for analyzing the curriculum and adapting it to fit the unique needs of the school.

ACTIVITIES

1. Reflect on the curriculum structure and offerings in your own school. Can you identify areas where restructuring should take place? Why do you believe so? Apply the concepts of this chapter to your school. How would you proceed to restructure your school's curriculum?
2. Review Cases Studies 5, 6, and 14 at the end of this book. Analyze the problems presented and apply the curriculum concepts developed in this chapter. What approach would you use in addressing the problems? Set forth a strategy to overcome the difficulties faced by the school as well as ways to deal with individuals in the cases.
3. Turn to the ISSLC Standards found in Appendix B. Review the knowledge, dispositions, and performances listed with Stan-

dard Two. Reflect on which of the standard items relate directly to the concepts of curriculum presented in this chapter. How do the concepts of curriculum development and organization match Standard Two? Identify one knowledge, one disposition, and one performance to link directly to a concept or idea discussed in Chapter 6.

ENDNOTES

1. Elliot Eisner, "What Is the Purpose of School?" *ASCD Update 32,* no. 19 (December 1990): 4.
2. Thomas Sergiovanni, *Moral Leadership: Getting to the Heart of School Improvement* (San Francisco: Jossey-Bass, 1992).
3. Christopher Hodgkinson, *The Philosophy of Leadership* (Oxford, England: Basil Blackwell Publisher, 1983).
4. John McNeil, *Curriculum: A Comprehensive Introduction* (3rd ed.). (Boston: Little, Brown, 1985).
5. Allan Ornstein, "Philosophy as a Basis for Curriculum Decisions" in *Contemporary Issues in Curriculum,* ed. Allan C. Ornstein and Linda Behar-Horestein (Boston: Allyn and Bacon, 1995).
6. Ibid., p. 16.
7. Ibid.
8. Ibid.
9. Abraham Maslow, "A Theory of Motivation," *Psychological Review* (July 1943): 388–389.
10. Carl Rogers, *Freedom to Learn for the 1980s* (2nd ed.). (Columbus, OH: Merrill, 1988).
11. Values clarification is a technique quite common in gifted education. It is based on the idea that the learners should be able to explore their own feelings and values and make their own choices.
12. Daniel Goleman, *Emotional Intelligence* (New York: Bantam Books, 1995).
13. Goldman credits Salovey as being the first one to coin the term *emotional intelligence* in an article with John Mayer entitled "Emotional Intelligence," in *Imagination, Cognition, and Personality* 9 (1990): 185–211.
14. Howard Gardner, *Multiple Intelligences: The Theory in Practice* (New York: Basic Books, 1993).
15. Robert Sternberg, *Beyond I.Q.* (New York: Cambridge University Press, 1985).
16. Goleman, *Emotional Intelligence,* p. 43.
17. Rogers, *Freedom to Learn.*
18. Effective schools research is usually divided into correlates. One of those correlates, the school climate, addresses many of the principles of humanistic curriculum in terms of setting the tone of the setting and the relationship between teacher and student.
19. Carol Rogers, *Client-Centered Therapy* (Boston: Houghton Mifflin, 1951) and *A Way of Being* (Boston: Houghton Mifflin, 1981).
20. William Glasser, *Schools Without Failure* (New York: Harper & Row, 1968).
21. Ibid.
22. Stewart B. Shapiro, "Developing Models by 'Unpacking' Confluent Education." Occasional Paper no. 12, *Development and Research in Confluent Education* (Santa Barbara: University of California, 1972).
23. Refer to the cohort concept and model discussed in Chapter 2 of this text.
24. McNeil, *Curriculum: A Comprehensive Introduction,* p. 32.
25. Michael Apple, *Education and Power* (Boston: Routledge and Kegan Paul, 1982) and *Teachers and Texts: A Political Economy of Class and Gender Relations in Education* (New York: Routledge & Kegan, 1986).
26. Henry Giroux, *Critical Pedagogy, the State, and Cultural Struggle* (Albany: University of New York Press, 1989).
27. Jeannie Oakes, "Limiting Students' School Success and Life Chances: The Impact of Tracking," in *Contemporary Issues in Curriculum,* Allan C. Ornstein and Linda Behar-Horenstein (Boston: Allyn and Bacon, 1999), pp. 227–234.
28. Harold Shane, *Educating for a New Millennium* (Bloomington: Phi Delta Kappan, 1981).
29. See Chapter 1 for a detailed discussion of transformational leadership.
30. The *hidden curriculum* refers to learning that takes place unintended from the formal curriculum.
31. McNeil, *Curriculum: A Comprehensive Introduction.*
32. Bridges, E., and Hallinger, P., *Implementing Problem Based Learning in Leadership Development* (Eugene, OR: University of Oregon, 1995), ERIC Clearinghouse on Educational Management.
33. McNeil, *Curriculum: A Comprehensive Introduction,* p. 39.

34. M. Frances Klein, "Alternative Curriculum Conceptions and Designs," in *Contemporary Issues in Curriculum,* ed. Allan C. Ornstein and Linda Behar-Horenstein (Boston: Allyn and Bacon, 1999).

35. Linda Darling-Hammond, "Teacher Evaluation in the Organizational Context: A Review of the Literature," *Review of Educational Research 53,* no. 3 (Fall 1983): 285–328.

36. McNeil, *Curriculum: A Comprehensive Introduction,* p. 53.

37. Klein, "Alternative Curriculum Conceptions and Designs," p. 31.

38. McNeil, *Curriculum: A Comprehensive Introduction,* p. 70.

39. McNeil, *Curriculum: A Comprehensive Introduction.*

40. Paul Hirst, *Knowledge and the Curriculum* (London: Routledge & Kegan Paul, 1974).

41. California State Department of Education, *Model Curriculum Standards: Grades Nine Through Twelve* (Sacramento: California State Department of Education, 1985).

42. National Diffusion, *Educational Programs That Work* (Lungmont, CO: Sopris West Inc. Network, 1984).

43. Instructional Objectives Exchange (IOX), Box 24095, Los Angeles, CA 90024. IOX has collections at the secondary level in language arts, including reading, comprehension, structural analysis, composition, reference skills, listening, oral expression; journalism; grammar, mechanics, and usage; and English literature. Other collections include general mathematics, business education, home economics, auto mechanics, electronics, general metals, mechanical drawing, woodworking, American history, geography, biology, and Spanish. A current catalog can be obtained by writing to the above address.

44. Benjamin S. Bloom and others, *The Taxonomy of Educational Objectives: Effective and Cognitive Domains* (New York: David McKay, 1974).

45. W. Fredrick, "The Use of Classroom Time in High Schools Above or Below the Median Reading Score," *Urban Education 11* (January 1977): 459–464.

46. John A. Goodlad, *A Place Called School* (New York: McGraw-Hill, 1983).

47. Report of the Harvard Committee, *General Education in a Free Society* (Cambridge, MA: Harvard University Press, 1945).

48. J. Lloyd Trump, *Images of the Future* (Washington, DC: National Association of Secondary School Principals, 1959).

49. Jack Frymier, *The Annehurst Curriculum Classification System* (West Lafayette, IN: Kappa Delta Phi, 1977).

50. D. J. Armor, P. Conry-Oseguera, M. Cox, N. King, L. McConnel, A. Pascal, E. Pauly, and G. Zellman, *Analysis of the School Preferred Reading Program in Selected Los Angeles Minority Schools* (Santa Monica, CA: Rand Corporation, 1976).

51. Charles Fisher et al., "Improved Teaching by Increasing Academic Learning Time," *Educational Leadership 37* (October 1979): 52–54.

52. *A Guide to the Advanced Placement Program,* The College Board, 45 Columbus Ave., New York, NY 10023-6992.

SELECTED READINGS

Amabile, Teresa. *The Social Psychology of Creativity* (New York: Springer-Verlag, 1983).

Anderson, L. "Improving Instruction: Policy Implications of Research on School Time." *The School Administrator* (Arlington, VA: American Association of School Administrators, 1983).

Blase, Joseph, and Peggy C. Kirby. *Bringing Out the Best in Teachers: What Effective Principals Do* (Newbury Park, CA: Corwin Press, 1991).

Eisner, Elliot. "The Art and Craft of Teaching," in *Contemporary Issues in Curriculum,* ed. Allan Ornstein and Linda Behar (Boston: Allyn and Bacon, 1999).

Eisner, Elliot. *The Educational Imagination* (3rd ed.). (New York: Macmillan, 1993).

Gardner, Howard. *Frames of Mind: The Theory of Multiple Intelligences* (New York: Basic Books, 1983).

Goodlad, J. L., *A Place Called School* (New York: McGraw-Hill, 1984).

Greene, Maxine. "Philosophy and Teaching," in *Handbook of Research on Teaching* (3rd ed.). ed. Merlin C. Wittrock (New York: Macmillan, 1986).

Griffin, Gary A. "Leadership for Curriculum Improvement: The School Administrator's Role," in *Critical Issues in Curriculum: The 87th Yearbook of the National Society for the Study of Education,* ed. Laurel Tanner (Part I, pp. 244–

266). Chicago: University of Chicago Press, 1988.

Hughes, Larry W. *The Principal as Leader* (New York: Macmillan, 1999).

Hoy, Wayne K., C. John Tarter, and Robert B. Kottkamp. *Open Schools/Healthy Schools* (Newbury Park, CA: Sage 1991).

Jacobs, Heidi Hayes (Ed.). *Interdisciplinary Curriculum: Design and Implementation* (Arlington, VA: Association for Supervision and Curriculum Development, 1989).

Kozol, J. *Savage Inequalities: Children in America's Schools* (New York: Crown, 1991).

Sergiovanni, Thomas J. "The Roots of School Leadership." *Principal 74,* no. 2 (November 1994): 6–9.

Sternberg, Robert, J. "A Three-Faced Model of Creativity," in *The Nature of Creativity,* ed. Robert J. Sternberg (New York: Cambridge University Press, 1988), pp. 125–147.

Wagner, Tony. "What's School Really for, Anyway? And Who Should Decide?" *Kappan 76,* no. 5 (January 1995): 393–399.

CHAPTER SEVEN

PROMOTING STUDENT ACHIEVEMENT

Goals, strategies, learners, and objectives have styles. Each style implies a different set of relationships between the teacher, the learner, and the curriculum.
—R. W. Stong, H. F. Silver, and R. Hanson[1]

If curriculum can be defined most simply as what is taught in the school, then instruction is the *how*—the methods and techniques that aid students in their learning. The emphasis in instruction should be on student achievement, not on teaching, but obviously both are significant.

Consideration of instruction as the process for providing content, or the *what,* to the learner presents several major problems to the thoughtful organizer of the school program. These can best be presented as five questions:

1. What is the nature of the learner and how can students best be organized?
2. What instructional processes are available to be used?
3. How do these processes accommodate individual differences?
4. What are the implications of these instructional processes for the other organizational components of the school?
5. How can these processes be improved?

In this chapter we answer these questions through the lens of the standard, or measured, curriculum discussed in the previous chapter. This orientation rests heavily on the academic and technological orientations to curriculum that assume a *discrepancy* view of teaching. Such a view suggests that one must first determine *what should be taught* and then plan accordingly. The true judgment of the effectiveness of that teaching then will be to determine *what is learned* based on what was intended.

Instruction is the lifeblood of the school. It is the process by which content, or curriculum, is transported to the student. Instruction, however, requires a learner who gains insight, acquires information, and forms values not only from the content of the curriculum but also through the processes by which the content is presented (i.e., instruction). Therefore, the entire learning environment of the school constantly provides content for learning. This entwining of curriculum and instruction forces school administrators to look very carefully not only at what they teach in the school but also at how they teach it, for the medium is truly the message.

How different are children from each other? What differences count when organizing a school? Differences can be found in children's abilities, height, weight, age, sex, interests, needs, ethnic backgrounds, learning styles, achievements, and personalities. But before determining which differences matter in school organization, we should consider what these differences really are. Obviously, as children mature, differences increase. Many characteristics can be measured against accepted fixed scales and spoken of in fairly concrete terms. Items such as gender or ethnic background remain fixed and can usually be described in specific terms, also. However, factors such as abilities, interests, needs, learning styles, and personalities are far more difficult to assess, for they are far more complex, varied, and changeable. As a result, efforts to classify people become more dependent on other constructs for definition and therefore less exact. For example, rarely will a single continuum suffice in a description of ability. Ability to do what? To be meaningful, ability descriptions must also be scaled in some way. Ability compared to what or to whom? Ability to do something or to do something better than someone else? Comparative information, then, is necessary in studying or determining differences in abilities because of the abstract nature of terms such as ability.

INDIVIDUAL DIFFERENCES AMONG CHILDREN

One reason for looking at individual differences is to determine the conditions they may set for organization. Individual differences obviously affect the way instruction and curriculum are organized. Contributing to these organizational decisions will be decisions relating to grouping children. *Achievement* is most often used as a basis for predicting *ability*. As a result, the two terms become inappropriately interchanged. Achievement can be measured with a fairly high degree of accuracy, but translating achievement into ability is fraught with danger because of the inability to always know of, or adequate place in the formula, those factors contributing to a student's opportunity to achieve.

For example, a child may have the ability to be an excellent computer programmer, but if he or she has never had the opportunity to even sit at a computer terminal, future performance is uncertain. Thus, to take past achievements with computers as a predictor of future success would be erroneous. More thought about the conditions or circumstances under which past achievement occurred needs to take place before making instructional decisions.

If one is going to look not at ability but at achievement as a determinant for organizing children for learning, what kind of differences should one expect to find in a school population? Studies done at the University of Minnesota in the early 1940s, that still hold today, established a simple rule of thumb to indicate an achievement range.[2] The rule is: The achievement range of an age group of children is equal to approximately two-thirds of their chronological age. A group of 6-year-old children will have an achievement range of four years; a group of 9-year-olds will have an achievement range of six years. In other words, the slowest 9-year-old will be approximately equal to an average 6-year-old (three years below), and the fastest 9-year-old will be approximately equal to an average 12-year-old (three years above). Figure 7.1 illustrates the formula for school-age children. Note particularly the overlap of achievement over any three-year age span. A group of 6-year-olds, a group of 7-year-olds, and a group of 8-

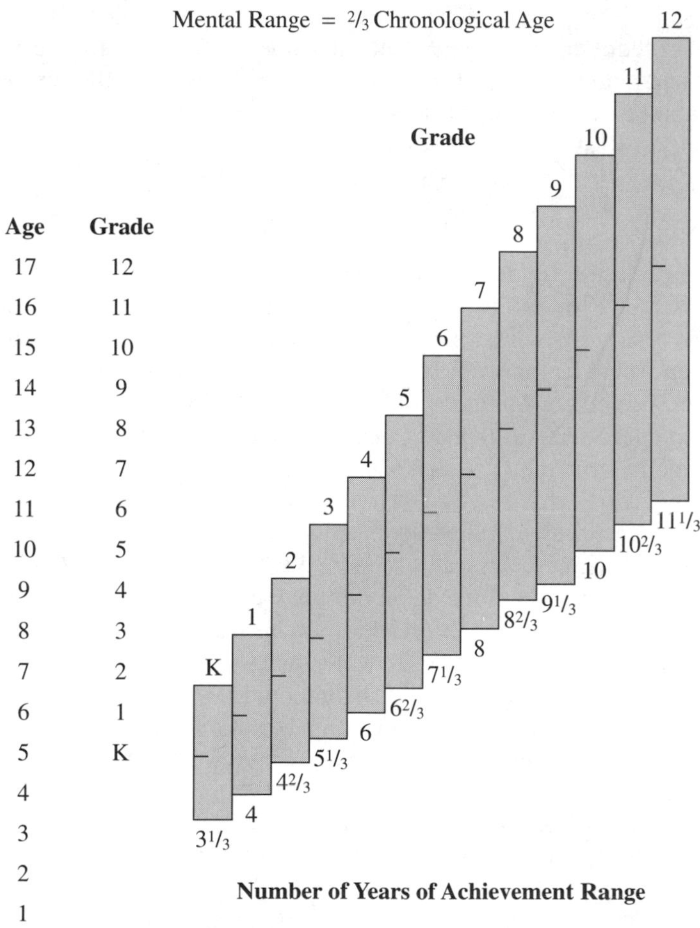

FIGURE 7.1 Achievement Formula for School-Age Children

year-olds have a broad range of achievements in common. The extremes contribute only fractional differences across the several years.

GROUPING STUDENTS

Instruction in any normal school setting requires numerous decisions about the grouping of children. Basically, these decisions will relate to three variables: group size, group composition, and group flexibility. The basic purpose of grouping students is to bring about the highest quantity and quality of instruction possible. Grouping practices should be consistent with curricular decisions and should be compatible with each student's needs and interests. These lofty goals must be tempered by two factors.

The first factor is the variations of abilities within each learner making homogeneous grouping very difficult. The second factor is the practical consideration of the cost of a particular organization design in comparison with its related effectiveness. For example, group size usually suggests certain staffing patterns that can be converted into dollar costs. A school might conclude that a staffing ratio of three-to-one would give the best quality and quantity of learning per student but that it would be too expensive. Instead, grouping designs must consider more economical staffing ratios, most likely in the range of 15 to 30 students per 1 staff member.

Group Size

Over the years, research studies on class size have produced mixed results. Two meta-analyses of class size, researched by Glass and Smith, published by the Far West Laboratory, have been widely interpreted as providing convincing evidence that smaller classes are better than larger ones. The basic finding of analyses on class size indicated that smaller classes resulted in increased achievement. However, the study showed that in classes ranging from 20 to 40 pupils, class size made little difference in achievement. The major benefits from reduced class size were obtained as size was reduced below 20 pupils.[3]

A more recent study in Tennessee,[4] using over 70 classrooms in a well-designed four-year study of primary classes (K–3) size 13–17, 22–25, and 22–25 with an aide, produced conclusive results. Students in the small classes made higher scores on both the achievement and criterion-referenced tests. The greatest gains were made in inner-city small classes. The highest scores were made in rural small classes. Teachers reported that they preferred small classes in order to identify student needs and provide more individual attention as well as to cover more material. The findings also suggest a cumulative and positive affect of small classes in later grades. Students in grade 4 who had previously been in the project's small classes demonstrated significant advantages on every achievement measure over students who had attended regular classes.

Teachers who had the smaller classes were observed to cover their basic instruction more quickly, providing increased time for additional material. They used more supplemental texts and enrichment activities. There was more in-depth teaching of basic content. More frequent opportunities were available for children to engage in firsthand learning activities using concrete materials. In summary, teachers were better able to individualize instruction. Smaller classes allow for more personal attention to the student encouraging a closer student-teacher relationship, as discussed in Chapter 6.

Group Composition

What should be the criteria for organizing children into groups? Obviously, efficient instruction requires groups; the needs of each student, however, should be the first consideration. This section will deal first with some of the more controversial grouping practices, such as homogeneous ability grouping and retention, and their accompanying problems. Then, on a more positive note, alternative grouping patterns based on interest, age, skill, and achievement, as well as group flexibility and tenure will be discussed.

Ability Grouping in the Elementary and Middle School. A common practice is to organize or group students on the basis of their supposed ability, creating a tracking system with a two-, three- or four-group continuum consisting of high-ability, average-ability, and low-ability students. The basic assumption underlying this pattern of student organization is that by subdividing children from the extremely broad-ability continuum found in any normal school population, teachers will be better able to focus instruction on the needs of the children in any particular group. Thus, ability groups supposedly narrow the range of abilities within any group and make it more possible for the teacher to organize and prepare materials for a narrower range of abilities.

Criteria used to determine group composition have included achievement test scores, IQ scores, previous grades, and teacher opinion. Serious problems develop when any of these criteria or combinations are used as the basis of organizing students on a permanent basis or for extended periods of time. This method of grouping is usually not effective. No common denominator can be found for long-term grouping across disciplines or even within disciplines. For example, interest can greatly change productivity within a discipline, overriding previous supposed ability measurements.

Children can be grouped successfully according to one factor to obtain a degree of homogeneity, but the group remains heterogeneous in all other aspects of curriculum and instruction. For example, homogeneity in mathematics can be obtained by placing in a group all children who know their multiplication tables through 12, but they remain a heterogeneous group for the rest of the curriculum, including other areas of mathematics.

When the descriptors of homogeneity are based on previous math achievements, an IQ test score, or all previous grades, almost all useful definition of homogeneity is lost, for in almost any specific skill or knowledge, some children placed in the lowest group on one basis will exceed the knowledge level of other children placed in the highest group on another. Therefore, homogeneous grouping as a broad-based or permanent grouping design simply does not work, and the homogeneity is a figment of the imagination of the staff.

Many teachers and administrators have argued strenuously that ability grouping does work and that definite differences exist among students. Of course, differences can be seen, but the point is that the overlap in abilities is far greater from group to group than most of us imagine, and, most importantly, homogeneous grouping overlooks the individual child.

Several attitudinal factors must also be considered in a discussion of homogeneous grouping. The phenomenon of the *self-fulfilling prophecy* enters into the ultimate outcomes of ability grouping. This prophecy says that children become what others say they are or what they think they are.[5] Research about self-concept has shown that children's own attitudes toward themselves as people and their assessment of their own abilities represent major factors in their ultimate success or failure in school. Teacher attitudes, as well as the student's self-concept, contribute greatly to the child's ultimate success or failure in school. The placement of a child in a group on the basis of perceived ability can seem to prove itself correct by adjustments in productivity on the part of the child that in fact take place as a result of the placement, thus fulfilling the prophecy. There is also the question of "reproductive theory" (discussed in Chapter 6)—the idea that children at different academic levels have different access to quality education, thereby perpetuating a stratified social order.

Over the past 40 years, numerous research studies have considered ability grouping. A massive review of many of these studies was reported in 1973 with the following conclusions:

1. Homogeneous ability grouping as currently practiced shows no consistent positive values for helping students generally, or particular groups of students, to achieve more scholastically or to experience more effective learning conditions. Among the studies showing significant effects, evidence of slight gains favoring high-ability students is more than offset by evidence of unfavorable effects on the learning of students of average and below-average ability, particularly the latter.

2. The findings regarding the impact of homogeneous ability grouping on affective development are essentially unfavorable. Whatever the practice does to build or inflate the self-esteem of children in the high-ability groups is counterbalanced by evidence of the unfavorable effects of stigmatizing those placed in average- and below-average-ability groups as inferior and incapable of learning.

3. Homogeneous ability grouping, by design, is a separative educational policy, made ostensibly according to test performance ability but practically according to socioeconomic status and, to a lesser but still observable degree, according to ethnic status.

4. In cases where homogeneous or heterogeneous ability grouping is related to improved scholastic performance, the curriculum is subject to substantial modification of teaching methods, materials, and other variables that are intrinsic to the teaching-learning process, and that, therefore, may well be the causative factors related to academic development wholly apart from ability grouping per se. Similarly, with respect to social development, evidence that points to variables other than ability grouping tends to relate substantially to personal growth or lack of growth.[6]

High School Grouping. In high schools, ability grouping functions somewhat differently than in the lower grades. Deficit and average students do seem affected by grouping but talented students achieve more and have better attitudes about subject matter when they are placed with others who are also talented. Ability grouping frequently occurs naturally in the selection of elective courses labeled "honors" or in advanced-placement courses. Advanced foreign language courses and higher-level mathematics courses also attract these students. More recent studies on grouping in the elementary school continue to support the position that heterogeneous grouping produces greater student learning than does homogeneous grouping.[7]

Retention

One form of ability grouping that is often overlooked is the result of the retention policies operating in many school districts. Retention places a child with a less intellectually and socially mature group based on the child's demonstrated ability or achievement. Therefore, it is actually an instance of ability grouping—adjusting the placement of the child to fit a curriculum and instructional level thought more appropriate, rather than bringing the appropriate curriculum and instructional level to the child.

Retention is as ineffective an approach to the grouping of children as the previously discussed method. A poorly achieving fourth-grader is not more like a third-grader. The affective development of the student must be considered along with the cognitive development. That student is still more like his or her peers and will be more successful with them than if retained and placed with a younger group of children. At any grade level, the achievement range will spread over a number of grade levels. The Cook studies of the 1940s concluded that:

> When pupils in the lower 10 percent of the classes are failed because of low achievement, they do not become better adjusted educationally or socially in the retarded position. The available evidence indicated that, on the average, they achieve as much or more by being given more regular promotions.

The study went on to point out that:

> When attempts are made to reduce the range of abilities and achievement in a school by retarding slow learning pupils and accelerating fast learning pupils, there is an increase in the proportion of slow learning pupils in each grade. Average grade achievement is lowered.

The study concluded, somewhat tongue in cheek, that:

> If the major concern of the teachers is to maintain grade level standards, the most effective way of increasing achievement standards in a school is to retard the bright and accelerate the dull pupils.[8]

Research on retention continues to show its inappropriateness as a means of adjusting for individual differences.[9] Nevertheless, it continues as a very popular policy in many schools. It does not work as a method of maintaining standards, nor does it work as a means of threatening children to perform. In Chapter 2 we discussed the concept of total quality management (TQM). Retention violates the TQM principle of not setting outcome goals. It is much better if a school uses instructional process solutions to adjust for individual differences of children.

Appropriate Bases for Grouping

Groups are necessary for school organization, but retention and homogeneous ability grouping as semipermanent forms of student organization are not effective. What should be the basis for grouping? The following principles and techniques for organizing students are sound:

1. Regular classrooms and teams should be based on heterogeneous grouping. Some means should be taken to ensure that all teams have an equal portion of students on various achievement and ability levels.

2. Achievement grouping for math and reading is appropriate, particularly if these subjects are taught from a skill continuum. However, achievement groupings should not result in tracking. Primary identity for a student should still be with the heterogeneous grouping pattern.

3. The principal has the responsibility of sharing with teachers the research on retention and grouping practices. "Conventional wisdom" misleads in this case. The principal also needs to be responsible for developing grouping patterns that serve the needs of the unique student population and should monitor teacher implementation of these grouping plans.

4. Grouping patterns must be flexible and, as a result of individual student assessment, allow change in student placement as needed.

5. Within each classroom setting, subgroupings should be kept small enough to ensure individual instruction.

6. Children of various ages may be grouped together if some other appropriate criteria such as skill development is utilized.

7. Particular care should be taken so that grouping practices do not become damaging to the self-concept of the child or create stereotypes in the eyes of other students or teachers toward particular children.

Group Flexibility

How long should an established group remain intact? When groups are reorganized, how extensive should that reorganization be? At what level within the organization should decisions for group reorganization take place? These questions relate directly to the ultimate flexibility that can be obtained for grouping within any school organization.

Groups should remain intact until they have accomplished their skills objective. Once the original purpose for the grouping has been achieved, the group must be reorganized. This may be after one hour of instruction in a skills group, or it might be after three years together as a heterogeneous, multiage group. Skill groups, interest groups, and achievement groups should be designed so they can be reorganized daily, if necessary.

Problems of Regrouping. The need for frequent regrouping in the school presents several problems in school organization. First, it is impractical to refer all grouping decisions to the principal since the quantity and frequency of needed grouping decisions would overwhelm that office. More significantly, most of the information needed for intelligent grouping decisions is found at the teacher-student level.

To give teachers and students an opportunity to make flexible grouping decisions, a school is best organized into learning communities consisting of two or more teachers, their students, and an extended time block. With this arrangement, students and teachers can group students. The unit design for school organization with a team of teachers, aides, and a group of 75 to 150 students is a good example of this organization.[10]

The important concept here is that the principal has passed on the power of decision making regarding grouping directly to the teachers. Once the components of the group have been designated, the principal's role becomes one of giving advice to the teams for internal grouping decisions. The teachers, in turn, then organize the groups.

Grouping Guidelines

Student grouping is necessary for all school organizations.

1. For purposes of assigning students to individual teachers or teams, a heterogeneous or mixed grouping plan is usually best.
2. Homogeneous grouping should take place in the classroom and should be done by teachers. The basis for internal class grouping can be interest, achievement, skill, age, or designed heterogeneity
3. Homogeneous grouping should be kept flexible with several different grouping patterns used each day. All homogeneous groups are usually of short duration. Flexibility is necessary because of the changing nature of groups and the problems of negative student self-concept or poor teacher attitudes that can develop from rigid homogeneous grouping patterns.
4. Homogeneous groups should not be used for more than one-third of each school day.

INSTRUCTIONAL PROCESSES AND TYPES OF INSTRUCTION

Instruction can take place in a variety of formats. Types of instruction can be divided into several basic categories:

1. Lecture presentation or demonstration

2. Discussion
3. Laboratory activities
   a. Group or individual
   b. Independent study

Each category presents a different mode for student learning. The purpose of instruction and the expected outcomes should be major factors in determining which instructional type should be used. For example, if the purpose of instruction is to introduce or present an overview of a topic, a lecture presentation to a large group might be best. On the other hand, if the anticipated outcome is the modification of values, then an instructional format that directly involves the learner (such as a laboratory or discussion) is most often more effective. The concept of "thinking meetings" discussed in Chapter 6 is a good example. Figure 7.2 presents the major purposes of these four categories of instruction. Note that each category also has certain group size recommendations.

FIGURE 7.2 Types of Instruction and Major Purposes

I. Presentation
Build concepts through information
Stimulate inquiry
Enrich course
Relate course to reality
Make assignments

Usually most efficient and effective in large groups

II. Discussion
Raise questions
Report experience
Discuss ideas
Generalize
Form opinions
Plan independent study

Usually most efficient and effective in small groups (7–15 persons)

III. Laboratory Activities

Individual Study	*Purpose*	*Independent Study*
Student performed directed	Build concepts and principles through action and viewing Practice skills	Student directed planned performed evaluated
Teacher directed planned evaluated managed	Apply ideas Develop investigative skills Develop problem-solving techniques Develop evaluation skills	Teacher advised

These activities may be small group (2 or more) or individual in nature and can be either scheduled or unscheduled.

In reality, in most lessons, all four types of instruction should probably be used. For example, the model lesson design proposed by Hunter uses all four types. The Hunter model suggests seven steps for a sequential learning model as shown in Figure 7.3.[11]

FIGURE 7.3 Sequential Learning Model

1. **Anticipatory Set**
   The teacher prepares students for the lesson. The first five minutes of a lesson are the most critical as that is when the teacher has the greatest degree of student attention.
2. **Statement of Objectives**
   The instructor should inform students of the objectives for a particular lesson: namely, Robert Mager's three elements of an instructional objective:
   a. State the task.
   b. Identify how the task is to be completed.
   c. Identify minimum level of competency to be achieved, if the teacher wishes to identify a minimum level.

   Instruction in the deductive style is recommended for students experiencing academic difficulty. The teacher would state the rule and give students adequate practice until they could demonstrate mastery prior to introducing a new concept.

   Guiding questions, prior to independent completion of an assignment, are recommended.

   The teacher should clarify for the students how one day's instruction ties into what has academically preceded and how it will influence the next day's instruction.
3. **Instructional Input**
   The teacher should move among the students, while they are working, providing additional reinforcement when needed.
4. **Modeling**
   The teacher should be illustrating concepts taught, providing many and varied examples, and responding to student questions.
5. **Checking for Understanding**
   Students should demonstrate 75–80 percent mastery on a concept before being taught a new concept.
6. **Guided Practice**
   The teacher can have children working in groups of five to seven, carefully monitoring their achievement while they are working. Particular attention should be given to those children who, in the past, have demonstrated difficulty in working independently.
7. **Independent Practice**
   Such practice should consist of only ten to fifteen minutes for a particular assignment. Independent practice should not be used as a teaching strategy; it should be used as reinforcement for concepts that are understood by the students.

Steps 1 to 3 of the Hunter model are usually in the form of a lecture to the entire group. Steps 4 and 5 are often in a discussion mode, initially with the entire group, but often with smaller follow-up groups as fewer and fewer children remain not having yet achieved mastery. Step 6 is a form of group lab activity, and step 7 is an individual lab or homework-type assignment.

RESEARCH ON TEACHING

Research regarding instruction and the development of a consistent view of teaching represents one of the major trends in education in the past decade. This change has come about as education has made a major shift in its attention from focusing on teacher traits to focusing on instructional skills. It is important to note that this trend represents only two of the four curriculum orientations discussed in Chapter 6. These are the technological and academic approaches. The other curriculum orientations (humanistic and social reconstructionism) require different instructional approaches. Since the standard curriculum in today's schools center heavily on academic and technological orientations, we discuss the methods that are applicable to them. Certainly, the curriculum can, and should be, enriched by the addition of the other orientations and the methods more suited to their delivery. The research on effective teaching has produced a list of recommended instructional skills that, when implemented effectively by teachers, produces observable, measurable gains in student learning. This emphasis on a directive teaching model is, of course, consistent with the measured curriculum discussed in Chapter 6. It is *not* always the most appropriate style for other curriculum orientations. A summary of the major teaching competencies, along with citations of their research, are listed for teacher competencies in planning, lesson implementation, cooperative learning, student motivation, evaluative feedback, evaluative methods, assigning grades, time on task, and individualized instruction.

Effective Planning Skills

Research on teachers' planning indicates that if teachers (1) identify instructional objectives, (2) set an appropriate level of difficulty for mastery, (3) plan out matching instructional methods, procedures, materials, and student activities, and (4) use good formative and summative evaluation techniques, the resulting preparedness can increase the probability of improving student achievement as measured by test scores. Such planning also ensures teacher confidence, direction, and security.

Some of the success of this planning can certainly be attributed to the improved curricular alignment that occurs from the detailed planning around objectives drawn directly from a prescribed curriculum. However, the *planning* for instructional implementation is believed to be the major cause of the gain found in student test scores.

The research on planning also provides a clear understanding of the stumbling block to planning.[12] Teaching for mastery demands a well-developed statement of goals and instructional objectives as well as appropriate criterion-referenced tests.[13] Although this makes good sense to administrators and many teachers, it requires a tremendous amount of work for teachers. Most teachers, however, intuitively base their success in the classroom on student interest and attitudes and not on cognitive gain. Therefore, the teachers do not obtain the personal reinforcement from the results of the students' test gains.[14]

Effective Lesson Implementation

The effective implementation of a lesson planned by the teacher is as important as the planning itself. The high-gain teachers use a variety of instructional methods, including drill, explanation, discussion, inquiry, role-playing, demonstration, and problem solving. One important element of good lesson implementation is the use of advanced organizers, which gives the learner an overview of the lesson. Hunter's concept of an anticipatory set is an example of an advanced organizer.

Other important elements of effective lesson implementation include asking relevant questions, giving explanations, and doing demonstrations in conjunction with frequent feedback to the teacher regarding student understanding. Feedback techniques, such as signing (thumbs up, thumbs down) or "if you know the correct answer raise your hand," can provide this information to a teacher throughout the lesson.

"Electronic classrooms," equipped with a keypad at each students work station, with a monitor for the teacher to see student responses, provide a means for each student to respond to questions. Such systems have the capability to record all the answers for later review by the teacher. The major limitation of these systems is that the questions must be only those that can be answered with multiple-choice responses, true/false responses, or numerically.

Increased wait time, the amount of time a teacher waits after asking a question, also has shown positive effects on student performance. Untrained teachers often wait only one to two seconds after asking a question. A longer wait time produces longer more complete student responses, more student confidence in their responses, increased factual evidence used by students in their responses, a greater number of slow students participating, and reduced teacher-centered presentations.[15]

Research also has produced surprising results about questioning techniques. First, many teachers do not use questioning of students during discussion very much, but it has been demonstrated that the frequency of factual, single-answer questions is positively related to gains in achievement.[16]

Quizzing and reviewing also have been shown to be elements in successful lesson implementation. When teachers give regular quizzes one or more times a week, scores on final exams go up. Frequent testing influences study behavior positively.[17]

The most effective teachers also use homework to enhance study habits of students. Studies support the view that frequently assigned homework, in small amounts to provide independent practice on what has been learned during the instructional lesson, has a positive effect on achievement.[18]

Cooperative Learning

This instructional strategy delegates some control of the pacing and methods of learning to student groups, usually composed of two to six persons. Students in the groups work together on assignments, sometimes competing with other groups. Individuals in the group assume responsibility for sharing knowledge and tutoring each other. It is an active-learning approach and has been shown to offer great opportunity for the development of higher-order thinking skills in all participants.

Classrooms that are organized for cooperative motivation instead of competitiveness produce a better classroom climate. Competitive organization permits aggressiveness, cheating, lowered motivation, and failure-avoiding behaviors; whereas cooperative environments are linked to positive peer relationships, higher achievement, positive self-esteem, and interracial acceptance.[19]

Student Motivation

Motivation concerns the "why" of behavior. Bloom suggests that motivational factors can account for 25 percent of the variation in student achievement.[20] The high-gain teacher, in motivating students, has a classroom environment that evidences a warm acceptance of students along with consistent rules and high expectations for student behavior. A special environment or climate must be created in the classroom that ensures involvement and success. It should move at a brisk pace, monitor all students, stimulate attention, and ensure accountability by variety and unpredictability in questioning patterns.[21]

It is an important motivator to use students' ideas in discussions by acknowledging student responses, repeating the responses in different words, applying their ideas, comparing their responses, and summarizing their responses.[22] Promoting students' beliefs in their own competence by carefully matching students' abilities to learning assignments is also a powerful motivator. The ALT (academic learning time) studies[23] suggest that materials allowing high and middle SES students to achieve approximately an 80 percent success rate and low SES students a 90 percent success rate will maximize student motivation. Teachers need to plan for and treat all students as if they were winners.

A good way to identify factors that may be affecting achievement and motivation is by using the instrument Comprehensive Assessment of School Environments (CASE) developed by the National Association of Secondary School Principals. The instrument also provides information about parent satisfaction.[24]

Providing Students with Evaluative Feedback

This competency consists of several tasks, including providing written comments to students on their progress in addition to grades, returning tests as quickly as possible, holding individual conferences with students, and interpreting test results to students and parents.

The research evidence is extensive regarding the importance of the frequency and timeliness of effective feedback to students. Formative feedback, done while the lesson and learning are in progress, is best done orally rather than in writing and is most beneficial when correcting wrong answers, both to correct the student and to allow the teacher to modify the lesson to cope with the problem.[25]

Feedback in the form of praise should be used extensively but within certain parameters. Low-achieving students may require more explicit recognition for their classroom participation; however, indiscriminate praise may not motivate learning. What is desired is real recognition for real achievement.[26] Feedback on tests and assignments also provides information both to the students on how their work is being evaluated and to the teacher on how successful the instruction has been.[27]

A high volume of feedback from the teacher is of value for reinforcement, as well as its information content.[28] The research also shows that immediate feedback from the teacher is important, as is a high frequency of testing on content material in the classroom.[29]

Preparing Appropriate Evaluation Activities

The effective teacher begins instruction by making the methods of evaluation clear to students; basing the evaluation on specific goals, objectives, and content of the course; and using both pretests and posttests in order to measure student gain. Student progress is measured through a series of both formative and summative evaluation techniques.

Specific statements of instructional objectives, in measurable terms announced to the students, become the first step in projecting toward the evaluation. These objectives need to be closely aligned with the stated curriculum and should be reflective of some diversity, as shown by some classification system such as the work of Bloom (cognitive domain), Krathwohl (affective domain), or Samson (psychomotor domain).[30] Surveys have shown that teachers generally select most of their objectives from the cognitive domain and most from the lowest level (knowledge) of that domain.[31] Greater diversity of objectives is usually desirable.

Formative evaluation, while instruction is unfolding, should be frequent and have as its purpose monitoring and guiding students to the correct learning as well as providing the teacher with data for monitoring instructional effectiveness.[32] Summative evaluation should be used to determine if the student has achieved the objectives. Mastery learning is a graduated approach to summative evaluation. Here, instructional objectives are divided into small units with specific objectives whose mastery is essential for the mastery of the major objectives. In mastery learning, frequent testing and evaluation are crucial. The research indicates that mastery learning evaluation techniques produce superior student achievement, learning retention, transfer of learning, and positive affective outcomes.[33]

Assigning Grades

High-gain teachers recognize the importance of assigning grades and take the responsibility seriously. They keep in mind what parents want to learn from student report cards, and they use grades to accurately reflect student progress rather than as a form of behavior modification. Teachers must test often and consistently to achieve good reliability of evaluative data.[34]

Marking systems using a maximum of five to nine discriminations are best understood by parents; therefore, a 5-point, letter-grade scale is probably a better communicator than is a 100-point scale.[35] Pass-fail grading system appear to lead to lower achievement.[36]

Two general approaches are used by teachers in assigning grades. The first is grading students on their performance relative to their classmates. The second is using an absolute scale of some type based on a standard, such as a predetermined number of objectives to be achieved. The first type, that of relative scores compared to other students, is commonly called *grading on a curve*. Students' grades are either based on raw scores drawn from posttest data only or gain scores based on the difference between pre- and posttest data. Gain scores logically provide a better measure of student achievement under the instruction of that particular teacher. However, this type of relative comparison of student scores to one another is appropriate only if there are very large groups of students included, and the students are not tracked. This is rarely the case in the normal classroom setting.

The second type of grading, that of using an *absolute scale,* is common to criterion-referenced tests and to mastery learning. Proficiency tests with minimum acceptable levels of performance also use this logic. Grades are based on a predetermined level of achievement necessary to obtain a particular grade, such as 8 out of 10 correct for a B, or 9 out of 10 correct for an A.

Grading must reflect student performance and growth. When it reflects something other than academic achievement, it cannot be considered valid. High-gain teachers do not abuse the assigning of grades but consider it a significant part of their communication with both parents and students.

Time on Task

The high-gain teacher uses the time allocated for the class in a highly efficient manner. Classwork begins promptly at the beginning of each period, management time and transition time are kept to a minimum, and the teacher reinforces students who are spending time on task. Studies report that low-achieving students are off task in excess of 50 percent of the time, whereas high-achieving students are off task less than 25 percent of the time.[37] Another study, of junior high students, showed that low achievers had engaged time of approximately 40 percent, whereas high achievers reached in excess of 85 percent engagement time.[38]

The research evidence demonstrates that time is a valuable resource in school, and when used efficiently, increases student performance.[39] The studies identify three levels of time used: allocated time—that assigned to a particular course or subject; engaged time—the amount of allocated time in which students actually are engaged in learning activities; and academic learning time (ALT)—a refinement of engaged time reflecting quality of learning. Factors included in the definition of *quality* are the appropriateness of instructional materials relative to the achievement level of the student, the best student's success ratio of learning (suggested is an 80 percent success ratio for most learners), and the amount of concentration the learner is actually contributing to the instructional process.[40]

The high-gain teacher is punctual and begins instruction for each class promptly, leaving management details until later in the hour, if possible. During seatwork time, the teacher monitors students closely, encouraging more time on task. It is suggested that at least 50 percent of each class period be devoted to active, direct instruction. This is significantly higher than what is found in most classes. For example, one study demonstrated that math teachers on the average used only 14 percent of their time for direct instruction, with 34 percent going for written work, 8 percent for review, and the balance being assigned to off-task activities.[41]

Individualized Instruction

Where does individualized instruction fit, in light of all the research findings supporting direct instruction in the form of demonstration-practice-feedback? How does the finding of the need for whole group instruction impact on individualized methods?[42] Although direct instruction has shown great results for the acquisition of specific skills, it cannot do it all; in fact, for higher-order learning and thinking skills, direct instruction may be counter productive.[43] An effective classroom must solicit student involvement in learning activities under appropriate conditions for mastery. This demands a proper climate and opportunity for the child to achieve success. These requisites demand that teachers provide appropriate opportunity for individual differences if maximum student productivity is to be maintained. Teachers can accommodate individual differences in a variety of ways:

1. By varying the level of teaching internal to the class through adjusting the level of questioning and varying the length of wait time
2. By providing varying amounts of allocated time to different students
3. By grouping within or between classes, as has been discussed earlier in this chapter
4. By consideration of different learning styles of children
5. By selection of classroom organizational methods, including learning centers, tutors, or study groups[44]

Instructional Tools for Individualization. We have emphasized individualized instruction and the need to provide a variety of instructional activities for students in order to make such a system functional. The logical question is how to organize or create materials for self-instruction.

Excellent commercial materials are now available for individualized systems, and more are becoming available each year. In areas such as reading and math, schools can purchase an entire system for a wide range of student achievement levels. Other materials can be organized and coordinated for instruction by teachers using those materials. Teachers, of course, should also continue to use their own materials.

The real problem, however, is organizing materials in a systematic way so that they are adequately available to students when they need them, adequately self-instructional so that teacher time can be appropriately balanced, and adequately organized to assure proper instructional sequencing, recording, and evaluation. Today's computers can aid greatly in managing records for individualized instruction. A number of methods of instruction have gained acceptance as ways to achieve individualization of instruction and to enhance learning. Among these are mastery learning, independent study, cooperative learning, and computer-assisted instruction.

Mastery Learning. Mastery learning, as described by Bloom,[45] has been a very successful form of individualized instruction.[46] Although this form of mastery instruction, as a means of obtaining individualization, has many benefits and has shown good success for certain types of learning, primarily skills development, a number of difficulties exist:[47]

1. Alternate instructional materials and tests are needed for those students required to recycle to achieve mastery.
2. Management problems of the increasing spread of achievements are caused by early masters and the extended recycling of others.

Independent Study. Two frequently stated goals for secondary student development are "the development of independence" and "the development of purpose." Traditional approaches to organization of instruction tend to limit, restrict, or inhibit these desired goals, however. Instruction that is heavily teacher directed, although it may be best for basic skill development, tends to foster dependence rather than independence. If student interdependence and independence with purpose are desired, then instruction must be organized to achieve it.

A variety of types of learning experiences may be considered as independent study program activities. Students may participate in homework and in-depth projects, walkabout challenge projects, enrichment courses, regularly scheduled classes, informal discussion, and other activities that are consistent with the purposes of the independent study phase of instruction.

Specific independent study objectives for students include the following:

1. Assume an increased responsibility for making decisions relative to his or her education.
2. Develop an increased control over his or her impulse behavior.
3. Become a more purposeful, independent learner by achieving a higher degree of interdependence, venturesomeness, resourcefulness, goal directedness, and persistence.
4. Develop an increased capacity to solve problems and learn to use critical and creative thinking processes.
5. Acquire relevant subject matter content.
6. Develop an increased interest in learning.
7. Achieve emotional independence of parents and other adults.
8. Achieve more and more mature relationships with peers of both sexes.
9. Desire and achieve socially responsible behavior by becoming more self-disciplined.
10. Acquire a set of values in an ethical system and a guide to behavior.

The implementation of an effective independent study program will be a new activity for many schools. Each student participating in advanced forms of independent study should sign an appropriate contract that states purpose, completion date, conference dates, and so on.

Computer-Assisted Instruction. This methodology has existed in theory for many years. However, new technological advances in both software and hardware make its daily use in the classroom practical and affordable. The graphical user interface (GUI), used now by much of the new computer software, along with mass storage capabilities of compact discs make this possible with the addition of full color pictures and sound to programs. Added to this is the capability of the software to offer instruction to students on the basis of their individual needs, monitor and adjust that instruction based on progress, and maintain progress records for each student. Although cost will always be a factor, it continues to drop dramatically while capability continues to rise.[48]

SUMMARY

In conjunction with any instructional system must come a plan for organizing and grouping students. Grouping considerations include group size, composition, and flexibility. Extensive preparation is needed to develop a variety of learning goals, objectives, and activities, so that appropriate instructional plans can be developed for all students.

Research on teaching indicates the importance of each teacher having skills in lesson planning, lesson implementation, student motivation, evaluative feedback, evaluative methods, assigning grades, maintenance of high time on task, cooperative learning, and individualization of instruction. The principal must have an understanding of diversified instruction and exhibit an expectation of such instruction from the teachers.

ACTIVITIES

1. Review Case Studies 2, 12, and 18 at the back of this book. Apply the instructional concepts expressed in this chapter. How might you proceed in addressing the problems cited in these cases? Set forth a strategy to overcome the problem.
2. Reflect on the instructional strategies and behaviors in your own school. Can you identify areas where restructuring should take place? Why do you believe so? Apply the concepts of this chapter to your school. How would you proceed to restructure your school's instructional program? How might you use the concepts of Chapter 9, Human Resources Development, to assist in your planning?
3. Turn to the ISSLC Standards found in Appendix B. Review the knowledge dispositions, and performances listed in Standard Two. Reflect on which of the standard items relate directly to the concepts of learning as presented in this chapter. How do the concepts of learning match Standard Two? Are there important concepts not included in the standard curriculum format? Identify one knowledge area, one disposition, and one performance to link directly to a concept or idea discussed in Chapter 7.

ENDNOTES

1. R. W. Stong, H. F. Silver, and R. Hanson, "Integrating Teaching Strategies and Thinking Styles with Elements of Effective Instruction," *Educational Leadership 42* (May 1985): 9–15.

2. Walter W. Cook and Theodore Clymer, "Acceleration and Retardation," in *Individualized Instruction, 1962 Yearbook of the National Society for the Study of Education,* ed. Nelson B. Henry (Chicago: NSSE, 1962), pp. 179–208.

3. Gene V. Glass and Mary Lee Smith, "Meta-Analysis of Research in the Relationships of Class Size and Achievement," in *The Class Size and Instruction Project,* Leonard S. Chaen, principal investigator (San Francisco: Far West Laboratory for Educational Research and Development, September 1978).

4. Helen Pate-Bain, C. M. Achilles, Jayne Boyd-Zaharias, and Bernard McKenna, "Class Size Does Make a Difference," *Phi Delta Kappan* (November 1992): 253–256.

5. A study by Rosenthal and Jacobson investigated the concept of the self-fulfilling prophecy and found that teacher attitudes and expectations about a child do have a direct bearing on the child's performance. Robert Rosenthal and Lenore Jacobson, *Pygmalion in the Classroom* (New York: Holt, Rinehart and Winston, 1968).

6. Dominick Esposito, "Homogeneous and Heterogeneous Ability Grouping," *AERA Journal* (Spring 1973): 163–179.

7. R. E. Slavin, "Grouping for Instruction in the Elementary School," *School and Classroom Organization* (Hillsdale, NJ: Lawrence Erlbaum, 1989).

8. Walter W. Cook, "Effective Ways of Doing It," in *Individualized Instruction, 1962 Yearbook of the National Society for the Study of Education,* ed. Nelson B. Henry (Chicago: NSSE, 1962), Chapter 3.

9. Margaret M. Dawson and Mary Ann Rafoth, "Why Student Retention Doesn't Work," *Streamlined Seminar, NAESP 9,* no. 3 (January 1991): 1–6.

10. *IGE Unit Operations and Roles* (Dayton, OH: Institute for Development of Educational Activities, 1970).

11. M. Hunter, "Knowing, Teaching and Supervising," in *Using What We Know About Teaching* (Alexandria, VA: Association for Supervision and Curriculum Development, 1984), pp. 169–192.

12. P. L. Peterson, R. W. Marx, and C. M. Clark, "Teacher Planning, Teacher Behavior, and Students' Achievement," *American Educational Research Journal 15* (1978): 417–432.

13. J. I. Goodlad, M. F. Klein, and associates, *Looking Behind the Classroom Door* (Worthington, OH: Charles A. Jones, 1974).

14. T. R. Mann, "The Practice of Planning: The Impact of Elementary School on Teachers' Curriculum Planning," *Dissertation Abstracts International 35* (1975): 3359A–3360A.

15. M. R. Rowe, "Relation of Wait-time and Rewards to the Development of Language, Logic, and Fate Control: Part II—Rewards," *Journal of Research in Science Teaching 11* (1974): 291–308.

16. J. Stallings and D. Kaskowitz, *Follow-Through Classroom Observation Evaluation,* 1972–73 (Menlo Park, CA: Stanford Research Institute, Stanford University, 1974).

17. P. Peterson and H. Walberg (Eds.), *Research on Teaching* (Berkeley, CA: McCutchan, 1979).

18. J. D. Austin, *Homework Research in Mathematics 1900–1974*. Paper presented at the 1974 Annual Georgia Mathematics Education Conference at Rock Eagle, GA, 1974.

19. D. W. Johnson and R. T. Johnson, "Instructional Goal Structure: Cooperative, Comparative and Individualistic," *Review of Educational Research 44* (1974): 213–240.

20. B. S. Bloom, *Human Characteristics and School Learning* (New York: McGraw-Hill, 1982).

21. T. L. Good and J. E. Brophy, *Looking in Classrooms* (New York: Harper and Row, 1973).

22. B. Rosenshine and N. Furst "Research on Teacher Performance Criteria," in *Research in Teacher Education: A Symposium,* ed. O. Smith (Englewood Cliffs, NJ: Prentice-Hall, 1971), pp. 46–56.

23. C. Fisher D. Berliner N. Filby, R. Marliave, L. Chance, and M. Dishaw, "Teaching Behaviors, Academic Learning Time, and Student Achievement: An Overview," in *Time to Learn,* ed. C. Denham and A. Lieberman (Washington, DC: The National Institute of Education, U.S. Department of Education, 1980).

24. CASE is available from the National Association of Secondary School Principals. Inquire: Publication Sales, NASSP, 1904 Association Drive, Reston, VA 22091-1598.

25. "Florida Beginning Teacher Program," Office of Teacher Education, Certification, and Inservice Staff Development, Tallahassee, FL, 1982. M. Mims and B. Gholson, "Effects of Type and Amount of Feedback upon Hypothesis Sampling Among 7–8 Year Old Children," *Journal of Experimental Child Psychology 24* (1977): 358–371. B. B. Hudgins et al., *Educational Psychology* (Itasca, IL: Peacock, 1983).

26. J. Brophy, "Teacher Praise: A Functional Analysis," *Review of Educational Research 51* (1981): 5–32. W. Brookover, C. Beady, P. Flood, J. Schweitzer, and J. Wisenbaker, *School Social Systems and Student Achievement: Schools Can Make a Difference* (New York: Praeger, 1979).

27. M. Hunter, *Appraising the Instructional Process.* Presentation for California Advisory Council on Educational Research, November 1973. Appears in *Resources in Education* (Washington, DC: ERIC Clearinghouse on Teacher Education, October 1977). B. Rosenshine, *Teaching Functions in Instructional Programs,* Airlie House Paper (Washington, DC: NIE Conference, 1982).

28. R. Bardwell, "Feedback: How Well Does It Function?" *Journal of Experimental Education 50* (1981): 4–9.

29. Peterson and Walberg, *Research on Teaching.*

30. B. S. Bloom, M. B. Englehart, E. J. Furst, W. H. Hill, and D. R. Krathwohl, *Taxonomy of Educational Objectives: The Classification of Education Goals. Handbook I: Cognitive Domain* (New York: Longmans Green, 1956).

31. Good and Brophy, *Looking in Classrooms.*

32. Peterson, Marx, and Clark, "Teacher Planning."

33. J. H. Block, *Schools, Society and Mastery Learning* (New York: Holt, Rinehart and Winston, 1974).

34. Clinton I. Chase, *Measurement for Educational Research* (Reading, MA: Addison-Wesley, 1978).

35. G. A Miller, "The Magic Number Seven, Plus or Minus Two: Some Limits on Our Capacity for Processing Information," *Psychological Review 63* (1956): 81–97.

36. L. A. Gatta, "An Analysis of the Pass-Fail Grading System as Compared to the Conventional System in High School Chemistry," *Journal of Research in Science Teaching 10* (1973): 3–12. W. L Claiborn, "Expectancy Effects in the Classroom: A Failure to Replicate," *Journal of Educational Psychology 60* (1969): 377–383. W. M. Stallings and H. R. Smock, "The Pass-Fail Grading Option at a State University: A Five Semester Evaluation," *Journal of Educational Measurement 8* (1971): 153–160.

37. D. Powell and M. Eash, "Secondary School Cases," in *Evaluating Educational Performance,* ed. H. Walberg (Berkeley, CA: McCutchan, 1974), pp. 277–293.

38. C. Evertson, *Differences in Instruction Activities in High and Low Achieving Junior High Classes.* Paper presented at the Annual Meeting of the American Educational Research Association, Boston, 1980.

39. J. Stallings, "Allocated Academic Learning Time Revisited, or Beyond Time on Task," *Educational Researcher 9* (1980): 11–16. W. Frederick, "The Use of Classroom Time in High Schools Above or Below the Median Reading Score," *Urban Education* (1977): 459–464. T. L. Good, "How Teachers' Expectations Affect Low Achieving Students," *American Educator* (December 1982): 22–32.

40. Peterson and Walberg, *Research on Teaching.*

41. J. Stallings and A. Robertson, "Factors Influencing Women's Decisions to Enroll in Elective Mathematics Classes in High School." Final Report to the National Institute of Education (Menlo Park, CA: SRI International, 1979).

42. W. R. Borg, "Time and School Learning," in *Time to Learn,* ed. C. Denham and A. Lieberman (Washington, DC: The National Institute of Education, U.S. Department of Education, 1980).

43. P. L. Peterson, "Direct Instruction Reconsidered," in *Research on Teaching,* ed. P. L. Peterson and H. J. Walberg (Berkeley, CA: McCutchan, 1979).

44. Good and Brophy, *Looking in Classrooms.*

45. Bloom, *Human Characteristics.*

46. B. B. Hudgins et al., *Educational Psychology.* Itasca, IL: Peacock, 1983.

47. Peterson and Walberg, *Research on Teaching.*

48. D. Stansberry, "Taking the Plunge," *New Media: Multimedia Technologies for Desktop Computer Users* (February 1993): 30–36.

SELECTED READINGS

Adams, Buck, and Gerald D. Bailey. "School Is for Teachers: Enhancing the School Environment." *NASSP Bulletin 73* (January 1989): 44–48. (ERIC Document Service No. EJ 382 023).

Berliner, David, and Ursula Casanova. "When Are Two Heads Better Than One?" *Instructor 98,* no. 4 (1988): 22–23.

Bracey, Gerald. "The Social Impact of Ability Grouping." *Phi Delta Kappan 68,* no. 9 (May 1987): 701–702.

Braddock, Jomills H. "Tracking the Middle Grades: National Patterns of Grouping for Instruction." *Phi Delta Kappan 71,* no. 6 (February 1990): 445–449.

Carroll, Joseph M. "The Copernican Plan: Restructuring the American High School." *Phi Delta Kappan 71,* no. 5 (January 1990): 358–365. (ERIC Document Service No. EJ 400 584).

Colvin, Shirley Beard. *Creating Effective Learning Environments for Disadvantage Learners: Implications for the Design of Educational Programs.* Paper presented at the Annual Meeting of the American Educational Research Association, New Orleans, LA, April 8, 1988. (ERIC Document Service No. ED 293 969).

Cruickshank, Donald R. *Research That Informs Teachers and Teacher Educators* (Bloomington, IN: Phi Delta Kappa Educational Foundation, 1990).

Davidson, Neil, and Pat Wilson O'Leary. "How Cooperative Learning Can Enhance Mastery Learning." *Educational Leadership 47* (February 1990): 30–33.

Eisner, Elliot W. "The Ecology of School Improvement." *Educational Leadership 45,* no. 5 (February 1988): 24–29. (ERIC Document Service No. EJ 368 822).

Fennimore, Todd F. *A Guide for Dropout Prevention: Creating an Integrated Learning Environment in Secondary Schools* (Columbus, OH: National Center for Research in Vocational Education, 1988). (ERIC Document Service No. ED 298 323).

Grace, Linda, and Robert L. Buser. "Student Motivation." *The Practitioner 14,* no. 1 (September 1987): 1–12. (ERIC Document Service No. ED 286 284).

Gursky, Daniel. "On the Wrong Track?" *Teacher* (May 1990): 42–51.

Hillerick, Robert L. "What Does 'Grade Level' Mean?" *Principal 69,* no. 3 (January 1990): 47–48.

Howe, Geery S. "Expecting Miracles: How to Develop a Learning Consciousness in High School Classrooms." *Social Studies 79,* no. 5 (September–October 1988): 228–231. (ERIC Document Service No. EJ 379 343).

Johnson, D. W., and R. T. Johnson. *Learning Together and Alone,* 2nd ed. (Englewood Cliffs, NJ: Prentice-Hall, 1987).

Knapp, Michael S., and Patrick M. Shields. "Reconceiving Academic Instruction for the Children of Poverty." *Phi Delta Kappan 71,* no. 10 (1990): 753–758.

Lake, Sara. *Instructional Practices for Middle Grade Students: Developing Self-Directed Learners.* Sacramento, CA: California League of Middle Schools, 1988. (ERIC Document Service No. ED 304 232).

McPartland, James M., and Shi-Chang Wu. *Instructional Practices in the Middle Grades: National Variations and Effects* (Baltimore, MD: Center for Research on Elementary and Middle Schools, 1988. (ERIC Document Service No. ED 301 321).

Miller, William. "Are Multi-Age Grouping Practices a Missing Link in the Educational Reform Debate?" *NASSP Bulletin 79,* no. 568 (February 1995): 27–32.

Porter A. and J. Brophy. "Synthesis of Research on Good Teaching." *Educational Leadership 45,* no. 8 (1988): 74–85.

Rodes, Marcia, and Jody Scott. "The Promise of Cooperative Learning as an Instructional Strategy to Help Students Think and Work Together." *Curriculum in Context* (Summer 1988): 14–15.

Schulz, Elizabeth. "Smaller Is Definitely Better." *Teacher 1,* no. 3 (December 1989): 332–333.

Sharan, S., and C. Schachar. *Language and Learning in the Cooperative Classroom* (New York: Springer, 1988).

Sharon, Shlomo, and Yael Sharon. "Group Investigation Expands Cooperative Learning." *Educational Leadership 47,* no. 4 (December 1989–January 1990): 17–21.

Sikorski, Melanie F., Richard P. Niemiec, and Herbert J. Walberg. "Best Teaching Practices: A Checklist for Observations." *NASSP Bulletin 78* no. 561 (April 1994): 1–6.

Slavin, R. E. "Are Cooperative Learning and 'Untracking' Harmful to the Gifted?" *Educational Leadership 48* (February 1991): 63–74.

Slavin, R. E. *Cooperative Learning: Theory, Research, and Practice* (Englewood Cliffs, NJ: Prentice-Hall, 1990).

Strong, R. W., H. F. Silver, and R. Hanson. "Integrating Teaching Strategies and Thinking Styles with Elements of Effective Instruction." *Educational Leadership 42* (May 1985): 9–15.

Thomas, John W., Robert G. Curley, and Amy Strage. *Course-Related Impediments to Effective Study Practices.* Paper presented at the Annual Meeting of the American Educational Research Association, Washington, DC, April 1987. (ERIC Document Service No. ED 293 810).

Van Deusen, Jean Donham, and Robert van Deusen. "Don't Buy Computers Unless...." *Principal* 69, no. 2 (November 1989): 10–12.

Weaver, Rosa Lee. "Separate Is Not Equal." *Principal* 69, no. 5 (May 1990): 40–42.

CHAPTER EIGHT

SPECIAL STUDENTS AND SPECIAL SERVICES

Historically, special education has been synonymous with separate education. Fundamental changes in America's schools have resulted in education for special children becoming an integral part of the total schooling picture. And, all educators now share responsibility for teaching all children.

—Michael Brady[1]

Children may come to school with many problems that will make learning difficult. Some are hungry, some need decent clothing, some have been abused at home physically or psychologically, and others have physical or mental disabilities that make learning difficult. Often, the need for special assistance is first signaled by low attendance. In many cases, school personnel have a legal responsibility to provide the resources to improve students' learning opportunities. In other cases, school personnel may feel a moral responsibility to function as a quasi-social services referral agency in order for some of the children of that school to have an adequate "quality of life." This is often necessary before learning can take place.

The principal or designated members of the staff need to develop a network of contacts in the community where assistance can be obtained. Many communities are fortunate to have governmental agencies both within and outside the school system available to provide most needed services to children. Special education services are mandated nationwide by the Individuals with Disabilities Education Act (IDEA).[2] Section 504 of the Rehabilitation Act of 1973[3] and the Americans with Disabilities Act[4] (ADA) also impact on the kind of services that must be provided to children with special needs. All states have child abuse laws administered, most often as part of a social services agency or welfare department. Public health departments often are charged with providing special health services to needy children as well as providing health screening and immunization monitoring of school-age children. Many private agencies also have available services for needy children, such as the Lions clubs that provide eye care or church groups that have emergency food or used clothing available.

Although some will argue that these needs of children should not be the responsibility of the school, often the school—the gathering point for all children—is the first to become aware of problems. When the physical or emotional needs of children get in the way of learning, the school has a direct stake in seeking a solution. The principal, the guidance counselor, the school nurse, the social worker, the special education staff, the regular classroom teachers, as well as others, all have a part to play. But when reaching beyond those activities required by law, or when taking fullest advantage of services from available agencies, the leadership of the principal in setting the direction for the school in providing services to special children is critical.

THE 1997 IDEA AMENDMENTS

The 1997 Amendments to IDEA introduced significant changes in the services provided to special education students. Basically, these changes revolve around three main themes:

1. Strengthening parental participation in the educational process
2. Accountability for students' participation and success in the general education curriculum and mastery of IEP goals and objectives
3. Remediation and rehabilitation of behavior problems at school and in the classroom.

SPECIAL EDUCATION AND RELATED SERVICES

The IDEA requires school districts to provide a free appropriate public education (FAPE), including special education and related services, in the least restrictive environment (LRE), as determined by a multidisciplinary team (M-team) and written in an individual education program (IEP). These services are mandatory for all children from age 4 to the end of the school year in which the student turns 22, or, in the case of a child who is deaf, age 23, who can be certified by an appropriate specialist as having a disability or exceptionality and verified by a multidisciplinary team of educators as needing special education services. Exceptionalities include:[5]

Mental retardation
Learning disabilities
Hearing impairment
Orthopedic impairment
Autism
Multidisabled
Developmental delays
Serious emotional disturbance
Visual impairment
Other health impairment
Speech impairment
Deaf-blind
Traumatic brain injury

The law requires that certain due process procedures be followed, assuming the right of the parent and child to be fully informed and included in the decision making at all steps in identification, child evaluation, planning, programming, and program evaluation. (See Chapter 16 for a more complete review of the law regarding special students.)

Program Steps

Particular steps must be followed in implementing a special education program. These include:

Step 1: Screening. The school has the responsibility to monitor the development of each child in order to know as early as possible if any child is having problems with his or her school work. Screening checks are to be made for the child's medical health record as well as the child's progress in school. Medical screenings are usually scheduled by the district special education departments or appropriate health agencies. Educational checks are initially the responsibility of the regular classroom teacher to observe and identify children with potential disabilities.

Step 2: Prereferral Actions. When a student presents a particularly unique problem, the classroom teacher often needs somewhere to turn for help. The problem may surface as a disciplinary problem, a learning difficulty, poor attendance, or what seems like a lack of interest in planned classroom activities. None of the strategies tried by the teacher have seemed to work. If the child is referred to special education, weeks can pass before a formal assessment is completed and a staff meeting is held to recommend a plan. In some cases, a formal referral may identify a student as disabled and recommend placement in a special education instruction program. Other students may be identified as mildly disabled, but not in need of special education programming, while others will not be identified as disabled at all. For these last two groups, the delay in providing immediate support to the teacher and student may not have been necessary at all.

It is suggested that prereferral procedures be developed that will allow for more immediate action and assistance in most cases and that would be less costly than the formal referral and assessment process. The prereferral procedure should begin with the collection and review of classroom data gathered by the teacher. Included should be attendance information, available standardized and classroom test data, teacher observations of student effort, attention, ability to follow directions, listening, social skills, self-confidence, peer relationships, and so on. Teaching strategies attempted should also be documented.

Step 3: Support Team Review. Each school should organize a school support team (S-team) to function as an intermediate step between the recognition of a problem by a classroom teacher and a formal referral for a comprehensive educational evaluation. For students who are obviously disabled, this support team review is bypassed and a formal referral is made immediately. On the other hand, the teacher who is experiencing less severe difficulty with a student should request the team's assistance. The information gathered through the prereferral action is received by this team. The team that meets regularly to discuss such cases considers the problem, generates possible remedial actions, and recommends specific intervention strategy. The support team (S-team) should be made up of experienced teachers qualified to teach that age child, possibly the special education teacher, and other appropriate staff members such as a Title I teacher or guidance counselor. One member should function as the S-team coordinator to schedule meetings, organize records, and ensure that the team's recommendations are implemented.

The S-team should be viewed as problem solvers, bringing to focus the expert resources of the school on those issues that fall just short of resulting in a formal special education referral. Those students deemed to have educational or emotional problems beyond the normal capability of the school staff and program to adequately address ultimately will be given a formal referral to the other education specialists for further evaluation.

Step 4: Formal Referral for a Comprehensive Evaluation. An evaluation to specifically determine the severity of the child's deficits is scheduled. An assessment team may include all or any of the following: school psychologist, occupational therapist, physical therapist, other special educators, physician, regular classroom teachers, and/or medical specialists. Parents have the right to obtain an independent evaluation at their own expense if they so choose; however, depending on the nature of the events, the school must sometimes eventually assume these costs. Ultimately, the assessment team determines if the student is eligible for special education. Eligibility is based on the child fitting the certification requirements for a particular special education category.

Step 5: The Multidisciplinary Team. The multidisciplinary team (M-team), made up of a group of at least three school professionals and the parent/guardian, is responsible for developing an appropriate educational program for the student based on a careful review of all diagnostic data. The M-team's responsibilities include: (1) reviewing the present level of educational performance as derived from the assessment data, (2) developing the individualized educational program (IEP), and (3) making a recommendation for placement.

The M-team approach is designed to ensure that decisions concerning a student's program will be made by a team of persons whose primary goal is to accommodate the interests, needs, learning styles, and abilities of that student. Careful consideration should be given to the selection of M-team members who are most qualified to contribute to the development and implementation of the IEP. Those individuals who must be part of the initial M-team include the principal or his or her designee; the teacher who recently or currently has the student in class; the assessment specialist(s), such as the psychologist or audiologist, who conducted the assessments as part of the evaluation; the parent/guardian of the student; and the student, when appropriate.

Individual Education Program (IEP). The individual education program, or IEP (or for preschool children, an individual family service plan [IFSP]), is a written record of the decisions reached by the members of the multidisciplinary team at the IEP meeting.

It sets forth in writing the commitment of resources necessary for the child who has disabilities, functions as a management tool to ensure services, is the compliance/monitoring document for government monitoring of the law, serves as the evaluation device in determining the child's progress, and functions as the communication document with the parent. The IEP must contain the following components:

1. The present level of educational performance
2. Certification that student meets disabled requirements
3. Annual program goals and interim program objectives
4. Regular program participation and modifications
5. Special education placement and justification
6. Multidisciplinary team signatures of participants
7. Parent signature and statement of review/appeal rights
8. Indicated date for annual review

Recommendations for Placement. It is required by the IDEA that the individual educational program developed by the M-team be provided in the *least restrictive environment.* Today, that generally means inclusion. *Inclusion* differs from *mainstreaming* in that the latter term usually refers to integrating children with disabilities and children without disabilities for only a portion of the day, which may be during nonacademic times. In a fully inclusive model, students with disabilities, no matter how severe, are taught in the regular education classroom of their home school with their age and grade peers for the full day with support services provided within the classroom.[6] In short, inclusion means bringing support services to the child rather than moving the child to a segregated setting to receive special services.[7] This means that each child should be placed in a setting where he or she can be with noneligible children as much of the time as possible. The act allows for 10 different placement options but demands that the least restrictive option appropriate for the child be used. The act requires that a continuum of service options be provided. A typical sequence of options would include the following:

1. Full time in the regular classroom with special supplies and/or equipment.

2. Full time in the regular classroom with consultative services for the teacher.

3. Full time in the regular classroom with additional instruction by a special education teacher in the regular classroom.

4. Part time in the regular classroom (as much as is appropriate) and part time in a special *resource program* coordinated with the regular classroom activities.

5. Full time in a special *comprehensive development classroom (CDC)* provided to meet the needs of the severely/profoundly involved students who require intensive planning and programming.

6. Part time in the regular school program with a special education aide supervising the child with disabilities while in the regular classroom.

7. Other related services, including transportation; speech pathology and audiology; psychological, physical, and occupational therapy; recreation; counseling; medi-

cal (for diagnostic and evaluation purposes); school health; social work; parent counseling and training; assistive technology devices and services; transition; nursing; interpreter; as well as others not specified.

8. Ancillary services provided by agencies outside the school to provide services a minimum of four hours a day in order to maintain the child in the regular program.

9. Residential services to provide for a child whose disabling conditions are so profound or complex that continuous intervention is required to meet his or her educational needs and no special education services offered in a CDC or self-contained program can meet these needs. While these programs are very costly, if the IEP calls for this service, the school system is responsible for the total program.

10. Home or hospital instruction may be provided to continue the educational advancement of eligible students who are unable to attend school.

Step 6: Implementing the Plan. Options numbered 1 through 6 from the preceding list are often implemented in the regular school, whereas the services of options 7 through 10 are more often provided by school district staff, by special schools, or by contract with outside agencies. The concept of *least restrictive environment* is being applied to greater and greater numbers of special education children, bringing more low-functioning and children with disabilities into contact with the regular education program. As a result, many more children with severe disabilities, previously housed in segregated special schools, are becoming part of the regular school and are spending at least a part of their day in regular classrooms, often accompanied by an attendant.

In some cases, building modifications are required to provide access for wheelchairs and health-related and other equipment required to support these special students and their program needs. Special Education Vocational Rehabilitation Laws (PL 93-113, sec. 504) require that buildings be made accessible to all children.

Often, the initial reaction of the staff to students with severe disabilities in their classrooms is one of fear because of the health concern for such a child and the concern that he or she will disrupt the normal classroom environment. A good in-service training program for the staff frequently turns the fear of special students into a learning opportunity. This is especially true when regular classroom children are taught about the classmates who are joining them. Often, a compassion and understanding develops in children that could not be taught as effectively any other way. Rather than children who are disabled detracting from the learning of other children, they often enrich it with the development of new values and understanding for all children.

The principal should take advantage of the opportunities provided by the special education program and its integration into the regular education activities and be very careful not to allow these to develop into separate programs.[8]

Program and Assessment Reviews. Each special education student's IEP is reviewed annually by the M-team for the purpose of determining the continuing appropriateness of the program placement, goals, and objectives. These review dates must be monitored so that the annual reviews take place on schedule. The intent of the review should always be to move the child toward a less restrictive environment with less special education assistance if this is appropriate. The effort should be to try to move the child back toward the regular program whenever possible. The evaluation process for each special education student must be repeated every three years. A new assessment plan must be developed and carried out, recertification must take place, and the M-team must once again develop a new IEP.

Safeguarding Special Education Records. Special education records must be maintained separate and apart from a student's regular school cumulative record folder. Access to the special education records is to be carefully controlled, with availability restricted to only those school personnel who have direct contact with the child or to whom the parents have given written permission for access, such as an outside psychologist. Sign-out sheets should be used and permission letters kept on file. Regular education records are not supposed to reference the existence of a special education file. The purpose of this regulation is to protect the special education student from later discrimination that might occur if it became known the child had some type of disability. This makes it extremely difficult for records maintenance, however, and it is easy to misfile or not be able to locate information. Some schools code their regular cumulative folders with some special mark to indicate the existence of a separate special education folder.

Rights of Parents and Due Process Requirements. The requirement of involvement of the parents of the potential or verified special education student has been noted through this entire section describing special education procedures. From the notification of the initial referral, through the assessment process, to the writing of the IEP,[9] and finally to the approval for placement, as well as future access to their child's records, parents must give their informed consent as participants in the process. Failure to notify or obtain this consent is a violation of the rights of parents under the law.

DISCIPLINING STUDENTS WITH DISABILITIES

Discipline of children in school is an important concern of all principals. In most situations, the day-to-day decisions regarding the control of children has been the prerogative of the principal supported by the staff. However, in the case of children with disabilities, intricate federal and state regulations govern the administration of punishment of these students; these regulations are based solely on federal court cases interpreting the IDEA.

Children who are attention deficit hyperactive disordered (ADHD) may receive educational services and protection under Section 504 regulations. These children, by the nature of their disabling condition, often show up in the principal's office as discipline cases. Great care must be taken in establishing discipline procedures for these children because they often defy normal school behavior expectations. One cannot discipline children with disabilities in the unilateral fashion generally used for other students. In 1989, in *Honig* v. *Doe,*[10] the U.S. Supreme Court ruled that students with disabilities cannot be unilaterally suspended or expelled for more than 10 days without

FIGURE 8.1 Conditions of Disciplinary Action for Children with Disabilities

Disciplinary Action	Conditions of Use
Verbal reprimand	OK
Written warning	OK
Payment for damages	OK as long as the child's behavior does not suggest IEP changes.
Time out	OK
Detention (lunch, recess, after school)	OK
In-school suspension	OK if supervised by a certified special education teacher and/or the child's IEP is being carried out.
Corporal punishment	Many states prohibit its use. If permitted, it must be administered fairly. It is not recommended for children with disabilities.
Aversive therapy/Devices	Only if specified in IEP.
Bus suspension	Counts as part of 10-day maximum if busing is included in child's IEP.
Exclusion from extracurricular activities	OK as long as it is not central to IEP goal.
Suspension/Expulsion	OK for 10 school days per offense so long as "pattern of exclusion" does not exist.* For longer periods, the M-team must determine the offense not to be related to the child's disability.
Alternate school placement	OK as long as the change is made through the regular IEP process.

Any disciplinary action must have no adverse effect on IEP goals and objectives and must not be applied in a discriminatory manner.

*In addition to the 10-day limitation imposed by *Honig* v. *Doe*, the Office of Civil Rights (OCR) reminds districts that Section 504 requires a student reevaluation prior to every significant change in placement. Therefore, any change in placement, including a suspension/expulsion, for more than 10 days or any consecutive 10-day suspensions must be evaluated by the M-team.

provision of due process. This case triggered a array of procedural restrictions on local schools. Figure 8.1 summarizes basic disciplinary actions often used in school and indicates under what conditions they may or may not be used for children with disabilities.

DEALING WITH PARENTS OF SPECIAL CHILDREN

The identification of a child as a potential special education child is always stressful for parents, and the principal and staff must be prepared to deal with a variety of reactions from parents. The parent has probably been aware for some time that a problem exists for his or her child. This knowledge may have been suppressed or the parent may already have a long history of dealing with the child and the school about the problems. There are at least four general patterns of parental reaction for which the school, the M-team, and the principal, whether part of that M-team or not, must be ready.

The Supportive Parent

This parent is understanding of his or her child's problems, is concerned about the child's education, and respects and appreciates the efforts of the school to develop an appropriate educational plan for that child. He or she generally is most supportive during M-team meetings, attending faithfully and asking how he or she might best support the school's efforts at home. Some always accept the recommendations of the school staff without question, while others may begin to question M-team recommendations if they feel services are not adequate. This latter type may become a demanding parent if the school fails to carefully present a rationale for its recommendations.

The Denying Parent

This is the parent who is unaccepting of the possibility that his or her child has a disability. He or she is offended by the request for a referral, often initially refusing to sign the permission for testing, and frequently demanding to submit outside independent evaluations to refute the school's claim that the child is disabled. In some cases, he or she begins to resist actions of the school by not attending meetings, by refusing to sign documents, and generally by becoming purposefully nonresponsive. The denial of the disability may be due to a feeling that the child's disability is a reflection on his or her own intelligence or on his or her ability as a parent to raise the child. In these cases, parent education must often be an additional consideration before meaningful assistance can be provided for the child.

The denying parent is often extremely frustrated with the child, and his or her demands of the child are often impossible, given the identified disability. It is sometimes helpful to counsel with the parent privately, reviewing assessment data and pointing out that disabling conditions know no social or intellectual bounds (Albert Einstein had a learning disability, the Kennedy family has a retarded sister, and President Roosevelt was confined to a wheelchair). Additional support needs to be provided to these families because these feelings of denial die slowly and new strategies for dealing with the disability at home must be learned if the home is to be a supportive environment. Parent education and counseling is an appropriate consideration in the development of the IEP for these situations.

The Nonresponsive Parent

The problem of the nonresponsive parent is probably the saddest of all. Notices are sent out, phone calls are attempted, and certified letters are sent in order to meet the due process informed-consent legal requirement for parent notification. Some schools will even attempt to arrange a home visit in order to elicit a parental response. In some cases, the work schedule of the parent interferes; in others, child care makes school visits difficult. If these are really the problem, the school should make every effort to arrange a schedule or situation that will allow the parent's participation. However, there are situations where there is little or no interest on the part of the parent in the child's schooling. In these cases, it is often appropriate to identify some other responsible adult to work with this child and to provide an adult advocate and educational support system outside the classroom environment.

The Belligerent, Demanding Parent

This parent is going to attempt to obtain more than the school (the M-team) believes is necessary to provide appropriate options for program placement. He or she will question the assessments provided by the school staff to the point of demanding independent evaluation or bringing in his or her own psychologist. He or she will challenge the recommendations of the M-team, and if his or her demands are not met, will threaten to or actually will bring his or her lawyer to the M-team meeting. He or she will sometimes contact EACH (Effective Advocacy for Citizens with Handicaps)[11] and bring a representative of that organization to the M-team meeting. As might be expected, this parent is very aware of his or her due process rights and will demand a hearing to contest the recommendations of the M-team if his or her demands are not satisfied.

When, as a principal, you see this type of parent, be prepared to participate fully in the M-team process yourself. Don't leave your teachers to deal with this situation without strong support. If you can see that a particular staffing is going to be very difficult or complicated, request that someone from the district-level special education office join the M-team. Remember: You must keep in mind the best interests of the child, tempered by the needs of the parents, staff, administration, and other children in the school. Your goal is to provide each child with an appropriate educational program in the least restrictive environment possible, given that child's disabling conditions.

THE ROLE OF THE PRINCIPAL

For the principal, the M-team represents a very visible form of involvement with the special education program and the special needs children in the school. Although it is possible for the principal to designate a representative to serve on M-teams, direct participation by the principal in the M-team process signals an interest in this program to students, teachers, and parents. It also provides to the principal very direct feedback regarding the adequacy of the special education program in meeting the needs of the children in the school and an opportunity for leadership in improving the program where needed.

THE ROLE OF THE REGULAR CLASSROOM TEACHER

Many students with special needs are in regular classrooms. The teachers in these classrooms have certain responsibilities for these children, including the following:

Identifying and referring potentially disabled children
Taking part in due process and M-team procedures
Collecting assessment data about children with disabilities
Assisting children with disabilities with special equipment
Participating in a team effort with special education staff
Helping all children work and play together
Communicating with parents

Whenever a child with disabilities is placed in the regular classroom, the responsibility of the regular classroom teacher for that child is the same as for any other child in the room. Because all children differ with respect to the amount, rate, and style of learning, minor modifications in methodology, curriculum, or environment are often necessary for children, disabled or not. When a child's IEP specifies modifications in methodology, curriculum, or environment from the regular class, the development of such specially designed instruction is the responsibility of special educators. Regular educators are responsible for assisting in carrying out the program. Overall classroom management remains the responsibility of the regular educator.

Educating children who are severely disabled in the regular classroom can often be difficult. It is here where problems sometime arise. Given the requirement of the law for providing programs in the least restrictive environment and inclusion, more children with severe disabling conditions are now being educated in the regular school setting, both in the regular classroom as well as in the special education classroom but housed in the neighborhood school. Regular classroom teachers are sometimes frightened by the responsibility they feel for children who have special physical or emotional needs. Wheelchairs and other special manipulative equipment to transport children are seen as problems. Assisting children with bodily functions—helping to place a child on a toilet, changing diapers, and monitoring catheterizations—is felt to be beyond their level of training or interest. With the onset of acquired immune deficiency syndrome (AIDS) and the need to wear laytex gloves as a precautionary measure, additional fears are generated. When difficult physical situations exist, the IEP should specify the need for special assistance for the classroom teacher both through special training and through the provision of a special education assistant in the classroom or one who is on call and immediately available.

Children with mental disabilities provide an even greater problem for many teachers. Many of the learning disabilities, though mild in a sense, cause great difficulty for the child and require great understanding and skill on the part of the teacher. Some children used to be referred to as discipline problems and sent to the office, or others were regarded as lazy and not motivated to do their work. Educators now know that many of these students actually have a type of learning disability such as attention deficit disorder, dyslexia, dysnomia, or one of a host of others. In many cases, the problem has gone undiagnosed for many years and becomes compounded by the repeated failure to succeed on the part of the student who now has advanced to middle or even high school. Teachers often have not been trained either to diagnose these problems or know how to deal with them properly when they are known. Additionally, many teachers feel overwhelmed by the number of children and problems they face daily in the classroom.

Good staff development activities are needed by most school faculties in many aspects of working with children with special needs. Training in diagnosing and treating learning disabilities can be a help to virtually every classroom teacher. Knowledge in the use of supplementary aids and services such as brailled worksheets for students who are blind, provision of tape recorders or word processors for children who cannot write, or the operation of physical aids such as wheelchairs, walkers, and hearing aids is helpful. Skill in the use of cooperative learning techniques in conjunction with special educators or the management of disabilities in the classroom needs to be learned.

Most needed of all, perhaps, is the need for good human relations training for teachers to help them understand and deal with their own fears and biases concerning people who are disabled and how to help children in their classes to do the same. Finally, teachers need to be trained about their role in special education, state, and national special education policies, their role in referrals, evaluations, IEP development, due process, working with parents, and working with special educators regarding such things as student grading, scheduling, and record keeping.

OUTSIDE PUBLIC AGENCIES

A variety of public agencies in every community have direct access to the school. Local states and communities will have different names for these agencies and offer somewhat different services, but each school must recognize the demand and need to interact with these other services.[12] The three that are common to almost every school are public welfare or human services departments, public health agencies, and judicial systems (usually represented by police departments and juvenile court systems). Each of these agencies has certain legal responsibilities and authority. The authority of each of these agencies transcends the walls of the school, and the school principal is not always "master of the house." It is important not to get into a "turf battle" with the representatives of these agencies, but rather to develop a supportive network with them to serve the children of the community better. When the police come to pick up or question a child regarding a local crime, the principal is summoned to juvenile court to testify on a matter dealing with one of the school's children, or a representative of the protective services unit of the local welfare department shows up to investigate a child abuse case, not only is it important for the principal to know his or her rights and the rights of the children but also to have a good working relationship with the representatives of these other agencies so that all can work for the benefit of the children and the community.

The development of a network of contacts with private agencies and other public agencies is also important. Who should be in a principal's network is somewhat dependent on the nature of the local student clientele, but important network contacts for many schools would include groups that can provide clothing or food on an emergency basis, both emergency and nonemergency medical treatment, and both public and private mental health professionals.

Public Welfare or Human Services Agencies

Child abuse cases are one of the most common school-related involvements with public welfare or human services agencies today. A problem that a few years ago was normally considered "only a family matter" now is recognized as an area of responsibility for our society. Most states now require schools to report suspected child abuse cases to the appropriate authority for investigation. The classroom teacher who notices heavy bruising on a child or the pattern of absences along with extreme emotional behavior on the part of a child is required by law to report it. The school is, in fact, the one place outside the home where a child can take some refuge from an abusive home environment. Confidentiality regarding the reporter of abuse is generally guaranteed. However, it is this confidentiality issue, along with the sensitive nature of child abuse investigations, that sometimes causes some difficulty.

Child abuse investigators often consider the school to be an appropriate safe location to conduct initial interviews. It is a safe place to contact a child without alerting a suspected abuser, and it is a place where the child is more comfortable and hopefully willing to discuss the problem. The problem is that it can also disrupt the ongoing instruction in the school. The intrusion into the school by an outside investigator can also be taken as an interference in the school's domain.

Most state laws give authority to child abuse investigators from public agencies outside the school to interview children on school premises and, in some cases, to take them into their custody. These investigators also have the authority to conduct the interviews in private with no school official present and generally do not have to reveal the content of an interview after it is concluded. For some principals, this contradicts what they consider to be their responsibilities for their children. The first reaction may be not to want to take a child out of class, and, second, not to want to let an "outsider" conduct a private interview with a child for whom the principal is responsible. The laws of most states, however, give the public social services agency this authority if it chooses to use it. The following suggestions are appropriate ways to manage requests from outside investigators:

1. Always ask to see credentials.
2. Attempt to convince investigators of the importance of having a school representative present during any interview. Some workers will allow you to be present.
3. Control the time and place for the conference. You are generally allowed to protect instructional time.
4. Document the conference, noting date, place, names of persons present, and length of the conference.
5. Refuse to give access to student records without a signed release from the parent, guardian, or a court order.

In almost all cases, it is to the school's long-range advantage to develop a good working relationship with these outside agencies. They have a job to do and are also trying to safeguard the well-being of the children. Most often, you need each other.

Working with Law Enforcement Agencies

The major school involvement with law enforcement agencies will be requests by officers to interview children while they are at school. Of course, schools also often employ off-duty officers as security guards for ball games and other evening school activities. The basic suggestions listed for investigator procedures apply to police officers as well and are for the school's protection as well as the protection of the children.

Developing a good working relationship with police officers who work in the school zone can be most helpful to both the school and the police. The occasional informal discussion with them can sometimes cut bureaucratic paperwork and procedures and solve a problem where formal procedures could not.

The school principal will also be called on to testify in juvenile court in conjunction with children from his or her school. Every community has a juvenile court system ranging in size from a part-time judge in smaller communities to large buildings and multiple judges in larger communities. School children may be brought into juvenile court for three different types of situations. The first is for felony or misdemeanor charges similar to charges brought against an adult. However, juvenile court handles the disposition of a case somewhat differently: Publicity of juvenile crimes is kept at a minimum and prescribed treatment has rehabilitation as its purpose rather than punishment.

Status offenses, the second category, make up the largest number of cases that will involve school officials. *Status offenses* can be defined as actions that are considered violations of laws for children but not adults. Nonattendance at school (truancy) and running away from home are the most common. For school officials, instigating truancy charges becomes the last resort among efforts to obtain regular attendance from a child. In many cases, the real problem is the parents. Juvenile courts have the power to order certain action from the parents to improve or control their child's behavior, such as requiring the parent to ensure the child's presence at school each day or be held in contempt of court. A contempt charge against the parent could result in the parent being jailed. Once again, a good working relationship between the school principal and the juvenile court can be most helpful in solving such problems.

The third type of case dealt with by the juvenile court involves the problems of neglected and/or abused children. In these cases, the children are the victims rather than the offenders. School employees are often reporters of suspected child abuse and may be called on to testify in juvenile court regarding their observations. Testifying in these situations can be particularly traumatic. Reporting child abuse is generally kept confidential, or at least confidentiality is attempted. However, when the accused are the parents or someone else closely associated with the school, testifying can be difficult.

Outside Agencies and Closed Records. In an effort to protect the reputation of children and their families, many of the agencies who work with children are required by law to maintain strict confidentiality of the records they develop and maintain. This is true, for example, with the special education records maintained by the school. When a child has been in the custody of the juvenile court or has been a ward of the welfare department's Children's Protective Services unit and is then returned or placed in your school, it is extremely difficult, it not impossible, to get any information about the child's recent history. In some cases, this makes it extremely difficult to know how to deal with a child or even if the safety of other children should be a concern. Some local areas have developed coordinating councils for the several children's agencies in an effort to improve the communication among them. The individual principal will probably find his or her efforts to develop an informal network among the workers of the various agencies to be an extremely useful communication link to information not available through the formal channels.

Drawing on the Services of Outside Social Welfare Agencies. Mental health agencies, chemical abuse agencies, civic clubs, local churches, and so on, all have an interest and a role to play in the welfare of school children. Networking once again becomes the byword for the principal and staff. Situations always develop that fall short of eligibility for one or more of the formal service agencies to the school. It may be a parent who becomes aware that his or her child is doing drugs, or it may be the child who appears to be suffering from severe depression; however, until children take some overt act to harm themselves, there is no regular agency support available. It is in these situations that it is important to have contacts with professionals from other agencies from whom the principal can get advice and learn where the school or the parents might turn for help.

What can be done for middle school-age children who don't want to come to school, such as the boy who doesn't have any shoes or the girl who has had a front tooth knocked out and is ashamed of her looks? The best way to solve the attendance problem is to help solve the child's personal problem. If the school is fortunate enough to have a public agency that can meet these needs, that is wonderful, but often it must be met by the principal getting a pair of size 8 sneakers from the local church clothing service or working out a deal with a local shoe store or the salesperson from whom the principal buys athletic equipment. For the girl who needs dental work, but the school does not have a formal procedure for obtaining assistance, the principal may call a local dentist, explain the problem, and ask for some free service. Obviously, a preestablished relationship with these community members and agencies is critical to the success of these attempts. Once again, the importance of establishing a network of contacts in the community is apparent.

Public Health Departments and Local Schools. The services provided by public health agencies directly to school children vary greatly throughout the country. In some states, the only contact may be to monitor immunization records to ensure the health of the general public, while in other areas, services may include provision for public health personnel to provide direct services to children in the school. Nurses stationed in the school, health presentations in classrooms, dental services, immunizations, and some emergency medical care may be provided. Once again, there may be more services available for the asking than the average school receives. It is up to the principal to make the contact, develop the relationship, and add these professionals to his or her network of available persons to be called on when needed.

SUMMARY

Schools have many special children with many special needs. The quality of school life is dependent on the collective satisfaction of the needs of all the children. The principal cannot personally meet the needs of each and every child, but he or she can set the tone, develop the network of contacts who can assist in providing for the children's needs, and be a facilitator of resources for its achievement. Once again, the symbolic leadership of the principal in showing concern for all children will demonstrate to the staff the significance and importance of their efforts.

ACTIVITIES

1. Review Case Studies 4 and 13 at the end of this book. Analyze the problems presented and apply the special services concepts developed in this chapter. What approach would you use in addressing the problems? Set forth a strategy to overcome the difficulties faced by the school as well as ways to deal with individuals such as Ricky.
2. What are some ways the services required by special education laws can be implemented, while minimizing the time required of the regular classroom teacher for special education activities?
3. What are the agencies in your community that provide services to children? In what networks does your school participate to help link together these services?
4. Turn to the ISSLLC Standards found in Appendix B. Review the knowledge, dispositions, and performances listed with Standard Two. Reflect on which of the standard items relate directly to the needs of special students. How do the concepts of special education and special needs children match Standard Two? What other standards speak to the needs of special students? Identify one knowledge area, one disposition, and one performance to link directly to a concept or idea discussed in Chapter 8.

ENDNOTES

1. Professor Michael Brady, University of Houston. Department of Educational Psychology, to a graduate class of aspiring principals, summer 1991.

2. The Individuals with Disabilities Education Act (IDEA) Part B and its amendments were passed in 1990 and 1991. It is located in 34 CFR Part 300 and 304.

3. 34 CFR Part 104, Section 504, has become a means of obtaining special attention or services for children who do not fit into one of the discrete IDEA categories of handicapping conditions. Children with a wide variety of disabling conditions such as acquired immune deficiency syndrome (AIDS), attention deficit disorders (ADD), or children with a temporary disability such as a broken leg can obtain services under this section.

4. The Americans with Disabilities Act, 42 U.S.C S 12101, et seg., basically indicates that a school district cannot discriminate against/exclude an otherwise qualified individual with a disability on the basis of his or her disability.

5. As this material is being written, the U.S. Department of Education is considering a dramatic

retooling of IDEA that would greatly modify the current funding system and eligibility categories. The intent of the 1995 proposed changes is to refocus the law from merely guaranteeing access to education to improving the results for students with disabilities. The most fundamental change proposed is the replacement of the 13 disability categories in IDEA with a disability definition similar to the one in Section 504 and ADA.

6. National Association of State Boards of Education, *Winners All: A Call for Inclusive Schools* (Alexandria, VA: NASBE, 1992).

7. See Joy Rogers, "The Inclusion Revolution," *Research Bulletin 11,* Phi Delta Kappa Center for Evaluation, Development, and Research, May 1993, p. 1.

8. In Chapter 8 will be found several suggestions to aid in the development of an integrated special education and regular education program.

9. A draft copy of the IEP should be developed in advance of the M-team meeting to be presented and explained to the parent. Following this meeting, and any appropriate parental modification, refinements are made and the document executed.

10. *Honig* v. *Doe,* EHLR 559:231 (U.S. 1988)

11. EACH (Effective Advocacy for Citizens with Handicaps) is a nationwide volunteer organization that provides assistance for disabled individuals to ensure their legal rights are met.

12. See J. P. Comer, *School Power* (New York: The Free Press, 1980). Comer presents a powerful thesis for developing integrated community services for inner-city children, with the school being the delivery point for these services.

SELECTED READINGS

Anderson, Ronald J., and Robert H. Decker. "The Principal's Role in Special Education Programming." *NASSP Bulletin 77,* no. 550 (February 1993): 1–6.

Darrell, Larry D. "At-Risk Students Need Our Commitment." *NASSP Bulletin* (January 1989): 81–83.

Dixon, Virginia L., and David E. Greenburg. "Assessment in Special Education: Administrators' Perspectives." *Diagnostique 10* (1985): 161–175. (ERIC Document Service No. EJ 334 426).

Dragan, Edward F. "Accountability and Special Education: Planning for Results." *NASSP Bulletin 78,* no. 565 (November 1994): 1–5.

Dubin, Andrew. "Through the Administrative Looking Glass: The Special Needs Child." *Thrust for Educational Leadership 16,* no. 4 (January 1987): 36–37. (ERIC Document Service No. EJ 347 177).

Ellis, Joseph and Daniel Geller. "Disciplining Handicapped Students: An Administrator's Dilemma." *NASSP Bulletin 77,* no. 550 (February 1993): 22–38.

Epstein, Michael H. et al., "Improving Services for Students with Serious Emotional Disturbances." *NASSP Bulletin 76,* no. 549 (January 1993): 46–51.

"Feds Eye Major Changes to IDEA." *The Special Educator 10,* no. 13 (February 4, 1995): 206–207.

Golden, Diane Cordry. "Discipline of Students with Disabilities: A Decision-Making Model for Principals." *NASSP Bulletin 77,* no. 550 (February 1993):12–20.

Greenburg, David. *A Special Educator's Perspective on Interfacing Special and General Education: A Review for Administrators.* Reston, VA: ERIC Clearinghouse on Handicapped and Gifted Children, 1987. (ERIC Document Service No. ED 280 211).

Jachard, Charles. "Researching the Underchallenged, Marginal, or At-Risk Student." *Clearing House* (November 1998).

Katsiyannis, Antonis. "Individuals with Disabilities: The Role of the School Principal and Section 504." *NASSP Bulletin 78,* no. 565 (November 1994): 6–10

Lasky, Beth, Belinda D. Karge, Suzan M. Robb, and Marjorie McCabe. "How Principals Can Help the Beginning Special Education Teacher." *NASSP Bulletin 79,* no. 568 (February 1995): 1–14.

McCarthy, Martha M. "Inclusion and the Law: Recent Judicial Developments." *Research Bulletin 13.* Phi Delta Kappa Center for Evaluation, Development, and Research, November 1994, pp. 1–4.

Newby, John. "Parent-School Partnerships: Breaking Down the Barriers," *The High School Magazine 2,* no. 3 (March 1995): 17–18.

Sires, Carolyn, and Sandra Tonnsen. "Special Education: A Challenge for Principals." *NASSP Bulletin 77,* no. 550 (February 1993): 8–11.

VanSeiver, James H. "From Intimidation to Participation: Making Parents feel Welcome at Special Ed Proceedings," *The High School Magazine 2,* no. 3 (March 1995): 19.

CHAPTER NINE

HUMAN RESOURCES DEVELOPMENT

Teacher development in school districts does not take place in a vacuum. Its success is influenced in many ways by the district's organizational context.

—M. McLaughlin and D. Marsh[1]

Human resource development is both a concept and a process. As a concept, it is concerned with the full development and utilization of an organization's most valuable resources—its human ones. As a process, it is an integrated continuous flow of functions that make up a dimension of principal responsibility known as *personnel administration*. The various functions are integrated through the philosophy, policies, procedures, and practices involved in the human resources development (HRD) process. We address only two of those functions in this chapter: professional development and personnel evaluation.

Although most educational leaders espouse a dedication to the enhancement of individual potential, organizational practices may, in fact, be counterproductive to human resources development. In this chapter we discuss the impact of organizational context on the HRD process, explore various teacher differences that impact the design of professional development, investigate the nature of professional development and its various delivery models, and examine the relationship between professional development and personnel evaluation.

HUMAN RESOURCES DEVELOPMENT AND ORGANIZATIONAL CONTEXT

In order to understand human resources development as a concept, as well as a process, it is necessary to have some understanding of the context in which the human resources functions take place. Various contextual frames lend very different meaning to the term *development.* In Chapter 1 we explored three contextual frameworks based on metaphor: the machine, the organism, and the brain. These are helpful to reconsider as contextual frames for understanding how human resources development is enacted.

The machine metaphor, based on a rational systems model, is a closed system operating from a standardized structure based on predictability, and the best model for teaching, learning, and evaluating. In this context, policies and procedures tend to drive all decisions. These policies and procedures are designed in top-down fashion, with little input from those closest to implementation. Practices, therefore, tend to be halfheartedly applied because they operate from mandates rather than commitments and are often contrary to the very philosophies that direct them. Philosophy, though it may have initially guided the structure, soon takes a back seat to the policies and procedures, and evaluation and professional development takes on a routine, rational operation that assumes that what *is being* done is what *should be* done.

Of particular emphasis in this context are the notions of predictability, measurement, detail, and sequence. These characteristics are reflected not only in the way that evaluation is designed and conducted but also in the manner in which professional development is viewed.

The organism and brain metaphors, representative of a natural system's model,[2] lend a quite different perspective to human resources development. Philosophy, developed collectively from shared values, becomes the guiding factor in the process, with commitment to that philosophy enabling the process to flow and yet respond to changing needs. The structure that is developed by policies and procedures facilitates and enables practice rather than constraining it. Practices reflect more deeply the intended philosophy.

In the organism metaphor, much emphasis is placed on individuality, flexibility, and adaptation. Rather than a "one size fits all" mentality, teaching, learning, and evaluation are designed and applied in modified forms, with more attention being given to the whole rather than to the detailed parts. These characteristics are reflected not only in evaluation but also in staff development. Teaching is viewed as an *emergent*[3] process adapted to various learning groups in various ways. Evaluation is holistic, rather than merely criterion-referenced based,[4] and teachers are encouraged to design professional development experiences according to various models of staff development.

The brain metaphor shares many of the same characteristics with the organism metaphor, since both are natural systems. It adds, however, an important dimension of a thinking/learning organization. In this context, great emphasis is on shared knowledge and understandings, collaboration, and inquiry. Human resources, committed to organizational purpose, enable the organization to reach its highest level of performance. In all of these contexts, there is an overarching need to integrate the individual in a meaningful way with the work of the organization. The following discussion centers on this issue.

Integration of the Individual and the Organization

The work of Schein[5] provides much insight into the complex process of integrating the individual and the organization in ways that will effectively meet the goals and needs of both. Schein views this integration process in three stages: entry, socialization, and mutual acceptance.

During the *entry* stage, the individual endeavors to make the right career choice, train for the occupation, and search for the appropriate position. As illustrated by Figure 9.1, it is a time, as well, when the organization is determining the nature of the job that is needed, identifying the skills that the individual will need to possess, recruiting a pool of candidates, and ultimately making an appropriate selection of the best person to fit the job. The thoughtfulness and skill with which both parties approach this stage will be a determining factor for the next stage: socialization.

The *socialization* stage marks a point at which "the individual builds a picture of the organization and his or her future in it."[6] At the same time, the organization comes

FIGURE 9.1 The Integration of the Individual and the Organization through the Functions of HRD, According to Schein

THE ORGANIZATION	HRD FUNCTION	THE INDIVIDUAL
Organizational philosophy, mission, and sense of *what should be*	1. Planning	Individual philosophy mission, and sense of *what should be*
Organizational analysis of *jobs* and *skills* required to accomplish purpose and exhibit effectiveness; a determination of *what is*		Individual analysis of *jobs* available and *skills* required in those jobs in comparison to individual competence; a determination of *what is*
Matching defined skills/qualities of applicant to job requirements to job requirements; determining person-job fit	2. Recruitment	Selecting appropriate organizational setting/ job position to match individual skills, preparation, and competencies; is career fit based on personal aspirations?
An offer is extended to the individual with *high expectations* for his or her success in the organization	3. Selection	An offer is accepted by the individual with *high expectations* that he or she will be successful in the organization
The organization *reaffirms* its selection of the individual or becomes *disappointed* in its choice and chooses to (1) show resentment toward the individual or (2) assist the individual		The individual *reaffirms* his or her acceptance of the organization's position or becomes *disappointed* in his or her choice, resulting in leaving, rebelling, conforming, or trying to make a difference in the organization

to view the individual in terms of his or her future role within the organization. Though both parties may have viewed their union with high expectations for success, the realities of the situation are often far different from what they seemed initially for either or both parties. Often, the disenchantment has to do with lack of competence or unclear performance expectations. At other times, it may be strong differences related to the values held by the organization or the individual. At the point of disenchantment, the organization has two choices. It can either sever its relationship with the new employee or it can commit its resources to the improvement of the person *the organization* chose for the position.

The individual in a similar situation also has choices. Obviously, the person can leave the organization or stay and rebel. Not so obvious is the second choice, which is to stay and conform to the values and expectations of the group. The individual's last choice, and one that enables the growth and development of the organization, is to stay and try to make a difference in the conditions and/or values that exist.[7]

The final stage, *mutual acceptance,* is a time for granting full membership to the individual through such rites of passage as special privileges, increased responsibilities and a type of "psychological contract."[8] As Schein suggests, "All that has been established is that there is enough of a match between what the individual needs and expects and what the organization needs and expects to continue the career in the organization."[9]

INDIVIDUAL AND GROUP NEEDS

Understanding Individual and Group Needs

The organism metaphor serves as a way of appreciating the uniqueness of individuals. This uniqueness has major implications for the work that principals must do in the area of human resources development. Teaching, evaluation, and staff development are all affected by the individuality of teachers.

Since teachers vary in their readiness levels and in their motivational needs, principals should consider these variables when determining teachers' development needs. As the research suggests, "The circumstances most suitable for one person's professional development may be quite different from those that promote another individual's growth"[10]

Three very important variables determine level of need: teacher age, years of teaching experience, and readiness or maturity level. Certainly, interests and learning/personality styles are additional factors that play a part. Teachers collectively, as adult learners, also have certain needs that should be considered when designing any professional development programs. Perhaps the most appropriate place to start in this discussion is with the needs of teachers as a group.

The Adult Learner

Knowles[11] provided a thoughtful perspective to the area of adult learning. His work suggests that as adults, teachers learn best when:

- They have opportunities to plan and design their own learning/development opportunities.
- There is relevance to the learning experience.
- Learning is problem centered rather than content centered.
- Past experience can be incorporated in experiential learning settings.

Although there are needs that teachers do have as a group, there are also unique differences among teachers based on their years of teaching experience and their developmental levels. We will consider the research of Huberman[12] as a beginning point in understanding these differences among teachers.

Teacher Needs Determined by Experience

Huberman[13] classified teachers based on their years of teaching experience into five stages of development. Although the model is based primarily on research of secondary teachers with little or no administrative experience, it does suggest a *process* through which teachers are likely to progress in their career. Principals should not assume that all teachers would progress through these stages in exactly the same sequence. As Huberman suggested, some may develop in a linear fashion while others may exhibit "plateaus, regressions, dead-ins, or spurts."[14] The model is helpful to principals as they work with teachers, however, for it allows them to understand more fully the impact that individuals and groups have on each other. It also assists principals in planning professional development that is more suited to teacher need. In the following section, each teacher career stage is considered.

Survival and Discovery Stage (1–3 Years). In the first career stage, survival and discovery coexist; ironically it "is discovery that allows the novice teacher to tolerate survival."[15] Although this teacher career stage is dotted with reality shock and self-preoccupation, it is also a time when teachers are excited about their first classroom and are elated by feelings of being a "colleague among peers."[16] It is important for teachers during this time to be guided in ways that help them see teaching from a broader perspective. They need to arrange fragmented tasks of method and strategy into a large context. Teachers have learned many skills from their university preparation programs at this point, but they have had little opportunity so far in their development to integrate those skills and apply them to their own teaching. Supervisors and principals can guide them in making connections between the theories they have recently been taught and their actual practice in the classroom. Holland and Weise[17]provide useful suggestions to guide principals in working with novice teachers.

Stabilization Stage (4–6 Years). Teachers take on the mantle of "teacher" and take major steps toward professionalism during the stabilization stage. Not only do they assume responsibility for their immediate classrooms but also for the profession of teaching. Teachers begin to feel comfortable in their basic knowledge of good teaching (most have moved from probationary to tenured status) and they are ready to experiment and create their own teaching styles. At this time, teachers should be provided more opportunities for *capacity building*.[18] As they make more decisions related to their own teaching and professional development, they move more toward teacher empowerment and an individual view of their career. (See Chapter 2 for a more complete discussion of this concept.)

Experimentation and Activism (7–18 Years). Teachers begin to experiment at this time, for they have gained skill and competence in their teaching. They have established a comfortable knowledge base about good teaching and are eager to experiment with new ideas that they hope will maximize their impact on student learning. This stage is a natural time for involvement, contribution, and challenge as well as a time when teachers want a greater voice in those things that impact their teaching. It is a time for accepting new responsibilities; however, it is a period for many when they begin to question their professional choice. Some wonder if they truly want to remain in the profession, and disenchantment occurs for many, resulting in either a search for new responsibilities or a complete job change.

Serenity/Relational Distance and Conservatism (19–30 Years). At this time many teachers who have previously been innovative and dynamic in their instructional methods begin to shift to a more mechanical response. Teachers no longer exhibit the energy and enthusiasm previously exhibited. Although they do have increased serenity and self-confidence, this is also a time marked by "relational distance from students."[19] The age gap between teacher and student widens and there is less connection than before. Often teachers at this stage become reluctant to embark on anything new or innovative and seem greatly concerned with maintaining the status quo.

Principals need to be aware of this tendency toward the line of least resistance and withdrawal and look for ways to involve these teachers in meaningful activities. This is an important time in the lives of many teachers when they need real leadership and inspiration to raise their levels of values consciousness,[20] inspiring them to continue contributing to the organization in productive ways. In Chapter 1 we discussed the importance of a school leader working to transform not only the organization but also the individuals who serve within that setting.

Disengagement (31–40 Years). This stage is pronounced by either serenity or bitterness. There is increased withdrawal and internalization—a gradual disengagement and absorption in one's own interests is evidenced. There are also feelings of pressure to move over for younger employees and fresher ideas. Many teachers in this stage still have much talent and expertise that they could contribute to the organization if they were properly challenged and encouraged. Often teachers can become revitalized during this stage by having opportunities to contribute to the growth of others in such activities as mentoring and peer coaching.

The important thing to consider from Huberman's research is that teachers will have different needs at various times during their careers. This fact has significant implications for school principals and suggests that professional development must be tailored to meet teachers' differing needs. A model very similar to Huberman's, although not connected to defined years of experience, is discussed in the next section.

Maturity and Readiness Levels

De Moulin and Guyton[21] identified four levels of teacher maturity or stages of development: provisional, developmental, transitional, and decelerating. Their study suggested that the age factor does not necessarily determine a teacher's level of growth in the profession. For instance, some teachers might remain in the developmental level for the majority of their career, whereas the transitional and decelerating levels might include teachers represented by various age levels. These stages will be briefly discussed as a way of supporting the concept of developmental phases for teachers.

Provisional. Provisional teachers experience great stress based on their uncertainty in the teaching situation. Their inexperience and limited knowledge of child psychology contributes to a trial-and-error approach to performance. As these teachers gain experience, their comfort and confidence increase. This stage is quite similar to Huberman's entry and survival stage; however, it does not relate necessarily to the number of years that the teacher has taught, as other factors may compound the situation. Teachers at this stage, regardless of their years of experience, should be provided with the *levels of opportunity*[22] necessary to build skill and confidence. Matching these teachers with a mentor reinforces their skill acquisition and provides them with opportunities to receive the important feedback necessary for learning transfer. The concept of collegiality and collaboration, discussed at length in Chapter 2, has tremendous implications for meeting the needs of teachers at this level.

Developmental. These teachers exhibit self-confidence, direction, and structure. A great deal of satisfaction and sense of direction is balanced by curiosity and refinement of instructional practice. This is a wonderful time for exploration and growth! At this stage, teachers enjoy the opportunities provided through peer coaching, teamwork, study groups, and action-based research. It is ironical that although the majority of the teaching staff in most schools tend to be at this level, the bulk of time spent in professional development is spent in "training programs" provided through traditional in-service education!

Transitional. Teachers at this stage begin to decline in classroom effectiveness. Many begin to question their desire to remain in the teaching profession. There is little desire to participate in professional development and most are content to operate from a day-to-day perspective. Many of these teachers have reached a plateau in their careers where there seems to be nothing challenging and inspiring. These teachers need to be inspired to look for opportunities for personal and professional growth that have previously been unrecognized. There is much overlap between this stage of development and the Huberman stage of disengagement.

Decelerating. At this stage, teachers have little motivation for work and exhibit a "clock-watching" perspective. Burnout is a classic symptom, with more traditional methods being the choice for instructional format. Again, competent teachers must become "reengaged" in the educational process. Finding a way to inspire their contributions and continued growth becomes a major challenge for today's school leader.

PROFESSIONAL DEVELOPMENT

What part does staff development play in helping to meet the emerging developmental needs of teachers and how does their individual and collective development contribute to the increased effectiveness of the school's educational program? These are important questions to consider as we view the nature and scope of staff development. A working definition of *professional development* is necessary to begin. For the purposes of this chapter, we will use the terms *professional development* and *staff-development* simultaneously.

Staff development has been called many things, including *in-service training, professional development,* and *human resource development.* But in all cases, it is considered to be something "done to" teachers in a compressed period of time (e.g., a fall workshop or special conference) that makes them more content and effective in the classroom setting. A major paradigm shift concerning staff development, however, has been brought about by three major ideas: (1) results-driven education, (2) systems thinking, and (3) constructivism. Each of these, individually and collectively, is causing school principals to view staff development much differently than they did in past years.[23] We will explore these paradigm shifts and examine their impact on the design and delivery of staff development.

- *Results-Driven Education.* Just as accountability has become the emphasis for the classroom, so too has it impacted the nature of staff development. The true measurement of the effectiveness of any staff-development program is currently being judged by how it affects the instructional behavior of teachers in a positive way that benefits the learner.
- *Systems Thinking.* What happens in any one part of the organization has an effect on all other parts of the organization and on the organization as a whole. Staff development now encourages a broader view of the impact that changes in any one aspect of curriculum, instruction, or assessment might have on all aspects of the organization.
- *Constructivism.* The emphasis has shifted from the nature of learners as passive receivers of information to one in which learners are actively involved in making sense of their own learning. The need to provide learners with the necessary skills to build their own knowledge structures has caused staff development to be viewed in a similar fashion. Teachers, viewed as adult learners, collaborate with peers, students, and others to share knowledge and to construct new knowledge based on collective understanding.

Figure 9.2 outlines the major shifts that have occurred because of the trends suggested.

Models of Staff Development

A current review of the literature related to staff development suggests that it must become multifaceted in its delivery. Sparks and Loucks-Horsley[24] have suggested that five models of staff development are currently being delivered. It is important for prin-

FIGURE 9.2 Paradigm Shift in Staff Development

FROM	TO
Individual development	Individual and organizational development
District-centered approaches	School-centered approaches
Fragmented, piecemeal efforts toward change	Improvements based on school improvement plans
Focus on adult needs	Focus on student needs and learning outcomes
Externally delivered training	Comprehensive, multifaceted staff-development models incorporating the talents and resources of staff
Staff development provided by one or two departments	Staff development as a critical function and major responsibility performed by all administrators and teacher leaders
The transmission of knowledge and skills by "experts"	The study by teachers of the teaching and learning process
A focus on generic teaching skills	A combined focus on generic and content-specific skills
Staff development as a "frill" dependent on availability of financial resources	Staff development as an essential component of the educational process

Source: Adapted from D. Sparks, "A Paradigm Shift in Staff Development," *The ERIC Review 3,* no. 3 (1994): 2–4.

cipals to understand these models and their applications to the professional development of teachers and be able to appropriately apply the models to match individual teacher need. These five staff-development models are discussed next.

Individually Guided Staff Development. This model, based on the assumption that teachers can best determine their own developmental needs and that they are motivated to direct their own learning experiences, casts teachers as self-motivated individuals who learn best when they can guide the relevancy of their own experiences. The model consists of several phases:

1. Identification of a need
2. Development of a plan to meet that need
3. Activities outlined to accomplish the plan
4. Evaluation of the plan

Examples of the individually guided model include individual study of an issue of special interest, development of a special project, curriculum-improvement activities, and other activities tied to a teacher's particular interest.

Observation and Assessment. As discussed in Chapter 1, feedback is a major component leading to the development of an *individualized view* of one's teaching career. Without directed feedback, a major link to motivation is lost. The observation-assessment model provides opportunities for teachers to provide the feedback to each other that may not always be available from the principal. The model is based on the assumption that reflection and analysis are critical avenues that facilitate professional growth and that teaching can be improved by observation and feedback from another. Not only does the reflection benefit the targeted teacher but the observation and analysis of the teaching act is mutually beneficial to both teacher and observer. When teachers are given positive feedback, their efforts are reinforced and motivation increases.[25] Examples of observation and assessment that might be included in a school setting are peer coaching, team building and collaboration, and clinical supervision. In peer coaching, teachers alternate visits to each other's classrooms, gather and analyze data, and give feedback. Both teacher and observer are targets for improved classroom performance, since reflection is mutually occurring.[26]

Involvement in a Development/Improvement Process. This model takes the form of curriculum improvement and development. It relates directly to school improvement projects designed to improve classroom instruction or to solve a specific problem related to school effectiveness. The model is based on the assumption that teachers, as adult learners, want to be engaged in the resolution of problems in which they have a direct professional interest. It assumes, also, that teachers are in a position to best identify the issues that need resolution. In this approach, teachers become researchers, independent learners, and shapers of solutions to their own curriculum/instructional problems. The model proceeds according to the following steps:

1. *Problem Identification.* Either the individual or a small group of teachers identify a need.
2. *Response Formulation.* The individual teacher or the group brainstorm possible alternatives to consider in resolving the issue.
3. *Information Gathering.* The need for further study or investigation of the issue is determined and study is completed.
4. *Plan Formulation.* Based on the information gathered, a plan or program is developed.
5. *Plan Assessment.* Data are gathered to determine the effectiveness of the plan. Information gleaned from the assessment is used to further refine or modify the existing plan.

Training. Long the most common form of staff development, the training model is synonymous in the minds of many with the entire concept of staff development. In addition to its familiarity, it is the most cost effective of all models in terms of initial delivery. A major caution in its use, however, is the notion of *transfer of learning.* Modifications of the external, or visible, teaching behaviors of staff are desirable and tend to be the major focus of initial training. There is an underlying more important purpose with any staff-development effort, however, and that is to change the *thinking* of teachers. The important issue with training, then, is how to enable the transfer of the learned skill to the classroom setting. In order to ensure proper transfer, any training must be reinforced with other follow-up procedures, such as mentoring or peer coaching, to be assured that learning transfers to the teacher's classroom.[27]

Inquiry. In the inquiry approach, the teacher, either individually or in a small group, inquires into an issue of concern relative to classroom instruction or a related school problem. This inquiry may be either a formal or informal process in which valid questions are formulated and researched. This model allows for collective study by a group of teachers and encourages the combined analysis of many individuals pooling their ideas and resources. It is based on the assumption that teachers do question their own practices and search for valid answers to their problems. It assumes, as well, that teachers can develop new understandings and practices based on the discoveries made. The model, often referred to as *action-based research,* has been made popular through the Japanese concept of quality circles and total quality management (TQM). The concept was discussed in Chapter 2.

Matching Teacher Differences and Staff-Development Opportunities

These five models of staff development have great potential for providing a synthesized approach to total professional development within a school setting as well as capitalizing on the unique needs that teachers have based on experience, or the developmental level.

These staff-development models, because of their different areas of emphasis and method, become fertile ground for developing professional development opportunities for teaching staff based on the unique needs discussed in the second section of this chapter. It is one thing to know *how* to help a teacher through development; it is quite another to identify the needs that should be addressed. It is important, then, that the nature and design of personal evaluation and supervision are considered.

PERSONNEL EVALUATION AND SUPERVISION

What will be *judged* from the evaluation results? What *purpose* will the evaluation serve? We will consider these questions through a discussion of *merit* and *worth.*

Merit and Worth

It is important to understand these two terms and their relationship to one another when considering evaluation. In the evaluation of personnel for decision-making purposes, both are applied.[28]

Merit is the more common of the two concepts and is concerned with measuring the effectiveness of the individual's performance within a given setting, such as a teacher in the classroom performing job-related tasks. When a comparison of an individual's performance is made against a standard, or in many cases a comparison of the individual's performance against the performance of others in similar roles, then the individual's merit within the position has been judged.

Worth, on the other hand, is a determination of how valuable that teacher's particular position is to the rest of the organization and to the fulfillment of the organization's mission. It is an assessment of that value based on need. As Scriven stated, "Worth must be determined by comparing resources in education with needs in education."[29] It is possible, therefore, for a teacher, or other staff member, to be judged as having merit but to be in a position of little worth to the organization. It is not possible, however, for any position to have worth without the presence of merit. Very little merit also implies very little worth. Judgments of performance are based on both issues, and this can sometimes cause conflict. It is possible, because of scarcity of resources or changes in organizational need, for teachers to lose their positions even though they have great merit. It also happens that at times teachers who are less than meritorious are allowed to continue in positions that have value or worth to the organization. The question then becomes: At what point does lower merit affect position value? These are troublesome issues that face principals as they attempt to evaluate teacher performance.

These are important concepts to consider, as well, when evaluating teachers as a group. As societal resources become scarce, there is an increasing need to justify the cost of education to the public. Performance evaluation becomes one way of substantiating teachers' merit to suggest the worth of education. Herein lies one of the greatest challenges of personnel evaluation: How does one justify accountability to the public and at the same time maintain the trust and cooperation of individuals within the school setting that will enable the performance one so desires? How can an evaluation occur in both a summative and formative manner without neglecting one of the stated purposes? How does one foster change once the problems have been identified?[30]

Summative and Formative Evaluation

Personnel evaluation has two purposes: summative and formative. The summative process, often called *teacher appraisal,* is designed to provide a basic foundation for making decisions that can be justified. It is used to make a judgment relative to the *merit* of an individual's performance. Since it is administrative in nature, it is usually the predominate responsibility of the principal and/or the principal's designee. Decisions based on summative evaluation might include any or all of the following:

- Should the teacher be hired for a particular position?
- Should the teacher be dismissed?
- Should the teacher be placed on tenure?
- Does the performance of the teacher justify merit pay?

Because these are important decisions that affect the lives and careers of individuals, the assessment instrument, procedures used, and practices applied in the process need to stand the scrutiny of legal challenge. We deal with these issues in Chapter 16. It is important here to note that these legal issues are relevant only in the case of summative evaluation or teacher appraisal.

In recent years, many states have mandated forms and processes by which teacher appraisal will take place. Many of these mandates have resulted in standardized rating scales and designed checklists. Care must be used in basing an entire appraisal system on this or any other specific model. There is danger that the criteria will become too narrow to encompass the teaching of subjects that incorporate higher-order thinking skills or that require a high level of creativity on the part of students.

Tom McGreal has proposed alternatives to the rating scales appraisal designs to make them more useful as a clinical tool.[31] He has suggested that an appropriate appraisal be based on a cooperative goal-setting model, and that the appraiser and the teacher identify specific instructional improvement goals on which to work together. In working together, the techniques of clinical supervision are used and a supportive environment is established. Appraisal thus is the basis for staff development. The collaborative goal setting based on the formal appraisal that ensues at the postobservation and later conferences is critical to the development process. This suggests some important ways, then, in which the two purposes of evaluation may differ.

Formative evaluation is concerned primarily with professional growth and development. It is administered much more frequently than summative evaluation, and because it does not concern itself with administrative judgments for decision making, it can be, and most often is, a joint responsibility shared among teachers. Formative evaluation is often termed *clinical supervision* although this is only one of the many forms that formative evaluation can take. It does, however, make an important entry point considering formative evaluation.

Clinical Supervision

Clinical supervision is a collaborative process. The term *clinical supervision* gained national prominence in the 1960s through the writings of Robert Goldhammer and Morris Cogen.[32] Originally, the model was proposed for use with student teachers. Its applicability in the formative evaluation of practicing teachers was soon recognized.

Five steps comprise the model. Each step helps both the supervisor and the teacher in focusing on the teaching-learning process. An examination is made of the strengths and weaknesses of a lesson and then the process involves identifying specific activities to improve future lessons or teaching practices. The final step is formal feedback to the teacher.

Step 1: The Preobservation Conference. The purpose of the preobservation conference is to provide focus to the upcoming observation. The teacher outlines for the principal the plans for the lesson and helps identify specific aspects to which attention will be directed during the observation. The teacher's plan is expected to contain learner objectives, introductions, teaching strategies to be employed, resources to be used, evaluation plans, and lesson closure.

During this discussion, there is opportunity for the principal to clarify the various components of the lesson and to offer suggestions about other possible approaches. The discussion about the initial observation should focus on specific areas of interest or concern to the teacher rather than areas or concerns of the principal. Later observations and discussions will provide ample opportunity to address principal concerns.

It is important that the teacher understand the purpose of each step in the clinical model. The teacher needs to know that the observer will be taking notes during the observation and that this is for the purpose of giving accurate feedback. Before the conclusion of the preobservation conference, both a time for the classroom visit and a time for the postobservation conference should be established.

Step 2: The Classroom Observation. The teacher's task is to teach the lesson as planned. The observer's task is to record those items specifically identified in the preobservation conference as well as the events surrounding the lesson. Specific happenings should be scripted and in the language of the teacher. Activities relating to the lesson—student verbal and nonverbal behavior, for example—should be noted. Opinion and summary statements need to be avoided; the language of the participants and specific events are what the principal needs to provide useful feedback. It is important to be on time and to stay for the entire lesson.

Step 3: Analysis of the Lesson. To prepare for the postobservation conference, script notes need to be analyzed. Were the objectives obtained? How did the various intended teaching strategies work? What unusual circumstances were observed? What seemed to work? What didn't? What comments can you make about the teacher's verbal and nonverbal (physical) behavior? How about student verbal and nonverbal behavior? What did the teacher do well? What specific aspects might be improved? What should the teacher work on for the next observation?

Step 4: The Postobservation Conference. The conference needs to take place in a comfortable and private location. The teacher's classroom itself is often appropriate. A good opening line, after the amenities, is: "What do you think went well?" Then, the teacher should be asked to clarify the objectives of the lesson, review what happened, and assess whether the objectives were attained and to what degree. At this point, the principal will relate some of his or her specific observations supported by the notes that were taken. Successes will be discussed.

Agreement should be reached about what went on. Together, the teacher and the principal should decide on some strategies that might be worth trying. Information should be solicited from the teacher. Every conference should conclude with some growth objectives and some agreed-upon plans for improving any deficiencies.

Step 5: Postconference Analysis. The final step in the clinical model is an evaluation of the process and the outcome. Information is solicited from the teacher. How could the process be improved? Are the growth objectives clear? What assistance is available to the teacher? After the teacher leaves, the principal needs to reflect on the process and his or her own behavior and skill. Did the conference go well? Why or why not? The process is intended to promote both improved instruction and supportive relationships. One likely will not occur without the other.

As previously mentioned, staff evaluation has two basic purposes: (1) to improve the performance and provide direction for the continued development of present staff and (2) to provide a sound basis for personnel decisions such as awarding of tenure, promotions, transfers, or dismissals.

These two purposes create a dilemma for many administrators, even though both support quality education. Staff improvement is largely a helping relationship most effectively carried out when built on trust between the teacher and the principal. Personnel decisions are judgmental in nature and can cause teacher apprehension.

Several authors[33] have suggested that supervision and teacher appraisal styles become situationally specific; that is, situational factors determine the approach used by the principal in working with each staff member. This situational approach is similar to situational leadership models proposed by Blanchard[34] and Glatthorn.[35] A differentiated system of situational supervision has four levels:

1. *Clinical supervision,* as described in the previous section
2. *Collaborative professional development,* as a collegial process in which a small number of teachers work together for professional growth (the quality circle idea from TQM will integrate well with this approach)
3. *Self-direction,* in which the teacher prepares an individual development plan (IDP) with the assistance of the principal who serves as a resource person
4. *Administrative monitoring,* where the principal makes a series of brief, usually announced visits as "quality control" assurance

The fourth approach, commonly used by administrators, is one that should not be considered a supervisory method because it does not provide improvement opportunities to the teacher being observed. However, each of these approaches has its appropriate place in certain circumstances, depending on the maturity and needs of the teacher. The chart shown in Figure 9.3 points up many of the differences in the three supervisory approaches from the preceding list.

Staff development and evaluation are essential activities of the elementary school principal. Just as a teacher manages student learning by using a diagnostic prescriptive model, so can the principal direct staff development using staff evaluation as a diagnostic tool and an evaluation-by-objectives approach as a prescriptive tool. For proper staff development and evaluation, the principal must take an initiating, rather than reacting, role, and the comprehensive plan for staff evaluation must be based on a sound rationale.

THE STAFF EVALUATION CYCLE

Staff evaluation and development is a cyclical process. Staff evaluation leads to a staff-development prescription that is checked once again through evaluation. Seven basic steps in the evaluation cycle focus on the ultimate purpose of improving instruction. The cycle begins when the teacher and principal plan goals and targets for the year and include other people in the evaluation process during the year (see Figure 9.4). The seven steps of the evaluation cycle are as follows:

1. Prepare an individual development plan (IDP).
2. Select specific objectives or activities for observation or review.

FIGURE 9.3 Situational Models of Supervision

	CLINICAL	COLLABORATIVE	SELF-DIRECTED
Teacher Initiative	Low	Moderate	High
Supervisor Initiative	High	Moderate	Low
Approach	Formal, systematic	Collaborative	Self-directed
Goal of Learning	Create rationality/order	Problem solving	Goal directed
Knowledge	Predefined set of life-survival skills	Concrete results that "work" for individuals	That which is discovered
Learning	Condition individual by outer environment	Outcome of learner/environment interaction	Unfolding process within learner
Foundation	Behaviorist	Cognitivist	Humanist
Learning Theory	Conditioning	Experimentation	Self-discovery
Teacher Risk	Low	Moderate to high	Moderate to high

Source: Adapted from A. A. Glatthorn, *Differentiated Supervision* (Alexandria, VA: Association for Supervision and Curriculum Development, 1984).

3. Determine the observation method, time, and place.
4. Observe and collect data.
5. Analyze data and provide feedback.
6. Summarize and interpret collective observational data.
7. Report evaluation results, target achievement, and make recommendations for individual and staff development at an annual conference.

The following sections provide discussions of important processes or models that support this cycle. Central to these components is the individual development plan.

Individual Development Plans

An IDP is a written schedule of experiences designed to meet a person's particular goals for development. It is a method of systematically planning for training and other experiences in order to develop necessary skills and knowledge. Rather than haphazardly chancing time and money on what may not be a useful learning experience, the IDP gives both staff member and administrator an opportunity to set reasonable objectives and then plan experiences that support those objectives.

The IDP is realistic and feasible because its construction includes both administrator and staff member perspectives. The staff member's personal and professional goals are considered insofar as these are organizationally feasible. The staff member

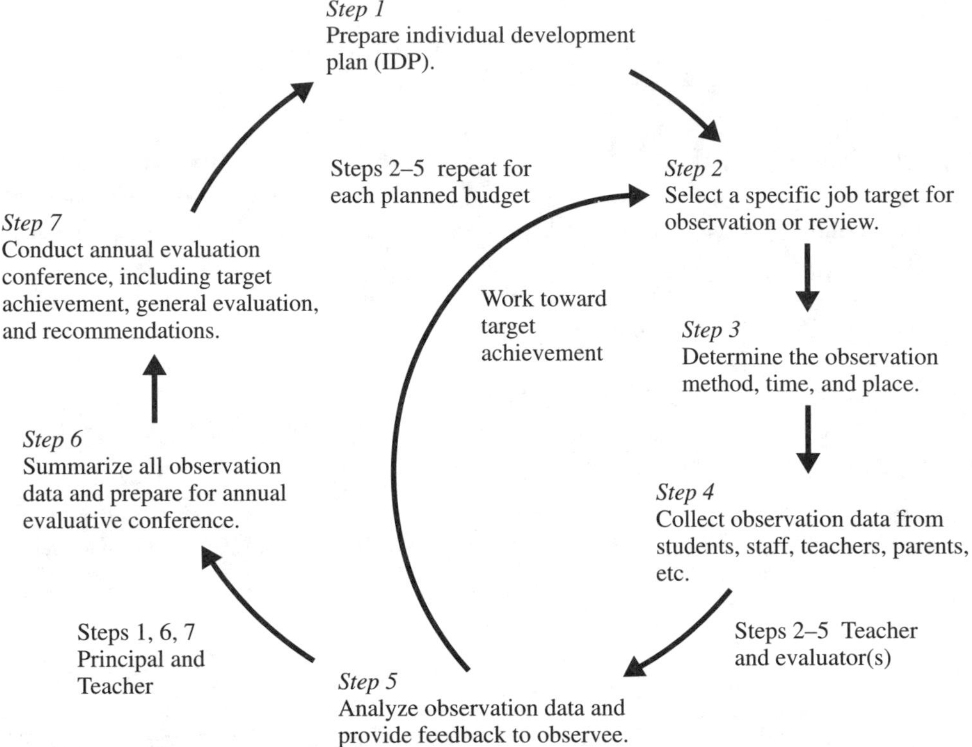

FIGURE 9.4 Staff Evaluation and Development Cycle

Source: Larry W. Hughes and Gerald C. Ubben, *The Elementary Principal's Handbook: A Guide to Effective Action,* 4th ed. Boston: Allyn and Bacon, 1994, p. 261. Used with permission.

also gets information and feedback so that goals can be set that are organizationally necessary and reasonably achievable.

Individual development is a joint responsibility of the administrator and the staff member. As such, it is a logical extension of the clinical supervision and appraisal process. The principal's responsibility is to arrange the work environment to capitalize on the skills and interests of the staff so that the important tasks get accomplished in the most efficient and effective way. To do so requires that the principal and staff member work together to identify skills deficiencies (developmental needs), strengths, and professional and organizational goals. The IDP is a joint commitment to address these issues.

The IDP includes first a self-assessment. The individual staff member reviews his or her professional qualifications, skills, and interests. A personal judgment is made about how these skills may be capitalized on in the organizational setting and how any skill deficiency can be best addressed. The second step in this process is for the individual to think about his or her professional career and begin to establish long-term career goals.

The responsibility of the principal is to conduct an analysis of the staff member's strengths and weaknesses as well. This analysis is always conducted from the perspective of what is good for the school. It frequently occurs that an individual's self-assessment will overlook important organizational demands and skills needs.

Following the two analyses, a development conference is held and the IDP begins to take specific form. Important information is exchanged at this conference. The two parties may not see all things similarly. Congruence is never likely to be achieved without a discourse about job-related expectations. At this time, the principal becomes aware of the goals of the staff member and, where possible and feasible, may provide assistance through establishment of a mentoring process.

MENTORING

The focus to this point has been the relationship between the principal as supervisor and individual staff members. Mentoring proposes a relationship between peers—however, generally not peers of equal stature and experience. Mentoring is often used to assist in the orientation of new employees.

The term *mentor* comes from Greek mythology. Mentor was the friend and counselor to whom Ulysses entrusted his son when Ulysses set off on a 10-year odyssey. It was a complex role: Mentor was protector, advisor, teacher, and father-figure to the inexperienced boy. The relationship was one of trust and affection.

In today's organizational setting, a formalized mentor program typically involves a relationship between a veteran employee of some stature and a younger inexperienced colleague. When it is an aspect of a human resources development effort, the focus of the relationship is on career counseling, advanced skills development, and learning the culture of the organization from a broadened perspective. Less formal relationships, which are conceptually similar, are typified by labels such as *sponsor, coach,* and *senior advisor.*

Mentoring has come to take on a more precise role than that suggested by the other labels. Often, the practice is reserved to those who have been identified early as "fast trackers" or potential leaders. However, the concept is easily applied at the building level, albeit perhaps not quite as formally, but nevertheless to good effect. It can substantially improve the clinical approach to supervision and become a very sophisticated *peer* supervision program. It does require a cadre of excellent experienced staff, however.

As in any relationship, both parties in the mentoring process have important responsibilities. It is critical that the relationship be managed so that maximum benefit is achieved. The responsibilities of the mentor include:

- *IDP Counseling.* Specific guidance and suggestions are given for developmental experiences to be included in the protégé's IDP to strengthen competencies.
- *Monitoring and Feedback.* An active role must be taken by the mentor in monitoring the progress and performance of the protégé. Regular feedback sessions

need to be held at which time the IDP is reviewed, clinical observations made, and formative evaluation considerations discussed.

- *Career Strategy Advisement.* The mentor provides general guidance and insight regarding the kinds of opportunities available in the organization and the career background and path necessary to qualify for such positions. In this capacity, the mentor brings to bear an extensive knowledge of the history and culture of the system, as well as of projected trends. Many school systems, for example, have differentiated staffing patterns, extended-year contract opportunities, special assignments for staff with special qualifications, different salary arrangements depending on certification, interesting opportunities for those whose teaching areas are in high demand/short supply, as well as the usual administrative positions with opportunities for broadened leadership responsibilities. The mentor advises about these.
- *Sponsoring and Mediating.* This aspect of the mentor's responsibility is to provide direction and assistance in arranging particular developmental assignments and promotion opportunities. The second dimension is to serve as a mediator in any conflicts that may arise that involve the advisee and others in the organization, including the "boss."

The developing person has responsibilities as well. Any productive relationship is mutually supportive and requires the active attention of both parties. The advisee needs to take the lead in several ways: by initiating meeting and actively seeking advice, by remaining open to the advice and suggestions of the mentor, and by a willingness to share personal and professional problems and aspirations.

Developing a Productive Relationship

Productive relationships are not automatically obtained. There is always the issue of the "interpersonal chemistry" of the involved individuals, for example. This notwithstanding to the contrary, there are several other factors that can greatly facilitate the relationship. Administrators interested in developing productive mentoring arrangements need to consider such aspects is careful matching, good initial orientation, and a feedback and monitoring system.

Careful matching of individuals is essential. The administrator should develop an initial list of potential mentors before considering the process further. Important factors that result in a good mentor include willingness to act as a mentor, personal commitment to helping others develop, commitment to the school, extensive knowledge and insight about how things get done in the organization, solid experience, good professional relationships beyond the immediate building or system, and a proven record of success.

For example, when using a mentoring system as part of the orientation of new teachers, it is often best to select as mentors relatively young but experienced teachers. As mentors, they will generally relate well to entering members of the profession having enough experience to share good advice, including a good memory for the problems of a first-year teacher.

Fundamental to a long-term relationship is an early orientation to the program at which the involved parties can, within a school system and school building policy, work through role definitions and expectations of each other. This process will clarify initial commitments to help foster the climate of trust and openness important to success.

The establishment of a regular feedback and monitoring system is essential. This must be encouraged and supported by organizational mechanisms. One approach is to schedule regular monthly luncheons, in addition to other spontaneous sessions, at which lengthier discussion can take place in a more relaxed atmosphere away from the usual interruptions.

ORGANIZATIONAL DEVELOPMENT

Organizational development (OD) is a process designed to improve the interaction and productivity of work groups. The work group may be a team of teachers, the staff of a particular school, or some other configuration of employees. OD methods work well as initial activities for newly formed teams or with established groups that are refocusing their efforts. Quality circles as part of a Total Quality Management (TQM) program can use OD methodology to facilitate their interaction.

Although HRD and OD are different and are employed for different outcomes, they are related. An OD intervention frequently results in the development, or improvement, of the human resources development program. Frequently, as well, a well-functioning HRD program will bring about conditions that result in a better-functioning work group—an intended outcome of organizational development. Some theorists may argue otherwise, but for the practitioner and the student of management it is most useful to view the two approaches as parts of a whole.[36]

Healthy organizations systematically and regularly engage in introspective analyses of organizational activities, the purpose of such introspection is to maintain viability—to continue to effectively respond to client needs. Three questions must be asked:

- *Why are we doing what we are doing?* This is a goals question. Healthy organizations have well-developed and well-understood goals and objectives. From time to time there is need to reexamine these in the light of changing conditions—to reaffirm them, add to them, or modify them.
- *What are we doing?* This is a question about the nature and kind of processes that are being implemented to achieve the goals and objectives. This has to do with such things as the nature of the curriculum, scoping and sequencing of subject matter, policy and procedures, and a host of other things that comprise the formal organizational structure and deliver, systems.
- *Can it be done a better way?* This is an evaluation question. Once the goals have been clarified, and reaffirmed or modified, and once the processes have been identified and analyzed, it is necessary to decide what, if anything, could be done differently to achieve the goal more efficiently. Such issues as decision-making practices, communication practices, allocation of resources and/or additional resources needed (personnel and material), changes in organizational structure

and curricular delivery, systems, staffing arrangements, and any individual developmental activities are among the processes that must be examined.

As with any complex process issuing from the behavioral sciences, there is not complete agreement about just what organizational development is. Nevertheless, there are some common characteristics about which most in the field would agree.

Organizational development is systematic and involves a total organizational system *or* subsystems. The entire organization need not be involved. Any unified subsystem—a school building or a decentralized school system unit, for example—could engage in such a process *provided* the unit was relatively autonomous (i.e., free within wide bounds to determine its own long-range plans), and *top* management was aware and committed to the effort.

It has as its main focus that of changing the attitudes, behaviors, and performance patterns of work groups rather than individuals. The emphasis is on realistic group goal setting, systematic planning, and problem solving. Such aspects of effective work groups as how best to work together, how to capitalize on the skills of members, how to communicate effectively, and how to manage and resolve intra- and intergroup conflict are among problem areas addressed.

Organizational development is an ongoing and long-term process. People learn to work effectively together only as they face real problems and develop effective problem-solving skills. This cannot be accomplished quickly; behavior change and the skills needed are acquired only after much practice. Frequently, it is best to have a process consultant facilitate the work of the group. This person can be from within the parent organization but should be external to the target work group.

An OD process relies on action research and experiential learning. The data that are of most use are data about the ongoing system—its characteristics, issues, problems, and resources. This information is collected, analyzed, and returned in summary form to the work group. It forms the basis for problem identification, goal setting, and systematic problem resolution. The survey-feedback method of data collection/data analysis action planning is most frequently employed to facilitate this process.

Survey-feedback methods have a rich history. The method is essentially a systematic way of collecting information about the entire organization across several organizational dimensions. The process involves the development of an organizational questionnaire that is administered anonymously to organizational members.

The usual approach is to include questions about worker demographics and work group characteristics, as well as items that provide insight about such organizational dimensions as the nature of communication practices, organizational goal setting, decision-making practices, motivation and reward systems, and control practices, among other possible dimensions. In the often used survey of organizations, there is space for the organization to add its own questions about purely local issues and concerns.[37]

Once the data are collected, a computer analysis is performed and the information, appropriately categorized, is returned to the organization for the feedback/problem-solving effort to begin. Usually a consultant will feed the information back to the top administrative team first and then move through the organizational hierarchy. The process involves discussing the data, what the information means, and what might be done about it. Each administrator then meets with his or her own work group to interpret the data further and to develop corrective action plans.

Thus, just as HRD is far more than a cafeteria list of in-house seminars and on-the-job training, so is OD more than a few problem-solving groups working with a process consultant. Understanding and providing for the complexities of these two approaches brings sophistication and productivity to the staff and organizational development effort.

IMPLICATIONS FOR LEADERS

The role of the principal in human resources and organizational development is a crucial one. Even if the school district is not operating on an enlightened development model, there is much that can occur at the school building level to address staff development systematically and provide for a responsive organization.

The Needs Assessment

What does the staff need? What does the staff want? Where is this expertise available? It is appropriate to survey the staff formally and such surveys should be more than a once-in-a-while activity.

A formal survey is not the only source of information about staff needs. If principals have been regularly and routinely engaging in clinical supervision, then they clearly will be in a good position to know what some of the important needs are on the faculty. Moreover, reviewing data in a systematic way about such things as pupil progress, demographic aspects of the community, changes in state law, federal programming, and impending curricular changes, among any number of other impinging forces, will be suggestive of current or impending development needs. The point here is that a principal must not feel bound to a survey when it is clear that there are pressing needs other than those recognized immediately by the staff.[38]

Making staff aware of changes on the horizon is one way to elevate a sense of need. Moreover, if the principal has been engaging in the postobservation feedback sessions essential to a clinical supervision process, this too is an awareness-raising activity. Urick and his colleagues prescribe the ARC model. The acronym stands for Awareness, Readiness, and Commitment, and the point of their manuscript is that these are the sequential building blocks to the success of any in-service development activity.[39]

Structuring and Monitoring the Development System

Whether the aspect of the human resources development program that is being addressed is individual in nature or is focused on the work group, there is a need for administrative support, an appropriate structure, and a monitoring system. Administrative support begins with needs assessment, of course. It continues when the expectations are established. It is buttressed by a willingness to engage others in the planning of the development efforts and a willingness to secure time and dollar resources to support the effort.

The nature of the need, who is to be involved, and whether the development is to be work group focused or individually oriented will, for the most part, determine the structure of the programs. If the program is an individually oriented one, then the IDP is probably the best approach. If the program is focused on the work group (schoolwide, department, grade-level, teaching team, or whatever), then the structuring of the experiences becomes somewhat more complex. Once it is clear what it is that the group needs to know, and assuming that the group is at the stage of commitment, it is probably best to turn the planning of the development events over to the group itself. The principal's role then becomes one of facilitation rather than direction.[40]

Monitoring progress at regular intervals is important. In the instance of the IDP, regular conferences with the individual and/or the mentor, if there is one, is essential. This keeps the process a formative one and allows for appropriate adjustments. In the instance of group-development programs, it is equally essential that formative evaluation practices be present. All human resources development programs need regular assessment.

Positive Reinforcement

Learning and development—whether adult, adolescent, or child—are facilitated by positive reinforcement. Among a number of findings reported in a research synthesis about effective school practices was the following characteristic of leaders in these schools:

Leaders set up systems of incentives and rewards to encourage excellence in student and teacher performance; they act as figureheads in delivering awards and highlighting the importance of excellence.[41]

These findings highly correlate with those about successful management in the private sector:

> The excellent companies have a deeply ingrained philosophy that says, in effect, respect the individual," "make people winners," "let them stand out," "treat people as adults."[42]

In sum, then, there are four implications to the principal who wants a well-developed, highly motivated staff:

- Development needs of the staff must be accurately assessed. Self-assessment is a starting point, but the principal must also conduct an investigation, using clinical observations in classrooms, student data, and current and foreseeable school and community concerns among other data sources.
- High standards of performance must be established and advertised. Setting performance standards in cooperation with staff members has been revealed to be the most effective practice.

- Human resources development systems require careful planning and a variety of approaches. IDPs as well as group development events must focus on recognized needs and be regularly monitored.
- Positive reinforcement techniques need to be consistently and continually employed. Public pats on the back, award ceremonies, private thank yous, bonuses for jobs well done—what Peters and Waterman call "hoopla"[43]—all serve to keep people congruent with the needs of the organization, and productively motivated.

SUMMARY

Negative responses to organized efforts in the name of staff development are the result of a history of bad experiences with activities that have gone on in the name of inservice training. However well-intended such activities may have been, too frequently they have not addressed either the needs of the individual staff members or the needs of the organization.

Better approaches exist, and these approaches issue from a model of human resources development that recognizes the varied needs of individual organization members; the needs of the organization; the nature of adult learners; the time and effort required, depending on the nature of the knowledge, skill, or attitude to be acquired; and the impact that individuals have on the very nature and culture of the workplace.

ACTIVITIES

1. Review Case Study 4 at this end of this book. Apply the goal-setting and strategic planning concepts of Chapter 4 and the human resources development concepts expressed in this chapter. How might you proceed in addressing the problems cited in this case? Set forth a strategy to overcome the problem.

2. Review Case Study 7 and 12. Analyze the problems presented and apply the concepts of human resources development presented in this chapter. What approach would you use in addressing the problems? Set forth a strategy to overcome the difficulties faced by the schools in these cases.

3. Turn to the ISLLC Standards found in Appendix B. Review the performances listed with Standard Three. Which of the performance statements best support the human resources concepts discussed in this chapter? What weakness do you find in your school's human resources management? How would you go about correcting them?

ENDNOTES

1. M. McLaughlin and D. Marsh, "Staff Development and School Change," *Teachers College Record 80,* no. 1 (1978): 69–94.

2. Linda Darling-Hammond, Arthur Wise, and Sara Pease, "Teacher Evaluation in the Organizational Context," *Review of Educational Research 53,* no. 1 (1983): 285–328.

3. Ken Peterson, "Methodological Problems in Teacher Evaluation," *Journal of Research and Development in Education 1,* no. 4 (1984).

4. Tom McGreal, "Effective Teacher Evaluation Systems," *Educational Leadership 39,* no. 4 (1982): 303–305.

5. Edgar Schein, *Career Dynamics: Matching Individual and Organizational Needs* (Reading, MA: Addison-Wesley, 1978).

6. Ibid.

7. Ibid.

8. Ibid.

9. Much of the difficulty in organizational and individual incompatibility could have been eliminated up front if a more careful selection and placement process had been done.

10. Dennis Sparks and Susan Loucks-Horsley, "Five Models of Staff Development in Teachers," *Journal of Staff Development 10,* no. 4 (Fall, 1989): 40–57.

11. M. Knowles, *The Modern Practice of Adult Education* (Chicago: Association/Follett Press, 1980).

12. Michael Huberman, "The Professional Life Cycle of Teachers," *Teachers College Record 91,* no. 1 (Fall 1989): 32–57.

13. Ibid.

14. Huberman, "The Professional Life Cycle of Teachers," p. 131.

15. Ibid.

16. Ibid.

17. Patricia Holland and Kaye Weise, "Helping Novice Teachers," in *Principal as Leader,* ed. Larry W. Hughes (Upper Saddle River, NJ: Merrill, 1999).

18. McLaughlin and Yee, "Schools as a Place to Have a Career," in *Building a Professional Culture in Schools,* ed. Ann Lieberman (New York: Teachers College Press, 1988).

19. Huberman, "The Professional Life Cycle of Teachers," p. 134.

20. This concept was discussed in Chapter 1. Part of the role of the principal is to provide opportunities for organizational members to develop the means necessary for moving to higher levels of values awareness.

21. Donald De Moulin and John Guyton, "An Analysis of Career Development to Enhance Individualized Staff Development," *National Forum of Educational Administration and Supervision Journal 7,* no. 3 (1990).

22. McLaughlin and Yee, "School as a Place to Have a Career." These authors discuss the need to provide teachers with two opportunities that will inspire their development as professionals: *level of capacity* and *level of opportunity.*

23. Sparks and Loucks-Horsley, "Five Models of Staff Development in Teachers."

24. Ibid.

25. Beverley Showers, *Peer Coaching: A Strategy for Facilitating Transfer of Training* (Eugene, OR: Center for Educational Policy and Management, University of Oregon, 1984).

26. B. Showers, B. Joyce, and B. Bennett, "Synthesis of Research on Staff Development: A Framework for Future Study and a State-of-Art Analysis," *Educational Leadership 45,* no. 3 (1987): 77–87.

27. Beverly Joyce and Beverly Showers, "The Coaching of Teaching," *Educational Leadership 40,* no. 1 (1982): 4–10.

28. Michael Scriven, "A Unified Approach to Teacher Evaluation," *Toward a Unified Model: The Foundations of Educational Personnel Evaluation* (Center for Research on Educational Accountability and Teacher Evaluation: Western Michigan University, 1994), pp. 2–15.

29. Scriven, "A Unified Approach to Teacher Evaluation," p. 1.

30. Linda Darling-Hammond, Wise, and Pease, "Teacher Evaluation in the Organizational Context."

31. Ronald Brandt, "On Teacher Evaluation: A Conversation with Tom McGreal." *Educational Leadership 4,* no. 7 (July 1987): 20–24.

32. See Robert Goldhammer, *Clinical Supervision* (New York: Holt, Rinehart and Winston, 1969); and Morris Cogen, *Clinical Supervision* (New York: Houghton Mifflin, 1973).

33. A. A. Glatthorn, *Differentiated Supervision* (Alexandria, VA: Association for Supervision and Curriculum Development, 1984); and Carl D. Glickman, *Developmental Supervision* (Alexandria, VA: Association for Supervision and Curriculum Development, 1981).

34. K. Blanchard, D. Zigarmi, and P. Zagarmi, "Situational Leadership: 'Different Strokes for Different Folks.'" *Principal 66,* no. 4 (March 1987): 12–16.

35. Glatthorn, *Differentiated Supervision.*

36. A good treatment of the relationship of individual development organizational development can be found in Edgar H. Schein, *Career Dynamics: Matching Individual and Organizational Needs* (Reading, MA: Addison-Wesley, 1978).

37. The Institute for Social Research at the University of Michigan has a "Survey of Organizations" designed specifically for schools. A good source to learn more about survey-feedback methodology is David G. Bowers and Jerome L. Franklin. *Data-Based Organizational Change* (La Jolla, CA: University Associates, 1977).

38. The Survey should not be discounted, however. Commitment to improve is always more easily

obtained when the individual to be improved personally recognize the need.

39. Ronald Urick, David Pendergast, and Larry W. Hillman. "Pre-Conditions for Staff Development," *Educational Leadership 38,* no. 7 (April 1981): 546–549.

40. As always, it is important to establish the ground rules when delegating such tasks. The principal will want to work with the group at the beginning to set the essential conditions that any development process must meet. Such things as budget, impinging systemwide policies, and so on that must be lived with in order for the plan to be implemented should be discussed and understood

41. Northwest Regional Educational Laboratory, *Effective Schooling Practices: A Research Synthesis.* (Portland, OR: The Laboratory, 1984), p. 8.

42. T. J. Peters and R. H. Waterman, *In Search of Excellence: Lessons from America's Best Run Companies* (New York: Warner Books, 1982).

43. Ibid.

SELECTED READINGS

Acheson, Keith A. and Meredith, Gall. *Techniques in the Clinical Supervision of Teachers* (2nd ed.). (New York: Longman, 1987).

Bernstein, H. T., L. Darling-Hammond, M. W. McLaughlin, and A. E. Wise. *Teacher Evaluation: A Study of Effective Practices* (Santa Monica, CA: Rand, 1984).

DePasquale, Daniel, Jr. "Evaluating Tenured Teachers: A Practical Approach." *NASSP Bulletin 74* (September 1990): 19–23.

Educational Research Service. *Teacher Evaluation: Practices and Procedures* (Arlington, VA: Educational Research Service, 1988).

Educational Resources Information Center. *The Best of ERIC on Educational Management: Teacher Evaluation.* NASSP Edition (Eugene, OR: Clearinghouse on Educational Management, College of Educational, University of Oregon, October 1989).

Goldstein, Irwin L. *Training in Organizations: Needs Assessment, Development and Evaluation* (2nd ed.). (Monterey, CA: Brooks/Cole, 1996).

Glatthorn, Allan. *Supervisory Leadership* (Glenview, IL: Scott, Foresman, 1990).

Glickman, Carl D. *Supervision of Instruction* (Boston: Allyn and Bacon, 1989).

Gordon, Bruce G. "Making Clinical Supervision a Reality: Steps Toward Implementation." *NASSP Bulletin 76,* no. 542 (March 1992): 46–51.

Harris, Ben M. *Supervisory Behavior in Education* (Englewood Cliffs, NJ: Prentice-Hall, 1985).

Hartzell, Gary N. "Avoiding Evaluation Errors: Fairness in Appraising Employee Performance," *NASSP Bulletin 79,* no. 567 (January 1995): 40–50.

Herman, Janice L., and Jerry J. Herman. "Defining Administrative Tasks, Evaluating Performance, and Developing Skills." *NASSP Bulletin 79,* no. 567 (January 1995): 16–21.

Hughes, Larry W., Mary Murphy, and Martha Wong. "Quality Assurance: Positive Approaches to Teacher Improvement." *Record in Educational Administration and Supervision 5,* no. 2 (Spring 1985): 11–13.

Hunter, M. "Knowing, Teaching, and Supervising." in *Using What We Know About Teaching,* ed. P. L. Hosford (Alexandria, VA: Association for Supervision and Curriculum Development, 1984), pp. 169–192.

Joyce, B., and B. Showers. *Student Achievement Through Self Development* (New York: Longman, 1988).

Katims, David S., and Richard L. Henderson. "Teacher Evaluation in Special Education." *NASSP Bulletin 74* (September 1990): 46–52.

Lane, Bruce A. "Personnel Evaluation: From Problems to School Improvement." *Journal of Research and Development in Education 23,* no. 4 (Summer 1990): 243–249.

Millman, Jason. *Handbook of Teacher Evaluation* (Beverly Hills, CA: Sage Publications, 1981).

Murphy, J., and P. Hallinger. "The Characteristics of Instructionally Effective School Districts." *Journal of Educational Research 81,* no. 3 (1987): 175–181.

National Association of Elementary School Principals. *Effective Teachers: Effective Evaluation in America's Elementary and Middle Schools* (NAESP, 1988).

Olthoff, Richard J. "The Principal as Instructional Coach-Providing Quality Education." *NASSP Bulletin 76,* no. 542 (March 1992): 6–12.

Pope, Carol A. "Indirect Teaching and Assessment: Are They Mutually Exclusive?" *NASSP Bulletin 74* (September 1990): 1–5.

Scriven, M. "Validity in Personnel Evaluation." *Journal of Personnel Evaluation in Education 1,* no. 1 (1987): 9–23.

Shelton, Maria M., Kenneth Lane, and Patt Yuhasz. "Great Beginnings." *The Executive Educator* (January 1992): 27–29.

Sikorski, Melanie F., Richard P. Niemiec, and Herbert J. Walberg. "Best Teaching Practices: A Checklist for Observations." *NASSP Bulletin 78* no. 561 (April 1994): 1–6.

Stufflebeam, Daniel L., Chair. *The Personnel Evaluation Standards: How to Assess Systems for Evaluating Educators.* The Joint Committee on Standards for Educational Evaluation (Beverly Hills, CA: Sage Publications, 1988).

Thorson, J. R., et al., "Instructional Improvement Through Personnel Evaluation." *Educational Leadership 44* (April 1987): 52–54.

Wood, Carolyn J. "Toward More Effective Teacher Evaluation: Lessons from Naturalistic Inquiry." *NASSP Bulletin 76,* no. 542 (March 1992): 52–59.

Zumwalt, K. *Improving Teaching* (Arlington, VA: Association for Supervision and Curriculum Development, 1986).

PART III

MANAGING THE ORGANIZATION

The school leaders of the twenty-first century must have knowledge and understanding of theories and models of organizations and principles of organizational development, operational procedures at the school and district level, principles and issues relating to school safety and security, human resources management and development, principles and issues relating to fiscal operations of school management, principles and issues relating to school facilities and use of space, legal issues impacting school operations, and current technologies that support management functions. They should also believe in, value, and be committed to making management decisions to enhance learning and teaching; taking risks to improve schools; trusting people and their judgments; accepting responsibility; having high-quality standards, expectations, and performances; involving stakeholders in management processes; and assuring a safe environment. ISLLC Standard Three supports these.

> **Standard 3: A school administrator is an educational leader who promotes the success of all students by ensuring management of the organization, operations, and resources for a safe, efficient, and effective learning environment.**

Part III addresses this standard and the knowledge, dispositions, and performances that accompanies it.

CHAPTER TEN

STAFFING THE SCHOOL

Recruitment, Selection, and Termination Processes

Selecting quality teachers may be the single most important thing you do as an administrator. A beginning high school teacher who stays in the class room for a thirty-year career can have had almost 5,000 students under their instruction by the time they retire.

—G. C. Ubben[1]

Recruitment and selection policies of school districts vary. The local school's involvement in the recruitment and selection process will depend on how the school district administrators perceive their role. If the machine metaphor is used where the efficiency of the organization is best served with a centralized approach to personnel administration, then the central office for the school district is likely to play the major role in the recruitment, selection, and placement of new and transferring employees. The principal becomes the gatekeeper for the local school, with the role of confirming or objecting to the decisions of the central office. On the other hand, if the brain metaphor is applied with a learning organization as the preferred model, the local school—teachers, principal, parents, and even students—become the decision makers in the selection process, with the central office playing a supporting role.

Organizational tension created from personnel decisions exists in many organizations because the issue of *locus of control* has not been carefully delineated. Central personnel offices operating from the machine metaphor wish to play a major hand in personnel decisions to ensure efficiency as well as compliance with the law. This model suggests a highly centralized decision process.

Principals wishing to use the learning organization concept prefer to follow the brain metaphor, reserving personnel decisions for the members of local learning community. This is a highly decentralized model. This chapter takes the position that the learning organization model is preferred, with most of the personnel decisions made by stakeholders at the building level, but also points out many of the tension points that occur with this approach.

RECRUITMENT

The major recruitment efforts by the school begin with good position and person descriptions. Figures 10.1 and 10.2 depict sample position and person descriptions. If the school finds it difficult to locate appropriate candidates, central office personnel should be contacted to review the recruitment process. For example, if the principal, in an effort to diversify the staff, has asked for a teacher from somewhere other than the local college, and the personnel office has not posted vacancies at other colleges, the recruitment drive will be ineffective. The principal must assume responsibility for seeing that recruitment policies are broad enough to meet personnel needs.

The selection of personnel should be a cooperative effort between the district personnel office and the local school. The central-office role should be to screen applicants and then to send those best matching the position descriptions to the school for final selection. In some large school districts, a personnel office may employ teachers unassigned to specific buildings, but even in this case, the building principal and staff should have the final decision regarding who works in the building.

The greatest problem in the selection of new staff members often comes from the need of the central office to place "transfers." These are generally tenured employees who must be moved from a previous assignment in the district. Since they are tenured,

FIGURE 10.1 Person Description

Lakeview Schools
219 Lakeview Ave.
Lake City

Person Description
Position: Elementary Teacher
Sex: Prefer male
Teaching Experience Necessary: None
Training Requirements: BS; prefer graduates from other than local college
Certification: Elementary, K–3
Teaching Strength: Strong reading training; interest in social studies
Other Skills: Prefer someone with training or experience with team teaching or cooperative learning
Other interests: Prefer someone with a vocational interests that would appeal to young boys such as camping, hiking, model airplane making, and so on

Source: Larry W. Hughes and Gerald C. Ubben, *The Elementary Principal's Handbook: A Guide to Effective Action*, 4th ed. Boston: Allyn and Bacon, 1994, p. 238. Used with permission.

FIGURE 10.2 Position Description

Lakeview Schools
219 Lakeview Ave.
Lake City

Position Description

Position Title: Teacher (team) grade-level elementary 1–3
Purpose of Position: To plan, organize, and instruct primary children
Starting Date:
Salary Range: Beginning teacher, B.S.—$28,000
M.S.—$32,000

Principal Duties: The teacher will be a member of a four-teacher team working with six-to-eight-year-old children. Instruction is organized on an interdisciplinary basis with cooperative planning units. The team has four assigned classrooms and schedules children in a flexible manner into these spaces. Major instructional responsibilities will include reading and mathematics as well as participation in the integration of other subjects.

Performance Responsibilities:

I. Instructional Skills
- **A.** Knowledge and Training
  1. Is academically competent in assigned teaching areas.
  2. Keeps abreast of new findings and current trends in the field.
  3. Remains open-minded and willing to grow and change.
  4. Provides opportunities for all students to experience success.
- **B.** Classroom Environment and Management
  1. Maintains a classroom environment conducive to learning (by using special interest areas, learning centers, units, themes, furniture arrangements, proper lighting, heating, ventilation, and structured rules and regulations understood and accepted by all).
  2. Monitors individual pupil progress and adapts the pace of instruction accordingly.
  3. Uses democratic procedures that show consideration for the rights of others.
- **C.** Methods and Techniques
  1. Uses a variety of stimulating instructional techniques (such as the lecture method, demonstration, self-directed activities, both small and large group activities [drill and rote activities], and community resources, audiovisual aids and individualized programs).
  2. Demonstrates and fosters the growth of communication skills.
  3. Presents subject matter in a functional manner.
  4. Makes homework assignments for meaningful instructional purposes.
- **D.** Planning
  1. Establishes short- and long-range goals with well-defined objectives and identifies appropriate procedures to accomplish them. (Example: A minimum competency and curriculum guide.)
  2. Provides opportunities for all students to experience success.
  3. Has a well-defined alternative plan for substitute teachers.

Continued

FIGURE 10.2 Continued

- **E.** Evaluation
  - **1.** Provides feedback to students on their accomplishments and progress with positive and effective reinforcements.
  - **2.** Uses instruments based on activity, objective, or goal-oriented criteria.
  - **3.** Guides students toward self-motivation, self-evaluation, and self-direction.

II. Student Attitudes and Performance
- **A.** Demonstrates consistency, firmness and impartiality in dealing with students in a professional manner.
- **B.** Appreciates individuality.
- **C.** Shows positive attitudes toward students by helping all children experience success, possibly through the use of tutorial and counseling activities.
- **D.** Promotes desirable standards of work and behavior within the classroom.

III. Personal Qualities
- **A.** Demonstrates a positive and enthusiastic attitude and a genuine interest in students, colleagues, curriculum, and the education field in general.
- **B.** Recognizes and capitalizes on his or her own assets, thereby projecting a good model for students in dress, demeanor, and speech.
- **C.** Is able to profit from constructive criticism.
- **D.** Shows qualities that reflect the importance of punctuality, efficiency, dependability, accuracy, and congeniality.

IV. Professional Growth and Development
- **A.** Participates in enrichment activities, including such activities as study in his or her field and/or travel.
- **B.** Actively pursues avenues of personal and professional growth through workshops, classes, professional organizations, and seminars.
- **C.** Establishes personal goals for professional development.

V. Teacher Relationships
- **A.** Teacher-Parent
  - **1.** Establishes an effective line of communication between home and school via notes, conferences, written reports, work samples, telephone conversations, and meetings of groups such as the PTO that stress discussion of students' strengths and weaknesses.
  - **2.** Encourages parents to form a partnership with the teacher in the total education of their child—mentally, emotionally, physically, and spiritually.
- **B.** Teacher-Community
  - **1.** Works effectively with legitimate community organizations and identifies and utilizes community resources to augment the educational opportunities of the children.
  - **2.** Projects a positive image of the total school program to the community; liaison function is served.
- **C.** Teacher-Teacher
  - **1.** Cooperates fully with colleagues in shared responsibilities.
  - **2.** Shows tolerance for peer differences.
  - **3.** Shares experiences, ideas, and knowledge with peers.
  - **4.** Communicates effectively with other teachers who have shared or will share the same students for the purpose of developing smooth continuity between grade levels and subject matter.

FIGURE 10.2 Continued

D. Teacher-Administrator-Supervisor
   1. Understands and adheres to the chain of command.
   2. Participates in decision making when appropriate.
   3. Demonstrates cooperation in performing both classroom and extra duties.
   4. Seeks advice and counsel when needed.
   5. Forms a partnership to develop good public relations in the school district.

E. Teacher-Student
   1. Recognizes the uniqueness of all students.
   2. Guides and encourages students in a friendly, constructive, and impartial manner.
   3. Initiates procedures that will invite regular feedback for students.
   4. Maintains a classroom atmosphere conducive to mutual respect, one that adequately establishes appropriate roles.

Source: Larry W. Hughes and Gerald C. Ubben, *The Elementary Principal's Handbook: A Guide to Effective Action*, 4th ed. Boston: Allyn and Bacon, 1994, pp. 238–240. Used with permission.

the school district must place them ahead of any new hires. Although there may be many legitimate reasons for the transfer of employees within a school district, some school districts have a bad habit of playing "pass the trash." This is the practice of allowing the transfer of poor or incompetent teachers from school to school rather than going through the process of dismissal. Once again, the principal must evaluate each candidate for a position in the school on the basis of what he or she thinks is best for the school.

The principles of learning organizations and the concepts of teacher empowerment strengthen the principal's position in employing new staff members. Involving the leadership team in setting policies for the selection of new staff members and involving members of the teaching staff in the interview and selection process will increase the principal's power base in resisting undesirable placements of staff by a central personnel office.

Federal Regulations to Prevent Employment Discrimination

Care must always be taken to abide by the federal laws regarding recruitment and selection of staff. The Civil Rights Act of 1964 and the Equal Employment Opportunity Act of 1972 and their several amendments as well as the more recent Americans with Disabilities Act (ADA) of 1992 make it unlawful to discriminate on the basis of race, color, religion, sex, age, national origin, or disabling condition.

EEOC Regulations. It is unlawful to ask about the following on either a written application or during an interview:

1. Complexion or color of skin.

2. Applicant's religious denomination, affiliation, church, parish, pastor, or religious holidays observed.
3. Applicant's sex, marital status, name or other information about spouse, or ages of children if any.
4. Whether applicant has a disability or has been treated for any of certain diseases. However, you may ask if the applicant has any physical impairments that would affect the ability to perform the job for which the applicant has applied.
5. If the applicant has ever been arrested. You may ask if the applicant has been convicted of a crime.
6. Any previous name that the applicant has used. You may ask if he or she worked for your organization under a different name, (e.g., a maiden name).
7. Birthplace or birthplace of applicant's parents or spouse; birthdate or certificate of naturalization papers, and so on.
8. Require the applicant's photograph before hiring.
9. Whether the applicant or a relative is a citizen of a foreign country. You may ask if the applicant is a U.S. citizen, intends to become one, or has a legal right to be in the United States.
10. The applicant's native language. You may ask which languages the applicant speaks and writes.
11. Questions or information about the applicant's relatives. Prior to employment, you may not even ask the name of a person to contact in case of emergency.
12. The clubs, societies, and lodges to which the applicant belongs. You may ask the applicant to list organizations he or she believes to be pertinent to the job.

After the individual has been employed, many of these items of information can then legally be asked on an employee information form but cannot appear or be asked on an application or during an interview.

Americans with Disabilities Act (ADA). The Americans with Disabilities Act prohibits employers, public and private, from discriminating against any individual with a disability. The law covers the full range of employment activities, including recruiting and hiring, termination, compensation, job assignment and advancement, and training. The law requires that employers make reasonable accommodation in the workplace to enable the individual to perform fundamental job duties of a position. This may require providing properly positioned chalkboards and new technology to allow the person to function successfully. Often, the workplace itself is more of a barrier to the physically challenged than job skills and knowledge. Care must be shown not to exclude anyone from consideration for employment because of his or her disabling condition if he or she is capable of performing the essential functions called for by that position.

THE SELECTION PROCESS

The selection process for the employment of new staff members has several steps or stages.

Screening

The first step is application clarification. Prior to an interview, the principal should carefully review the candidate's application file, comparing the application with the personal description. Few candidates will possess all the qualifications that have been specified, but the principal should try to find candidates with most of them.[2]

Discrepancy Analysis

The second step in the selection process should be a discrepancy analysis of the application materials. Remember, applicants usually present themselves in the best manner possible, minimizing weak points. One technique used to uncover discrepancies is to search the file for missing information. Common problem areas are (1) efforts to conceal unfavorable past activities by excluding dates and (2) not listing appropriate reference sources. Other things to check for include health and legal problems.

The reviewer should look particularly at references from previous employers to make sure each employment situation is represented. Read between the lines on health records. Look for gaps in employment or school records. The interviewer can request more detailed explanations concerning those areas where possible discrepancies have been identified. Most often, candidates will give perfectly acceptable explanations regarding the discrepancies, but occasionally interviews uncover serious problems by a discrepancy review.

Reference Check

If the job candidate has had previous teaching experience and is one of the final candidates being considered for the position, a personal telephone contact with the previous principal or some other school administrator who is acquainted with the candidate is usually helpful. Often, interviewers can obtain more information during a phone call than from a written reference.

Care must be taken, however, in the manner in which questions are asked. Similarly, one must be careful in answering any questions regarding a previous employee. The courts have held that in cases of employee nonreemployment where no charges have been officially brought and where no dismissal hearing has been held, an employer is restricted in the negative comments he or she may make about a previous employee. This is based on the concept that such comments could limit the opportunity of that former employee to obtain employment elsewhere and therefore place a limit on that former employees "liberty," a right that is protected under the amendments to the federal Constitution.[3] Therefore, employers must use care in stating opinions regarding former employees' performance.

These court decisions, however, do not prevent one from either asking for references or in answering questions. Nevertheless, they do signal that one must stick to the facts rather than delving into opinion or gossip. Similarly when asking for information from a previous employer, recognize that this individual is under the same limitation, and should hesitate in answering questions of a speculative nature. Ask for factual information about the previous employee. One very telling question that the former employer can answer is: "If the person in question would seek a job in your school again, would you rehire him or her?" If the answer is anything but extremely positive, it should raise a caution flag for you.

The Job Interview

The job interview has several basic functions. It provides an opportunity for the candidate to clarify any apparent discrepancies found in the written job application. The job interview, however, goes beyond the written application by allowing the principal and staff to gather information in greater depth than can be obtained from written materials only.

The interview also allows the principal and staff to gain insights into the personality and interpersonal skills of the applicant. Teaching is a "people" business, and teachers must be able to relate well to other adults and children. Research has shown that good verbal skills are particularly significant in determining the quality of a teacher. These skills can best be assessed through an interview. Whenever possible, an employment recommendation should be based on group interaction with the principal and the existing staff.

Interviews should be arranged to involve teachers, department heads, and team members in the process. This is one additional way to empower teachers. Some will argue that under the concept of site-based management, your local site board should also be involved. We believe that staff selection is a task to be delegated to the professional staff based on policy set by the local site board, but that board members should not be involved directly in the selection process. The one exception to this might be if the central office continues to dictate personnel placements for the school. Then the clout of site-based management might be needed to veto unwanted placements.

When staff members are asked to participate in the interview process, they also are obligated to follow the EEOC guidelines regarding appropriate questions. It is usually wise to hold a short refresher course before staff members interview candidates to remind them of appropriate and inappropriate questions.

Interviews can be conducted using a variety of different formats. Here is an interview agenda that is well accepted:

1. *Establish the atmosphere*. Open the interview slowly and try to create a warm, pleasant relaxed atmosphere that will reduce the candidate's anxiety.

2. *Ask focused questions*. Such questions will elicit the knowledge and information needed about the candidate. The principal and staff want to learn of his or her perceptions of personal strengths and weaknesses, his or her understanding and philosophy of education, his or her verbal fluency, and his or her ability to project enthusiasm. The use of "what if" questions often works well to get the candidate indirectly to share these beliefs and attitudes with you.

3. *Be an active listener.* Ask open-ended questions rather than yes-no questions. Support the candidate verbally with "uh-huhs," or "tell me more." He or she should be contributing about 70 percent of the conversation to the interviewers' 30 percent during the interview.

4. *Share school information with the candidate*. Remember the candidate also has a decision to make ("Do I want to come to work for you?"). Tell him or her about the specific job vacancy; with whom he or she may be working, particularly if those individuals met the candidate; the kinds of children enrolled in the school; particular programs that the school may have; and information about the school community if the candidate is not from that area.

5. *Close the interview.* Thank the individual for his or her time and openness. Share the next steps in the selection process including when he or she might expect to hear from the school or how he or she might keep up with the decision process.

6. *Write out your notes.* Gather information from the others who participated in the interview process. Often a team discussion works well. If several candidates are to be interviewed before a decision is made, the use of a checklist or some formatted method of recording perceptions is wise so that later comparison can be more objective.

EMPLOYEE PROBATIONARY STATUS

The selection process for staff continues through the probationary phase for new employees. Most states have a one- to three-year probationary period during which the employee is on a continuing contract before receiving tenured employment. During this period, the principal and staff must reaffirm the original decision to employ a particular staff member. Usually, the contract renews automatically around April 15 unless notification is given to the teacher for nonrenewal. Through the continuation of the orientation phase and evaluation of instructional competence, which is discussed in more detail in a subsequent chapter, the emphasis for staff development is on improving the quality of teaching. The selection process is usually considered complete only when tenure is granted. During this probationary period, the principal must consider the possibility of termination or nonrenewal of the contract when there is reason to suspect that the original selection was not wise.

TEACHER TENURE

One of the most misunderstood concepts in education is tenure. It is not, as often believed, a guarantee of a job from which dismissal is all but impossible. Rather, in most states, tenure is simply a statement of the guarantee of due process assuring exercise of academic freedom for the teacher by allowing dismissal only for specific causes listed in the tenure law. Tenure does not guarantee the right to a job. If the job is abolished or a teacher is found to be incompetent, insubordinate, or guilty of a variety of socially unacceptable behaviors, that teacher can be dismissed, with proper due process.

In the last few years, federal courts have broadened their decisions regarding due process and human rights to the point that due-process guarantees, including many of the guarantees found in the tenure laws, have been extended to most employees. As a result, probationary teachers are now guaranteed many of the same due-process rights afforded tenured teachers in the past.[4]

INVOLUNTARY TERMINATION

An extremely poor or incompetent teacher should never be kept on the staff of a school simply because dismissal is difficult. The law establishes definite rights for employer and employee. Procedural due process is guaranteed, but due process does not mean that teachers cannot be dismissed. What it does mean is that teachers have specific rights, such as the right to a hearing, the right to be treated in a fair and nondiscriminatory fashion, and the right to require that just cause be shown for a dismissal action. The law may be more specific about the causes and process of dismissal for teachers under tenure, but dismissal can still be accomplished.

Every step in a dismissal action should be carried out on the assumption that it will ultimately go to court. This attitude is the best way to prevent court action. Rarely will an attorney engaged by a dismissed teacher or provided by a teacher association take a case to court if the school district has prepared its action carefully. When the courts reject the dismissal and order reinstatement of a teacher, it is most often because of improper procedure on the part of the school district and less likely due to teacher behavior.

Preparation for Dismissal

Dismissal decisions should not be made quickly. A tentative decision not to rehire a first-year teacher for the following year should be contemplated three to four months before the deadline for contract renewal. For a tenured teacher, often two or three years are needed to build a case defensible in court to reverse earlier recommendations that were positive enough to have resulted in tenure, even though the earlier recommendations may have been a mistake. Unfortunately, poor personnel records and poor evaluation procedures are common in school districts.

The defense attorney will often demand to see the entire personnel file for a teacher being dismissed. If positive evaluations have been given in the past, even though they were unjustified, a greater collection of data of a negative nature is required to offset them. Evidence that the teacher received specific notice of inadequacy and was offered help is important.

In a hearing, the courts will try to answer the following questions: Was procedural due process used? Is the evidence appropriate and supportive of the case? Was the employee discriminated against? Were efforts made to help the employee? Did the employee have prior knowledge that his or her work was unsatisfactory? Was the employee provided time and the opportunity to improve or correct whatever deficiencies existed?

Due Process

Teachers must be given timely notice of the decision not to rehire. If contract renewal comes on April 15, with a two-week hearing notice deadline, employees should be notified by April 1. A certified letter is the best way of assuring a record of such notification. Employees must be informed that they have the opportunity for and the right to a hearing. The hearing time, date, and place should be stated in the letter. If the teacher is tenured, the letter should also include the specific causes or charges for dismissal. Recent due process decisions from the courts in some cases make it highly advisable to provide this opportunity for a hearing to nontenured teachers as well as to those who have tenure.[5, 6, 7]

Appropriateness of Evidence

Evidence should be firsthand, factual, and documented accurately with appropriate dates. If the offense is cumulative in nature, the collection of data should also be cumulative. Descriptive notes of supervisory meetings and conferences—for example, expressing agreed-upon outcomes and a statement describing the extent of the implementation or the lack thereof on the part of the teacher—should be included. The statements should be objective. Rather than stating, "This teacher did a poor job of teaching today," the note should state that in presenting a lesson on the Civil War the teacher did not hold the interest of the class, the students did not understand the lesson as presented, and the class became unruly while under the teacher's direction. Include the date; the time; the events that led up to the conference, such as the previous involvement of a supervisor; and any immediate follow-up action that was taken. A note might simply read, "Mr. Smith arrived at school at 8:30 on December 2, 3, and 4. His designated time of arrival is 8:00. He has been notified of this deficiency." This is not a judgmental statement but a simple statement of fact. Such items, properly collected, can be used to support a claim of incompetence, neglect of duty, or insubordination. The important thing to remember is to record facts, not opinions, and to do this in a timely fashion.

Equal Rights

Was the employee treated in a fair and nondiscriminatory manner? Was anything done to or for this employee that was not done or available to other employees? Was the assignment unfair? Was the teacher asked to do more or less than the rest of the staff? Was supervision uniform? A grossly unequal schedule for supervision, for example, can be construed to be harassment. When problems arise, however, it is not unreasonable for supervision to increase as long as the time sequence can be demonstrated. Supervisory appointments and documentation included only in the file of the teacher being dismissed with no evidence of supervision included in the files of the other members of the staff, however, will often be looked upon as discriminatory action by the courts.

Efforts to Help the Teacher

The courts will want to know what was done to make this individual an effective employee. Was adequate supervision of a helping nature developed? Was adequate time given for the improvement effort? If not, the courts may not uphold the dismissal action but may reinstate the employee, suggesting that the supervisory staff provide assistance.

Most often, when the principal is well prepared and has central-office support, teacher dismissal, while serious, will take place quietly. A teacher who knows that school officials are well prepared most often will not request a hearing and will simply resign. Most cases resulting in the failure to dismiss are a result of poor preparation and improper procedure on the part of the school district. See Figure 10.3 for a flowchart for employee dismissal procedures.

VOLUNTARY TERMINATION

Each year staff members will resign from a school for a variety of reasons: retirement, transfers, better jobs, starting a family, going back to school, and incompetence. In every case the principal should hold a termination interview before that person departs. Several basic purposes exist for such an interview. Of primary concern is the help the school might offer the individual in adjusting to a new life situation.

Second, the interview should be an opportunity to investigate the perceptions of the departing employee regarding the operation of the school. At times, principals have difficulty getting good information about the operation of the school and the existing climate within the staff. Often, departing employees will be very candid about their perceptions concerning existing problems. They may even identify some previously hidden reason for leaving.

Finally, the interview can be useful in identifying prospects for substitute, part-time, volunteer, and future employment when the departing employee is planning to remain within the community. Retired teachers, or those who are staying home to rear a family, are particularly good candidates for part-time employment or volunteer positions.

SUMMARY

The search for and the employment of new staff members is one of the most important tasks of a school administrator. The process begins with the determination of staff needs—including recruitment, selection, orientation, and staff development—and culminates with the placement of the employee on tenure.

Termination of employees, voluntarily or involuntarily, will occur in most schools each year. The principal needs to conduct exit interviews with all terminating employees. Involuntary termination is usually a difficult, but sometimes necessary, task. An important point in staff dismissal is following due process and ensuring that the employee's rights have not been violated.

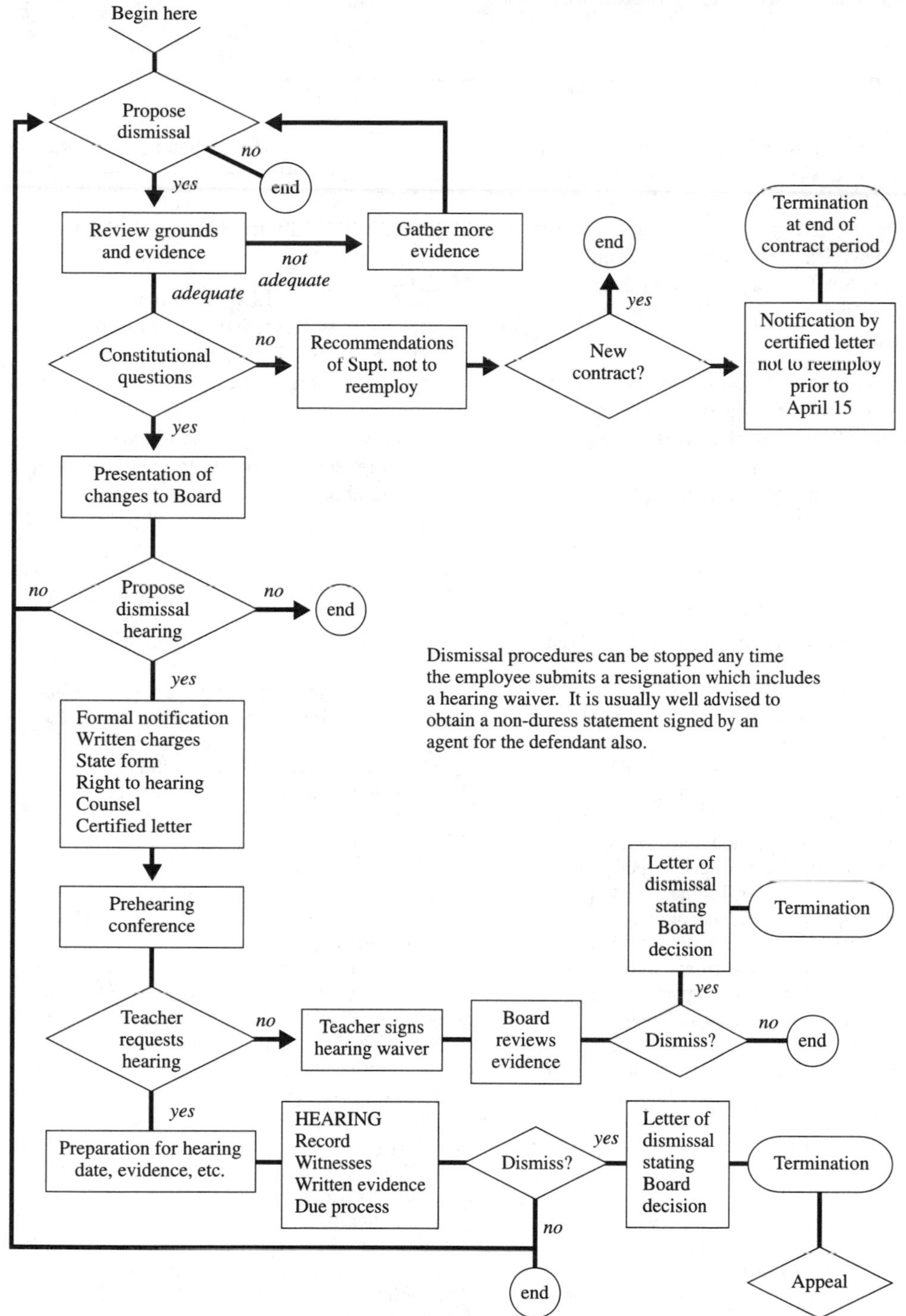

FIGURE 10.3 Steps in Dismissal Procedures

Source: Larry W. Hughes and Gerald C. Ubben, *The Elementary Principal's Handbook: A Guide to Effective Action*, 4th ed. Boston: Allyn and Bacon, 1994, p. 248. Used with permission.

ACTIVITIES

1. Review Case Studies 7, 12, and 16 at the end of this book. Analyze the problems presented and apply the concepts of staff evaluation developed in this chapter. What approach would you use in addressing the problems? Set forth a strategy to overcome the difficulties faced by the individuals in these cases.

2. Develop a plan for the evaluation of the staff in your school. Over what portion of the year should it run? How much of your time will it take to conduct an evaluation of your faculty members? Should you evaluate all teachers each year? If not, which teachers get priority evaluations? What about other nonteaching staff members? What is your responsibility for their evaluation? How much of your time will this take?

3. Turn to the ISLLC Standards found in Appendix B. Review the performances listed with Standard Three. Which of the performance statements best support the human resources concepts discussed in this chapter? What weakness do you find in your school's human resources management? How would you go about correcting them?

ENDNOTES

1. G. C. Ubben, class lecture, University of Tennessee, Knoxville, October 1995.
2. Gerald C. Ubben, "Selecting Personnel," *Principal's Audio Journal 1* (December 1974). Cassette Services, St. Paul, VA.
3. *Board or Regents* v. *Roth,* 92 S. Ct. 2701 (1972). This case dealt with the nonreemployment of a nontenured teacher who had difficulty obtaining another job because of comments made by the administrators of the nonreemploying school. The teacher charged that his right to "liberty" was violated by his inability to obtain other employment because of his lack of opportunity to defend himself against unheard charges. The Supreme Court found that his due process rights were violated and ordered that he be given a hearing and back pay.
4. See Chapter 16 for information about the steps in procedural due process.
5. See Chapter 16, especially the reference to *Illinois Education Association* v. *Board of Education,* 320 N.E. 2nd 240 (Ill. App. 1974).
6. Cases Related to Due Process—Teacher Dismissal
   - **a.** *Board of Regents* v. *Roth,* 92 S. Ct. 2701 (1972) and *Perry* v. *Sunderman,* 928 Ct. 2694 (1972). These are the precedent-setting cases regarding due process just as *Brown* v. *Board of Education* set the precedent for discrimination cases.
   - **b.** *Paul* v. *Davis,* 424 U.S. 693 (1976); *Bishop* v. *Wood,* 246 U.S. 341 (1976); and *Meachum* v. *Fano,* 427 U.S. 215 (1970).
   - **c.** 7th Cir., the Court of Appeals in *Confederation of Police* v. *City of Chicago,* 547 F. 2d 375 (1977).
   - **d.** *Codd* v. *Velger,* 97 S. Ct. 882 (1977).
   - **e.** *Arnet* v. *Kennedy,* 416 U.S. 134 (1974).
   - **f.** *Peacock* v. *Board of Regents,* 510 F 2d 1324 (9th Cir.)
   - **g.** *Withrow* v. *Larken,* 421 U.S. 35 (1975).
   - **h.** Hortonville 96S Ct. 2308.
   - **i.** *Mt. Healthy City School District* v. *Doyle,* 97 S. Ct. 568 (1977).
7. Although most state tenure laws and continuing contract laws in and of themselves do not require a hearing for nontenured staff, the federal Constitution and the Civil Rights Act of 1964 might. According to a series of court decisions over recent years, a teacher is considered to have certain rights under the First and Fourteenth Amendments to the Constitution. While nonrenewal of a contract does not require a hearing, dismissal does. If a denial-of-freedom-of-speech claim is made, a hearing is advisable, and if the case is receiving much publicity so as to endanger the individual's opportunity for other employment, a hearing should be held. Also, if discrimination is charged, a hearing should be held. If an opportunity for a hearing is not granted, the teacher may later file a complaint charging violation of due process.

SELECTED READINGS

Allen, Dwight W., Roy D. Nichols, Jr., and Alyce C. LeBlanc. "The Prime Teacher Appraisal Program: 2 + 2 for Teachers," *The High School Magazine 4,* no. 4 (June/July 1997).

Faltz, Darlene. "Innovative Programs Affect Recruitment of Teachers." *Black Collegian 28,* no. 2 (February 1998): 151–152.

Ganser, Tom, and Ruth Koskela. "A Comparison of Six Wisconsin Mentoring Programs for Beginning Teachers." *NASSP Bulletin 81,* no. 591 (October 1997): 71–80.

Jackson, Cleaster M. "Assisting Marginal Teachers: A Training Model." *Principal 77,* no. 1 (September 1997).

Lewis, A. C. "Just say no to unqualified teachers." *Phi Delta Kappan 80* (November 1998)

Marshall, Patricia, Debra Baaucom, and Allison Webb. "Do You Have Tenure, and Do You Really Want It?" *The Clearing House 71* (May/June 1998): 302–304.

Martin, Cynthia. "Hiring the Right Person: Techniques for Principals." *NASSP Bulletin 77,* no. 550 (February 1993): 79–83.

Norton, Scott M. "The Work of the School Principal in the Area of Human Resources Administration in Arizona." *NASSP Bulletin* (January 1999): 108–113.

Pawlas, George E. "The Structured Interview: Three Dozen Questions To Ask Prospective Teachers." *NASSP Bulletin 79,* no. 567 (January 1995): 62–65.

Ralphcyril, Edwin G., Kesten Hellmut, and Lang Douglas Smith. "Hiring New Teachers: What Do School Districts Look For?" *Journal of Teacher Education 49,* no. 1 (January/February 1999): 47–56.

Sullivan, Kathleen A. and Perry A. Zirkel. "Documentation in Teacher Evaluation: What Does the Professional Literature Say?" *NASSP Bulletin 83,* no. 607 (May 1999): 48–58.

Vann, Allan S. "The Pre-Employment Interview: Asking the Right Questions." *Principal 73,* no. 3 (January 1994): 38–41.

Weld, Jeffery. "Attracting and Retaining High Quality Professionals in Science Education." *Phi Delta Kappan 79* (March 1998).

CHAPTER ELEVEN

RESTRUCTURING THE DEPLOYMENT OF INSTRUCTIONAL PERSONNEL

Inherent in any good staffing design is optimal utilization of staff. Staff planning must take into account the present needs and functions of the members of the organization, as well as the school's long-range goals and plans that might modify hiring practices in the future.

—J. Lloyd Trump[1]

One of the greatest responsibilities assigned to a principal is organizing and assigning staff in the school. Included in normal staffing responsibilities is the deployment of all employees and volunteer workers to the instructional program and service functions of the school. Central office administrators and supervisors often have a hand in these assignments, but especially with the advent of site-based management, the responsibility, and particularly the final decision, rest with the principal and staff. Inherent in any good staffing design is optimal utilization of staff. Staff planning must take into account the present needs and functions of the members of the organization as well as the school's long-range goals and plans that might modify hiring practices in the future.

Professional employees in school organizations often have great insight and usually excellent ideas of how a school could be improved. They also have the need for both personal development and professional growth through interaction with other professionals in the school. School organization, however, often works against this opportunity for interaction because of self-contained classrooms that isolate teachers for up to six hours each day. The development and vitality of the school as a learning community is also dependent on the opportunity and ability of the school staff to interact with each other. One way for school professionals to interact with each other is to participate in management decisions at the building level that affect the school's curriculum and instruction.

EMPOWERMENT

Ultimately, what is wanted of teachers is quality instruction and for learning to take place between teachers and students. There are many functions within the school organization that must be properly balanced for this to be maximized. Too little attention on the part of administration regarding what goes on in each classroom can lead to lack of coordination of the curriculum, great variation in the quality of teaching, and great variation in the motivation of teachers. On the other hand, too much control or structure over teachers or centralization of authority over the classroom might produce some uniformity but take away teachers' autonomy, negatively affecting teacher motivation and thus reducing the quality of instruction among the better teachers.

What is desired is a fine balance that can adequately empower teachers to exercise appropriate professional judgment while still ensuring the coordination of the curriculum and supervision of instruction. The appropriate empowerment of teachers must lie in the amount of authority granted, methods of accountability used to ensure responsibility, and the organizational structures created to maintain the proper communication flow necessary to carry out these tasks.[2]

LEARNING COMMUNITIES

The organization of the staff within the school and the opportunities faculty members have to interact with other faculty members in shared responsibilities is important to the growth and development of the school as a learning community. The organization of the faculty may enhance or inhibit communication among staff members and the development of shared values and beliefs. In his writing on learning organizations, Peter Senge[3] suggested that systems thinking needs be employed for improvement and growth to take place within organizations. Sergiovanni[4] further expanded the idea in his writing on learning communities. He described a preferred school learning community to include parents, students, teachers, and administrators who have shared values, purpose, and commitments and to bond together around this common cause.

Learning community norms become major motivational forces for determining the best strategies for improving the systems of teaching and learning. To create an environment within the school that enhances the nurturing of learning communities, principals must practice a very different kind of leadership behavior than is typically found in traditional corporate top-down organizational structures. The norms of the group give meaning to the community life. The norms become motivators and guide the group together as colleagues. The role of the leader becomes one of facilitating group conversation and helping guide the members of the learning community to an acceptable set of values and beliefs. Teachers become leaders and in turn work to instill the values of a learning organization in their students and parents.

ORGANIZING FOR LEARNING COMMUNITY DEVELOPMENT

A staff cannot be ordered to be a learning community. It must be grown as a culture, with common values, beliefs, vision, and mission. This growth and maturation takes time. A culture can be enhanced, however, as one would enhance a biological culture by creating an environment that encourages growth. The development of the culture of the school can be accelerated or retarded by the way the school is organized.

Traditionally, staffing has been by simple unit-classroom analysis—that is, one teacher, one group of students, one room, sometimes one instructional format, and sometimes one subject. Staffing plans have been built and modified from year to year using this basic classroom unit. Such a procedure is very restrictive for learning community development, particularly when used in conjunction with some of the curricular, instructional, and grouping ideas presented in previous chapters. Organizing teachers into teaching teams offers several desirable alternatives to single classroom units.

Team staffing has been used with varying degrees of success in schools for years. Persuasive arguments can be given both for team staff organizations as well as self-contained classrooms. Arguments favoring team teaching are:

1. A teaching team provides variation for the children because the students have contact with a set of teachers.
2. Teacher productivity generally increases under a team arrangement since teachers tend to support each other in the achievement of the goals of the learning community.
3. Flexibility of grouping becomes possible and building-level scheduling can be greatly simplified when teachers are working together in a team.
4. The advantages of both specialization and generalization can be obtained when teachers specialize in either or both the curricular and instructional dimension within the team and still have the opportunity to observe the whole child as that child works with the team over the major portion of the day.
5. Individualized instruction can more easily be attained with the team of teachers sharing the variety of instructional tasks necessary to successfully implement an individualized program.

On the other hand, some still argue that self-contained classes are better. Reasons favoring self-contained classrooms are as follows:

1. Teacher training and experience traditionally has been for the self-contained classroom. Many teachers favor it because they know it best.
2. Buildings are designed for self-contained classrooms, not for team arrangements, and they simply do not lend themselves to team teaching.
3. When placed on teams, teachers develop difficulties in interpersonal relationships because of different personalities, teaching styles, or philosophies.

4. Team teaching requires a great deal of additional time in planning on the part of the teacher that could be devoted to children or to preparation of lessons in the self-contained classroom.

However, when consideration is given to the overall management of instruction, the arguments favoring team staffing patterns are clearly superior because of their ability to foster learning community development.

STAFFING PATTERNS FOR ELEMENTARY AND MIDDLE SCHOOLS

An elementary or middle school staff can be organized in a variety of different ways depending on its desired results. Learning communities that utilize teams of teachers with responsibility for a common group of students are favored by the authors. The integrated contributions of several teachers, the teacher growth enhanced by common planning and quality circles, and the collective team concern for the growth of their students generates a synergism that is difficult to match in the traditional self-contained classroom.

Variations in Staff Assignments

A variety of different staffing options are possible for a given student population, ranging from the traditional self-contained classroom under the direction of one teacher to a variety of learning community models involving regular teachers, specialists, instructional assistants, parent volunteers, student helpers, etc. For our examples, we use an elementary school enrollment of:

Kindergarten	75
Grade 1	80
Grade 2	95
Grade 3	85
Grade 4	100
Grade 5	90
Grade 6	75

Some elementary schools may have a preschool, grade 6 may be in the middle school, and so the enrollments will be different, but the task is to organize the students and staff into instructional assignments that will provide the best learning environment.

Traditional Self-Contained Classrooms

A traditional staffing pattern with total reliance on self-contained classrooms based on a student-teacher ratio for each classroom of approximately 30 to 1 is shown in Figure 11.1. As is often the case, tough dollar decisions determine when to exceed the 30-

FIGURE 11.1 Staffing for Grade-Level Teams

GRADE	STUDENTS	STAFF TEAM	
K	75	3	
1	80	3	
2	95	3 or 4	
3	85	3	Sp. Ed. 1
4	100	3 or 4	
5	90	3	
6	75	3	Sp. Ed. 1
Specialists	Art, Librarian, Music, P.E.	4	
Principal		1	
	Staff Totals	28	overall ratio: 1–21.4
		30	overall ratio: 1–20.0

pupils-per-classroom figure and when to hire additional staff to reduce the ratio. For a totally self-contained program, the only additional support staff would be the principal and possibly a librarian.

Teachers and Specialists

Usually, a school prefers specialists in certain areas such as special education, art, music, and physical education. Figure 11.2 illustrates a specialist staffing pattern with two special education teachers each taking a class load of 10 to 15 students, thus reducing class size by approximately 1 or 2 students in each room. The art, music, and physical education specialists, on the other hand, either come into the classroom with the regular teacher once or twice a week or take the children from the regular teacher for several periods each week, giving the regular teacher a break. The total staff size is increased by the number of specialists added, increasing the total staff in this example to 28 or 30.

Team Teaching

Teaching teams can easily be implemented as an alternate pattern to those just outlined using the same number of students and staff positions (see Figure 11.2). Each team consists of three or four teachers in grade-level arrangements. The special education teachers attach themselves to either the primary or intermediate teams, dividing their time among the several groups. The art, music, and physical education specialist and the librarian also form a team for staff organization. Advantages as well as disadvantages of team organization have been discussed earlier.

FIGURE 11.2 Grade-Level Teams with Instructional Assistants

		TEAMS		
GRADE	**LEVEL**	*Teachers*		*Instructional Assistants*
K	75	3		+ I.A.
1	80	3	Sp. Ed. 1	+ I.A.
2	95	3		+ I.A.
3	85	3		+ I.A.
4	100	3		+ I.A.
5	90	3	Sp. Ed. 1	+ I.A.
6	75	3		+ I.A.
Specialists: art, music, P.E., librarian		4		+ I.A.
Principal		1		
	Staff Totals	28		8 instructional assistants
		overall staffing ratio: 1–16.7		

Eight instructional assistants can be hired for the salary of two teachers.

Team Teaching with Instructional Assistants

Grade-level teaching teams can be enhanced if each team adds an instructional assistant (I.A.). In many communities, aides can be hired for a minimum wage, or in some cases, volunteers can be used to support the team. The cooperative organization of a team approach permits sharing students. Teachers often prefer to employ instructional assistants rather than additional teachers to reduce class size. If, as shown in Figure 11.2, grades 2 and 4 could function with three-teacher teams instead of four, the salary dollars saved could pay the salary for eight aides (part time if necessary), one for each of the school's teams (see Figure 11.3).

FIGURE 11.3 Staff Utilization in a Team or Learning Community

20 teachers (5 teams, 4 each)	5 instructional assistants
4 teacher specialists	3 clerical assistants
1 principal	8 paraprofessionals
2 special education	overall staffing ratio: 1–16.7
1 librarian	
28	

Teaching staff to support these five groups would be deployed as shown in Figure 11.4. The organizational pattern illustrated in Figure 11.5 results in the same staff requirements but distributes responsibilities more evenly. This type of team organization, coupled with multiage grouping, allows for an extremely even distribution of students. Even when the enrollment numbers vary greatly or when staffing ratios are

Unit 1 4 teachers 1 instructional aide ½ clerical aide 120 children K, 1, 2	**Unit 2** 4 teachers 1 instructional aide ½ clerical aide 120 children K, 1, 2	**Unit 3** 4 teachers 1 special ed. teacher 1 instructional aide ½ clerical aide 120 children 2, 3, 4
Unit 4 4 teachers 1 instructional aide ½ clerical aide 120 children 3, 4, 5	**Unit 5** 4 teachers 1 special ed. teacher 1 instructional aide ½ clerical aide 120 children 4, 5, 6	**Specialists Unit** 1 music teacher 1 art teacher 2 P.E. teachers 1 librarian ½ clerical aide

FIGURE 11.4 Learning Community Design for Staff and Students

FIGURE 11.5 Learning Community Staff Assignments

TEACHER A	TEACHER B	TEACHER C	TEACHER D	P.E. SPECIALIST
25 advisees Team Leader Advisement Coordinator	25 advisees Reading Coordinator	25 advisees Math Coordinator	25 advisees Learning Center Coordinator	20 advisees
Reading (3) Math (2) Writing Crafts Language	Reading (3) Math (2) Science Spelling Learning center	Reading (3) Math (2) Social studies Library Learning center	Reading (3) Math (2) Science Health	

unfavorable, balance can be provided, ensuring uniform availability of instructional services.

Options on Using Staff Specialists

The addition of specialists for special education, reading, math, learning disabilities, physical education, art, and music has been a mixed blessing. Most schools have desperately needed the extra help but have not been able to make maximum use of the talents that specialists can provide.

Part of the problem of using specialists arises from single-classroom organization. The specialist in a "pullout" program is a fifth wheel and often is never fully integrated into the program. Many times, specialists have been set apart in little rooms by themselves to call children out of regular classrooms, disrupting the regular program for the child as well as using their own time very inefficiently.

A team organization leads to a variety of ways to use specialists. In some cases, specialists can best be utilized by dividing their time into fractional units and assigning them to teams for each unit. Following are three examples of how a team organization can utilize the services of specialists or the services provided by special programs.

School 1: Resource Teachers. A school organized in a multiunit fashion similar to the school just discussed was allocated two additional reading and math positions out of federal funds. One was for remedial reading and the other for mathematics. The school decided to integrate these positions fully into the teams so that no specialist would work with more than one team. In order to do this, the specialist positions were divided into fractional units and student loads were adjusted accordingly. Instead of hiring new people for these positions, interested faculty from the existing staff were identified and given the special training necessary for the new assignments. The two positions were divided into four units of time and distributed among the existing staff. Each team was assigned a one-fourth-time reading specialist and a one-fourth-time math specialist. The released staffing money was used to hire two more regular teachers. Specialist services were integrated into each team to make the available instruction relate closely to the organized program. Federal guidelines were met by assigning designated students to these specialists for the appropriate times.

School 2: Special Education—Full Inclusion. In order to provide for full inclusion for children with disabilities within this school, organized according to a multiunit pattern, these children were assigned on an age basis to the appropriate learning community. The two special education teachers for the children with disabilities in this school worked together as a team with the instructional teams in the school. They attended team planning meetings when appropriate and scheduled their visits to coincide with the skill-grouped reading program of the team. During the reading schedule, they became part of the team and took the children with disabilities into expanded reading groups, thus bolstering the reading staff. The children of this school never identified and labeled these two specialists as special education teachers, even though they spent almost all of their time with certain children. A way to save time for the special education staff is to place all the children with disabilities into two or three specified learning communities, reducing the number of different teams with which specialists must work.

School 3: Art, Music, and Physical Education Specialists. In the third school, the art, music, and physical education specialists served two major functions: (1) They served as student advisors along with each of the other four teachers on the team to which they were assigned. They did this during the early minutes of the school day, the noon hour, and the last 30 minutes of the afternoon. (2) During an approximately 2½-hour block in the morning and again each afternoon, two physical education teachers, an art teacher, and a music teacher worked on a unit-rotating basis, taking half of the children from two of the units for instruction in their specialties. Thus, for 2½-hours once or twice a week, each team had a block of time with only half the children and could concentrate on small group instruction activities.

Learning Community Organization

The full integration of a team's instructional program is the key to its success as a learning community. All teachers must share in organizing the curriculum, preferably with an interdisciplinary approach with each teacher carrying a specific independent assignment. The teachers must share the children and together discuss their problems. Specialization in curriculum can be used to reduce the planning required of any particular teacher, but not to the extent that it causes departmentalization of the curriculum. Figure 11.5 illustrates how one learning-community staff divided the workload after much discussion and planning. All of the children were organized into 12 skill groups for reading and 8 for math. Thus, each of the 4 regular teachers had 3 reading skill groups and 2 math skill groups. In addition, each teacher took several other curricular responsibilities for learning-center development as well as for direct instruction. Each team member also assumed some administrative responsibility. The physical education teacher worked directly with the team only part of each day. Each week a schedule was planned.

STAFFING PATTERNS FOR SECONDARY SCHOOLS

General ideas have been presented for staffing design, curricular arrangements, and instructional strategies in elementary and middle schools. How does a high school operating in a traditional mode begin to make the transition to incorporate some of these ideas into its operating model and gain benefits from a learning community model. We begin with an existing high school with a staff of 67 professionals and 1,260 students and show a number of staffing alternatives for their organization. Each staffing pattern takes into account some of the ideas previously discussed in the chapters on curriculum, instruction, and grouping of students. The first model shows how the school might be organized at the present time in a traditional departmental staff organization.

Departmental Staff Organization

The standard departmental staffing arrangement shown in Figure 11.6 divides the high school into nine departments: language arts; social studies; science; math; foreign language; physical education, health, and driver education; fine arts; vocational; and special services. The school is a comprehensive high school with a large vocational program. The special services department is somewhat unique. It includes guidance counselors, one vocational rehabilitation counselor, one special education coordinator, two instructional media specialists, and one person to coordinate both the independent study program and action learning program. The three principals share the school's administration, with one of the assistants responsible for buildings, grounds, lunch-

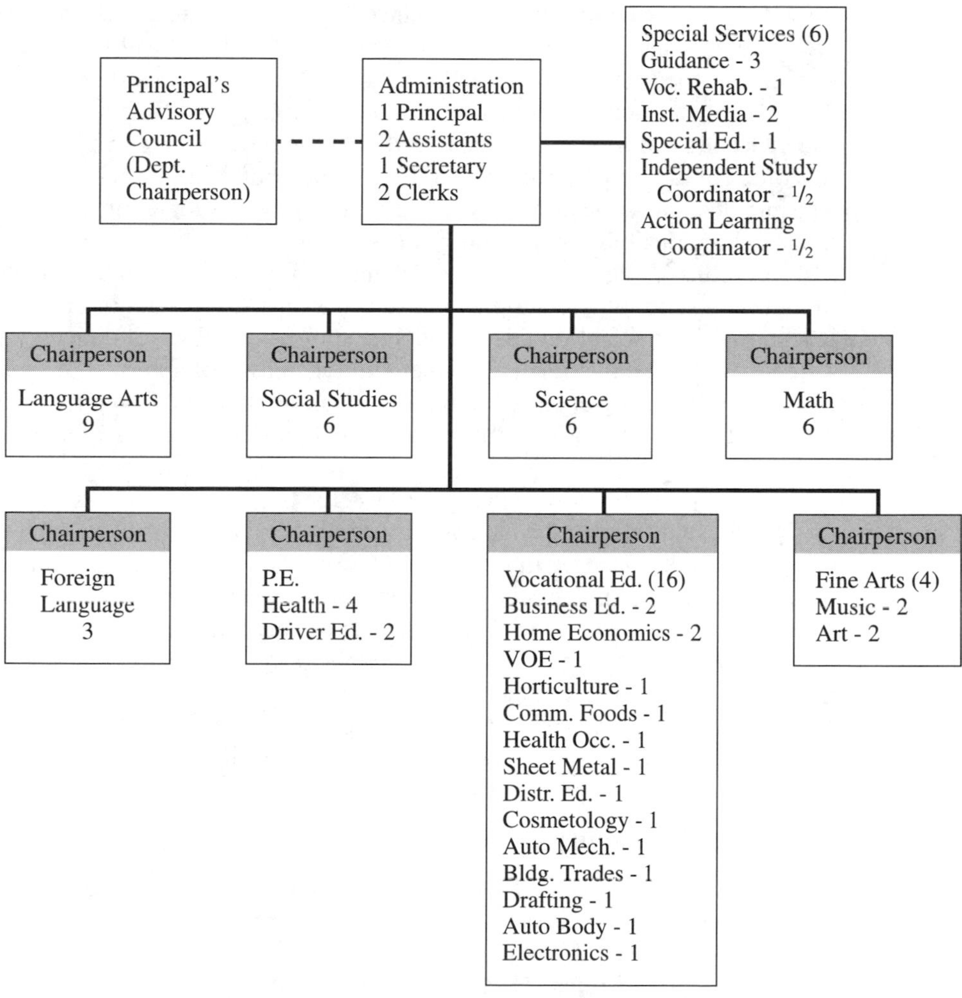

FIGURE 11.6 Standard Departmental High School Staffing Pattern

room, transportation, office management, and some discipline. The other assistant's major responsibility is the curricular and instructional program and the coordination of volunteer services.

Department Head—Role and Responsibilities. A department head coordinates the activities of each department and serves as a member of the principal's advisory council. Figure 11.7 lists possible department head responsibilities.

Learning Community Staffing Patterns

The basic staff of a typical high school, as shown in Figure 11.8, can be used to create numerous variations in team arrangements. Appropriate team designs, however, must provide a good relationship with a planned curricular design, good instructional strategies, and desirable patterns for student grouping. A summary of previous information concerning good design for curriculum, instruction, grouping, and staffing includes the following: team members from two or more disciplines; a differentiated staff including a team leader, team members, aides, clerks, and so on; and a group of 75 to 150 students in a block of time appropriate in length to the number of subjects included in the team. The interdisciplinary team allows for the best options in integrating the curriculum, ease of schooling, flexibility in grouping, and student control.

Interdisciplinary teams can be organized in a variety of ways. One high school organized a series of two-subject, four-teacher teams, consisting of two language arts teachers and two social studies teachers in a three-hour block of time coordinated with a free-floating elective. Each team met with one group of approximately 120 students in the morning and worked with another block of students during the afternoon. The other half of the day for the students involved participating in a regular elective program.[5]

Using the staff outlined in Figure 11.8, the fluid block design organized language arts, social studies, and science teams. One of the main advantages of the fluid block design is its allowance for three basic styles of instruction, ranging from traditional, to team approaches, to individually paced labs.[6] Most of the teachers in the basic required subjects of language arts, social studies, and possibly science must be willing to work in a team arrangement for a fluid block schedule to work. Teachers in other subject areas may join teams, may wish to set up their instruction as an individually paced laboratory (typing, art, foreign languages, and certain math courses lend themselves nicely to individualized labs), or may operate in a traditional-type schedule as in the past.

Learning Community Planning

Learning communities suggest the active participation of staff members in decisions that affect their own areas of responsibility. This includes an expanded role in curriculum and instructional decisions, evaluation decisions, and the day-by-day organizing and scheduling functions. These tasks are most effectively carried out on a team or learning community basis.

FIGURE 11.7 Department Head Responsibilities

Job Description—High School Department Head

1. Coordinate the inventory of textbooks and audiovisual materials.
2. Coordinate the development of an instructional budget for the department.
3. Provide the department staff with information regarding advances and subject matter and promising instructional materials.
4. Coordinate the placement and supervision of student teachers and interns in the department.
5. Recommend special resources and personnel needed to aid the department's instructional staff.
6. Direct department staff in selecting or preparing a written behavioral objective for each curricular area.
7. Seek the advice of a counselor or principal in handling special department problems.
8. Assume responsibility for completing routine reports.
9. Participate in the development of the school's in-service teacher education program.
10. Observe on request the instructional presentations of department staff and provide feedback aimed at improving instruction.
11. Provide individual assistance to new and beginning teachers.
12. Hold the staff accountable for student achievement.
13. Evaluate paraprofessionals assigned to the department.
14. Attend all meetings of the principal's advisory council.
15. Schedule and chair department meetings.
16. Channel information from a variety of sources to the department teachers.
17. Conduct demonstration lessons for department staff members using new materials and procedures.
18. Coordinate the assessment of students and the department based on individual objectives.
19. Plan with appropriate personnel to research activities for the department.
20. Schedule department meetings for goal setting, problem solving, and evaluation.
21. Coordinate the assessment of students' characteristics prior to any grouping.
22. Cooperate with other department chairpersons in coordinating schoolwide facilities and resources.
23. Confer informally with department staff members to discuss ways of improving instruction.
24. Facilitate communication between central office personnel, consultants, and department staff.
25. Participate in the selection of professional staff assigned to the department.
26. Participate in the evaluation of professional staff assigned to the department.

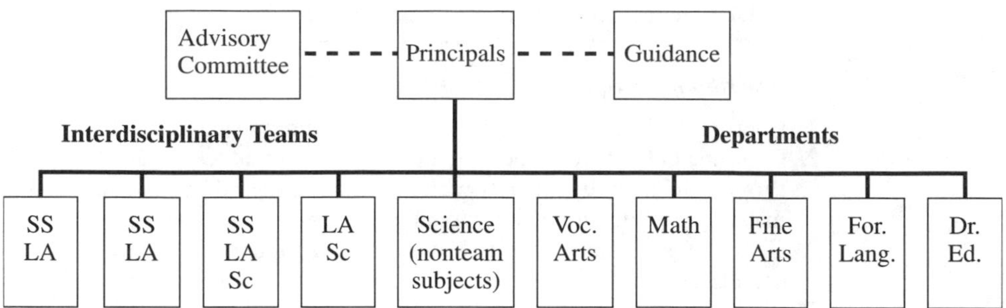

FIGURE 11.8 Interdisciplinary Team Staffing for Fluid Block Schedules

One of the most crucial factors in a successful team operation is adequate planning time and efficient utilization of that time. If at all possible, team planning should occur during the regular school day. Planning should be regularly scheduled; at least two hours per week are needed in a minimum of one-hour blocks. Building an agenda for team meetings needs to be an opportunity for all team members to share in the planning for the team. One good way is to place an agenda planning sheet in a central location for the team to list items they wish to discuss at the next scheduled meeting. Some principals have the teams prepare their agenda so that copies can be quickly reproduced and distributed to team members, as well as to other key people such as the librarian, special education teacher, or the principal, all of whom may want to attend the team meeting. Each meeting should have a designated chairperson, and a secretary for the team should keep minutes of the meeting. Figure 11.9 is an example of a form to be used for agenda building.

Team Planning Tasks

A variety of different planning tasks of both a long- and short-term nature need to be carried out by each team. Effective use of planning time can usually be enhanced by focusing on a particular purpose during a meeting. The following five types of planning meetings are suggested with recommendations regarding frequency:

1. *Goal-Setting Meeting.* One goal-setting meeting should be held each semester to look at the philosophy of the school, the curriculum guidelines existing for its direction, and the identification of goals for the particular group of students for whom the team is responsible. These goals would be long range in nature and would be things to work toward over a semester or year.

2. *Design Meeting.* A design meeting is a planning meeting to select instructional topics and develop instructional units. Principles and objectives as well as general ideas for the unit are considered. After the topic has been selected, one team member is usually assigned the responsibility of drafting the unit. When the draft is ready, the team modifies and builds on the design. Specific objectives are listed, overall responsibility for each member of the team is outlined, and the calendar of events is developed

Team: 4 - A Date of Meeting: 10/14

I. Students

Name	*Person Presenting*	*Concern*	*Est. Time Needed*
Bill Fox	Mary	attendance	5 m.
Nancy York	Jane	uncomp. assign.	5 m.

II. Program Development

Area	*Person Presenting*	*Est. Time Needed*
Unit—election	Gary	20 m.
Unit—health	Mary	to next time

III. Staff Development

Area	*Person Presenting*	*Est. Time Needed*
accelerated learning	Pat	20 m.

IV. Administrative

Area	*Person Presenting*	*Est. Time Needed*
lunchtime	Pat	5 m.
Friday's assembly	Pat	5 m.

FIGURE 11.9 Form for Agenda Building

with specific target dates. Methods of student evaluation are also planned. One of these meetings is necessary for each new unit, and a minimum of one each quarter or marking period is essential.

3. *Grouping or Scheduling Meeting.* This planning meeting outlines activities for the next week or two, defining specific instructional plans, organizing students into appropriate groups, and constructing the weekly calendar and daily schedule. One of these meetings is needed at least once every two weeks, if not weekly.

4. *Situational Meeting.* This meeting focuses on individual children. Various children within the group are discussed by the various members of the team to coordinate information and develop plans for learning activities for that child. The teacher advisor for the particular child has the responsibility of carrying out team decisions. These meetings should probably be held each week, with each teacher advisor determining which children need to be discussed by the team.

5. *Evaluation Meeting.* The major focus of this meeting should be the evaluation of the instructional program and units. Questions to be asked are: Did we achieve our goals? What were our strengths? What were our shortcomings? How well did we function together as a team? One of these meetings should be held each quarter immediately after the close of the quarter or immediately after the completion of a major unit.

Team Meeting Schedule

Assuming a planning schedule that allows for two planning meetings per team each week in a six-week instructional period, a schedule of team meetings for the period might look like Figure 11.10. Extra grouping and scheduling meetings as well as situational meetings are scheduled early in the year to work through changes in enrollment and to place children better as more data are available.

THE SCHOOL AS A LEARNING COMMUNITY

This chapter has focused on the small clusters of teachers and staff linked with students and parents as the nucleus of a learning community. However, in practice, the entire school should be one large learning community linked with common values, beliefs, vision, and goals working across departments, grade levels, or interdisciplinary teams. Management teams or schoolwide councils become a way of establishing communication links to help in the development of *community* across the school.

A learning community, to function successfully, requires greatly increased participation in school decisions on the part of staff members. An excellent way to involve the faculty is through the formation of a faculty council to improve the school's curricular and instructional program. If the school has a multiunit learning community design, as described in this chapter, this faculty council should be made up of the head of each learning community and the principal (see Figure 11.11); otherwise, department heads or grade level chairpersons would be appropriate. Topics appropriate for consideration

FIGURE 11.10 Schedule of Team Meetings

Two team meetings should be held each week.

Prior to school year	■ Goal setting for the semester ■ Design of units for the first grading period ■ Initial grouping and scheduling of students assigned to team
Week 1	■ Situational meeting ■ Grouping and scheduling meeting
Week 2	■ Situational meeting ■ Grouping and scheduling meeting
Week 3	■ Situational meeting ■ Grouping and scheduling meeting
Week 4	■ Situational meeting ■ Design meeting—plans for the next period meeting
Week 5	■ Situational meeting ■ Design meeting
Week 6	■ Situational meeting ■ Evaluation meeting (of teaching)
Week 7 (repeats Week 1)	■ Situational meeting ■ Grouping and scheduling meeting

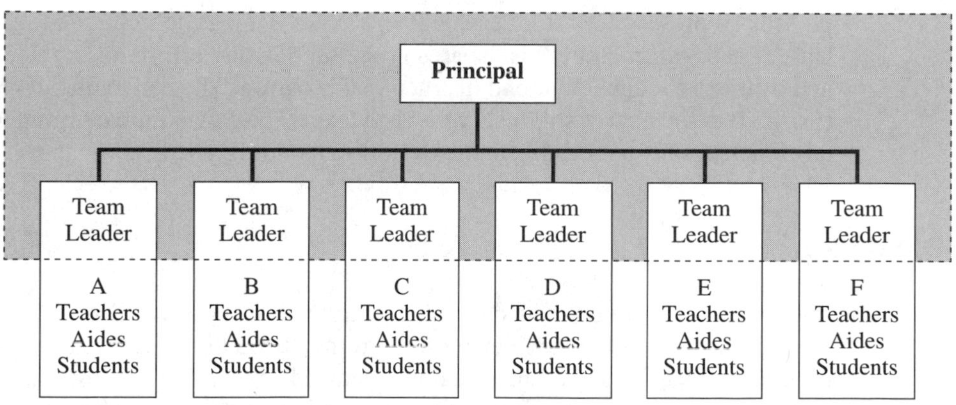

The staff within the dotted line makes up the Faculty Council.

FIGURE 11.11 Faculty Council

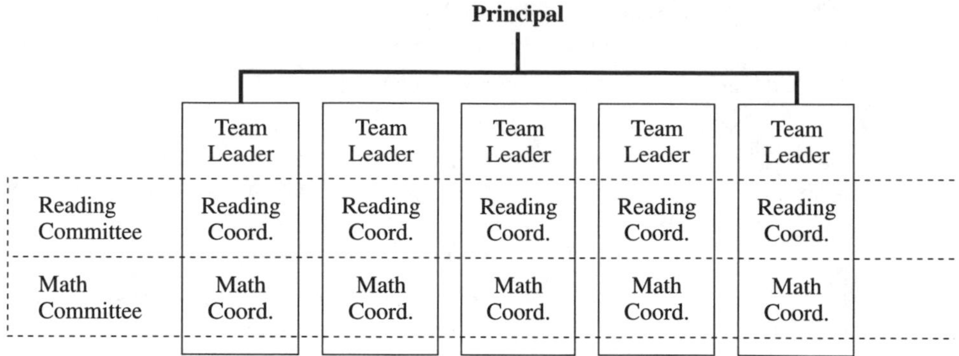

FIGURE 11.12 Multiunit Curricular Coordinating Committee's Matrix Management

by this advisory council to the principal include virtually any significant decision that will require staff cooperation and is in their field of expertise. A quality circle approach is appropriate for some of the advisory council activities.

Matrix Management

In a similar fashion to the faculty council, special coordinating committees should be organized to deal with curricular areas such as reading, math, social studies, or any area that requires cross-unit coordination. These committees may be permanent or temporary in nature, depending on the assignment.

If a multiunit staffing design is used, these committees can best be formed with one teacher from each team (Figure 11.12). The curriculum committee, thus formed, provides representation from each of the teams as well as communication back to each team. Each staff member also shares in the schoolwide efforts to provide community and thrust to the curricular and instructional program. The major line of responsibility (vertical) in the matrix still rests with each team. The curriculum committees (horizontal) function only to coordinate the overall school program.

SUMMARY

The principal has many plans to make regarding how best to utilize the staff. Many of these plans rest on earlier decisions regarding curriculum, instructional formats, and grouping of students. Teaching teams organized as learning communities offer maximum flexibility for instructional programming but attention must be given to good team planning for it to work. The appropriate use of specialists must also be considered in elementary and middle school staffing. Secondary school staffing patterns can be designed with flexibility in mind as well. A variety of staffing patterns can be used to facilitate learning communities with teaching teams or departmental units. Schoolwide learning community structures for overall management should take several forms, including a school management council and curriculum or grade-level committees.

ACTIVITIES

1. How would you proceed to restructure your school's staff deployment? Why would it be important to integrate your plans on instructional and curriculum restructuring with your plans on staff restructuring?
2. Review Case Studies 1, 7, and 20 at the end of this book. Analyze the problems presented and apply the staff deployment concepts developed in this chapter. What approach would you use in addressing the problems? Set forth a strategy to overcome the difficulties faced by the school as well as ways to deal with individual teachers.
3. Turn to the ISLLC Standards found in Appendix B. Review the performances listed in Standard Three. Which of the performance statements best support the learning community concepts proposed in this chapter? How could you better organize your school's staff to facilitate learning community development?

ENDNOTES

1. J. Lloyd Trump, *Images of the Future,* Experimental Study of the Utilization of Staff in the Secondary Schools and the National Association of Secondary School Principals, 1959.
2. Gene I. Maeroff, "A Blueprint for Empowering Teachers," *Phi Delta Kappan 69,* no. 7 (March 1988): 472–477.
3. Senge, Peter M., *The Fifth Discipline: The Art and Practice of the Learning Organization* (New York: Doubleday/Currency, 1990).
4. Thomas J. Sergiovanni, *Moral Leadership: Getting to the Heart of School Improvement.* (San Francisco: Jossey-Bass, 1992).
5. Gerald C. Ubben, "A Fluid Block Schedule," *NASSP Bulletin 60* (February 1976): 104–111.
6. See the section in Chapter 12 on block schedules.

SELECTED READINGS

Cromwell, Sharon. "Critical Friends Groups: Catalysts for School Change." *Education World* (November 1999).

Denault, Linda E. "Restructuring? Keep It Simple...Consider Looping!" *The Delta Kappa Gamma Bulletin 65,* no. 4 (Summer 1999): 19–26.

Donaldson, G. A. "Working Smarter Together." *Educational Leadership 2* (1993): 12–16.

Donavel, David F. *Restructuring the High School: The Renaissance Program.* Written version of presentation at the Annual Meeting of the National Association of Secondary School Principals, San Diego, CA, February 1990. (ERIC Document Service No. ED 321 390).

Erb, Thomas O. "Meeting the Needs of Young Adolescents on Interdisciplinary Teams: The Growing Research Base." *Childhood Education, 73* no. 5 (1997): 309–311.

Fullan, M. G., and A. Hargreaves. *What's Worth Fighting For: Working Together for Your School* (Andover, MA: Regional Laboratory of the Northeast and Islands, 1991).

Fullan, M. G., and C. Rolheiser-Bennett. "Linking Classrooms and School Improvement." *Educational Leadership 8* (1990): 13–19.

Hansen, J. Merrell, and John Childs. "Creating a School Where People Like to Be." *Educational Leadership* (September 1998): 14–17.

Herbert, Elizabeth A. "Rugtime for Teachers: Reinventing the Faculty Meeting." *Phi Delta Kappan 81,* no. 3 (November 1999).

Idol, L., A. Nevis, and P. Paolucci-Whitcomb. *Collaborative Consultation* (Austin, TX: Pro-Ed, 1994).

Kessler, R. "Shared Decision Making Works!" *Educational Leadership 1* (1992): 36–38.

Little, Thomas and Dacus, Nannette. "Looping: Moving Up with the Class." *Educational Leadership 57,* no. 1 (September 1999): 42–45.

Maeroff, G. I. "Building Teams to Rebuild Schools." *Phi Delta Kappan 7* (1993): 512–519.

Senge, Peter M. *The Fifth Discipline: The Art and Practice of the Learning Organization* (New York: Doubleday/Currency, 1990).

Sergiovanni, Thomas J. *Moral Leadership: Getting to the Heart of School Improvement* (San Francisco: Jossey-Bass, 1992).

Silver, William S., and McGowan, Robert P. "Stage 3: Adventures in Team Teaching." *Journal of Management Education 20* no. 4 (November 1996): 435–446.

Smith, Stuart C., and James J. Scott. *The Collaborative School: A Work Environment for Effective Instruction* (Eugene, OR: ERIC Clearinghouse on Educational Management, 1990).

Strong, Richard. "Keeping It Simple and Deep." *Education Leadership 6,* no. 56 (March 1999).

CHAPTER TWELVE

RESTRUCTURING TIME

Scheduling

The school schedule is considered by many to be the command performance of the principal. It is here that the ability to conceptualize, to organize, and to carry out detailed planning is most visible. If well done, the schedule will strongly support the instructional and curricular program of the school. On the other hand, if poorly designed, the schedule will be a roadblock to a balanced curriculum and instructional flexibility.

—L. W. Hughes and G. C. Ubben[1]

Scheduling can be defined as the plan to bring together people, materials, and curriculum at a designated time and place for the purpose of instruction. Its basic purpose is to coordinate the requirements laid down by previously reached decisions regarding curriculum, instruction, grouping, and staffing.

The effective schools research has much to say about the use of time in school. The concept of academic learning time (ALT), discussed in earlier chapters, describes scheduled time as its umbrella component from which the "actual" instructional time and "engaged" time are achieved. It is therefore imperative that scheduled time be maximized so that ultimately high amounts of instructional and engaged time can also be obtained.

Several important concepts in scheduling should be reviewed before actually beginning the construction of a schedule. The concepts are equally important for elementary, middle, and high school schedules. These include the flexibility, simplicity, and complexity of the schedule, the decision level at which schedule changes are made, efficiency in the use of time, and the timeliness of the schedule. Other concepts to consider are previously made decisions concerning the design of curriculum and instruction; staffing and grouping patterns; and space availability and utilization.

SCHEDULE FLEXIBILITY

The schedule should have either the potential of being legitimately changed with great frequency or have the internal elasticity of meeting a variety of curricular and instructional requests within its regular structure. For example, the teacher who would like to take a group of children on a half-day field trip should be able to do so without disrupting the entire school schedule. Likewise, the group that needs an extra hour to complete a project should be able to have that hour with an easy adjustment in the schedule.

Simplicity and Complexity

The schedule needs simplicity to prevent interdependence of the components of the schedule, so that the modification of one component does not require the modification of several others. Complexity, on the other hand, is also needed in order to meet the demands of individual differences of students. To meet individual differences, intricate schedule designs need to be constructed. This seemingly creates a paradox, but it is another application of the loosely coupled/tightly coupled concept of organization. An analogy that seems fitting to describe this relationship is found in modularized electronics. The complexity of their circuitry is an amazing example of modern-day technology, but, on the other hand, this complex design is constructed in such a way that if a failure occurs, or a modification is desired, a circuit board can be removed and replaced very quickly, once the trouble spot has been identified or the desired modification determined, without having to disassemble the entire set. So it is with schedules: A good schedule must permit the complex construction required for individual differences while maintaining simplicity to allow easy changes.

Efficiency and the Use of Time

The effective schools research points out the need for time efficiency. There are many ways greater efficiency can be obtained within the schedule. Several specific suggestions are as follows:

1. Minimize the use of nonspecific study time during school hours. This means the reduction—or better yet, the elimination—of study halls. Too often children who cannot get into scheduled classes are put in study halls—a reflection of the principal's inability or unwillingness to design a tight, efficient schedule. In a good schedule, study halls should be virtually eliminated. At the elementary and middle school levels, activity periods must be carefully designed so they do not also become holding areas for children otherwise not engaged in a supervised learning activity.

2. Minimize the time used for movement from classroom to classroom. Techniques will vary greatly depending on building arrangements and instructional design. Specifics might include the use of two- or three-hour blocks of time with no student passage required, as well as clustering of classrooms and lockers to minimize travel on the part of students for the development of efficient hall traffic patterns and the reduction of the time between classes.

3. Available instructional time can be enhanced with the development and implementation of an efficient policy regarding the use of the intercom system. Within the school, restrict its use to the first and last few minutes of the day so as not to interrupt potential instructional time.

Other efficiencies in the use of teacher and children's time in school may include good use of lunch time (including a duty-free lunch for teachers and the opportunity for students to relax as well) and the effective use of before and after school waiting time on the part of students (waiting for buses, parents, etc.). Every minute of the school day counts. The rule must always be "What is the best possible use of this time?"

Timeliness of Scheduling Decisions. Timeliness is part of flexibility. Schedules must be designed so that daily and weekly instructional and curricular needs can be met as they occur.

Decision Level—Loosely Coupled

The decision level is the point in the hierarchy of an organization where decisions are made. A basic rule for good decision making in most organizations is that decisions should be made at the lowest level within the organization where adequate information exists for that decision (loosely coupled). The application of this rule to scheduling suggests that students and teachers should have maximum involvement in scheduling decisions. At the building level, scheduling should be kept as simple as possible so that the various components can be changed without disrupting the entire school. Also, each building should have maximum control over its schedule and not be frequently subject to the schedules of other schools in the school system. Some traditional areas of conflict such as coordinating bus schedules between schools or scheduling shared teacher specialists require higher-level decisions. The major conflicts will arise over making up specialists' schedules within the school, in coordinating special areas such as gymnasiums and music rooms, and in scheduling schoolwide programs such as lunch.

SCHEDULE DESIGN

There are several approaches to achieving a good schedule. Although the detail of scheduling certainly differs among elementary, middle, and high school, the basic tenets are largely the same. One of the best methods is to provide relatively large blocks of time unencumbered by outside influences to teams of teachers and groups of students so they can develop a detailed daily schedule to meet curricular and instructional needs. Such a schedule must accommodate a few special activities such as lunch, physical education, or music (see Figure 12.1).

Inside these large blocks of time, the team of teachers and students functioning as a learning community plans all of the learning activities. These internal schedules can differ from one day to the next as plans are made by the team reflecting the instructional format, curriculum, groupings, and staffing assignments. Because each of these instruc-

<table>
<tr><td rowspan="2">Morning</td><td rowspan="2">Team Scheduled Block</td><td rowspan="2">Team Scheduled Block</td><td>T.S.B.</td><td>P.E. MUSIC</td></tr>
<tr><td>P.E. MUSIC</td><td>T.S.B.</td></tr>
<tr><td></td><td>LUNCH</td><td>LUNCH</td><td>LUNCH</td><td>LUNCH</td></tr>
<tr><td rowspan="2">Afternoon</td><td>Team Scheduled Block</td><td>P.E. MUSIC</td><td rowspan="2">Team Scheduled Block</td><td rowspan="2">Team Scheduled Block</td></tr>
<tr><td>P.E. MUSIC</td><td>Team Scheduled Block</td></tr>
</table>

FIGURE 12.1 Team Scheduled Block

tional blocks stands alone, changes within them do not affect the remainder of the school.

Figure 12.2 illustrates a simple form of scheduling within the block of time that can be used by a team of four teachers following a basic rotating design. In this schedule, each teacher has access to each group of children operating in a semi-departmentalized school-within-a-school design. The schedule does not meet all of the curricular, instructional, and grouping recommendations made in the previous chapter, but neither does it preclude further development to meet the additional criteria. The team has a high

Period	**Group A**	**B**	**C**	**D**
1	R	SS	SC	M
2	SS	SC	M	R
3	SC	M	R	SS
L	L	L	L	L
4	M	R	SS	SC
5	P.E.	P.E.	Music Alternate Days	

RReading
SSSocial Studies
SCScience
LLunch
MMath

Four teachers responsible for groups A–D

FIGURE 12.2 Block Rotating Schedule

degree of autonomy to plan its schedule as it sees fit and can modify it as frequently as every day if it chooses.

Numerous schedule variations can be created from this basic design. It offers an excellent opportunity to create groups that vary in size as well as the ability to group students according to a variety of special interests and skills patterns.

At the elementary level, a team might create small groups for reading instruction by assigning children to instructional groups on a skills basis. Each team member can teach a small group of children by sharing activities and placing children in several different learning activities. To have reading groups of a reasonable size, three teachers of a four-member team can each take 10 children in their reading group while the fourth teacher supervises the other children in some form of teacher-planned instructional activity (see Figure 12.3). Sharing responsibility among teachers within a schedule permits the group variation necessary for good instruction. During additional periods, the schedule can shift so that each teacher has some large-group direct instruction time as well as small reading groups for skills instruction (see Figure 12.4). An instructional aide could assist in supervising computer centers and independent study activities while the regular staff does direct instruction.

FIGURE 12.3 Staffing for Small Skill Groups

	TEACHER A	TEACHER B	TEACHER C	TEACHER D
9–9:30	Reading Group 1, 10 children	Reading Group 2, 10 children	Reading Group 3, 10 children	90 children, direct instruction

FIGURE 12.4 Reading Skills Group Schedule

	TEACHER A	TEACHER B	TEACHER C	TEACHER D	AIDE
9:30–10	R–4 10 children	R–5 10 children	Direct instruction, (30) children	R–6 10 children	Learning centers, (60) children
10–10:30	R–7 10 children	Direct instruction, (30) children	R–8 10 children	R–9 10 children	Learning centers, (60) children
10:30–11	Direct instruction, (30) children	R–10 10 children	R–11 10 children	R–12 10 children	Learning centers (60) children

Twelve groups, including those in Figure 12.3—30 minutes directed instruction of each group plus a small reading skills group.

Grouping patterns can remain flexible. As the learning community's planning develops, the internal schedule can change as frequently as needed. Variations for math, the addition of science, social studies, or language arts activities (including independent study work), and the scheduling of field trips can be built in and designed by teachers without requesting approval from an outside authority. Only when special teachers, facilities, and services for these activities are needed must the team consult and coordinate with the principal at the building level.

Ultimately, how the block schedule is to be used depends on the decisions regarding curriculum, instruction, grouping, and staffing. If teachers are organized in teams, the curriculum has a broad base of subjects, the instructional program is individualized, and the grouping is designed to allow change frequently, the block schedule may be designed to accommodate those needs with ease.

LEARNING COMMUNITY PLANNING TIME

One of the most important features of any schedule involving a team of teachers working as a learning community is the provision of adequate team planning time. Every teacher should have a minimum of five hours each week for planning and materials preparation. Much of this time should be in common with other members of the team. Teachers usually prefer to arrange this time in several large blocks rather than divide it into many small segments. Teachers and aides can occasionally alternate supervision, giving each team member some time for planning or materials preparation. However, extended planning sessions where all team members are present is also a must.

Parallel Scheduling

Team planning can usually be best arranged on a schoolwide basis using parallel scheduling. Parallel scheduling provides large blocks of planning time through the use of specialists. The elementary school or middle school staff must include three or four full-time specialists such as music teachers, art teachers, and physical education teachers. These teachers are scheduled in a design paralleling that of the regular teaching staff so the specialists can replace each of the regular teaching team members, freeing them from all of the children in their learning community for a given block of time. The specialists then work in rotation with these children from one team for a period of one or more hours (see Figure 12.5). Specialists can handle additional children if there are more specialists available or if an aide can work with a specialist and increase group size. The specialists work with each group of children so that, within a one- or two-day period, they replace each team (the team organization used here is the one shown in Figure 12.3).

These examples of schedules are meant only to be suggestions to generate ideas. Many variations can be developed from these different models. Each school and each team must develop a schedule of its own, tailored to meet its individual needs. It is important to let the schedule follow the demands of the curricular and instructional program and the student grouping and staffing patterns and not allow the schedule to dictate the rest of the program.

	Monday	Tuesday	Wednesday	Thursday	Friday
Morning	Specialist Replace Team A	Replace Team C	Replace Team E or Specialist Planning	Replace Team B	Replace Team D
Afternoon	Replace Team B	Replace Team D	Replace Team A	Replace Team C	Replace Team E or Specialist Planning*

FIGURE 12.5 Team Parallel Schedule

*In a five-team school, the specialists use an extended duty-free lunch for planning.

ELEMENTARY SCHOOL SCHEDULES

Self-Contained Elementary Classrooms

There is renewed interest in one-teacher, self-contained classrooms. This has occurred as a reaction to what is considered by some to be overspecialization, "pullout" programs such as Title I, and the seemingly myriad other special programs that fragment the activity of the regular classroom. It is true that the special programs and the utilization of instructional specialists have often been uncoordinated and apparently directionless. As noted in an earlier chapter, eliminating many of the specialists and converting these staff lines to regular classroom instructional lines in order to reduce class sizes to 15 or fewer has seemed to make a difference in student achievement in some schools.[2]

The drawback to doing this is that many teachers do not have the requisite skills to meet the very special needs of many of the children in their classes. Moreover, a good case can be made on other grounds for the use of specialists as a part of the school team. It is neither useful nor productive to operate at either extreme. Clearly, though, there is a need for great coordination when large numbers of specialists are to be found on a school staff.

An alternative to pullout programs is the integrated team approach. Here, the specialist is integrated into the regular instructional team and the team itself develops the schedule and instructional activities for the students assigned to it. Block scheduling, discussed in the previous section of this chapter, is consistent with this kind of staffing arrangement.

Block Scheduling—Elementary

A sample internal block schedule is shown in Figure 12.6. It is designed to meet the time needs based on the following major tenets:

1. A flexible curriculum (different subjects with varying amounts of allocated time for different students)

	Teacher A	Teacher B	Teacher C	Teacher D	Teacher E	Aide
8:00	PREPARATION FOR DAY AND FINAL TEAM COORDINATION					
8:30	Children Arrive Group Advisement					Lunch Count Attendance
9:00	Reading 1 (10)	Reading 2 (10)	Social Studies Large Group (50)	Science (50)	Learning Centers (30)	Science
9:30	Writing (25)	Learning Centers (95)	Reading 3 (10)	Reading 4 (10)	Reading 5 (10)	Learning Centers
10:00	Reading 6 (10)	Reading 7 (10)	Social Studies Large Group (50)	Science (50)	Learning Centers (30)	Science
10:30	Writing (25)	Learning Centers (95)	Reading 8 (10)	Reading 9 (10)	Reading 10 (10)	Learning Centers
11:00	Reading 11 (10)	Reading 12 (10)	Social Studies Large Group (50)	Social Studies Large Group (50)	Learning Centers (30)	Science
11:30	Writing (25)	Learning Centers (95)	Reading 13 (10)	Reading 14 (10)	Reading 15 (10)	Learning Centers
12:00	Lunch (duty free)	Lunch (duty free)	Lunch (duty free)	Lunch Supervision	Lunch Supervision	Supervision
12:30	Playground	Playground	Playground	Lunch (duty free)	Lunch (duty free)	Lunch (duty free)
1:00	Math 1 (15)	Math 2 (15)	Math 3 (15)	Health (25)	Learning Centers (80)	Learning Centers
1:30	Learning Centers (55)	Spelling (15)	Learning Centers (50)	Math 4 (15)	Math 5 (15)	Learning Centers
2:00	Math 6 (15)	Math 7 (15)	Math 8 (15)	Health (25)	Learning Centers (80)	Learning Centers
2:30	Learning Centers (55)	Spelling (15)	Learning Centers (50)	Math 9 (15)	Math 10 (15)	Learning Centers
3:00	Group Advisement Cleanup					
3:30	Dismissal	Dismissal	Dismissal	Dismissal	Room Supervision	Bus Load
4:00	PREPARATION TIME					

FIGURE 12.6 Sample Daily Schedule

Note: The number in parentheses indicates the number of children for that activity. Learning centers are supervised by the teacher indicated but all teachers contribute to their preparation.

2. Individualized instruction (use of mastery learning, cooperative learning, small skills groups, independent study, and student interest groups)
3. Varied and flexible grouping (skills groups of 10 to 15 for reading and math instruction, interest groups with student advisor direction for learning centers, large heterogeneous grouping for directed instruction, such as in science, social studies, and health)
4. Organization of the staff, a team of five teachers, and an aide in a learning community

This schedule is meant only as an illustration of a particular day. The reading and math schedules are fairly constant for the teachers each day, but the groups change for the children as they master their skills and are regrouped in both math and reading.

The schedules for the other subjects change frequently as instruction is planned and group sizes are determined. Students use learning and computer centers for drill and practice activities previously assigned during directed instruction when they have not scheduled group activity.

A child's daily schedule is based on skills groups. Since children are grouped in the morning on a skills basis for reading, reading then becomes the grouping basis to direct children to all other subjects during the morning. In the afternoon, the math groups become the organizational block in which children are directed to the other group activities. This provides homogeneous grouping according to skills in reading and math and heterogeneous grouping in all other subject areas. The only exception to this rule occurs when children are grouped on an interest basis for other activities while not in reading or math.

The schedule can be simplified or made more complex as the situation changes. Teachers' skill in scheduling these internal team activities evolves with practice and time. Adequate team planning is an essential component to making the schedule function properly.

MIDDLE SCHOOL SCHEDULES

Middle schools have unique problems in scheduling students and staff. Greater subject area specialization on the part of teachers is required than is generally the case in the elementary school. However, it is preferred that each student have a limited number of teacher contacts. This means that each teacher still must be capable of teaching several subjects.

The range of differences in the achievement levels of middle school children is also greater. This means that to meet the individual skills needs of the children, greater efforts must be made to individualize instruction either through skills grouping, cooperative learning, or some other technique. Care must also be taken not to overuse homogeneous grouping because of its detrimental effects on student attitudes and achievement when overused.

The block schedule shown in Figure 12.1 is probably the best design for a schoolwide schedule in the middle school, along with the following ideas to be used for the internal team schedule.

Achievement grouping is recommended for use in reading and math instruction because of the relatively large span of abilities in the middle school. The fact that curriculum tends to be organized according to skill levels in these two subjects makes them the best candidates for this technique. Most other areas of the curriculum should use heterogeneous grouping.

Homogeneous grouping is more successful in improving learning when the curriculum is modified for the homogeneous grouping (i.e., when reading and math skills learning continues). When homogeneous grouping is used, the criteria for grouping must specifically match the curricular area (e.g., total reading scores for reading groups and math scores for math groups). Grouping on the basis of an IQ score, for example, is much too general and should not be used.

It is almost impossible from a scheduling standpoint to group more than two subjects if each teacher teaches a separate subject. The schedule shown in Figure 12.7 will allow homogeneous grouping in reading with good flexibility in assigning and moving students because all four teachers will be teaching reading at the same time. In this schedule, the math teacher homogeneously groups children during periods 2 through 5 into four or eight levels for mathematics. However, this schedule fails to meet the specification of heterogeneity for social studies, science, and language arts because the math grouping spills over into these subjects, allowing the good math students to stay together in science, period 3; social studies, period 4; and language arts, period 5.

Teacher Period	A	B	C	D
1	Reading Groups A–E	Reading Groups B–F	Reading Groups C–G	Reading Groups D–H
2	Math 1	Science	Social Studies	Language Arts
3	Math 2	Science	Social Studies	Language Arts
4	Math 3	Science	Social Studies	Language Arts
5	Math 4	Science	Social Studies	Language Arts

FIGURE 12.7 Middle School Team Schedule with Tracking

Additional refinements to the schedule can help solve the problem of homogeneous grouping carrying over in an undesirable manner, however. In order to create heterogeneity, a matrix must be designed that will undo the grouping created by a subject such as math that runs parallel to social studies, science, and language arts. The matrix must reassign the math groups to bring about the desired heterogeneity. This can be done by assigning each of the math classes a series of scheduling numbers and placing children in groups of four or five (called *modules*). These subgroups for the math grouping can then be dispersed through the other classes in an orderly manner.

The first column (math) of Figure 12.8 assigns each succeeding group of five math students a number. The top five math students are assigned number 1. The lowest five math students are given number 24. This number assigned to them in math class is then used to disperse them, thus creating heterogeneous grouping in the other three subjects.

A schedule for a four-teacher middle school team might carry the following specifications; many variations of these assignments are possible, however:

All teachers teach reading—reading is divided into eight skill levels.
One teacher teaches math—math is divided into four or more skill levels.
One teacher teaches social studies.
One teacher teaches science.
One teacher teaches language arts.
} These classes are to be grouped heterogeneously and not reflect either the math or reading grouping.

SECONDARY SCHOOL SCHEDULES

Secondary school schedules, although somewhat more complex, can often be viewed as extensions of elementary or middle school schedules. The secondary school schedules can be classified under the following types: group schedules, mosaic schedules, and block schedules.

Group Schedules

A group schedule of single subjects is most often used to place in groups those students who are registered for the same subjects and where the elective offerings are very few. Students are scheduled by groups and stay together through the day. Only two steps are required for this scheduling procedure: Determine the number of students taking the same subjects and identify how many sections are needed; and arrange the classes into a schedule according to their groups, rotating through the subjects in a similar fashion to Figure 12.2. Only physical education and music or some other elective would also rotate.

The group schedule is used most often for traditional junior high school schedules. Its major advantages are its ease in scheduling and simplicity of design. Disadvantages are that students do not mix outside of their basic assigned groups and all classes are single-teacher responsibilities with very limited time flexibility. The block schedule, also discussed in this chapter, is a variation of the group schedule.

Home Base: Heterogeneous groups 2 subjects each teacher
Reading: Skill groups—8 groups
Math: Skill groups—each math module contains 5 students—120 total
Other Subject: Heterogeneous groups

Teacher Period								
1	**Home Base Heterogeneous**		**Home Base Heterogeneous**		**Home Base Heterogeneous**		**Home Base Heterogeneous**	
	(Heterogeneous groups are created by rank ordering on reading scores with each home base receiving every fourth card.)							
2	Reading Skill Groups A,E		Reading Skill Groups B,F		Reading Skill Groups C,G		Reading Skill Groups D,H	
3	Math Homogeneous Groups		Language Arts		Science		Social Studies	
	1	4	7	16	8	17	9	18
	2	5	10	19	11	20	12	21
	3	6	13	22	14	23	15	24
4	Math		Language Arts		Science		Social Studies	
	7	10	15	24	13	22	14	23
	8	11	18	3	16	1	17	2
	9	12	21	6	19	4	20	5
5	Math		Language Arts		Science		Social Studies	
	13	16	20	5	21	6	19	4
	14	17	23	8	24	9	22	7
	15	18	2	11	3	12	1	10
6	Math		Language Arts		Science		Social Studies	
	19	22	1	12	2	10	3	11
	20	23	4	15	5	14	6	13
	21	24	9	17	7	18	8	16

7,8 Lunch-activity period—Art—Music—PE—Health—Guidance—etc.

FIGURE 12.8 Middle School Team Schedule: Four-Teacher Team—Heterogeneous Grouping

*These numbers are based on the math groupings of 5 students each and are used to recreate the heterogeneity for Language Arts, Science, and Social Studies.

Mosaic Schedules

The most popular form of secondary school scheduling, mosaic scheduling, is designed to allow the scheduling of a large number of student electives. It is based on the concept that students register for courses first and then a schedule is built that fits *all* their requests. The term *mosaic* comes from the method of schedule construction. Each course to be offered is written on a small card or tile and moved about on a scheduling board so that it can be assigned a teacher, a time, and a room that is free of conflicts from other parts of the schedule. When the board becomes full of these small squares, it resembles a mosaic. The steps in building a mosaic type schedule are as follows:

1. Determine the educational offerings of the school. Each year, a needs assessment is conducted to determine what the curricular offerings for the following school year should be. New courses may be proposed by new district or state requirements or by the requests from students and staff. The initial list should consist of courses that are desired and for which there is some probability that they can be taught. With computer scheduling, all possible courses can initially be put on request.

2. Provide an appropriate means for students and parents to review the curricular offering and to select courses for students to take with appropriate guidance from teachers and counselors. A booklet listing all courses with a brief description can be prepared. The booklet can also list requirements for graduation and suggested courses of study. Tentative planning worksheets for each year of a student's school career may also appear in the booklet so that complete programs can be worked out. Figure 12.9 shows a sample planning sheet for individual high school curricular planning. Student requests should be gathered on a standard registration sheet that allows for easy tallying. A form such as the one in Figure 12.10 can be used for either manual or computer scheduling.

3. Tabulate student choices by subject to determine the number of students in each subject as a basis for the needed number of sections in each subject. The tabulating can be done either by hand, placing the tallies on a sheet similar to the ones the students have used for registration, or by preparing input data for the computer indicating the student's request. The computer can provide an accurate total listing of all subjects and the number of requests for each.

4. Determine the number of sections needed for each subject. This can be determined by selecting a maximum class size for each subject and dividing the total students by that number. In the case of small enrollments, a determination must be made of adequate staff numbers to offer all requested courses. In some cases, small enrollments may require dropping some electives and asking those students to select another option. The feedback from the computer can aid the principal in rapidly determining the enrollment feasibility of offering a particular course. The computer specialist can assist the principal in reviewing course offerings. The number of small enrollment electives that can be offered is ultimately determined by the total student-staff ratio.

FIGURE 12.9 Senior High School Course Guide

Instructions: Use this form to plan your three years in high school. Circle the courses that you tentatively plan to take each of your three years in high school. Record next years courses on the registration form and return this sheet to your homeroom teacher.

SOPHOMORE	JUNIOR	SENIOR
English 10 (Required)	English 11 (Required)	English 12 (Required)
American History (Required)	World History (Required)	Creative Writing
World Geography	World Geography	Social Studies (Required)
Physical Education (Required)	Elementary Algebra	World Geography
Elementary Algebra	Integrated Mathematics	Humanities
Integrated Mathematics	Plane Geometry	Elementary Algebra
Plane Geometry	Higher Algebra	Integrated Mathematics
Biology	Biology	Plane Geometry
French I, II, III	Chemistry	Higher Algebra
German, I, II, III	French I, II, III, IV	Trigonometry/Advanced Algebra
Latin I, II	German I, II, III	Advanced Mathematics
Russian I	Latin I, II, III	Biology
Spanish I, II, III	Russian I, II	Chemistry
	Spanish I, II, III, IV	Physics
		French II, III, IV
		German II, III, IV
		Latin II, III, IV
		Russian II, III
		Spanish II, III, IV
Art I	Applied Physical Science	General Mathematics
Commercial Art I	Art I	Applied Physical Science
Typing I	Art II	Art I
Beginning Business	Commercial Art I, II	Art II
Electricity I	Typing I	Commercial Art I, II
General Metals	Office Skills	Typing I
Power I	Secretarial Skills	Office Skills
Wood I	Shorthand I	Secretarial Skills
General Graphic Arts	Bookkeeping & Accounting	Sales and Merchandising II
Home Economics I, II, III, IV	Architectural Drawing	Office Education
Journalism	Electricity I, II	Shorthand II
Speech	General Metals	Bookkeeping and Accounting
Gym & Choir (Alt. Days)	General Graphic Arts	Law/Sales
Gym & Band (Alt. Days)	Machine Drawing I	Architectural Drawing
Gym & Study (Alt. Days)	Machine Shop I	Electricity II, III
Orchestra	Power I, II	Machine Drawing I, II
	Wood I, II	Machine Shop I, II
	Home Economics I, II, III, IV	Power II
	Journalism	Wood II, III
	Speech	Home Economics I, II, III, IV
	Band	Journalism
	Choir	Speech
	Orchestra	Drama
	Boys' Physical Education	Band
	Girls' Physical Education	Choir
	Sales and Merchandising I	Orchestra
		Boys' Physical Education
		Girls' Physical Education

Graduation Requirements

1. English 10, 11, 12
2. American History
3. World History
4. Social Studies
5. One mathematics course
6. One science course
7. Passing grade in 10th grade phys. ed.
8. Total of 14 credits plus 10th grade phys. ed.

FIGURE 12.10 Registration Code Sheet and Teachers Tally Sheet

Student Course Requests

Student's Name:

Directions: Encircle the code number, *in red,* of all subjects for your next year's schedule as approved on your Proposed Program of Studies sheet. Recheck for accuracy. The homeroom teacher may reserve the responsibility of checking those subjects where ability grouping is involved.

Miscellaneous

___060 Unassigned
___065 Driver Education
___067 Library Training

Work Periods

___071 First
___072 Second
___073 Third
___074 Fourth
___075 Fifth
___076 Sixth
___077 Seventh

Special Education

___081 & 082 Spec. Educ.
___083 Individual Acceler. Prog.

Coop. Voc. Training

___091 Job not yet assigned
___092 Dist. Ed. (assigned)
___093 Ind. Coop. (assigned)
___094 Ind. Coop., Part G.

Mathematics

___321 Alg. 2R
___330 Analysis A
___331 Analysis R
___351 Analy. Geom. (1/2)
___352 Probability (1/2)
___354 Comp. Prog. (1/2)
___355 Comp. Prog. (1)
___356 Comp. App. (1/2)
___358 Trig. (1/2)
___360 Calculus
___361 Calculus AP

Science

___400 Spec. Ed. Biol.
___430 BSCS Biol. A (1/2)
___431 BSCS Biol. B (1/2)
___435 Botany (1/2)
___440 Biol. 2A (1/2)
___441 Biol. 2B (1/2)
___445 Radiation Biology (1/2)
___430 BSCS Biol. A (1/2)
___450 Chemistry A (1/2)
___451 Chemistry B (1/2)
___454 Chemistry 11 A
___455 Chemistry 11 B
___461 Physics A
___462 Physics B

Business Education

___604 Typing IV (1/2)
___605 Office Practice
___606 Pers. Use Typing (1/2)
___608 Voc. Off. Ed. —Jr.
___610 Shorthand I
___611 Shorthand II
___612 Voc. Off. Ed. —Lab.
___613 Voc. Off. Oc. —Coop
___620 Acct. 1
___621 Adv. Acct.
___631 Bus. Law (1/2)
___632 Off. Mach. (1/2)
___641 Bus. Arith.
___642 Cons. Ed. (1/2)
___643 Bus Comm.
___099 Cl. Off. Aide

Homemaking

___681 Homemaking 1A (1/2)
___682 Homemaking 1B (1/2)
___683 Homemaking 2A (1/2)
___684 Homemaking 2B (1/2)
___685 Homemaking 3A (1/2)
___686 Homemaking 3B (1/2)
___687 Chef's Course (1/2)

5. Determine the teaching staff needed and compare with the teaching staff believed to be available, considering areas of certification, budget, and so on. Teaching staff available can be determined roughly by multiplying the number of classes taught by each full-time teacher plus the number of sections taught by part-time personnel. This can then be compared to the number of sections indicated as being needed in the course tallies calculated in step 4.

Sections needed based on student requests 350

Teacher sections available based on total staff 335

Sections that must be cut from student request tabulations or provided for by the employment of three additional teachers 15

A more detailed analysis must now be carried out to properly match teacher assignment requests and certification areas to student course tabulations. This is done by comparing specific subject section needs with available staff. Some flexibility is usually available in determining staff assignments where additional positions are to be filled or staff turnover exists. Figure 12.11 is an illustration of the matching teacher specialties and student requests.

Assignments may need to be moved around in order for all to be matched with qualified staff. In some instances, modifications may be made based on appropriate assignments for staff yet to be hired or yet to be employed by putting together logical assignments for new faculty (i.e., math-science, social studies-physical education-coaching, etc.). Ultimately, job descriptions for new staff can be formulated from these data.

FIGURE 12.11 Teacher Assignment Worksheet

STAFF ROSTER	DESIRED ASSIGNMENT	AREAS OF CERTIFICATION	PROPOSED ASSIGNMENT
Bailes, Cris	English 10–11	L.A.	L.A. 3–10, 2–11
Bray, Gail	S.S. 10	S.S., L.A.	5–10th
Brewer, Max	Sc. 11–12	Sc., Math	2–Chem. 1–Phys. 1–Biol.
Crockett, Reba	Typing, Bkk.	Business Ed.	4–Typing 1–Bkk.
Dietz, Pat	SS. 10–11	S.S., P.E.	S.S. 5–11
Edison, Freda	Algebra	Math, Spanish	Alg.–4 Germ.–1

6. Determine the number and length of class periods and the time for extracurricular activities. The number of periods in the school day should now be determined. Six or seven periods is usually typical for mosaic-type schedules. Additional school periods over and above the number of classes taken by the average student usually become study halls or early dismissal opportunities. In most cases, experience has shown that unless students are on work assignments of some type, these additional hours are not used productively. Therefore, it is suggested that the number of periods in the school day match fairly closely the number of courses for which each student registers. It is somewhat more difficult to build a no-study-hall or limited-study-hall schedule requiring students to take courses each hour, but the productivity for a student is usually improved; thus, such tightly organized schedules are worthwhile. A five- or six-period day is recommended, which includes a large block of time plus several hour-long elective classes.

Extracurricular activities are most often scheduled after the regular school day. This works well when the students either walk to school or provide their own transportation. When a large number of students ride school buses, an after-school activity period greatly restricts the number of students that can participate. A number of schools have had good success in establishing midday activity periods during the early afternoon. All students are then expected to select and participate in an activity, club, or intramural program, or they may use the period as a study period if no other opportunities are available.

7. Make a conflict chart to determine the subjects that must not be scheduled at the same time if pupils are to have the program they have selected. Subjects, for which only one section is offered, that are placed in the schedule at the same time prevent students from taking more than one such course. Therefore, in order for single-section subjects not to conflict, they must be scheduled at different hours of the day. Two-way conflicts can also frequently occur. This happens when two single-section offerings are matched with a request for a double-section course offered the same hours as the singles. Three-way conflicts are also possible, but the probability is relatively low (see Figure 12.12).

FIGURE 12.12 Conflict Matrix

COURSE NO.	107	111	121	142	451	455	621	697	704
107		3	2	78	17	17	2	9	0
111			1	0	2	0	12	22	0
121				1	2	7	9	4	0
142					8	0	0	1	
451						3	2	0	
455							54	14	
621								0	12
697									2
704									

The underlying philosophy of a good mosaic schedule is to design a schedule that is capable of honoring all student requests and to then build a schedule that eliminates all possible conflicts. The smaller the number of unsolvable conflicts within the schedule, the more perfect the schedule is considered to be.

A well-designed mosaic schedule should be able to reduce unsolvable conflicts to around 2 percent of the total student population. An *unsolvable conflict* is defined as a set of student course requests that cannot be honored because of conflicts within the schedule and that requires the student to select one or more alternate courses in order to complete a program.

A conflict chart sets up a matrix of the least single-, double-, and triple-section offerings and shows how many students have signed up for the various possible combinations. The conflict matrix in Figure 12.12 shows that three students want to take both courses 107 and 111.

While a conflict matrix is a vital part of the mosaic scheduling procedure, it is also an extremely time-consuming task if done by hand—particularly in a large school. It is accomplished by taking each student course request and comparing it to the other courses also requested by that student. The comparison is indicated by placing a tally mark on the matrix at the bisecting point. Up to 15 comparisons could be required for six course requests from one student if they were all single subjects. Computer-assisted scheduling will produce a complete conflict matrix for all subjects generated from the same data that were used to determine student tallies. The computer scheduling consultant will often circle those conflicts that he or she feels to be particularly significant.

8. Assign classes to the master schedule in terms of the conflict matrix. Even where computer-assisted scheduling is being used, this is a necessary manual task. A small card, approximately one-inch square, should be prepared for each section of each subject to be offered in the schedule. It is often desirable to color code the card by predominant grade levels, also reserving an additional color for classes that draw heavily from all or several grades. The mosaic cards should contain the course title and the section designation such as 1–1, 1–2, or 2–3, indicting which section the card represents in the number of sections of that type. The mosaic cards are now to be placed on a scheduling grid, listing all proposed teacher positions and the periods of the day.

The following order is usually helpful in constructing the schedule with a minimum of conflicts. Use the conflict chart for all decisions.

- **a.** Assign 12 grade sections, proceeding downward in grade order. This is desirable because often the greatest number of singletons are twelfth-grade courses. Also, it is often thought desirable to design the twelfth-grade schedule first to ensure no conflicts since it is the seniors' final year in high school.
- **b.** Assign subjects having only one section, scattering them throughout the school day. The scattering will reduce conflicts. Next, check each single-section course against other single sections offered during that hour to ensure no conflicts. If some exist, move sections until all are free of conflict.
- **c.** Be careful not to assign two or more classes to one teacher during the same period.

d. Classes having double or triple periods should be assigned next. Included are the core classes, vocational classes, team-taught block classes, and so on. Because of the larger block of time for these subjects, fewer options exist for scheduling; therefore, it is necessary to place them in the schedule early.

e. Subjects having only two or three sections should be scheduled next, checking each placement against the conflict matrix. By now, some moving of earlier placed sections will probably be necessary. Be sure to follow each through an analysis on the conflict matrix with other sections offered that hour.

f. Finally, multiple-section subjects should be filled in, taking care to properly balance teacher load. Care should be taken to assure reasonable balance each hour for teacher preparation time, as well as to ensure adequate availability of staff for teaching purposes. Each time a previously placed mosaic is moved, care must be taken to check out all other ramifications of that move on the conflict matrix. Consideration must also be given to available special facilities each hour, such as music rooms, science rooms, typing rooms, and so on.

9. A room assignment sheet is prepared to prevent the assignment of two or more classes to the same room the same hour. A chart can be used simply by replacing the top row of teachers' names with classroom numbers and entering each room assignment on the appropriate mosaic of the master schedule.

10. Students may now be assigned to the classes of the proposed master schedule. As each student is assigned to a class, the information needs to be recorded on the student's individual assignment sheet, as well as on the separate class tally worksheet in order to balance class size. Each student must be scheduled individually for each of his or her course requests. Previously undetected conflicts will now come to light if the information from the conflict matrix was not completely adhered to or if certain conflicts were overlooked.

Computer Scheduling

Computer-assisted scheduling procedures can save hours of clerical time by electronically loading students into a manually planned master schedule. Excellent scheduling software is also available for microcomputers that will actually construct a master schedule.[3] However, a particular advantage of using only computer loading is the opportunity for the scheduler to maintain greater control over the schedule design. Trial runs can be processed with computer printouts indicating any problem with student requests that cannot be scheduled. These student conflicts can now be reviewed by the schedule designer and result in additional scheduling modifications to avoid previously overlooked conflicts. All schedule modifications at this time are to the master schedule only. Until the master schedule is perfect, no individual student schedules should be changed. Unsolvable conflicts are reviewed later.

A good master schedule should result in required schedule changes on an individual basis for no more than about 2 percent of the students. The scheduling specialist, if used, frequently will offer additional suggestions as to how the schedule can be improved. Any number of simulated runs of the schedule can be made with additional schedule modifications each time. This method will finally confirm its soundness with minimum conflict levels before all other forms are printed.

In addition to the tally lists and conflict matrix previously mentioned, computer packages can include study hall control; common course scheduling (the same students in more than one class); simulated runs; alternate course schedules in case of conflicts; balanced class enrollments as to size; and class lists of students for each teacher for each hour of the day, as well as generation of the master schedule itself. Costs of these software programs range from several hundred to over one thousand dollars, but it is generally believed that when a school reaches an enrollment of three to four hundred, the clerical and administrative time saved by the use of a software program more than offsets the cost.

Student and teacher schedules can be electronically transferred directly into the student record database each year, saving the clerical time necessary for data entry (see Chapter 14). The individual student schedules can be printed in multiple copies on paper as well as on cardstock, providing one copy to the student, one for the office, and additional copies for school files such as attendance, counseling, and the like. Individual schedules can also be printed with home addresses for summer mailing if this is desired (see Figure 12.13).

Block Schedules—Middle and High School

The traditional six- or seven-hour day schedule of the typical middle or high school creates a very hectic, fast-moving, disruptive day for most teachers and students. Frequent class changes constantly disrupt available academic learning time (ALT). An excellent alternative to the traditional six- or seven-period day is the use of block scheduling. Block schedules generally increase the length of a class by doubling it and reduce the number of classes a student and teacher participates in on a given day usually by one-half. To achieve this one-half reduction, classes generally meet every other day or are one semester in length.

Block schedules offer a number of distinct advantages over traditional schedules. They reduce the number of class changes that students must make during any one school day. They reduce the number of students for whom a teacher must prepare each day and/or term. They also reduce the number of assignments, tests, and projects that the student must address at the same time, and decrease the fragmentation inherent in single-period schedules. Block schedules also provide teachers with blocks of time that allow and encourage the use of a variety of teaching strategies. Students have extended amounts of time for learning. In addition, the schedule provides the opportunity for interdisciplinary teaching, which is a much sought after curriculum goal of the middle school.

Academic learning time is also enhanced with the use of block scheduling. Chapter 10 discussed the ALT concept and the importance of reducing the amount of "start-up" and "close-down" time at the beginning and end of each lesson. Two-period classes reduce by more than one-half the lost time by eliminating a class change. Block schedules are also relatively easy to implement. They do not require student assignment procedures much different from those already on place for a six- or seven-period schedule. Only the relative changes of hours and days that classes meet must be modified.

13939 WILBURN ANGLIA R	10	F	01-02	MARYVILLE
STUDENT NAME	GRADE	SEX	NUMBER	HIGH SCHOOL

PERIOD	SUBJECT NUMBER	SUBJECT	ROOM NUMBER	SEM.#	TEACHER	028	
						HOME ROOM	TELEPHONE
1	121	ENG 2 COL PR	014	3	014		
2	606	GEN BUS 1/2	013	1	117		
2	605	PERS TYP 1/2	017	2	117		
3	925	PHYS ED 1/2	025	1	106		
3	929	DR ED SFM 2	105	2	105		
4	821	HOME ECON 2	001	3	001		
5	211	ALGEBRA 1	020	3	020		
6	311	BIOLOGY	023	3	023		

13940 WILBURN DAVID M	10	M	01-02	MARYVILLE
STUDENT NAME	GRADE	SEX	NUMBER	HIGH SCHOOL

PERIOD	SUBJECT NUMBER	SUBJECT	ROOM NUMBER	SEM.#	TEACHER	028	
						HOME ROOM	TELEPHONE
1	211	ALGEBRA 1	020	3	020		
2	925	PHYS ED 1/2	025	1	104		
2	929	DR ED SEM 2	005	2	205		
3	121	ENG 2 COL PR	014	3	014		
4	311	BIOLOGY	023	3	023		
5	491	LATIN 2	015	3	115		
6	021	BAND	026	3	026		

FIGURE 12.13 Computer-Printed Student Schedule

Alternate-Day Schedules

Alternate-day block schedules may be adopted to meet the needs of schools that offer six, seven, or eight courses per year. In schools where six or eight classes have been taught, half of the classes are taught every other day. Classes might have a Monday-Wednesday-Friday schedule one week and a Tuesday-Thursday schedule the next; or Monday could be maintained with single-period classes and double-period classes operate on Tuesday-Thursday and Wednesday-Friday. The seven-course block schedule uses six courses that meet in double periods while one course meets as a singleton. Often, the singleton is scheduled in conjunction with the lunch hour. Figures 12.14 and 12.15 illustrate the six- and seven-course alternate-day block schedules.

The 4/4 Semester Plan

In the block schedule semester plan, the school day is divided into four instructional blocks of approximately 90 minutes each and the school year is divided into two semesters. Each semester, students are enrolled into four courses that meet daily for a full 90-minute period. Instruction that was previously stretched out over 180 days is now taught in 90 days. The two-period block reduces the lost academic learning time more than enough to make up for shorter assigned minutes of instruction. In fact, it is argued that more instructional time is really available under this 90-minute, one-semester plan than the traditional two-semester, one-period schedule.[4] Figure 12.16 illustrates the basic 4/4 model. Proponents of the 4/4 semester plan suggest that the plan has the following advantages:

FIGURE 12.14 Alternate Day Six-Course Block Schedule for Five-Day Schedule

DAYS/PER.	MONDAY	TUESDAY	WEDNESDAY	THURSDAY	FRIDAY
1	1	2	1	2	1
2	2	2	1	2	1
3	3	4	3	4	3
4	4	4	3	4	3
5	5	6	5	6	5
6	6	6	5	6	5

Days/Per	Day 1	Day 2	Day 3	Day 4	Day 5	Day 6
1	1	2	1	2	1	2
2	1	2	1	2	1	2
3	3	4	3	4	3	4
4	3	4	3	4	3	4
5	5	5	5	5	5	5
6	7	6	7	6	7	6
7	7	6	7	6	7	6

FIGURE 12.15 Alternate Day Seven-Course Block Schedule for Six-Day Rotation

FIGURE 12.16 The Basic 4/4 Two-Semester Block Schedule

PERIOD	SEMESTER 1	SEMESTER 2
1	Course 1	Course 5
2	Course 1	Course 5
3	Course 2	Course 6
4	Course 2	Course 6
5	Course 3	Course 7
6	Course 3	Course 7
7	Course 4	Course 8
8	Course 4	Course 8

1. Teachers have to work with only 50 to 90 students at a time.
2. Teachers have only three classes and maybe fewer preparations.
3. Students are responsible for only three or four subjects at one time.
4. Students failing a course may have the opportunity to repeat it immediately the next semester.
5. Students have opportunities to accelerate their study in specialty fields.
6. More elective opportunities exist for high school students who now have as many as 32 choices over a four-year period of time.
7. As many minutes of instruction (ALT) can be built into the schedule as single-period schedules.

Variations in block schedules are many. Lunch schedules, single-schedule needs for subjects that need to meet for the entire year, vocational programs that require blocks of time for "school-to-work" activities—all of these represent special impacts to the schedule. There is no available space in this chapter to provide the answers to each of these variables. An excellent resource, however, is the work of Canady and Rettig,[5] who provide a great number of schedule adaptations illustrating their book on block schedules.

YEAR-ROUND SCHOOLS

Another dimension of time deals with the length of the school year and the school calendar. Although U.S. schools traditionally have 180- to 200-day school years, many other calendar options are possible. Knowing that academic learning time is a critical element for student achievement, simply lengthening the school year would, in most cases, improve achievement scores. However, budget limitations and traditions get in the way. In a publication about year-round education, Ballinger (1999) stated:

> If year-round education were the traditional school calendar and had been so for 100 years or more, and if someone came along to suggest a "new" calendar wherein students were to be educated for only nine months each year with another three months free from

> organized instruction, would the American public allow, or even consider, such a calendar?[6]

Lengthening the school year has an immediate impact on student achievement both by providing more time for learning and by shortening the summer, allowing less time for forgetting. Schools devote a significant amount of instructional time each fall to the review of material taught the previous year because children forget over the summer. Some schools have modified the school calendar, not by increasing the number of school days but by shortening the summer and providing longer vacation periods during the school year.

One common time organization is the 45-15 day plan. In this plan, students attend school in cycles of 45 days on, 15 days off. Such a plan allows for a six-week break in the summer. Some schools elect to extend the time in school with special intersessions during the off weeks. Other schedule arrangements are a 60-20 day plan and a 90-30 day plan.

Once the sequence of days is decided, the school must determine if all students will start and stop at the same time or if there will be a staggered form of attendance. The staggered attendance is usually used in schools where space is a critical issue. This plan allows the school to use the classrooms during vacation times for other groups of children still in attendance.

The advantages of year-round programs include continuity of learning, better flow and retention of learning, intersession opportunities for tutoring and/or enrichment activities, reduction in student retentions in grade, and less teacher stress/burnout because of the more frequent breaks in schedule. Stated disadvantages include family conflicts from children in different schools who may be on different schedules, difficulty for teachers to get extra training in the summer, interference with summer jobs and summer camps, and potentially higher costs of keeping the building open all year.

SUMMARY

Scheduling has as its basic purpose the bringing together of curriculum, staff, and students for the purpose of instruction. It must be kept flexible, allowing for changes in group size and instructional time. Schedules must also provide for adequate staff planning and allow major scheduling decisions to be made by the team. Block-of-time schedules assigned to the team and parallel scheduling for team planning offer good solutions to scheduling demands.

This chapter has developed several different concepts of scheduling a high school, from a simple group schedule to the complex modular schedule of some of our more experimental institutions. Complexity is not always best, however. More traditional mosaic schedules, when properly constructed, are most functional. When all aspects of school organization are considered, such as staffing, student grouping, curriculum, instruction, and student advisement and control, the block schedule must be given a high rating.

Under all circumstances, scheduling is a major determinant of the school program. While it should not control, it must be designed in such a way as to not limit the desired instructional program for the school.

ACTIVITIES

1. Reflect on the use of time and the schedule in your own school. Can you identify areas where restructuring should take place? Why do you believe so? Why is it important to consider the planned decisions for curriculum, instruction, and staffing along with rescheduling decisions? Apply the concepts of this chapter to your school. How would you proceed to restructure your school's use of time?
2. Review Case Studies 4 and 20 at the end of this book. Analyze the problems presented and apply the concepts of restructuring time developed in this chapter. What approach would you use in addressing the problems? Set forth a strategy to overcome the difficulties faced by the schools in these cases.
3. Turn to the ISLLC Standards found in Appendix B. Review the performances listed with Standard Three. One of these performances states "time is managed to maximize attainment of organizational goals." What are your school's organizational goals relative to the use of time? How are these goals being met?
4. Another ISLLC Standard Three performance states "there is effective use of technology to manage school operations." Does your school use computer technology to schedule students or to manage student records? If so, what does it do and what software is used?

ENDNOTES

1. L. W. Hughes and G. C. Ubben, *The Secondary Principal's Handbook* (Boston: Allyn and Bacon, 1980), p. 173.

2. Elizabeth Ward et al., "Student/Teacher Achievement Ratio (STAR)," *Tennessee's K–3 Class Size Study 1985–1990* (Nashville: Tennessee State Department of Education, 1990).

3. Isabelle Bruder reviews six microcomputer-based administrative software programs that handle scheduling, grade reporting, and attendance tasks—(1) Alpha II, (2) Harts III, (3) Mount Castor, (4) the Osiris System, (5) the School System, and (6) STARS (Student Academic Records System)—and lists companies producing the programs, the systems they run on, and price information. (Isabelle Bruder, "Users Speak Out: A Look at Six Administrative Software Programs," *Electronic Learning 7,* no. 8 [May–June 1988]: 54–56.)

4. See Chapter 2 of Robert Lynn Canady and Michael D. Rettig, *Block Scheduling: A Catalyst for Change in High School Scheduling,* Princeton: Eye On Education, 1995. Canady and Rettig present an interesting rationale for longer classes providing more than twice the academic learning time of that provided by 50-minute classes. (Robert Lynn Canady and Michael D. Rettig, *Block Scheduling: A Catalyst for Change in High School Scheduling* [Princeton: Eye On Education, 1995]). See especially Chapter 2.

5. Ibid., p. 300.

6. Charles Ballinger, "Specializing in Time and Learning," The National Association for Year-Round Education (1999) On-line. <www.nayre.org>.

SELECTED READINGS

Alam, Dale, and Roger E. Seick, Jr. "A Block Schedule with a Twist." *Kappan 75,* no. 9 (May 1994): 732–733.

Ballinger, Charles. "Specializing in Time and Learning" The National Association for Year-Round Education (1999) [On-line] Available: <www.nayre.org>.

Bloom, B. S. "Time and Learning." *American Psychologist 29* (May 1974): 682–688.

Braddock, Jomills Henry, III, and James M. McPartland. "Alternatives to Tracking." *Educational Leadership 47,* no. 7 (April 1990): 76–79.

Brundrett, Mark. "Transforming Learning with Block Scheduling." *School Leadership and Management 19,* no. 3 (August 1999).

Canady, Robert L. "Parallel Block Scheduling: A Better Way to Organize a School." *Principal 69,* no. 3 (January 1990): 34–36.

Canady, Robert Lynn, and Joanne M. Reina. "Parallel Block Scheduling: An Alternative Structure." *Principal* (January 1993).

Canady, Robert Lynn, and Michael D. Rettig. *Block Scheduling: A Catalyst for Change in High School Scheduling* (Princeton: Eye On Education, 1995), p. 300.

Canady, Robert Lynn, and Michael D. Rettig. "Restructuring Middle Level Schedules to Promote Equal Access." *Schools in the Middle* (Summer 1992).

Canady, Robert Lynn, and Michael D. Rettig. "The Power of Innovative Scheduling." *Educational Leadership 53,* no. 3 (November 1995).

Carroll, J. M. (October 1994). "The Copernican Plan Evaluated: The Evolution of a Revolution." *Phi Delta Kappan* (October 1994): 105–113.

Conway, M. A., G. Cohen, and N. Stanhope. "On the Very Long-Term Retention of Knowledge Acquired through Formal Education: Twelve Years of Cognitive Psychology." *Journal of Experimental Psychology: General 120* (1991): 395–409.

Daigle, Paul D., and Daniel C. Leclerc. "Turning a New Leaf: Flex Time for Teachers in a Restructured School." *NASSP Bulletin 81,* no. 588 (April 1997).

DiRocco, Mark D. "How an Alternating-Day Schedule Empowers Teachers." *Educational Leadership 56,* no. 4 (December 1998/January 1999).

Dow, Jeffery, and Paul George. "Block Scheduling in Florida High Schools: Where Are We Now?" *NASSP Bulletin 82,* no. 601 (November 1998): 92–110.

Edwards, C. M. "The Four-Period Day: Restructuring to Improve Student Achievement." *NASSP Bulletin 77* (1993): 77–88.

Hopkins, Harriet J., and Robert Canady. "Integrating the Curriculum with Parallel Block Scheduling." *Principal 76,* no. 4 (March 1997): 28–31.

Kane, Cheryl. *Controlled by the Clock.* Report of the National Education Commission on Time and Learning (April 1994). [On-line] Available: <www.ed.gov/pubs/prisionersoftime/yearround.html>.

Karweit, N. "Time-on-Task Reconsidered: Synthesis of Research on Time and Learning." *Educational Leadership 41* (May 1984): 32–35.

McKinney, Regina, Beverly Titlow, and Geoerganne Young. "The Academic Enrichment Block." *NASSP Bulletin 83* (May 1999): 79–81.

Queen, J. Allen. "First Year Teachers and 4X4 Block Scheduling." *NASSP Bulletin 83,* no. 603 (January 1999).

Staunton, Jim. "A Study of Teacher Beliefs on the Efficacy of Block Scheduling." *NASSP Bulletin 81,* no. 593 (December 1997): 73–80.

CHAPTER THIRTEEN

CREATIVE BUDGETING, FISCAL ACCOUNTING, AND BUILDING MANAGEMENT

Budgeting, around here, begins at the basic level. Teachers, counselors, athletic directors have a good idea how money could best be directed. So do collections of these same people in their departments. We all do but these folks have great insights into how we might get the greatest bang for the buck. And, we expect them to contribute these insights and develop good beginning budgets. I'm seldom disappointed.

—James May[1]

Managing and allocating funds at the building level has never been easy and even less so in these days of greater budgetary development and fund expenditures at that level. With greater control has come greater responsibility. Consider these sounds emanating from the school business office:

"Gary, Art has overspent his departmental budget again."

"And all it will cost for this supplemental reading program is $1,625 the first year. Sign here."

"The school band needs new uniforms."

"But you said the science program was high priority. So how come you're not approving this purchase order?"

"The commodes in the second floor girl's restroom are clogged again."

"You spent Title I monies for *what?*"

"I dunno, these accounts just don't balance."

"Miss Hoke, the auditor's office just called. Something about some misappropriated funds . . ."

"I don't care what it costs—get the maintenance department over here and get those swings fixed."

"Dr. Karpicke, the Citizens for Economy committee is here for their appointment. They look grim."

A headache begins. Building management ("mop, brooms, and playgrounds") budgeting instructional monies, and fiscal accounting are all functions of the principalship. When the spending program issues from the needs of the instructional program, when accounting procedures withstand audit, when the building is well equipped and maintained, great things can happen in a school. Although the principal does not have total control over who determines the monetary needs of all of the instructional units, or who keeps the books, or who fixes the toilets, it is the principal who ultimately is responsible for all of these things occurring in a timely and efficient manner.

In research syntheses about practices in high-performance schools, two findings that relate to resource and facility management are evident. In high-performance schools, resources were allocated to maximally support instructional and curricular improvement. Good financial planning and good budgeting were apparent. Also, schools that were excellent were invariably clean and physically attractive, inside and outside. There was obvious attention to the impact the physical environment has on educational outcomes.

This chapter comprises four parts. In the first part, important concepts about financial planning and budgeting are discussed. There is much attention given to ways to engage the staff in fiscal planning that has an impact on the instructional program. In the second part, good accounting and record-keeping practices are examined. The focus of the third part is on supplies and equipment management. The chapter concludes with a discussion about the care of the school plant, including a review of custodial schedules.

THE BUDGETING AND PLANNING PROCESS

There are four sequential steps to the budget development/budget implementation process: program planning and tentative allocation of resources by category; analysis and adoption of a final budget; administration and coordination of the budget, including record keeping; and review and appraisal of budget implementation with regard to the instructional goals of the school program. The budget process is continuous and cyclical. Figure 13.1 depicts this process.

Responsible financial planning rests on good program planning. It requires, as well, a substantial database about the nature of the student body; population projections and housing patterns; estimates of personnel needs; and historical information about average daily attendance (ADA) or average daily membership (ADM), whichever is the basis for the state reimbursement program, and reasonable projections thereof, among other information that would help determine the financial demands of the next fiscal period.

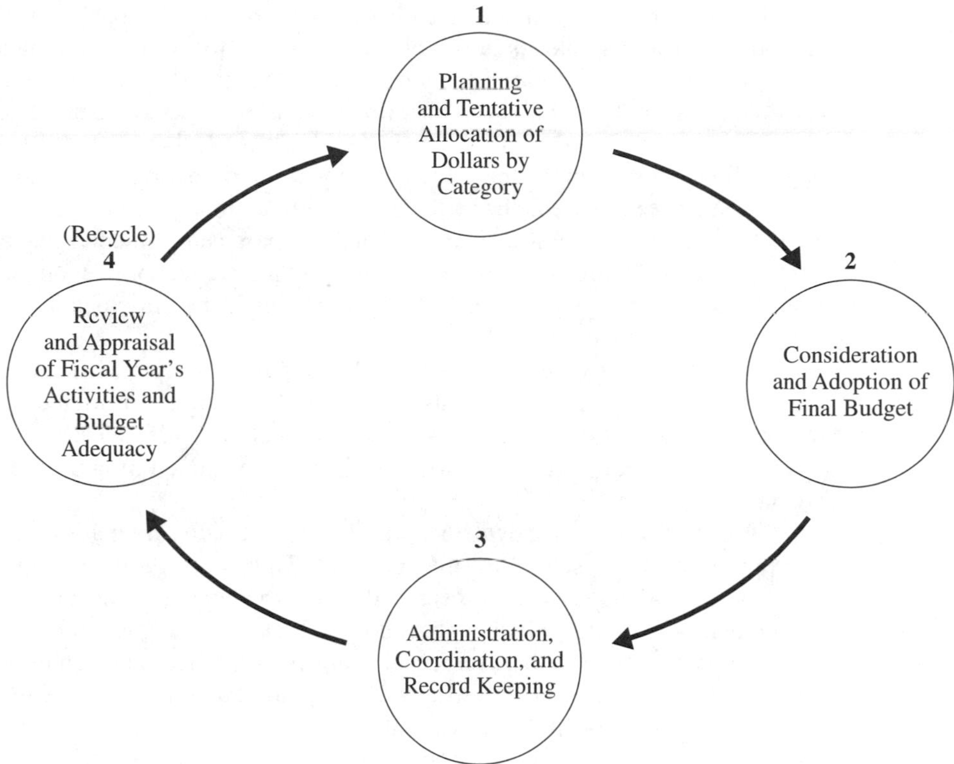

FIGURE 13.1 The Cyclical Nature of the Budgeting Process

Three Common Budgeting Processes

For the principal in school districts committed to site-based decision making, the budgeting process takes on critical importance. Three major techniques for budget development have emerged over the years, none of which is based on assumptions of decentralized decision making but any of which may be employed at the site. Two of these clearly are conducive to much staff participation in budget development and implementation. One is such a "mechanical" approach that only minimal staff participation would seem called for.

Incremental Budgeting. Incremental budgeting begins with the current year's budget and in its pure form is largely an "add-on" (or "subtract-from") process. It assumes stasis: stasis in the nature of the needs of the student body, stasis in curriculum organization, and stasis among line items. Within line items there may be shifts in proposed expenditures, to be sure, and staff decisions with regard to this might be encouraged.

Fundamentally, however, the next school year is assumed to be very much like the current year. Often, certain fixed charges that can be anticipated are excluded from building-level planning. That is, the district may do its own projections with regard to such things, for example, as utility bills and provide for uniform maintenance. These most often will remain centralized and accounted for in the district business office.

At the school site, however, the principal will be expected to project needs for the next year on a formula that most often is based on the number of students anticipated to be enrolled. This becomes the primary factor for anticipating the number of teachers needed, supplies required, support staff permitted, among other expenses that can be expected that go along with an increased or a decreased enrollment. Frequently, the student enrollment figure is based on average daily attendance or average daily membership for the current year and any changes that might be anticipated because of new housing starts, for example.

Special requests such as needed building repair or special facilities for special programs and specialized projects housed in the building are most often considered separately. Programs such as those funded by such outside sources as the federal government—"Title" programs, vocational programs, lunch programs, and the like—are handled separately.

When the totals are calculated, preliminary decisions are made with regard to the appropriation for the school for the next year. This is budget development at its simplest. It is also budget development at its most inadequate—because it assumes that what exists is working well enough. It does not take into consideration any changes in the nature of the students to be served, or changes in instructional technology, for example. It is status-quo driven, and structural, curricular, and instructional innovations are less encouraged than would be desirable. The amount of money to be spent is viewed as finite and dependent on the school allocation.

Zero-Based Budgeting. At the other end of the budget development continuum is zero-based budgeting. In its purest form, this technique assumes a new year, every year. The school organization is divided into program or budget units. The mere fact that a program was funded during the current year or in previous years is no assurance that it will be funded in subsequent years. The program unit and ultimately program heads are expected to justify their program and the dollars needed to support that program on an annual basis. The budget is "zero" until this is done.

Justifications are made on the basis of curriculum evaluations, demographic realities, research about instructional technology, shifting priorities in the light of the former, the established school and program goals. One important advantage of zero-based budgeting is that it forces continuous reevaluation of program objectives, needed resources, and the establishment of new priorities or reestablishment of existing priorities. A downside is that this is a very time-consuming process and does not recognize that any school has certain fundamental requirements. Everything is "up for grabs." Beware, neophyte principal.

Planning, Programming, Budgeting System. This is a better alternative to either of the other two processes. At its best, PPBS recognizes that there are needs for a consistent base of support and that a per-pupil allotment may best provide for a baseline. That is, there is enough experience in the district to know that irrespective of individual learner needs, demographic realities, changes in instructional technology, and curriculum revisions, certain per-pupil costs of an education can be anticipated.

Beyond this, however, PPBS begins to take on the elements of zero-based budgeting. Some planners and analysts insert an *E* between the *B* and the *S* to stand for *evaluation*. The PPBES approach explicitly emphasizes that the goals and processes used to address these goals are subjected to evaluation. We believe this is implicit in a PPBS approach, but if it makes the point more telling, that's all the better.

The PPBS technique requires the establishment of specific program goals and processes to achieve these goals; projections of needs—students to be served, new technology, and so on; the generation, analysis, and projection of data about program element costs; alternative processes to achieve the goals; other sources of funding; and any additional personnel or additional facilities needed and what that would cost.

IMPLEMENTING A PLANNING, PROGRAMMING, BUDGETING SYSTEM

At its simplest, PPBS involves five steps:

1. Establishing the general goals to be achieved
2. Identifying the specific objectives that define this goal
3. Developing the program and processes that it is believed will achieve the objectives and goals
4. Establishing the formative and summative evaluation practices
5. Implementing a review and recycle procedure that indicates whether or not, or the degree to which, the program and processes resulted in the achievement of the objectives and the goals, and, if not, to help determine other procedures, processes, and programs

The PPBS approach is designed to help the school staff decide specifically what is to be accomplished and how to go about it. The focus is on goal accomplishment. When sensitively and sensibly applied, an efficient expenditure of monies results.

Too often, educational planning has primarily been concerned with the "inputs" of education. PPBS differs substantively from other budget-building procedures because PPBS focuses on desired "outputs" of the effort (goals and objectives) and afterwards considers the numbers of staff, books, equipment, and buildings that must be engaged to obtain the desired end.

There are other values to a PPBS plan, however. The process provides great opportunity for staff involvement and staff development about an issue that many may be interested in and all are affected by. At the initial stages, individual departments, teaching teams, grade levels—however the building is operationally organized—essentially will be engaged in a "GII" decision process.[2] Later, as tough decisions need to be made—initial budget proposals almost always outstrip available funds—the principal may find the "CI" or "CII" process more appropriate. In any of these instances, good use has been made of the collective wisdom and subject matter expertise of faculty to arrive at a budget which all will work hard to implement.

Moreover, as PPBS is implemented, data are being collected about the productivity of distinct elements of the program. As the school enterprise has become more complex and more diversified, and more demanding of public funds, personnel, and time investments, there has been a resultant anxiety about results. There is a pressing desire on the part of the various publics to know more precisely what this investment is producing and where changes should be made. PPBS helps provide this important information and forms a solid basis for gaining public support. Among the outcomes of such a budget development process is a concern for the future and a continuous assessment of current curricular and instructional practices.

Step 1: The Five-Year Plan

The planning process begins with the development of a five-year plan well in advance of any specific budget proposals for the next fiscal year. This is not a document that is developed quickly. The process does provide a good basis for in-service workshops with staff and lends a substantive focus to faculty meetings and workshops held throughout the school year.

The process may begin by organizing the preschool workshop to focus on planning for the future. Several schoolwide or department sessions are held, at which time the topics to be addressed are often stated as: "What a student at the end of grade 6 should know" or "What this school needs is" or "What the outcomes of the 7–12 social studies program should be," or any number of other topics that are generative of ideas that focus on curricular or student outcomes.

Following the idea gathering, staff members convert the product of these sessions into a series of goals and objectives by a process of synthesizing, summarizing, and combining. Once the staff has refined the statements of objectives and goals, they identify the processes, materials, and personnel that will be necessary in order to implement these goals and objectives over the next five years. The tentative five-year plan has four major components:

1. A written description of the current state of the discipline. The staff simply describes, briefly, where the department, or subject matter, or curricular field is at the present time in relation to what the literature and research reveal is the ideal state.
2. Statement of goals, objectives, and the indicators that will be accepted as evidence of achievement of objectives for the department. It is important to establish objective indicators of achievement. However, this does not have to be done at this time; it can be done later. A staff could bog down at this point and become fatigued at developing long lists of performance objectives based on lower-level cognitive achievement. The five-year plan is subject to modifications through the formative evaluation that will occur as it unfolds.
3. A list of processes to implement the objectives.

4. A statement of needed equipment, materials, personnel, and other resources supportive of the processes.

Component 4 is the culmination of the five-year plan development. The plan is subjected to refinement and modification and is ultimately submitted for executive review and discussion. It does not contain any dollar figures at this point. Although care should be taken not to hurry the process, definite time lines must be established for the completion of this process. Otherwise, it may become a cumbersome intellectual exercise that never gets completed.

Step 2: The One-Year Plan

While the five-year plan for the school plots a general direction, the one-year building plan provides budgetary substance. The one-year plan is a proposal that specifically identifies what needs to happen next year if the five-year plan is to be realized. Figure 13.2 provides a suggested format for the one-year plan.

Department (or Grade Level): __________
Fiscal Year: __________
Prepared by: __________
Amount Requested: __________
Amount Allocated: __________

Request (indicate after each item which long-term objective it supports)	**Estimated Cost**	**Suggested Source of Supply**	**Suggested Source** (federal funds, local funds, donation, state experimental funds, etc.)
1. Needed personnel			
2. Needed equipment and materials			
3. Needed other resources (e.g., travel monies, consultants, etc.) N.B. list above in descending order of priority.			
Total Requested	__________		

4. Attach a brief statement describing how this proposed budget is consistent with and supportive of the five-year plan.

FIGURE 13.2 The One-Year Plan

The one-year plan describes equipment needs, supplies, supplementary materials, immediate changes of personnel or addition of personnel, remodeling, and other needed resources. Justification for each specific item is available in the one-year document. This justification need not be elaborate; it is a brief statement about how the budget proposal is consistent with the five-year plan. An additional feature is that the departments or grade levels are asked to list needs in order of priority. If it is necessary to reduce budgets because of insufficient dollars, such cutting begins with lowest priority items in each of the proposals.

Subsequent Steps

The next steps involve submitting the budget and the curriculum proposals of the department or unit to the principal and the administrative staff for its approval or return for clarification or modification. Ultimately, the preparation of a total school budget in summary form is made by the principal and the staff for submission to the central office. Following this, there are negotiations and approvals of the individual school budgets in some form by the ultimate fiscal authority in the school district.

Eventually, an approved budget is returned by the principal to each department or unit—a budget from which requisitions throughout the year will be submitted to the principal and purchase orders issued. Each month a recapitulation of purchases to date is returned to the department.

Expectations and Product

Involvement of instructional staff in budget building does not make the principal's job any easier. In fact, after going through the initial process, team leaders, department heads, and other instructional staff can be expected to develop formidable and well-conceived arguments in defense of their budgets. Needless to say, however, the principal will be supplied with much of the data needed in order to go to the superintendent or the board of education to justify an adequate budget. Moreover, the central office and the school board will become well informed as to outgo and the reasons behind the outgo.

The budget-building process just described attempts to accomplish three things. It gives the appropriate personnel a large measure of authority for initial budget preparation in their areas of instructional expertise. Second, it causes foresighted curriculum planning. Third, it provides substantiation to the central office, school board, and the community that tax dollars are being spent in an efficient and effective manner.

ACCOUNTING FOR FINANCIAL RESOURCES AND EXPENDITURES

General Issues

In school districts, resource allocation and expenditures are generally divided into three broad categories: capital outlay, long-term and short-term debt payment and interest, and current expenses. It is the latter category that is of greatest concern to the principal, although certain items that appear in a capital outlay account also require consideration. Let us first examine what goes into each of these accounts.

Capital Outlay. An item with a life expectancy of over a year generally goes into a capital outlay account. The account will therefore contain equipment and all permanent additions to the buildings and school site. Plant and site maintenance expenditures are not reported here—only those expenditures that represent an extension to the existing school building and site. Relative permanence is the key determinate.

Debt Service. All short- and long-term loans and the repayment of those, including the interest payments, are reported in these accounts.

Current Expenses. Current expenses include all expenditures made for things that are consumable during a single fiscal year. This includes such expenses as textbooks, supplies, and salaries—known as *operating expenses*. Most often, these expenses can be found in the district budget classified under four categories: *Instruction,* which includes all of the programs—regular, special, and adult; *Support Services,* which includes transportation, food service, student services, and student activities; *Nonprogrammed Charges,* which include any payments to other governmental agencies for services, including rentals; and *Community Services,* which include recreation programs and nonpublic school services.

Accounting for Financial Resources at the School Site

Once the budget is developed and approved, it becomes the responsibility of the principal to see that it is managed properly. Schools are big businesses. In many communities, the school system is the single largest employer of personnel and the largest industry in terms of capital flow. School districts receive and disburse huge amounts of money for a variety of services and materials over the period of a year.

Similarly, at the individual school buildings, principals have the responsibility for administering sizeable financial resources—resources that come from the central district office as a result of local, state, and federal support programs, as well as much smaller sums that come from places such as PTOs, school clubs, plays, and so on. Managing financial resources is a major responsibility of most school principals.

All school systems have a prescribed accounting procedure, and a principal will need to become familiar with it in order to properly oversee income and expenditures. Figure 13.3 displays a typical array of accounts for a high school, and Figure 13.4 is a similar display for an elementary school.

In general, school principals need to keep a journal of receipts and disbursements and provide proper monitoring of these (see Figure 13.5). The principal may also have federally funded projects located in the building and will be expected to maintain appropriate records for these. Certainly, too, the principal will be responsible for securing supplies and materials, either by requisition from a central warehouse, perhaps using a system of transfer vouchers, or directly from a supplier. Probably most, if not all, of the principal's accounting responsibilities will occur in the operations" (supplies, equip-

FIGURE 13.3 Outline of Typical Accounts for a Secondary School

General Activity Fund Restricted

INSTRUCTIONAL FEE
- Towel Fee

INSTRUCTIONAL FEE & SHOP
- Art

INSTRUCTIONAL SHOP
- Auto Mechanics
- Machine Shop
- Wood Shop

OTHER INSTRUCTIONAL
- Music
- Band Uniforms

MERCHANDISING SERVICE
- Bus Tickets

PROFIT EARNING
- Coke Fund
- Concessions

SPECIAL PURPOSE
- Hospitality
- Library
- College Credit Course
- Sports Camp
- Senior Trip
- Scholarship
- Science
- Training & Technology

STUDENT ORGANIZATIONS
- Anchor Club
- Bridge Club
- Class, Junior
- Class, Senior
- Combined Studies
- Debate Club
- DECA
- French Club
- German Club
- Gymnastics
- Home Economics
- International Relations Club
- Key Club
- Leader's Club
- Leo Club
- Literary
- Magazine
- Masquers
- Music: Band
- Music: Choir
- Musical Production
- National Honor Society
- Oak Leaf
- Oak Log
- Pep Club
- Red Cross
- Ski Club
- Spanish Club
- Student Council
- Tennis Club
- TOEC
- VICA

ment, etc.) part of the budget. Figure 13.6 displays a purchase requisition flowchart in common use in schools. (Principals usually are not required to account for capital income and expenditures. These accounts are commonly handled in the central office.)

In most schools, there will be a clerk on whom will rest the responsibility for keeping the books. Under the principal's direction, this person will generally make the journal entries and keep the records in order. This does not relieve the principal of executive responsibility, however. Regular review is essential, and we recommend an annual independent audit of all records.

For the first few months on the job, the principal is best advised to be involved directly in the accounting process to learn intimately the business side of the enterprise. Proper accounting and budget procedures are essential to a well-managed school. The accounting system exists in order that the school may expend its funds efficiently and in accordance with the plan incorporated in the budget document. It also provides a his-

FIGURE 13.4 Outline of Typical Internal Ledger Accounts for an Elementary School

MERCHANDISING SERVICE
- Bus Tickets
- Insurance
- Workbooks

PROFIT EARNING
- Coke Machine
- Pictures
- School Store

SPECIAL PURPOSE
- Field Trips
- Assemblies
- Hospitality
- Instructional Supplies

ORGANIZATIONS
- Faculty Club
- Student Council
- PTO
- Intramural Program
- All-School Chorus

tory of spending and may be used to evaluate how the plan developed in the budget document is proceeding.

Financial resources are always in short supply, and it is not likely that all of the budgetary requests in support of the instructional objectives and school goals can be met in any one year. Thus, it becomes most important for the principal to keep a close record of outgo, making sure that this outgo is consistent with the budget plan and that sufficient funds remain for the purchase of high-priority items throughout the school year. It is a sad fact that improper accounting procedures have too frequently resulted in an inadequate amount of money in April for the purchase of routine supplies necessary to complete the school year. Under such a system, teachers tend to overpurchase and hoard supplies in their rooms. These practices are neither healthy nor necessary in a well-ordered school.

Most school districts use an accrual accounting system, which means that as soon as a purchase order is initiated or a requisition for anything is approved, it is encumbered in the account book. Through such a process, the principal knows immediately how much money remains to be expended in any particular account. Under such a system, it is not likely that financial obligations will be made beyond the actual amount of money available.

It cannot be expected, however, that faculty and nonacademic personnel will understand the intricacies of the accounting system, and sometimes individuals on the faculty may view the entire process as a hindrance to the instructional program. Thus,

FIGURE 13.5 Monthly Report Form

Statement of Receipts and Disbursements

Report for ____________________ 20 ______ Prepared by ________________

Central Treasurer

Account	Cash on Hand 1st of Month	Receipts This Month	Total	Disbursements	Balance End of Month
TOTAL	$_____	$_____	$_____	$_____	$_____

Reconciliation of Bank Statement

Bank balance as of ________________________		$______
Plus deposits not shown on statement ____________		$______
Plus others ________________________		$______
Minus outstanding checks ________________	TOTAL	$______
________________________		$______
Book balance as of ________________________		$______
________________________		$______

the wise principal will spend some time in faculty and staff meetings generally informing the staff about the reasons why good record keeping and accounting procedures are important to an instructional program.

Beyond this, it is the responsibility of the principal to make sure the practices being followed are, in fact, efficient and do provide for quick delivery of materials and other services to the classroom. It is also the principal's responsibility to make sure that his or her decision making, with respect to expenditures, is consistent with the preestablished instructional budget.

Regular Review

Once systemized, the accounting procedures need not absorb a vast amount of time but will require only regular monitoring by the principal. Care should be taken that materials ordered are received and properly inventoried. Keeping a separate set of books for

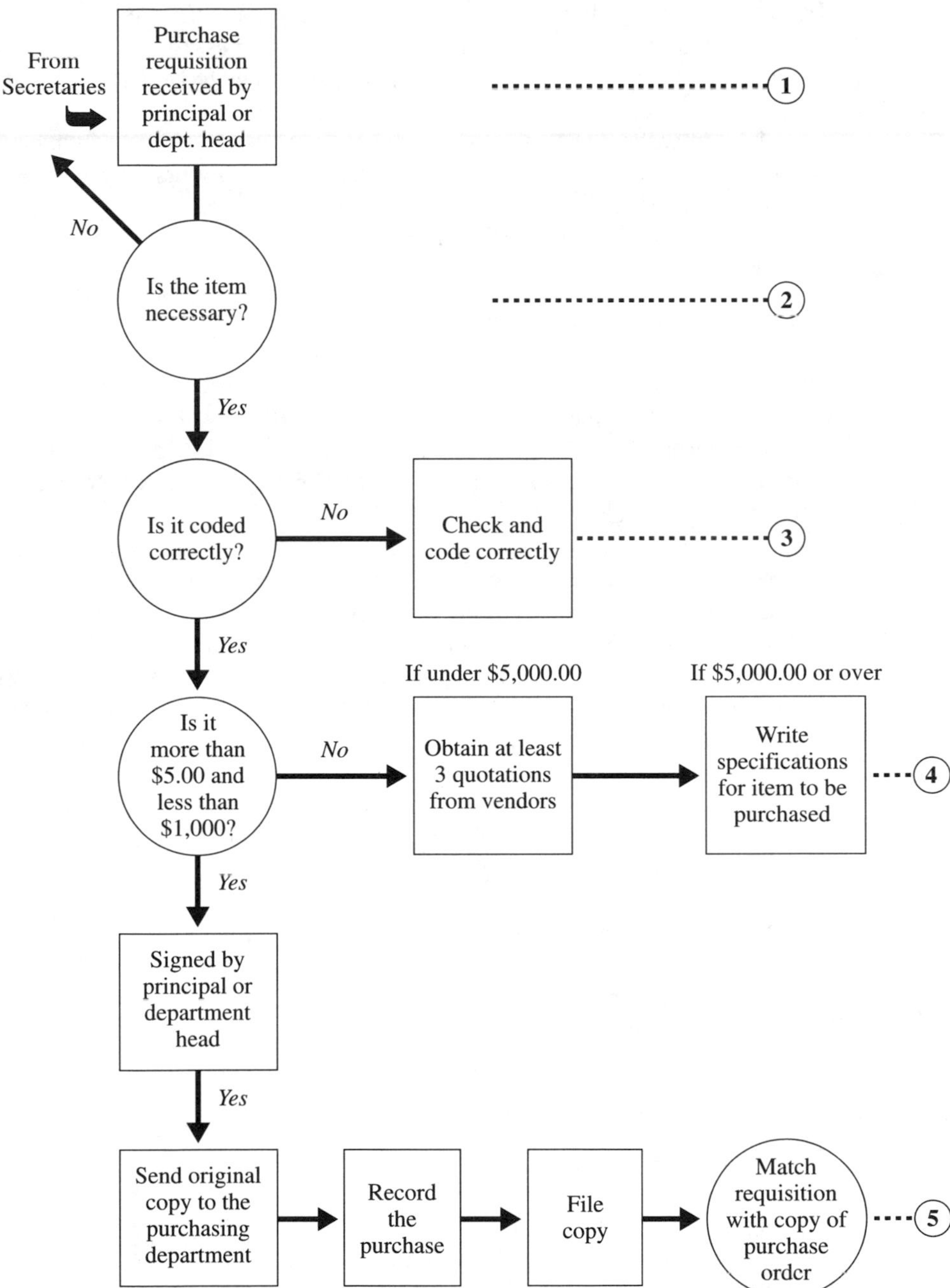

FIGURE 13.6 Purchase Requisition Flowchart for Principals and Department Heads

district funds will provide the principal with a good check on expenditures against the accounts of the school that are kept in the central business office. Mistakes do get made and when this occurs, it is to the principal's advantage to be aware of it and be able to rectify it.

In many school systems, the central business office will supply the principal with periodic financial reports in the form of ledger sheet printouts. These are easily checked against the school's set of books for accuracy. After reconciliation with the school's books, these will provide sufficient record of the financial aspect of the educational enterprise.

Activity and Other Funds

Most schools receive and distribute funds other than those disbursed by the district office. Such sources and accounts commonly include PTO funds, classroom accounts, insurance monies, candy sales, athletic funds, club treasuries, petty cash, funds from charity drives, gifts, and so on. Individually, the accounts may be quite small, but collectively they often amount to a considerable sum.

A separate set of books should be maintained for these funds. No less precise bookkeeping procedures are required for these than for the district funds. Many states have passed special legislative acts that require the establishment of orderly procedures for the administration of school activity funds. Some states, as well as local school districts, have developed policies and procedures to guide individual schools in such financial accounting. The absence of such policies and guidance in any particular school district is no excuse, however, for a principal to be any less careful—to the contrary, more care is required.

In general, specific procedures must be established to control the collection and disbursement of the variety of activity funds. The following procedures provide a good guide:

1. Official receipts should be issued for all money received.
2. All money expended should be expended by check, except for small cash purchases paid from the petty cash fund.
3. Supporting documents should be kept for all expenditures made.
4. Bank reconciliation statements should be made each month.
5. Monthly and yearly financial statements should be prepared.
6. An audit should be made each year, and copies of the audit should be filed with persons having administrative authority for the school.

Consistent with good financial practice is that each group having an account that the school is administering should file a simplified budget indicating anticipated income, anticipated expenditures, and persons designated to approve monies to be expended from the account. Further, all school employees who are responsible for handling funds should be bonded, the amount of the bond to be determined by an estimate of the amount of money that the school will manage. Many school districts provide a bond covering all employees in the school system who are responsible for such funds. Whether this is so in any particular district should be verified by the principal.

In some school districts, the principal is required to make a monthly report about the state of the internal funds in the school. Such a report commonly contains specific and general conditions of the accounts and expenditures. Regardless of whether this is required by district policy, it is an important procedure to be carried out by the principal and appropriately filed. It provides substantiation of the careful expenditure of funds and will assist in the annual audit. Figure 13.7 illustrates a monthly reporting procedure for an activity account.

School ______________________ Report for month of ______________________

Bank Reconciliation

Bank ______________________

Balance per bank statement ______________ $ ____________
Date

Add
Deposits in transit ____________
Other (specify) ____________
Total $ ____________
Deduct
Outstanding checks

$ ____________

Balance per general ledger ______________ $ ____________
Date

______________ ______________ ______________
Principal School Treasurer Date

FIGURE 13.7 Monthly Financial Report of the School Activity Fund

The Audit

The internal account books should be audited annually by an external accountant. The product of this audit should be filled with the district office. One should not misunderstand the purpose of the audit—it is not an attack on anyone's integrity. It has two primary purposes: It will provide good information for improving the accounting procedures, and it protects all of those who have been responsible for handling school funds.

Before accepting the position, the incoming principal should insist on an audit of all funds as a means of being informed about current practices and improving on these as necessary. The audit also establishes the state of the accounts before a person has responsibility for them. It red-lines the accounts, and the new principal starts with clean fiscal air.

SUPPLIES AND EQUIPMENT MANAGEMENT

A major responsibility of the principal is securing, making an inventory, and allocating supplies and equipment necessary to the educational program. It is essential that adequate quantities of soft goods (supplies) and the appropriate kinds of hard goods (equipment) be provided and available ahead of educational needs and secured in the most economical manner possible. It is equally important that a management system be provided that will not require an inordinate amount of supervisory time.

If the school is operating under a budget-development system as described earlier in this chapter, the selection and purchase of needed supplies and equipment in support of educational goals is easily routinized. At most, it should require a regular review to see that anticipated needs are being met on schedule; estimated costs are remaining within budget; advantage is being taken of the appropriate discounts allowed by suppliers; inventories are adequate; and equipment is being appropriately tagged, recorded, conveniently stored, and used.

Storage and Inventory Control

The daily needs of instructional staff are such that amounts of common educational supplies (art paper, chalk, etc.) can be predicted and kept in sufficient reserve to meet needs over a period of a few months. Responsibility for ensuring that the appropriate amount of day-to-day supplies are available can become that of the school clerk or another designated person. This task need not and should not require much attention by the principal. An inventory control procedure set up by the principal working with the designated individual will permit routine replenishment of supplies. Adequate inventories of educational materials and supplies unique to special aspects of the program can be maintained by the person who is responsible for that special aspect of the program.

Inventory control is greatly facilitated by using the school computer. Specialized programs can be written easily, and there are any number of commercial programs to which inventory control requirements may be readily adapted. All equipment, irrespective of where it is housed, should be tagged or identified in some manner and listed in the inventory.

Things break and wear out and disappear. Equipment must be kept in good repair and staff members made aware of their responsibility to report immediately any malfunction of equipment so that necessary action can be made. Routine ways to address these realities so that teachers are able to teach and learners are able to learn unencumbered by malfunctioning or missing equipment need to be established. The form depicted in Figure 13.8 uses a light touch to get the job done and done quickly.

HI!
CLAMOR HERE,
YOUR MAINTENANCE MOLLUSK

It's my task to hammer away at any jobs that need fixing in your room. Is there anything that requires attention?

Don't clam up now.
We want a smooth-sailing ship

Please fill out this form and leave at the custodial desk for quick service.

Room: ______________________________

Service Required: ______________________

____

____

____

____

For immediate needs, please call the office.

White: office
Pink: staff

FIGURE 13.8 Maintenance Form

Central Warehousing

The responsibilities for supply management in school systems are frequently handled at the central office level. Even if the principal has a considerable amount of responsibility with respect to supply management, large systems will have a central warehouse from which most supplies and equipment are secured. There is considerable advantage to this because systems can develop standardized lists of materials, with precise specifications. These need to be reviewed periodically to provide maximum use of school system dollar resources.

Certain kinds of educational materials may also be housed centrally in the school district. Materials such as film, filmstrips, audio and video tapes, and so on, which have use throughout the system but are not required in any individual unit of study except on an infrequent basis, are often cataloged and housed centrally in the school district. Where this is the case, teachers must understand the need for more lead time in requisitioning and securing these for classroom use. This is not to say that last-minute requests should not be acted on to the degree possible. It is an unhealthy school system that is not responsive to an unplanned "teaching moment," but in general it will be necessary for staff to anticipate the need for centrally housed educational materials.

CARE OF THE SCHOOL PLANT

> This building is clean and we keep it that way. It's not a new facility as you can see but that doesn't mean it shouldn't look good. And, that makes a difference on how our students and their parents feel about this place. We ask everyone—students, staff, parents—to help out. "If it drops on the floor, pick it up." "If you see it on the floor, pick it up." Graffiti in the restrooms? It doesn't happen much anymore, and when it does our custodians have it erased within the hour. Does this make a difference? You bet it does. We like this place. And for a lot of our kids, this is the most stable and pleasant thing in their world.[3]

Properly housing the educational program and equipping the school presents some management priorities for the principal. Innovative programs can be housed in traditionally designed buildings. Whether the building represents the latest in school design or reflects architectural thinking in the 1950s, the principal's responsibility is the same: to ensure the maximum efficient use of the school plant for the educational program. An inefficiently used building, a poorly kept building, a building with unpleasant, colorless rooms, or a poorly maintained site all inhibit the development of a good educational program. These have a negative impact on staff and student morale and productivity.

The principal has two important support groups: classified employees who are assigned to the building (custodians, cleaning personnel, cooks, kitchen personnel, etc.) and the districtwide maintenance department personnel. Working with nonacademic personnel to help them to do their jobs better will require the same kinds of human relations skills as working with academic staff.

Maintenance and Custodial Schedules

The building and grounds require much attention to create an attractive, safe learning-living-working environment for students and staff. Many large districts have a director of maintenance and operations whose overall responsibility is to see that skilled persons are employed and deployed to respond to refurbishment and major maintenance needs of all the buildings in the district. However, it is the responsibility of the principal, working with the custodial staff, to identify major needs and to ensure that those are systematically attended to. The day-to-day custodial and light maintenance functions will, even in larger districts, fall to the building custodial staff.

Effective supervision of building maintenance programs need not require an inordinate amount of time and can be regularized through the use of a simple checklist. Such a checklist is shown in Figure 13.9.

The principal and the custodial staff should give particular attention to common internal building flaws: inadequate lighting fixtures, roof or wall leaks, dirt in the corners, broken windows, torn sashes, and so on. The entire staff, including instructional personnel, should assist in identifying maintenance needs and reporting them immediately to the office for attention. Many times, annoying maintenance defects are allowed to continue simply because a teacher or another staff member has not reported them and they have gone unnoticed by the custodial staff.

Grounds and Playgrounds. The school site needs to be attractively maintained. The high cost of land often is reflected in small school sites and inadequate play areas. This is true especially in urban areas where children are often most in need of wide open spaces in which to play and experience nature. Size of site need not deter the latter, however. With a little ingenuity, arboreta and nature walks can be constructed in the most constricted of places. Effective design will often provide adequate play space. In both instances, however, attention needs to be directed to making the available space attractive and safe.

Frequent inspections are key. Debris-strewn school sites are inexcusable, and unsafe equipment is both unconscionable and perhaps an issue for litigation in the instance of student or staff injury.

Bell[4] has discovered that three types of equipment account for about 87 percent of all student injuries: swings and swing sets, climbing bars, and slides. Children are exuberant and like to show their prowess on such things. She indicates that 75 percent of all injuries occur from falls from this sort of equipment. The answer? Close supervision and equipment that is in good repair.

Evaluating the Appearance of the Building and Site

Routine work schedules and well-understood expectations are important to the maintenance of the school plant. Time lines and systematic planning for the completion of major maintenance and repair projects need to be supplemented with daily and weekly time schedules to ensure that routine custodial and maintenance tasks get done.

Description of Service	Frequency of Service											
School: ______ Name: ______	7:00 – 8:45	8:45 – 9:00	9:00 – 9:15	9:15 – 10:00	10:00 – 10:15	10:15 – 10:30	10:30 – 11:00	11:00 – 1:30	1:30 – 2:00	2:00 – 2:15	2:15 – 3:30	
Unlock building and turn off alarm												
Sweep all entrances and put out mats												
Police entire building												
Police all restrooms and flush out commodes												
Drop cafeteria tables down												
Dust-mop cafeteria, front and back hall												
Break												
Clean glass												
Set up for lunch												
Repolice restrooms before lunch												
Lunch												
Cafeteria Duty												
Dust-mop back and front halls												
Recheck restrooms and clean wash areas												
Break												
Clean downstairs lounge												
Clean upstairs lounge												
Recheck restrooms and clean wash areas												
Clean drinking fountain in cafeteria												

FIGURE 13.9 Day Schedule, Head Custodian: Elementary School

Regular evaluation of the building's appearance is important. An example of one district's evaluation survey can be seen in Figure 13.10. These survey forms are best developed in concert with the staff so that expectations are clear and standards well understood.

Principal: School: Custodian: Date:

Entrances:	S	G	A	P
Walks:				
Floor mats:				
Door facings:				
Glass:				
Transoms:				
Door tracks:				
Offices:				
Doors:				
Facings:				
Walls:				
Floors:				
Furniture:				
Windows:				
Fixtures:				
Trash:				
Hallways:				
Floors:				
Walls:				
Lights:				
Water fountains:				
Learning Centers:				
Shelves:				
Floor:				
Furniture:				
Glass:				
Door:				
Classrooms:				
Door facings:				
Walls:				
Lights:				
Floors:				
Boards:				

Windows:	S	G	A	P
Furniture:				
Fixtures:				
Teacher's station:				
Cafetorium:				
Floors:				
Windows:				
Fixtures:				
Lights:				
Fountains:				
Machines:				
Doors:				
Fixtures:				
Storerooms:				
Walls:				
Tool racks:				
Supplies:				
Equipment:				
Restrooms:				
Floors:				
Walls:				
Partitions:				
Windows:				
Commodes:				
Urinals:				
Wash basins:				
Mirrors:				
Floor drains:				
Ventilation:				
Lights:				
Furniture:				
Garbage Area:				
Incinerator:				

COMMENTS:

S — Superior
G — Good
A — Average
P — Poor

FIGURE 13.10 Custodian-Maintenance Survey: Building Inspection Checklist

WORKING WITH CLASSIFIED PERSONNEL

Custodians, maintenance personnel, cooks, aides, and secretaries all have important parts to play in the development of the productive learning climate. Frequently, the contributions of these people are not fully recognized. Unless attention is directed to the needs and contributions of support personnel, the risk is that, at best, a wary truce will exist between these personnel and the professional staff.

Evidence of such a condition will be found in the not-so-sly digs each will direct at the other in private meetings and in less-than-adequate services being rendered. Paper towel dispensers that always seem to be out of towels; corners of the cafeteria left unswept; inordinately long waits that occur for equipment to be delivered or repaired; and any number of other examples that any reader of this book could supply—are indicators that all is not well. In some instances, of course, this may be because of a lack of skill or a lack of clear understanding about organizational expectations. If so, that should be quickly remedied—either with "on-the-job" training or replacement.

Engaging support personnel in the same kinds of goal-setting and problem-solving activities that have been suggested for the professional staff is necessary. Administration by edict works no better with custodians and maintenance personnel than it does with the certificated staff. At the beginning of each school year, the principal needs to meet with the custodial staff to chart long-range objectives for building maintenance for the year and to work out a systematic plan for addressing these. Many of the custodial activities will be routine and daily or weekly in nature, of course. Some will not be. Also, the performance of even the routine custodial functions will be affected by such things as special events and even the time of day. Cooperative development of the work schedule is desirable and will result in the important things getting done, getting done well, and in a timely manner.

Selection and Retention of Classified Personnel

The selection, training, and appraisal of support persons is an important managerial task. Yet this has received very little attention in professional literature. Improperly trained workers or workers who are unsure of their responsibility—whether in the cafeteria, in the boiler room, or in the principal's office—are a liability. Similarly, the nonacademic staff member who does not understand or particularly like children, while perhaps not common, is also a liability that a school cannot afford.

Personnel policies for the employment, in-service growth, and retention of good nonacademic personnel should be carefully developed. Job descriptions, adequate compensation, and other benefits must reflect the school's interest in maintaining a nonacademic work force of the highest quality.

The standards of employment should not only evidence an interest in appropriate technical competence, but also a realization that most of these personnel will be working with children in some way or another. The latter simply suggests that appropriate attitudes and understandings about young people may be one of the most important employment and retention criteria. Evaluation of performance is essential.

SUMMARY

The focus of this chapter has been financial and building management. Financial resources are never in great supply. The proper allocation of available resources requires careful planning—the kind of planning that delivers resources in a systematic way to the point of greatest need. Long-range planning and a process for involving the staff are fundamental. Important aspects of school site-based budget building and implementation have been presented in this chapter.

Properly accounting for the available funds is a responsibility of the principal. Special attention must be directed to the training of other personnel to carry out this function, with oversight and monitoring by the principal. A thorough knowledge of district policies is essential. Special attention must be directed to the management of activity funds. Regular, independent audits are recommended.

The physical environment of the school contributes mightily to the learning environment. An attractive, well-kept school building is essential. It is also important that the principal ensure that there are appropriate response mechanisms so that teachers can go about their work with the right equipment at the right time.

An attractive school environment also depends on teachers, custodians, cafeteria personnel, and students. Principals need to work with all of these to create a pleasant place to work and learn.

ACTIVITIES

1. Case Study 3 at the end of this book presents a budget issue of some complexity. Members of your staff in some of the departments are ready to go to war over a share of the available budget dollars. Set forth a process for resolving the issue in a manner consistent with the budget concepts presented in this chapter. Assume your district is committed to decentralized decision making.
2. Issues of school security and maintenance permeate Case Study 11. Where will you start to address these issues?
3. Some money appears to be missing from one of your school activity accounts. This situation is described in Case Study 15. Make any reasonable assumptions and begin the problem resolution process. What steps will you take to prevent this from happening again? What might you have done to have not been "blindsided"?
4. Turn to the ISLLC Standards found in Appendix B. Review the knowledge, dispositions, and performances listed with Standard Three. Reflect on which of the standard items relate directly to the material presented in this chapter. Identify one knowledge area, one disposition, and one performance to link directly to a concept or idea discussed in Chapter 13.

ENDNOTES

1. Dr. James May, Principal of Kempner High School in Fort Bend (Texas) Independent School District.

2. See Chapter 3 for a complete discussion of the GII, CII, CI, AII, and AI decision processes from the Vroom-Jago model.

3. Lloyd Choice, Principal, Kashmere High School, Houston, Texas, Independent School District.

4. Sue Oliver Bell, "Making Playgrounds Safe," *Principal 73,* no. 2 (November 1993): 18–19.

SELECTED READINGS

Alexander, Kern, and Richard G. Salmon. *Public School Finance* (Boston: Allyn and Bacon, 1995).

Drake, Thelbert L., and William H. Roe. *School Business Management* (Boston: Allyn and Bacon, 1994).

Kell, Sue Oliver. "Making Playgrounds Safe." *Principal 73,* no. 2 (November 1993): 18–20.

Natale, Joseph. "A Design for Administering Maintenance Programs." *Planning and Changing 14,* no. 2 (Summer 1993): 83–90.

Thompson, David C., R. Craig Wood, and David S. Honeyman. *Fiscal Leadership for Schools* (New York: Longman, 1994).

CHAPTER FOURTEEN

TECHNOLOGY APPLICATIONS FOR SCHOOL MANAGEMENT

Moore's Law: "Computing capacity, as measured by the speed of microprocessors, doubles on the average of every eighteen months." Metcalf's Law: "The value of a network increases in direct proportion to the square of the number of machines that are on it."

—Thomas M. Siebel and Pat House[1]

As Jim sat down at his desk, he touched his computer keyboard to activate the screen. It had become almost as automatic as turning on the lights, except his computer stayed on all the time, except weekends. Jim first checked his e-mail for important messages. Although he belonged to a number of professional listservs, the filter on his e-mail program filed them automatically so they did not clutter up his incoming e-mail. He reviewed his incoming central office e-mail, noted that the new budget proposals for next year were to be sent today, and then looked to see if any of his staff members had contacted him. He then sent several notes to his secretary to include in the daily e-mail bulletin to teachers. Notices to students were posted on the school web calendar that appeared on monitors throughout the school but had the added advantage of being accessible to students and parents from home.

Jim next brought his "daily reminder" to the screen and added the budget reminder as item 8 to those previously listed. Touching another key, his daily appointments appeared, and Jim noted that his 8:30 appointment was with the parents of Dan Hoglund. Realizing he needed to review Dan's case, he entered the student database, entered his password, and requested the discipline file for Hoglund. He printed out the dates of incidents of the past year from Dan's discipline file as well as the detailed reports that had been entered by the counselor at Dan's suspension several days earlier.

In his few remaining minutes while waiting for the 8:30 conference, Jim made several edits on the screen to rough drafts of letters his secretary had typed for him the previous day. He did not work this way very much anymore, but rather found that for many shorter letters he could compose more quickly at the keyboard than on his old "yellow pad."

Later, upon completion of his conference with the Hoglunds, Jim returned to his computer and entered into the discipline record a short note indicating the result of Dan's conference. Jim next loaded his electronic spreadsheet into the computer on which he had been preparing his new budget. He entered the several changes he had been contemplating, checked his updated totals, and printed a copy of the revised budget document to share with his department heads in his afternoon meeting.

Continuing his preparation for his afternoon department head's meeting, Jim loaded his presentation graphics program. He quickly created four bulleted slides to illustrate the major points he wanted to emphasize in his meeting and saved them in a file that he could access from the conference room on the LCD projector via the school computer network.

The initial tasks completed, Jim next turned to a review of the final draft of the new student handbook. This edition will be published as a web document, saving the cost of paper printing, making the handbook available to students, parents, and staff at any time, and allowing for more frequent updates when desired. Paper printed copies will be printed from computer printers on an "as needed" basis.

Does this scenario seem farfetched? Every one of the functions identified during Jim's busy morning on his computer is already in common use by administrators today. Electronic mail as a part of a local area network (LAN), word processing, desktop publishing, daily reminders and calendars, student record systems, spreadsheets, and web applications, as well as many more useful applications, are available for school principals. Software and hardware are available and the cost is not high. The potential saving in time can be great, and the access to more information for more effective administration is tremendous.

HOW TO GET STARTED

By now, most schools have many computers. Chances are that the first computers, now relegated to the graveyard, went for instructional use directly by students. Often, computers were designated for office use; computers for teacher use then followed. Frequently overlooked was the issue of how all of these computers related to one another, how these machines really fit into the overall program of the school, and what form of training was needed to maximize the potential of this new hardware. Every school needs an overall plan for procurement and integration of technology.

TECHNOLOGY PLANS

Technology planning must be a part of the overall school improvement plans. It is not a stand-alone area. It should be based on a vision of what the school community wants the school to be in the future and include a specific set of basic beliefs that have been agreed upon by the school faculty and staff. Figure 14.1 shows a set of basic beliefs from a technology plan for a K–8 elementary school.

Plans should be developed to span a number of years. Five-year plans, annually updated, are commonly used time frames. Topics may include:

- Technology integration into the curriculum
- Technology integration into school management
- Teacher, student, and staff training in technology utilization
- Expected student technology competencies
- Expected faculty and staff technology competencies

FIGURE 14.1 Phi Beta Kappa's Five-Year Technology Plan: Basic Beliefs

In order to accomplish the goal of providing "diverse opportunities for students to learn to live in a rapidly changing and increasingly complex, multicultural society," technological resources must be utilized. Students must learn how to use the tools of the present to participate effectively in the economy of the future. Our school must identify important technological skills and make certain that our curriculum and instruction allow students to learn and practice those skills, while at the same time learning and practicing traditional academics. Technology provides the current tools that allow people to work, create, and communicate. Pi Beta Phi's responsibility is to integrate those tools into the larger web of math, language arts, science, social studies, visual arts, music, health, and physical education.

- The first step in this process is to develop how to most effectively use technology in teaching the rest of the curriculum.
- The second step is to determine what resources are necessary to accomplish that aim. In the selection and adoption of these resources, the following beliefs will serve as our guide.
  —Curriculum and instruction must be continually assessed.
  —Technology supports opportunities for significant student achievement.
  —All teachers and students need access to computer workstations.
  —All students must develop technological competencies.
  —All teachers need to utilize appropriate technologies for management and for instruction.
  —Students and teachers adapt to change at different rates.
  —Technological training should be ongoing in response to assessed individual needs and interests as well as to the identified needs of the school.
  —Effective use of world-wide educational resources requires utilization of current and appropriate technology.

- Specifications for hardware acquisitions
- Specifications for software acquisitions
- Source of funds for computer acquisitions

Although all of these topics are appropriate for consideration in a school technology plan, this chapter focuses only on those aspects of the plan that relate directly to school management, the development of faculty and staff competencies, and certain hardware and software considerations that relate specifically to school management.

TECHNOLOGY APPLICATIONS FOR A SCHOOL OFFICE

Word Processing

The typical school produces many documents that require periodic updating, demanding in many cases that the entire document be retyped in order for it to be properly formatted. Documents such as student handbooks, policy manuals, staff rosters, standard memos, and curriculum guides are generally modified and updated each year. These items are great candidates for the efficiencies of word processing. Many word processors allow users to save their documents in *hypertext markup language (html),* which is the computer language of web documents. This is what Jim was doing with his student handbook in the introduction to this chapter. In addition, many form letters are used regularly in most school offices for discipline reports, absence notices, scheduling appointments, and the like, usually with blanks to be filled in with the name of the student or parent, or meeting time, or whatever. These documents can be prepared very efficiently with a professional look using the "data merge" capability of the word processor.

The merge feature allows form letters to be personalized with individual names, addresses, and any other data desired directly into the body of the letter or the document. Some of the better programs will allow either the combining of a database such as a name and address file with a form letter, or screen entry into the occasionally used form letter that is needed infrequently or in few copies. A suspension or discipline letter such as the one found in Figure 14.2 is an illustration. The code names called variables found between the "&" symbol are replaced with the data for the particular person or persons who are to receive that letter. For example, for each of the three lines shown in Figure 14.3, a copy of the letter would be typed inserting the proper parent name, address, student name, date, and time in each letter.

Desktop and Web Publishing

Desktop publishing can be used for the many documents schools produce in multiple copies and distribute to faculty, students, parents, and other community members. There are many font styles and sizes and the capability exists to produce graphics and photographs. A variety of page layouts for multicolumn pages is available. The result is professional-looking booklets, newsletters, and forms. Desktop publishing software may also be able to produce html code for the direct publishing of documents on the

FIGURE 14.2 Merge Letter Illustration

&DATE&

&NAME&
&ADDRESS&
&CITYSTZIP&
Dear &NAME&:

Regular attendance at school is very important to children if they are to do their best work. It is also important that your child establish good attendance habits in preparing for future employment.

The state of Tennessee recognizes the importance of attending school regularly and has a law requiring children to attend from their seventh until their seventeenth birthday.

According to the law, you are held responsible for &STUDENT&'s school attendance. I know you are interested in &STUDENT&'s education, and those of us who have the responsibility for teaching and administering the educational program for your child want to assist in any way we can.

I have scheduled a conference in my office on &APPDATES&, &APPTIMES& so that we can discuss the absences of &STUDENT&.

If you have any questions concerning this conference, please call me at 555-5942.

Your cooperation with us in the interest of your child will be appreciated.

Sincerely yours,

Randall Jones
Assistant Principal

web, or special software specifically designed for web publishing is available. Web publishing software also provides assistance in how to design and organize an entire website and includes a number of publishing templates to assist in the design effort.

Database Management Systems

A *database management system* is a computer application that allows the user to enter information into the computer to be later sorted, selected, listed, recalled, manipulated, or printed. The information entered usually is of a uniform nature (such as a series of names, addresses, and phone numbers) and is probably currently filed on one of the many forms or cards that are maintained somewhere within the school. What the com-

FIGURE 14.3 Variables Used in Personalized Form Letters

&NAME&, &ADDRESS&, &CITYSTZIP&, &STUDENT&, &APPDATES&, &APPTIMES&

Mr. & Mrs. Jones, 1234 56th St., Birmingham AL 52318, Mary, "Monday, April 14, 2001," 9:15 AM

Mrs. Sally Snyder, Rt. 2, Jacksboro TN 38024, Robert, "Wednesday, April 16, 2001," 10:00 AM

Mr. & Mrs. Tom Jones, 121 So. 1st St., Sheffield IA 21233, Peter, "Friday, April 18, 2001," 8:30 AM

puter does best is to *sort* entries into a particular order, such as alphabetical or numerical, and/or select records that meet certain criteria from a larger set of records.

Schools generally maintain a tremendous number of record forms that are organized and maintained so that information can be retrieved when needed. Many of these files can be greatly enhanced when served by a computer and its ability to manipulate information. Examples of appropriate applications for the school office range from a simple list of staff names and building keys that they have been issued to a complex file of student cumulative records. Figure 14.4 is a list of possible applications for the school office.

Student Records. Schools collect and maintain a great deal of information on each of their students. This information is usually filed in the student's cumulative record folder, on an emergency card in the office, in the counselor's or teacher's file, or elsewhere. For each application, it is often collected again because there is no easy way to retrieve the information from the existing files and transfer it to the new user. A computerized student records system allows for easier record updating or maintenance, transfer of data to the new various users, and the preparation of many reports that require student counts, lists, and other forms of information organization. Such things as "How

FIGURE 14.4 Data-Based Applications for the School Office

Attendance	Student Record Files
Student Grades	Calendar of Events
Student Emergency Contact Information	Cost Accounting
Student Test Score File	Maintenance Records
Student Club Membership Lists	Bus/Transportation
Student Activity Accounting	Mailing Lists
Scheduling	Sports Accounting
Equipment Inventories	Staff Data Base
Building Key Assignments	Building Key Record

many Title 1 students do you have?" "How many special education LD students are there in your school?" "Which children ride bus 342?" and "We need alphabetical class lists for each ninth-grade homeroom!" can be answered quickly and accurately, saving many hours of clerical time. Management can improve because of the availability of accurate, up-to-date information.

There are several different approaches to establishing and organizing the computer database applications. They are all dependent on the purchase of a software program designed to accept and manage records of this type. The simplest and usually least expensive of these programs are the "file managers." The most elaborate software systems available for microcomputers are the relational database management systems tailored specifically for school records.

No matter what type of software system used, one consideration should be the capability of the software to provide data security. This is particularly true if the software is going to be run on a network with multiple workstations. The more elaborate relational file data systems are more likely to provide for a password system for access, and almost all of the management information systems created specifically for school records have security password control built in. Whenever student records are involved, the same level of confidentiality is required as there is for confidential paper records. However, computer files with multiple workstations compound the problem. Special security measures through the use of passwords to control access is a must.

File Managers

A *file manager* is a program capable of organizing the information for a particular topic into a single file or flat file.[2] Within this particular file, it is necessary to organize all of the information needed for that database because it is not capable of interconnecting with any other files. In other words, when constructing the file, care must be taken to think through all the needed fields, both as to what data are to be stored, and as to how big each file is to become. For example, a basic file for a student record might consist of the following:

FIELD NAME	FIELD LENGTH
Student Name	25 characters
Student ID	9 characters
Student Address	30 characters
Parent Name	25 characters
Home Phone	8 characters
Homeroom Number	3 characters
Total	100 characters

If this information is to be used as part of an emergency card file for all students in the school, additional information such as parent's work phone number, doctor's name and number, and serious medical problems needs to be listed as well. On the other hand, if the file is to be used to identify important in-school information such as homeroom teachers, which bus the student rides, and whether the child receives any special services such as special education or Title 1, then this information needs to be included in the file.

Relational Databases

Relational database management software allows a number of files to be related to one another by some key field placed within each file. This type of database management system is called *relational* because of its ability to relate separate files to one another on this key field. For example, each student's ID number might be the key field in both the name and address file as well as the grade file. Using the ID number to make sure the correct records were accessed, the parent's address could be pulled from one file and the grades from another file. Together, they could be printed out for the report card to be sent home.

With this plan, a series of files can be created with each file including the student ID number as the key field. One file could include basic student descriptive information, another grades, a third standardized test scores, and a fourth emergency medical information. Each record is relatively small in size but can be accessed by other files as needed. A total systems approach using relational data files can be created. It also allows for flexibility, expansion, and modification. As new needs develop, additional files can be created as long as they key on a common field from one of the other existing files. Powerful software such as a relational database management system generally requires more computer memory on which to operate than the simpler file handling programs.

Several database management systems that can be designed by a principal, interested staff member, or student without any previous computer programming experience are available on the market. Consultants are generally available to provide assistance in this design if desired. Many commercial programs for particular applications are available that create a ready-made records system. Each approach has advantages and limitations. For a school to configure its own records system from a purchased database management system will take some time and energy to learn and implement. A school might not realize the full potential of its software nor develop as efficient a system as possible. To hire an outside consultant to assist the school in software development will probably result in the best product but will require a greater outlay of dollars. The purchase of a prepackaged program may or may not give the school a product that is totally functional.

MANAGEMENT INFORMATION SYSTEMS

A well-designed management information system should be able to provide the principal, as well as other personnel in the school, rapid, accurate access to a wide variety of data stored in the school computer. These data may relate to students, staff, finances, materials, athletics, grades, or any other part of the school. Although a school might develop its own system from one of the database management packages, it usually is more efficient to purchase one of the commercial programs designed specifically for school use.[3]

These programs have many standard features—such as scheduling, class lists, and grade reporting—but the better ones also allow the principal to design reports for specific needs. The standard reports and forms provide for efficient data processing in the school, but it is often the special reports that provide the opportunity for the principal to use these electronic data for management decisions. The following special reports could serve this management decision role:

1. *Community Parent Profile*. This is a summary profile of all the parents of the children in the school, showing the percentage of each educational level, number of single-parent homes, type of occupations, percentage originally from outside the area, number of children in the family, and so on. The analysis of this type of information is very useful in developing a better understanding of a student population and its needs.
2. *A New Enrollee Analysis*. This report consists of a listing of the new enrollments for each year by month, with information regarding each student's previous school, condition of transfer, and success in your school using GPA or test score comparisons.
3. *Departing Student Analysis*. This is similar to the enrollment analysis.
4. *Excessive Absence List.* This is a list by name of all students with more than *X* number of days absent, showing total days enrolled and days absent. Also, dates and days of the week of each absence are indicated. The report might include which absences were not excused and if a disciplinary file, particularly truancy, exists on the student. A cross-check on the attendance of siblings is possible as well. If the list is to be used to contact parents, then their names, phone numbers, and addresses could be included as well to speed the follow-up process.[4]
5. *Excessive Tardy Report.* This report could be similar to the excessive absence report. It might also be the basis for notification letters sent home using the merge feature on the word processor (part of good information management is keeping parents informed as well).
6. *Exceptional Student Report.* This is a list by grade and teacher, at the end of each grading period, of all students with a grade point average greater than 3.5, 3.0 to 3.5, and less than 1.5. Special notations can be included for those who were not in these categories during the previous reporting period.
7. *Proficiency Test Report.* This is a list of those students by grade, teacher, and subject area who have not passed certain components of the proficiency test.[5]
8. *Student Disciplinary Report.* A student disciplinary report can be a list of recent disciplinary cases by student and offense, or perhaps only a summary report indicating the number of cases, stating offense category and case disposition.
9. *Achievement Test Analysis.* This is a list of students showing achievement test score gains higher than expected over previous achievement test scores. It is also a list of all students showing achievement test scores lower than expected from previous achievement test scores reported by subject area and teacher.[6]

Financial Accounting Systems

Financial accounting is one of the most common applications for computers. With the increasing demand for highly detailed accounting, the computer becomes a natural solution as a highly accurate labor-saving tool. Specialized packages for accounting are available from most computer stores. These packages are generally designed for business use, however. Most often, only the general ledger component is needed for school accounting and in many cases can be purchased as a separate component. Simple accounting procedures can also be created from a database management system or formulated on spreadsheet software.

Media Center Materials and Equipment

An excellent computer application for schools is the development of a computerized checkout system for library materials and media equipment. An inexpensive bar code reader attachment to a computer allows for easy processing of student and teacher requests. A file is created on the computer, listing all of the material and equipment items to be organized. A bar code label (similar to those used in grocery stores for product identification) is placed on each book or item of equipment.

Each student and staff member is also assigned a bar code number with a label attached to his or her ID card. To process a book or piece of equipment, the media clerk simply scans the book and the student ID card with the bar code reader to record the proper numbers. The date needs to be entered only at the beginning of each day. From this, lists can be generated for the identification of overdue materials. Equipment inventories can be similarly organized for identification and processing. Inexpensive, battery-powered portable computers with bar code attachments can be carried around the building to verify equipment placement at inventory time.

Document Retrieval System

Document imaging and management systems, along with document scanning hardware, allow a school to create a computer document file of records it receives as "hard copy" and retrieve it to the computer screen. Medical records, parent letters, certificates, and even student art work can be stored in such a system. Document descriptors are entered by which the document can be retrieved, sorted, or selected, just as one would do with a regular electronic database.

Management Planning

A variety of tasks and projects are carried out in school each year that involve many people, numerous resources, and detailed planning. Principals often find a key staff member to head up these annual projects and rely on his or her experience for a successful operation each year. The project may be the annual spaghetti supper, school yearbook, or planning the senior prom, but nevertheless, it requires a significant planning or coordination effort. The major difficulty for the principal often comes when the project advisor changes and the new director is not sure what to do.

Project planning software is available to assist in the organization and planning of major projects. It is useful for projects with as few as 15 to 20 steps and can be used for projects up to the size needed by the contractor planning for the construction of a new building. The program guides the user through a series of steps asking for the events, times, people, resources, and relationships to be carried out for the project. It then builds a Gantt chart or a critical path network (CPN) to highlight the necessary steps for project completion. Figure 4.8 in Chapter 4 is an example of a report generated by planning software.

For financial or numeric planning for items such as budgets or attendance projections, spreadsheet software is available. It uses the column-and-row format of an accounting sheet, but formulas can be entered for automatic recalculations as the numbers entered on the spreadsheet change. For example, the program could be used to show enrollment projections for future years based on a predetermined enrollment formula. Each year it could be easily updated to show new enrollment projections. Budget projections are also possible using a previous year's budget with new data. Some of these programs also have the capability of generating graphs from the data that have been entered to improve the visual impression. See Figure 14.5 for a budget example on a spreadsheet.

School Calendar

Calendar software is available for most computers to ease the task of scheduling events and producing graphic calendars on which to post daily, weekly, monthly, and yearly school activities. Keeping schedules clear of one another and the proper people notified is a monumental task in many schools. While master schedules can be posted on a planning board, producing calendars that are readable and that can be modified easily allows the entire school to have up-to-date schedule information. Figure 14.6 is an illustration of such a computer-generated calendar.

Standardized Test Scoring

Most schools have standardized tests scored and analyzed through their district office, through the state department of education, or by the publisher of the standardized test. For most situations, this may continue to be the preferred approach because of the need for these agencies to use the test data from each school in an aggregate manner for comparison purposes. However, test scoring and analysis programs are available along with low-cost, optical scan readers that will allow local schools to efficiently score these tests if they desire. To do so, the school will want to obtain scoring and norming data from the publisher. There are several advantages to local scoring of standardized tests. The results can be back the same day if desired. Also, additional analysis of the collective results of the school's scores are now readily possible with the data available in an electronic format.

FIGURE 14.5 Budget Spreadsheet

DEPARTMENTAL BUDGET, 2001
Mathematics Department
Southeast Elementary

Month October

Budget Area and Item	Allowable	Exp. This Month	Exp. to Date	Remainder
TEXTS (B-4)				
5th Modern Math	$ 500.00	497.00		3.00
Programmed Texts and Temac Binders 21 @ $10.50	220.50		220.50	—
Supplementary Texts	450.00		275.00	175.00
EQUIPMENT (D-4)				
Volume Distribution Set (1)	60.00		60.00	—
Graph Board (multipurpose) (1)	35.00			
Tightgrip Chalkholder (6)	6.00	1.00		5.00
Rack of Compasses	12.00		12.00	—
Rack of Protractors	15.00		15.00	—
SUPPLEMENTARY (B-6)				—
Universal Encyclopedia of Math (2)	20.00	20.00		
Other References	50.00			
AUDIOVISUAL (D-7)				—
Overhead Projector	175.00		175.00	
DISCRETIONARY SUPPLIES	100.00			
SUBTOTAL	$1,643.50	518.00	757.50	368.00
PERSONNEL (A-3)				
2 Consultants 2 days each for in-service expenses	900.00			
SUBTOTAL	$ 900.00			
TOTAL	$2,543.50	518.00	757.50	1268.00

Presentation Graphics

Teacher and administrators alike are constantly giving presentations for which illustrations, graphs, major bulleted points, or pictures or drawings are needed. Presentation software provides an easy, quick means of producing such illustrations with a very professional look. Backgrounds and formats are provided. Output can be to a regular printer for black and white transparencies or paper. Color transparencies can be produced even with a low-cost color ink-jet printer. A disk can be sent to a photo finisher to produce 35 mm slides or the output can be displayed through a LCD projector or large

NOVEMBER

Sunday	Monday	Tuesday	Wednesday	Thursday	Friday	Saturday
				1	**2**	**3**
4	**5** 3:20—Faculty Meeting	**6** ELECTION DAY Student Holiday	**7**	**8**	**9**	**10**
11	**12** 3:20—Faculty Meeting	**13** NUTRITION DAY WORKSHOP 3:20—Leadership Team Meeting	**14** MAKE-UP DAY FOR PICTURES	**15** STUDENTS FROM LITTLE WORLD TO TALK TO K–5 9:30–12:00	**16**	**17**
18	**19** 9:15—K & 1 Program Marty Silver Environmentalist 3:20—Faculty Meeting	**20** End of Third Month 9:00 2nd Grade Play K, 1, 3, & Multi-Age 9:15—4 & 3 Program Marty Silver Environmentalist 1:00 2nd Grade Play K, 4	**21** End of Six Weeks 9:15—2 & 3 Program Marty Silver Environmentalist 10:30 Singers leave for Gatlinburg 2:00 Singers Program at Gatlinburg	**22** **THANKSGIVING HOLIDAYS**	**23**	**24**
25	**26** 3:20—Faculty Meeting	**27** The Clue That Turned Blue 10:00–K, 1st, 2nd Multi 10:30–3rd, 4th, & 5th 3:20—Leadership Team Meeting	**28** Progress Reports go out 8:30–11:30 Bledsoe—Ijani's Park Bivens—Airport	**29**	**30** Kindergarten— "Nutcracker"	

FIGURE 14.6 Computer-Generated Calendar

computer monitor. Hard-copy printouts with a place for speaker notes or three-to-a-page printouts for participants can be produced also. Additionally, the more powerful packages can have sound or short movie segments associated with them.

LOCAL AREA NETWORKS (LANS)

Most schools are now networked, linking together computers in a variety of configurations. Some networks link together the computers in a computer laboratory, others link together several machines in the school office. The direction being taken by most schools is the creation of a schoolwide local area network (LAN) linking all classrooms and offices in the building to a computer server. A computer server operates as the hub of the computer network. It generally is more powerful than the typical workstation and is set up with special networking software. The server is often connected via high-speed phone lines to an Internet service provider and the Internet. This new connectivity presents many new communication and information opportunities, but also presents new problems.

Software Issues

Software specifications must be designed for network applications and care must be taken to be sure appropriate software licenses have been purchased for each workstation. More discussion of software specification can be found later in this chapter. Deciding who is to have access to what information becomes a major policy concern. Much information will reside in the school computer files. Decisions must be made regarding who should have access to this information. Then set up a password system within the building and firewall protection to guard against unauthorized access from outside the school.

Network Policy Issues

On the computer system may be found copies of student school records and correspondence, personnel files of employees, financial records of the school, e-mail documents, a variety of software applications, operating system software, and more. Much of this information is confidential in nature or could be damaged or disabled by an accidental or malicious act. Good network software provides a level of access to the software and information stored in the computer files so that staff members and students can have access to only those files they need to use.

Acceptable Use Policies

Decisions must be made regarding levels of use. What can each teacher access? What should the school clerical staff be able to see? What files should be the private property of the file creator? To what files, if any, should the principal *not* have access (e.g., personal teacher files residing on their workstation)? Which files are public files that every one can see? Do students have e-mail privileges? What about Internet access? It is a valuable learning tool, but should the school place controls or limits regarding the kinds of material that can be viewed? And how will these decisions be enforced? What information can be stored, by whom, on workstations and who manages this? All of these questions require thoughtful consideration.

One way of dealing with the myriad of policy questions that technology brings is to form a technology policy committee to review these and other questions that arise. Because of the concerns regarding Internet use, it is probably wise to include parents as well as teachers and other staff on the committee. Acceptable use policies that have been developed by other schools are available as part of overall technology plans.[7]

E-mail is becoming a major communication tool for busy principals. Once every teacher in the school has a personal workstation, e-mail can become a way of enhancing in school communication. For example, faculty and staff announcements can quickly be broadcast to all concerned. Teachers can raise issues and express concerns for the principal's consideration via e-mail, allowing the principal to respond as time is available. E-mail messages can be filed electronically for better record keeping. Software systems for e-mail can be placed on the local server for in-house use. Similarly, student privileges for the use of e-mail are becoming more common. This can aid communication between teacher and student, as well as between teacher and parent. It can be limited to an "in-house" use or it can be allowed as an open Internet activity. Once again, this is a policy issue for some debate.

WORLD WIDE WEB (WWW)

The Internet, and particularly the portion known as the World Wide Web (WWW), has changed society significantly. It is imperative that children learn of the resources and tools the WWW provides for their future lives, but the WWW has become a tremendously rich resource for learning, as well. Supporting many aspects of the traditional curriculum of the school—geography, math, English, foreign languages, art, music, history, vocational subjects—every subject now has a greatly expanded source of materials and resources. In addition, lesson plans, teacher training, professional articles, support networks, and discussion groups are available for the professional staff's development. Many of the subject area teacher associations now have excellent teacher resource websites. The National Association of Secondary School Principals (NASSP) and the National Association of Elementary School Principals (NAESP) have excellent sites for principals.[8]

School Website

A school website provides an opportunity to present a positive image of the school to the local community and to provide a solid information link to the parents of the children served by the school. It must be remembered, however, that not all families have access to the web, so other communication links must also be used.

A good school website can contain a variety of semi-permanent items, such as the school's mission statement; policies, rules, and regulations for the school; and names of the building administrators and staff members, including e-mail addresses and phone numbers. Similar information can be provided for key district administrators. Information can also be listed about school clubs and other school-related organizations. Parents can be encouraged to communicate with teachers and administrators via e-mail.

Part of the website should be expected to change frequently. It might include items such as a school calendar of events for the week, month, and year; classroom news and announcements, including planned activities and homework assignments for each class; special school or classroom projects; breakfast and lunch menus; and educational links that might provide helpful resources for students and parents at home. A special page used to celebrate school and student successes is also appreciated. Be sure to carefully consider in the school's technology policy any limits that need to be placed on children's identities in web publications.

A faculty member or technology coordinator should be placed in charge of webpage development and maintenance. This person is often called the webmaster. However, all teachers should be taught webpage construction so they can maintain a web component for their classroom, club, or activity. Any materials they develop can be forwarded to the webmaster to integrate into the school site. Special software is available to aid in the construction of multiple page sites.

STAFF DEVELOPMENT FOR TECHNOLOGY

A continuing plan of staff development is absolutely necessary if the investment in hardware and software is going to produce real benefits. Schools that have invested in hardware and software only usually find their investment underutilized.

With the rapid advances in technology, teachers as well as other staff member must constantly be in training in order to keep abreast of the advances. Teachers cannot be expected to teach to children what they themselves do not model or cannot do. Teachers only a few years out of college can fall far behind recent technology advances. Here are some suggestions for staff development in technology:

- Provide each staff member, in his or her classroom, a computer workstation connected to the school computer network. Teachers should have the newest technology in their rooms so that they can keep up with the newest technological developments.
- Provide several levels of technology training each year, depending on staff members' needs.
- The principal should participate in the technology training and practice good technology utilization.
- Ask all staff members to use their computer for inside communication (e-mail).
- Conduct an annual staff technology self-evaluation to determine level of competence and needed areas for future training.

A self-evaluation instrument for technology can be constructed by asking staff members to self-rate on a multipoint scale on topics such as:

- Basic computer operation
- File management
- Word processing
- Spreadsheet use
- Database use
- Graphics use
- Internet browser use—operation and Internet research
- Telecommunication use—e-mail, video
- Ethical use understanding
- Information searching
- Presentation skills
- Technology integration[9]

HARDWARE SECURITY

Computer equipment, being expensive but relatively lightweight and compact, is highly vulnerable to theft, particularly in the open setting of a school. Particular caution needs to be taken to reduce this threat. The following actions are recommended to reduce this loss:

1. Record all serial numbers on microcomputers and related equipment. This will assist police in their investigation should equipment be stolen. Serial numbers further allow the police to place listings of stolen property in the NCIC (National Crime Information Center).
2. Stencil or burn the school name and location on the exterior surface of the computer in plain view. Also place identification markings on an unexposed area of your equipment.
3. Obtain security anchor pads, if available, from your vendor at the time of purchase, noting that time and effort will be involved in removing a device. This will prevent equipment from disappearing from open offices or classrooms during the day.
4. Be security conscious but be careful not to be so restrictive that it becomes inconvenient to use the equipment.

SUMMARY

The areas of using the Internet, word processing, student records, financial accounting, scheduling, grade reporting, attendance, staff personnel, presentation graphics, media center materials and equipment, management planning, and survey form and teacher-made test analysis represent areas to consider when planning for the computerization of the school office. Today, it is not overly ambitious to attempt all of them simultaneously. This will help in both software and hardware selection so that program compatibility can be maintained and hardware expansion made possible.

ACTIVITIES

1. Review Case Studies 15 and 20 at the end of this book. Analyze the problems presented and apply the concepts of computer utilization developed in this chapter. How might these problems have been prevented if a good computer system had been in place? What approach would you use in addressing the problems identified in these cases? Set forth a strategy to overcome the difficulties faced by the school in each of these cases.
2. What are the greatest impediments to full computerization of our schools? Apply the concepts of strategic planning set forth in Chapter 4 and the ideas on human resources development outlined in Chapter 9 to the impediments you have identified. Outline your plan of action.
3. Turn to the ISLLC Standards found in Appendix B. Review the performances listed with Standard Three. How well are the technology and management performances carried out in your school? What would be some ways to improve the management of your school with technology?

ENDNOTES

1. Thomas M. Siebel and Pat House, *Cyber Rules* (New York: Currency/Doubleday, 1999), p. 8.

2. A database management system organizes information into three levels: files, records, and fields. A field is usually one piece of information for which a specific amount of space is allocated, such as a space for the name of an individual. A record is a collection of fields for one case, such as the name, address, and phone number for a particular individual. A file is a collection of records entered into the computer, all organized with the same format.

3. There are many kinds and brands of commercial software on the market for school record keeping, class scheduling, and to assist in project planning. Both IBM-compatible systems and Macintosh-compatible systems are available.

4. Automated phone-calling programs are available that can use the electronic absence report to call each home of the absentees during the evening hours to inform parents that their child was absent that day.

5. A proficiency test is the term for a state or locally administered criterion-referenced skills test often given in reading, math, language, and occasionally other areas, such as social studies and science.

6. Any attempt to use these test score data to review teacher performance must be done with extreme care. Using raw gain scores such as suggested here must be enhanced by special statistical treatments such as analysis of covariance, or some other means of adjusting gain scores.

7. Appropriate use of the Internet by teachers and students is a concern of many educators. In conjunction with a technology plan, school planners frequently develop an acceptable use policy that addresses how students, staff, and community members use the Internet. There are many websites that list examples of acceptable use policies. Here are a few selected acceptable use policies that can be found online: Northwest Educational Technology Consortium <http://www.netc.org/tech_plans/aup.html>, The Education Technology Journal <http://www.fromnowon.org/fnomay95.html>, K–12 Acceptable Use Policies <http://www.erehwon.com/k12aup>.

8. National Association of Secondary School Principals <http://www.nassp.org/> and National Association of Elementary School Principals <http://www.naesp.org>.

9. A number of self-assessment instruments for technology are posted on the web. This list was drawn from a scale developed originally by the Mankato (Minnesota) Schools and later modified by the Bellingham (Washington) Public Schools <http://www.bham.wednet.edu/assess2.htm>.

SELECTED READINGS

Anderson, Larry. *Guidebook for Developing an Effective Instructional Technology Plan,* Version 3, presented at NECC '99 (National Educational Computing Conference) available as a PDF file at <http://www.nctp.com>.

Bradshaw, Lynn K. "Technology-Supported Change: A Staff Development Opportunity." *NASSP Bulletin 81,* no. 593 (December 1997): 86–92.

Brooks, Susan. "Networking and the School Administrator's Role." *Technology and Learning 19,* no. 8 (April 1999): 44.

Crouse, David. "The Principal Rules for School Technology." *NASSP Bulletin 81,* no. 589 (May 1997).

Dempsey, Dennis F. "Professional Development: Linking Principals, Staff Members, Students, and Technology" *NASSP Practitioner 24,* no. 2 (December 1997).

Ginsberg, Rick, and Virginia McCormick. "Computer Use in Effective Schools." *Journal of Staff Development 19* (Winter 1998): 22–25.

Johnson, Doug, and Eric Bartleson. "Technological Literacy for Administrators." *The School Administrator 56,* no. 4 (April 1999).

Kaufman, Cathy C. "Using Technology to Upgrade the Principal's Role as Instructional Leader." *NASSP Bulletin 81,* no. 587 (March 1997): 98–101.

Laffey, Richard. "Saving Time with Technology." *Principal 79,* no. 1 (September 1999): 60–61.

Logan, Joyce E. "The E's of E-Mail: Tip for Effective and Efficient Use in School Administration." *NASSP Bulletin 83,* no. 603 (January 1999): 84–90.

McKenzie, Jamie. "The New Library in the Wired School." *From Now On, The Educational Technology Journal 9,* no. 5 (January 2000) <http://www.fno.org/jan2000/newlibrary.html>.

Newman, Denis, Susan Bernstein, and Paul Reese. "Local Infrastructures for School Networking." <http://www.nctp>.

O'Lone, Daniel J. "Student Information Systems Software: Are You Getting What You Expected?" *NASSP Bulletin 81,* no. 585 (January 1997): 86–93.

See, John. "Developing Effective Technology Plans." Minnesota Department of Education <http://www.nctp.com>.

PART IV

INTERACTING WITH THE EXTERNAL SCHOOL ENVIRONMENT

The school leaders of the twenty-first century must have knowledge and understanding of emerging issues and trends that potentially impact the school community; the conditions and dynamics of the diverse school community; community resources; community relations and market strategies and processes; and successful models of school, family, business, community, government, and higher education partnerships. They should also believe in, value, and be committed to schools operating as an integral part of the larger community, collaboration and communication with families, involvement of families and other stakeholders in school decision-making processes, the proposition that diversity enriches the school, families as partners in the education of their children, the proposition that families have the best interests of their children in mind, resources of the family and community needing to be brought to bear on the education of students, and an informed public. ISLLC Standard Four supports these.

> **Standard 4: A school administrator is an educational leader who promotes the success of all students by collaborating with families and community members, responding to diverse community interests and needs, and mobilizing community resources.**

Likewise, the educational leader must have knowledge and understanding of principles of representative governance that undergird the system of U.S. schools; the role of public education in the developing and renewing a democratic society and an economically productive nation; the law related to education and schooling; the political, social, cultural, and economic systems and processes that impact schools; models and strategies of change and conflict resolution as applied to the larger political, social, cultural, and economic contexts of schooling; global issues and forces affecting teaching and learning; the dynamics of policy development and advocacy under a democratic political system; and the importance of diversity and equity in a democratic society. ISLLC Standard Six supports these.

Standard 6: A school administrator is an educational leader who promotes the success of all students by understanding, responding to, and influencing the larger political, social, economic, legal, and cultural context.

Part IV addresses these two standards and the knowledge, dispositions, and performances that accompanies them.

CHAPTER FIFTEEN

THE SCHOOL AND THE COMMUNITY

Schools have a political dimension. . . . The actions of federal and state courts, federal and state legislatures, and federal and state agencies all impinge on the operation of the local school. The local school board of education within set parameters controls much of what goes on in the daily operation of the schools. Yet, each of the aforementioned will be influenced greatly by an informed and committed citizenry when that citizenry is well organized, well funded, and highly vocal.

—Larry W. Hughes and Don W. Hooper[1]

The subject of this chapter is school public relations. In a democratic society, public agencies must not only be responsive to the needs of the members but also cognizant of the distinctive (and sometimes exceptional) nature of the local community to be served. In a pluralistic society, with its myriad belief systems and prevalent skepticism, developing an effective public relations program will require great sensitivity to the varied perceptions that may exist in any given school community.

This chapter is organized first to provide some sociological underpinnings to explain why the public relations process is so complex and second to provide a grounding in effective public relations practices to address these complexities.

THE COMMUNITY

To use a line from *The Music Man:* "You gotta know the territory!" There they were: salesmen—old-time "drummers"—being jostled along, on board a train, moving from town to town, purveying their various wares. How best to sell the product? No matter what the product, went the refrain to the song in progress, "You gotta know the territory!" And that means understanding the customer.

We don't want to carry the analogy too far but there is much to be learned from the refrain to the opening number in the often revived *The Music Man.* And, for the educator interested in developing a good public relations program, the "territory" to be known is complex, indeed.

The entire school territory—the community—is involved in the process of education. A high-performing school requires broad-based community support, and support will come from communities that are well informed and well engaged in the educative processes that go on in the school. This does not happen automatically.

Communication between parents and other citizens, businesses, health and social-care agencies, several levels of government, teachers, administrators, and students is essential and is the glue that binds the learning community together. Establishing good communication processes is an essential task of the principal. It is not easy. Communities are diverse, attitudes vary, and formal and informal forces vie for attention and make demands on the school that are often contradictory and at cross-purposes. The territory is complex and so must be the school-community public relations program.

Schools do not exist apart from the society to be served. They get their support from the "outside" world, and those who make policy and those who permit policy to be made reside in the outside world. Inevitably and inexorably, individuals and groups attempt to establish policies and procedures in the school that are consistent with—indeed generative and supportive of—their values, beliefs, and ideals.

These are days of much individual school-based autonomy and in some places a mandated use of such decisional mechanisms as citizen and teacher advisory councils organized at the school level. The principal's role as a community relations expert has expanded and pressures have mounted for more effective ways to communicate with the "publics" comprising the school community. These pressures are visited on teachers as well.

To perform this role even adequately well requires both knowledge about the makeup of the school community and about how best to communicate with community members. It is increasingly apparent that the strongest support base for the school is "grass roots" in nature, but there are seemingly infinite varieties of grass to be found in the lawns of many school communities. Moreover, it isn't only parents who feel they have a vested interest in schooling practices.

Also, one need not be a graduate sociologist to be aware of the impact such phenomena as technocracy, urbanization, and the increasing complexity of social relationships have had on the nature of interaction between school and community. The increasing esostericism of professional educational practices, a concomitant of these changes, has widened the gap between school and community. The dissolution of the small, closely knit communities of years past has made schools and the people in the area unsure of the other. The same situation obtains in the medical and legal professions as well as other welfare delivery agencies that attempt to address the varied and complex needs of people who live in a community. The term *community* has been corrupted to simply mean groups of people living in close proximity and served by many of the same social and governmental agencies.

THE SCHOOL IN THE COMPLEX COMMUNITY: THE IMPACT OF THE GESSELSCHAFT SOCIETY

U.S. society is characterized by multiethnicity and cultural pluralism, and this age is characterized generally by criticism and skepticism about public agencies and the efficiency with which these agencies dispatch services. Thus, the particular need for the development of better mechanisms to provide for effective communication between the school and the community is glaringly apparent.

There is ideological unity in a "real" community. A *real community* is a community that reflects well-understood belief structures and mores, is relatively independent from other communities, has a common bonding, and is made up of individuals who manifest a personal sense of identity with the community that is eternal and true for all other members. This type of community is described as *sacred* in orientation and carries the label *gemeinschaft*. It doesn't describe very many places in the western world today.

What does describe life in most western world communities today is the term *gesselschaft*. In the gesselschaft community, people are unified largely by civil units rather than by kinship ties. There is a great division of labor and proliferation of organizations, each with special membership and interests. Formal social controls are set by law and enforced by various civil agencies. In such communities there is a basic anonymity and people may live *in* the community without being *of* the community. This is the *secular* community, and in this community there may be much overt conflict.

Few things that have to do with human society can be unerringly assigned. When one thinks of gemeinschaft and gesselschaft, it's conceptually sound to place these terms at opposite ends of a continuum and think of communities as appearing on various points in between. Where a community lies on the sacred-secular continuum influences the nature of decision-making practices in that community.

One problem in the largely gesselschaft society, with its evident cultural pluralism, is that various individuals and groups may reflect widely differing points of view and hold diverse perceptions of what the institutions serving their particular location ought to look like and ought to be doing. The politics of confrontation and conflict within which the school and other social institutions are often caught up in is simply a manifestation of this.

The school is the closest community agency to residents, in both a literal and figurative sense. In geographic proximity, the school is "just around the corner" and often becomes the first line of communication with the area served. It is closer than the mayor's office; in most cases, it is even closer than the fire station. And, the school affects mightily the community's most prized possessions—its children and its pocketbook. It should not be surprising then that the schools are frequently the subject of perusal and subsequent criticism, and sometimes the result of the perusal is more visceral than cerebral.

INFORMAL COMMUNITY FORCES

Influence and power are distributed unevenly throughout communities. Moreover, informal power must be distinguished from formal power. Formal power is manifest in the elected and appointed governmental offices of the community—the mayor, city council, police chief, superintendent, and board of school trustees, for example. *Informal power* refers to the ability of various individuals or groups to get certain things done in the community in a way that is satisfying to the individual or group. It may refer to individuals who are at or near the top of their respective social or occupational hierarchies. It may also refer to groups that are composed of, or individuals who represent, members of various special-interest groups, and who, on any given issue, mobilize substantial portions of the population to respond in a particular way.

The ability to influence is dependent on the presence of two elements: substantial resources and commitment. *Substantial resources* does not necessarily mean control of large sums of dollars: it may simply mean the control of large groups of people. People are a resource. Most of the early civil rights successes were characterized by displays of latent power and were conducted without huge sums of money, relatively speaking. *Commitment* refers to a singular belief in the basic rightness of whatever it is that is being proposed (i.e., the group "hangs together" no matter what), and when coupled with control of some resources, a formidable force is present.

Neighborhood Influence Systems

As communities have become more and more complex, neighborhood influence systems have become increasingly important. Such influence systems often reflect racial, ethnic, religious, or economic homogeneity.

Neighborhood influence systems may be especially important within the principal's sphere of interaction. We noted earlier that the individual school building remains, in most places, the closest community agency, certainly in terms of geographic proximity. Thus, it is handy, if nothing else, to members of the immediate neighborhood who have opinions to express. Moreover, school personnel, and especially the principal, are also in an excellent position to feel the pulse of the surrounding area, and to interact directly with that group.

Individual schools need to develop effective mechanisms to receive information from, and to dispense information to, neighborhood leadership. Research suggests that an individual community member's decision to support or not support any particular community issue is more often than not based on the influence of friends and neighbors rather than on the presence of any outside objective data. It would seem, therefore, that the school principal should become familiar with the leadership structure of the neighborhood the individual school may serve.

There is a leadership structure in any community or neighborhood, except the most anomic. This structure may be readily identified, often through reputational means by surveying the "store-front" churches as well as the well-known churches, the local welfare agencies, the better *and* less well known social clubs, and the membership of union locals, among any number of other somewhat formal sources. If a community is characterized by heterogeneity in racial, ethnic, or social makeup, more than the usual effort will be required because well-known organizations may not reflect this heterogeneity. Further, a neighborhood leadership structure may not be composed of, or contain very many, people who are also parents of children attending the schools.

Old mechanisms will not suffice for the principal interested in developing effective school-community relations programs based on mutual trust and a willingness to examine issues of mutual concern. Traditional community groups often do not have a membership composed of anything approximating the real nature of the community or the neighborhood served by the schools, and there may exist a leadership structure that has not yet been recognized but that has important things to say about schools. An examination of the membership of local, formal parent-teacher organization and a comparison of certain characteristics of these people with general demographic characteristics of the student body of the school may reveal that certain groups of people are missing. If different kinds of people are missing, one can be sure that many key neighborhood influentials are not being reached by school messages.

Community Groups

The most intense memberships are held in groups that can be classified as *blut und bod*. These are groups with kinship and territorial bonds rooted in certain ethnic, racial, or historical ties.

> A common language, a common dietary, a common neighborhood, common experience with outsiders, a common history, make people feel more comfortable with one another, more at ease. They understand one another, they read one another; they get one another's messages. They feel they can count on one another for support. They constitute an in group; everyone else is an out group.
>
> *The bonds that hold people together also separate them from others; invisible lines are drawn to protect the boundaries between them and outsiders* (emphasis added).[2]

Moreover, people in the community are also often members of an array of different formal and informal groups that may impinge on the schools. They are members of clubs and associations, some *blut und bod* in nature, characterized by such self-help groups as, for example, the American Indian Movement, the League of United Latin American Citizens, the NAACP, or the National Organization of Women. People belong, as well, to unions and professional associations, to political parties, and to neighborhood improvement leagues. All of these organizations demand loyalty from their members and may from time to time oppose certain school system procedures, policies, and practices. Membership in what at times may be adversary groups can be the source of much community-school conflict.

Pressure Groups

No discussion of community influence systems would be complete without some attention to the nature of pressure groups. Pressure groups can be distinguished from the usual community decision-making systems because of the relatively short-lived nature of their activities and their tendency to form and re-form around issues or causes. Often, a group will form because of a specific decision made by the school leadership which is perceived to have an impact on the certain group's life space or belief system.

Pressure groups should not be dismissed lightly. They are a source of great disruption in many communities and sometimes a source of productive change. It is difficult to put the term *pressure group* in a noninflammatory context. Immediately, thoughts of book burnings, witch hunts, placard-carrying demonstrators, and impassioned pleas from the pulpit or the podium come to mind. One may also imagine school boards and superintendents hastily capitulating to the onslaught of such charges that the schools are "godless," that the English department is assigning lascivious literature, and that sex education is corrupting youth, among a host of similar kinds of charges, emotion-ridden in context and within which rational behavior often is nearly impossible.

But a pressure group may also be composed of parents arguing persuasively for the return of an art program. It may be a collection of citizens raising important issues of equity or insisting on balanced reporting in textbooks about the contributions of minorities. It may be a group raising questions about district employment practices or the lack of bilingual programs, among other issues of equity. Most of the legislation and court orders ensuring or extending rights at local, state, and national levels have occurred because, early on, a small group of concerned citizens organized to call attention to an undesirable situation.

It is clearly the right of citizens to protest when they feel that the school is failing to accomplish the right thing. Conflict may not be inevitable, but it is frequent in any society. Conflict is also not necessarily disruptive or negative. Often, it is out of conflict that greater understanding results, provided the situation is characterized by openness, a willingness to compromise, and well-understood and agreed-upon procedures for resolution.

Negotiating with Pressure Groups. From time to time, all school administrators will be confronted with requests from organized groups of people who represent a particular point of view about a school-related issue. Frequently, such pressure groups begin their inquiries at the school level in the principal's office. The issues may run the gamut, from complaints about teachers, textbooks, or specific courses of study to alleged institutional racism and demands for more equitable staffing or pupil assignment decisions. These are often legitimate concerns, but legitimate or not, they must always be dealt with sensitively and sensibly.

The following guidelines may help a besieged principal:

1. *Identifying*. An early identification should be made of the group that is in opposition to, or is likely to be in opposition to, certain school programs. Who are they? More importantly, who are the leaders?

2. *Discussing*. Can the leaders be talked with? Once the opposing group and the leader(s) of that group have been identified, it is appropriate to engage in a closed-door session to explore the elements of the issue. The administrator may gain a more definitive notion of just what it is that is troubling the group. This meeting or series of meetings may result in ways, if the cause is legitimate, for the school to help the group achieve its goals. It may require great insight to find out what the real issue is because stated "reasons" for opposition to this or that school issue are often at variance with the real causative factors. (At this point, it is also important to apprise the central office of the potential hostile situation and to seek counsel.)

3. *Analyzing.* Following the informal meetings, it is important to reach a decision. Some important points must be considered at this time, including the question of how strong the opposition really is. Do they have a good chance to "beat" the school in its present position? Most importantly, do they have a solid point on which to differ with the school? It is at this time that the decision must be made about whether the issue will be fought on the basis of the initial position of both sides or whether some accord is possible.

In all situations, it is important to determine what the real goal is and what results or gains can be expected from the achievement of that goal. In other words, is the school's position or is the school administrator's position tenable? If so, evidence must be present to substantiate why it is tenable. Many school administrators have ended up in great difficulty because of a refusal to negotiate or compromise or because of an unwillingness to give up irrelevant points of contention.

4. *Negotiating.* Is there room for compromise? The political system under which a democracy operates functions on compromise. Politics is the delicate art of compromise. Desirable changes can be achieved without compromising principles and without loss of integrity.

Of course, compromising may not be necessary. Perhaps simply sitting down with members of the pressure group and explaining the school's position and the facts may dissuade the group from further action. However, administrators who have engaged in community conflict situations over the years would suggest that compromise and negotiation is the more likely process. The pressure group's motives may be highly complex. Its needs and goals are every bit as important to its membership as are the needs and goals of the particular administrator or school system in question.

In any effort to influence or achieve compromise, timing is important. One really can't wait until an organized campaign is under way to effect compromises or modify points of view. The time to influence a pressure group is before the particular group has launched its initial fusillade and before school personnel are totally and publicly committed to a position. Common sense suggests that it is increasingly difficult to change someone or some group when there will be much loss of face, real or imagined, by doing so.

5. *Marshaling Resources.* Seek help from other community members. Assuming that all efforts to negotiate with the opposition are unsuccessful, what does the administrator try next? The first step is to find out who is on the school's side, or who it appears ought to be on the school's side. Some community analysis can be conducted even at this stage and may prove fruitful. Who besides the school really stands to lose? Principals should not forget about other less-organized neighborhood groups of people who, though they seemingly may have a low potential for power, might have a high potential for unity on the particular issue and who could be called on for counsel and help.

Evaluating the Legitimacy of the Critic. Members of the community have the right to legitimately question and criticize the schools, although defining the word *legitimate* in this context is difficult. One of the best benchmarks for judging legitimacy is to observe the behavior exhibited by the particular group. Is the group willing to meet with appropriate educational system personnel out of the harsh glare of TV lights or without benefit of newspaper rhetoric? Is the group willing to consider other sides of the issue? Is criticism mostly characterized by reason and rationality, or does it seem mostly emotional in nature? Will the critics accept demonstrable facts? If these conditions are not met then one may question the "legitimacy" of the critic and prepare for battle.

Implications for the Principal

School leaders need to identify the influential people and groups in the community or neighborhood. Influence systems vary from community to community and neighborhood to neighborhood. There is an indeterminacy and amorphousness about influence systems. Regular monitoring of the community is important to do.

Anticipate Obvious Flashpoints. Why should a school leader be surprised when there are expressed concerns by some parents that some school books have themes or language that they consider inappropriate* or about a new school rule that requires a uniform dress code? Why should there be surprise when a school that has a multicultural or multiracial, or both, population evidences discord and prejudice or charges or "unfair" treatment on this or that occurrence? Or that there is concern about a poor showing on state- or districtwide tests?

These things have happened historically and recur frequently. One is left to wonder why anyone would be unprepared for this sort of thing. The solution, of course, is to realize that such flashpoints will occur and to develop policies and procedures to handle these fairly.

The Need for Well-Developed Policies. If conflict can be expected on educational issues, if ideological unity is not characteristic of very many complex communities, and if criticism can be expected as a part of the normal life of the administrator of any public institution, what can be done to modify the divisive effects of such actions and instead capitalize on the rich diversity of views and opinions to improve the schools? Foremost is to provide a broad set of policies, both at the school district level as well as at the school building level, that establish a framework within which diverging views can be heard in a regular and systematic manner. Such a framework provides, in effect, procedural due process whereby dissident factions in a community can formally register their concerns.

*Library materials as well as assigned published materials from the classroom are a constant source of parent and community complaint. The books in the J. K. Rowling *Harry Potter* series, for example, have come under fire from some members of the Religious Right. "Satanism and witchcraft" are the battle cries, attacking these books, all of which actually promote friendship, loyalty, good over evil and high ethical principles, and use great adventures to capture the attention of young readers.

Figure 15.1 is a sample form that some districts provide to those individuals who are objecting to the use of certain educational material. Such a complaint form could be adapted to other issues and, if used judiciously, provide a vehicle for citizens to make their views known in a rational and systematic way.

Working with Review Boards. Individual principals would be wise to establish some kind of review body on whom the principal could rely for advice, counsel, and the development of criteria for judging potentially controversial instructional materials. The importance of involving an array of appropriate personnel in the development of policies to anticipate problems is important because it provides the basis for information sharing and good decision making. Principals cannot be expected to know everything. No principal should expect to be able to respond instantaneously to a critic. The advice and counsel of the school staff, as well as the community, and the development of broadly based policies and policy review boards are needed to provide for effective

FIGURE 15.1 Citizen's Request for Reconsideration of Educational Medium

Title of medium ______________________________

Type of medium: (circle)

Book Film Filmstrip Recording ______________________________ (other)

Author/artist/composer/other ______________________________

Publisher/producer (if known) ______________________________

Request initiated by ______________________________ Phone______________

Address ______________________________

Complainant represents ______________________________

______________ Self

______________ (Name of organization) ______________________________

______________ (Identify other group) ______________________________

1. After having read/viewed/listened to the item in question, to what do you object, and why? (Please be specific; cite pages, frame, other)
____
2. What do you believe is the theme of this item? ______________________________
____
3. What do you feel might be the result of students reading/viewing/listening to this item?
____
4. For what age group would you recommend this item? ______________________________
____
5. Other comments ______________________________
____
____

______________ Date

______________________________ Signature of Complainant

decision making and intelligent responses to questions that may come from the community.

Working with Other Community Agencies. Many community agencies and organizations in addition to schools have—or could have—an impact on the quality of children's lives. The school principal is in an uncommonly good position to coordinate the efforts of these agencies.

It often happens that the principal serves in that role anyway because the elementary school is most often the closest social agency available to patrons. And patrons look to their schools for all sorts of help that has to do with their families' well-being. The "closeness" of the school is for many as much a matter of psychological proximity as it is a physical proximity. Many community members look to the school for help in matters neither of the school's doing nor jurisdiction simply because they know of no other place to turn.

The sad fact is that in our complex society the important and varied welfare delivery agencies often operate in a most uncoordinated way. Principals frequently find themselves dealing with court orders, child protective services, police departments, city and state health and human services departments, and businesses and industries in an effort to help just one particular child or family. Sometimes these agencies even conflict with each other in their efforts and in their policies.

We are not aware of any administrator training programs that specifically prepare principals for this "add-on" role. But it is there, and while it may not be a part of the job description, effective principals recognize the importance of developing good contacts with these outside agencies and providing referral and follow-up services to their patrons who may be in need.

Developing close relationships with the police department only makes good sense. Becoming personally connected with child protective services directors and counselors among other welfare delivery agencies will pay rich dividends. Business partnerships such as "adopt-a-school" can provide enriched educational offerings as well as create an intimate involvement of the private sector in community service and an important support base.

FORMAL COMMUNITY FORCES

Agencies at all three levels of government exert influence and control over the formal education system, often in direct prescriptive and regulatory ways. Even though locally managed and substantially supported by locally assessed taxes, as established by the law, public school districts are really state institutions; school boards of education members are state officers. In practice, of course, the support and control of the public school systems in this nation are vested in federal, state, intermediate, and local governments. A kind of partnership thus exists, although the nature and role of the partners vary among the states.

In the federal system of the U.S. government education is a function of the separate states. Of course, no state may provide for a school system that violates the constitutional rights of citizens.[3] The U.S. Constitution itself is strangely quiet about education. The state receives its authority to operate and control public education within its boundaries through the enactment of the Tenth Amendment to the U.S. Constitution.[4] Thus, the education system is established under powers reserved to the states, and the manner in which the system is maintained is a plenary responsibility of the state. Private and parochial schools also operate under the aegis of the states.

All of the state constitutions specifically provide for public school systems. The legal basis on which the schools are conducted and maintained may be found in state constitutional and statutory law and in the body of common law as it is established by judicial decisions. Opinions written by state attorneys general also affect the operation of the schools until such time as these might be set aside by statute or by the judiciary.

Several trends in school district organization that are in response to societal change have become evident in the last several years. The establishment of educational cooperatives wherein several independent school districts combine to share specified services while remaining functionally independent is one such development. In this type of arrangement usually undertaken by several smaller school districts, the local district remains relatively independent while enjoying some of the benefits of a larger school unit.

The establishment of *magnet schools* has also been a phenomenon. Magnet school operation creates especially complex community-school relations problems because of a widely dispersed school population. The decentralization of urban districts is also an effort to be responsive to more local needs.

The Local Board of Education

The policymaking body of a school district is the board of education. The board of education is a corporate and political body and has the power expressly and implicitly given to it by statute. In many communities, members of the board of education are elected by the people in the communities that they serve; others have appointed boards of education. The method of the selection of members for the lay governing boards of private and parochial schools varies widely.

Irrespective of the method by which members are selected, the duties of the school board are both legislative and quasi-judicial. The local school board has great latitude in daily operation of the schools, subject always, of course, to constitutional and statutory limitations.

The size of boards varies considerably both within states as well as between the various states. Although uncommon, some local school boards have as many as 17 members. Legal requirements for school board membership are minimal, usually including no more than such prerequisites as being a registered voter in the district, being nominated for the office, and being elected. Age requirements are common, and certain people often may not serve on a board of education if they hold some other governmental position that would be deemed to be a conflict of interest.

But as dear to the heart and as winsome the thought, local boards are constrained in their operation. First, what local boards of education can do is circumscribed by a host of state and federal law, court opinion at both levels, attorneys general opinions at both levels, and expressed local community expectations (see Figure 15.2).

We've already discussed the informal influences at the local level. Let us now turn to a discussion of school boards and the federal and state impingement on school board authority.

State Education Agencies

Within the limitations of a particular state constitution, the state's legislature has wide power to determine the purposes and the procedures for the subordinate levels of the education hierarchy. Usually, however, the laws issuing from the state legislature deal with general powers and purposes, leaving specific implementation to a state education agency and various intermediate and local school systems. The state education agency, or state department of education, itself is a creature of the legislature and is imbued with certain discretionary powers.

There are a vast number of other state agencies that have some influence on various aspects of the school systems in a state. In order to carry out various legislative and constitutional provisions about education, any number of other boards of control exist, including controlling boards for higher education, vocational education, tenure, retirement and similar activities. These are all in addition to a state board of education, which exists to determine policies that are then implemented by the state education agency. There are also a variety of agencies concerned with budgeting, accounting, building standards, health, school lunches, library services, civil defense, and myriad other activities in which the schools engage. In short, although the local school system is often viewed as an autonomous unit, it is subject to the controls and impingements from an array of other legally established community and state agencies.

All states have a chief state school officer who may be known as commissioner of education, state superintendent of schools, or a similar title. The number, term, and

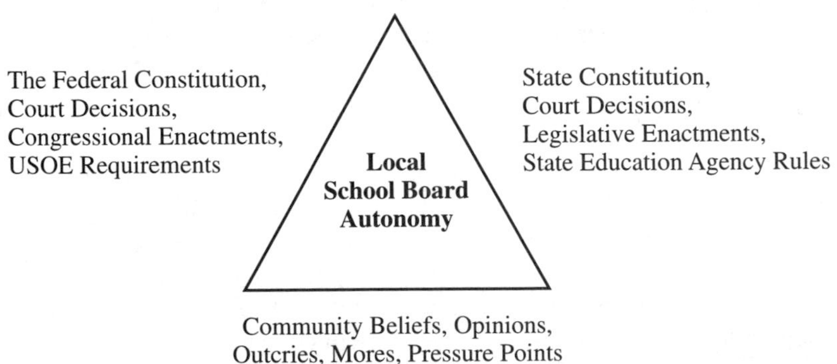

FIGURE 15.2 Circumscribed Local Authority for Schools

method of selection of State Board of Education membership varies. Similarly, the method by which the state superintendent is selected varies.

Federal Influences on Education

Even though the U.S. Constitution is silent about a public education system, it is clear to even a casual observer that the role of the federal government has developed from one of "silence" to active shared responsibility, with not a little control. The general welfare clause of the U.S. Constitution is most often cited as the constitutional provision that permits federal aid to public education. Federal programs tend to be categorical—that is, for an identified special purpose rather than generalized aid.

Categorical aid and specialized programs result in considerable federal influence and, inescapably, restrictions. Few would quarrel with the intent behind PL 94-142, the Education for All Handicapped Children Act, or with the legislation that resulted in the Occupational Safety and Health Act (OSHA),[5] for example. But the implementation of these pieces of legislation has not been without some administrative frustration. At times, positive legislative intent gets caught up in a maze of rules that seem to inhibit rather than facilitate. Nevertheless, the school administrator's task is to make it work the way it was intended to work.

The federal interest has also resulted in the use of the schools as a tool for major social reform. This can best be exemplified by the 1954 Supreme Court decision in *Brown* v. *Board of Education of Topeka* in which the Supreme Court determined that "separate but equal" state provisions and *de jure* segregated educational systems in the United States were unconstitutional.

The federal interest is pervasive, and while it rises or declines in emphasis—depending on the philosophic stance of the executive and legislative branches of government—it nevertheless impinges greatly on the direction that local systems take.

In Sum

In sum, then, the governance of education reflects the structural characteristics of the federal system of government. Each level of the government has its own areas of responsibility and autonomy. All of the levels interface, however, and there is both mutual obligation and dependence. Congress authorized many educational programs for those purposes that have been deemed to be especially important to the national interest. The U.S. Constitution itself grants to the states the responsibility for providing for public education; in turn, the states have delegated many of their powers to the local school district, while at the same time maintaining a vast number of regulatory controls over various aspects of the school operation, particularly in fiscal and program matters.

The previous sections have established a contextual base. It is to the subject of the relationship of the publics to their specific schools that we now turn. In the final part of this chapter, the focus is on school public relations practices and techniques. The subject is how principals can build a solid citizen support base and communicate effectively with school patrons.

PROMISING PUBLIC RELATIONS TECHNIQUES: DEALING WITH THE FORMAL AND INFORMAL FORCES

No one is in a better position to have a positive impact on the relationship between the school system and the community than the principal and the building staff. No single school district person is in a position to interact in person with greater numbers of community members than the principal. A district may spend huge sums of money on slick publications and a well-functioning, centrally located community relations office headed by a public information officer, but it is the principal who can be more influential on a day-to-day basis with individual school patrons. Even in this mass media environment it is still the face-to-face encounter that provides the best basis for understanding and is the most influential in molding public opinion.

The greatest opportunity to influence and persuade, and to hear and feel the community pulse, occurs in the more intimate and often face-to-face settings likely to occur at the building level. Nevertheless, although the next section of the chapter will focus on public relations at the building level, some attention will be given to districtwide public relations activities as well.

School-community communication endeavors may take several forms, any one of which has limitations. An effective school-community relations program will make use of a variety of media, and an alert principal will tailor the particular message to be conveyed to the appropriate medium.

GETTING THE MESSAGE OUT: ONE-WAY PUBLIC RELATIONS TECHNIQUES

There are numerous ways to broadcast a message from the school. Cooperative endeavors involving the print and electronic media, building or system-developed newsletters and brochures, and even the routinely sent report card can all be put to effective use. These are, however, one-way devices; there is little or no way to know if the messages were either received or understood.

Print and Electronic Media

Few communities are not served by at least a weekly newspaper, and no community is outside the reach of radio and television. These mass media are commonly used to impart information about the various agencies serving the community.

Newspapers vary from weekly or biweekly advertisers, with perhaps a few columns reporting highly localized activities, to urban dailies with several editions. Depending on the kind of newspaper, a principal's role will vary from writing news releases that will be published mostly word for word to meeting with news reporters who will recast the stories in their own words.

In any case, the development of good relations with the working press is essential. Reporters or editors will ask principals for information about developing stories or news items more often than for stories containing general information about what's going on in the schools.

The news media have their problems, too. Newspapers and television stations are businesses, with advertising to sell, bills to pay, and subscribers to satisfy. Some people are surprised to learn that 25 percent or less of newspaper space is devoted to stories and 75 percent or more to advertising. This percentage affects the amount of school news that will get printed. Moreover, news editors deal with many other agencies and pressure groups, each championing various causes or matters for the "public good," so there is competition for available space.

Also, it is a frequent complaint of reporters that schools tend to engage only in "gold-star" story writing. The charge is that many school administrators are only too eager to publicize praiseworthy news items but will back away from or become upset about legitimate adverse criticism. An adverse story *is* legitimate news, and when such a story breaks, the school official and the newspaper both have a job to do. Covering up a weakness or refusing to respond to a legitimate inquiry about a potentially embarrassing situation can only lead to bad press relations and a widening credibility gap.

Techniques for Dealing with the Mass Media. News releases need to be developed in a way that conforms to the requirements of the different media. Releases for radio and television must be shorter, more repetitious, and in a style that is more conversational than that used for newspapers.

Relationships with representatives of the various media, as well as district policy, will determine whether the person releasing the news concentrates on writing and distributing releases or on furnishing suggestions and information to journalists who in turn write their own material. In urban settings with large dailies and "live eye" television, reporters write their own stories but do need to be advised about promising sources, fast-breaking news, upcoming events, and policy changes. They also need to be provided with good "backgrounding."

In small towns and cities and in suburban and rural districts, local news will generally be disseminated by an array of daily, biweekly, and weekly newspapers, ranging from mini-versions of the large city dailies to four-page advertisers. In many of these places, a school official will frequently write an entire story with little assistance from an editor.

Articles and stories about scheduled events should be prepared well in advance, with photographs of speakers or others involved in the program provided to the news media *before* the event occurs. Often, as a matter of policy, newspapers will not print information about a past event. Follow-up reports should be prepared for the media as soon as possible after an event The school principal needs to know the various media deadlines. Missing a deadline will mean the story may never get printed.

Even small school systems are employing public information officers to facilitate and coordinate the flow of information from school to community. The duties vary and in some school systems the job may be only part time. Even where the job is full time and the public relations program well developed, for most of the public and the mass media it is still the principal who will be sought as the prime source of fast-breaking news, and in time of crisis. Figure 15.3 contains eight practices to facilitate a good working relationship with representatives of the media.

District Policy Considerations. The latitude a principal has with the press will depend in great part on the press policy of the school district. News media personnel, however, are most sensitive to what they perceive to be censorship and normally respond negatively to the suggestion that every story or every interview must be cleared with the central office. A policy that requires all school personnel to refer reporters and editors to the central office rather than answer questions, or that sends the news media to the central office for all information will damage press relations, if rigidly enforced. Obviously, fast-breaking news items of a potentially explosive nature will require discretion on the part of the school principal.

The public information program needs continual evaluation. It really isn't very valuable to send out large numbers of news releases if few are used, and submitting too much material in an indiscriminate way may result in few stories being published. The lesson is clear: The news media are most impressed by articles that contain only timely and worthwhile information. These will stand the best chance of getting reported.

School News Items File. There are many missed opportunities to get the school before the public in a positive way. The typical school is a beehive of activity, much of which would be of interest to one segment or another of the public. The difficulty is that

FIGURE 15.3 Working with the Media

- Give reporters story ideas and information but remember it is editors and news directors who decide what should be covered.
- Be aware of when reporters' deadlines fall and balance the time of releases so that morning and afternoon papers get an equal share.
- Articles about scheduled events need to be prepared well in advance and any photographs submitted at the same time.
- Releases for radio and television usually must be shorter, more repetitious, and in a more conversational style than those for the print medium.
- Avoid provoking reporters with "no comment" statements. Help reporters write potentially adverse stories by giving complete information and backgrounding.
- Anticipate the reporter's needs and have any background information written ahead of time for distribution. (Don't trust that a "general beat" reporter knows very much about schooling.)
- Avoid jargon and "in-house" language; it may not be understood, especially by a "general beat" reporter.
- Invite newspersons—reporters and their editors—to the school for lunch and periodic tours without trying to sell them on a story at the time. Get them acquainted with the school scene.

many schools have no central place where ongoing activities are recorded. Thus, when a reporter calls or an editor requests a story, media needs often cannot be adequately met.

An especially effective practice is the use of a School News Item File, depicted in Figure 15.4. Many activities in the school are probably newsworthy, but without encouragement and facilitation, they will otherwise go unreported. Each staff member should have a supply of the news item forms to jot down those projects that might be especially interesting, and on a regular basis these forms should be sent to the principal's office. The principal can then file the reports in a folder labeled according to the kind of project, and a news reporter can simply review the files, selecting any particular items to follow up. This helps both the reporter, whose responsibility it is to find news, and the principal, whose responsibility it is to provide news but not necessarily to write the story.

Newsletters and Bulletins. Frequently, the principal and the school staff will attempt to communicate with the home and outside agencies through newsletters and bulletins. These can be useful if employed judiciously and if well done. But a bad message is conveyed when a newsletter arrives home crumpled in the pocket of a student, hard to read, and containing out-of-date information. If newsletters and bulletins are to be employed,

It's news to somebody. Report it!

Type of News Item:

_________ Curriculum Project
_________ Activities of Staff
_________ School Awards
_________ Student Activities (field trips, special recognition, etc.)
_________ New or Interesting Instructional Techniques
_________ Continuing Difficult Problems
_________ Other

Title of Project or Item:

Description of Project or Item:

Persons Involved: (how many, and who—names, addresses, titles, etc.)

Dollars Involved and Sources of These Dollars:

Who to Contact for Further Information:

FIGURE 15.4 School News Item File

the format should be simple, the information conveyed should be written concisely, it should be free of educational jargon, and the method of getting these messages home should be via the mail. Newsletters sent home with children often do little but contribute to a neighborhood litter problem. If the newsletter is not produced with care and printed in an attractive manner, it is simply not worth the bother. Care should also be taken to recognize the multilingual nature of many communities.

It is easy to prepare newsletters and bulletins that appear professional in makeup. There are a number of desktop publishing programs available that are not difficult to learn and will result in an eminently attractive product—complete with graphics. Irrespective of the computer system that is being used in the school, good desktop publishing programs are plentiful.

Report Cards. Report cards are often overlooked as public relations mechanisms, but they are the single-most regular way in which schools desseminate information to the home. Both teachers and parents like them to be uncomplicated. Yet consideration of all of the ways in which a student is growing, developing, and learning defies summing up progress with a single letter grade. Thus, the development of an appropriate reporting procedure will require careful study by the staff and include the use of a faculty-layperson committee to develop a report form that is easy to understand but also contains important kinds of information relative to the student's progress.

If the purpose of a parent reporting system is to develop an effective communication link and if the parents highly values written reports, then the school should use some form of written report card. A written report of grades alone is not adequate, however, and a more personal communication link, such as additional comments written by the teacher on the report card or a parent-teacher conference, should be added.

To effectively report a child's progress, a report card should provide three kinds of information. First, it should estimate the child's overall ability compared to other children the same age. This can be done through standardized tests or the teacher's judgment of the child's ability based on diagnosis and observations. Second, the report card should indicate the child's individual progress. During the elementary and middle grades, this should be based on estimated ability and a measure of the child's achievement in the classroom since the last marking period. This statement is not a comparison to other children but the teacher's estimate of whether the child is achieving as much as possible. The sample report card uses A, B, C, D, F. Finally, the report card describes the child's conduct in school. Conduct may be rated with a check mark to indicate satisfactory behavior or with a code that indicates outstanding citizenship, satisfactory behavior, or unsatisfactory behavior.

It is much more meaningful to parents if an appropriate one- or two-sentence comment is written by a subject grade to provide parents with more detail regarding the progress of their children. Everyone knows that most teachers don't have the time to manually write a comment by each grade. They will generally do this only for extreme cases. However, with computer-generated report cards, it is possible for the computer to have on file a "comment bank" of commonly used appropriate teacher statements from which teachers may select a statement for each child. A list of 100 or so statements that the teachers themselves created would probably cover most contingencies. All the teacher needs to do is record the appropriate code number under the teacher comment section, and the computer then inserts that statement on the report card.

The Fog Index

Writing well requires careful consideration of who it is that will be receiving the message. We've called attention to the need to consider the multilingual nature of many school communities, but effectively conveying information in writing requires more than using the native language of the intended receiver; it requires using that language meaningfully. That dictates straightforward sentences, unencumbered nouns and verbs, and common language. Simplicity, lack of clutter, and avoidance of jargon and pedagogical phraseology are required. And this can be done without talking down to people. Newspapers accomplish it daily. The messages should not rely on someone having a high school education to understand them. The nearer the messages come to a sixth- or seventh-grade reading level, the better.

GETTING THE MESSAGE OUT AND BACK: TWO-WAY PUBLIC RELATIONS TECHNIQUES

Information dissemination is not synonymous with *communication*. Because of the failure to make this distinction, many public relations efforts fail. The final part of this chapter is a discussion and description of proven communication techniques.

The Message Was Sent—What Happened?

The *co* in communication suggests a closed loop. That is, communication means that the message was not only sent *but* that it was received and responded to in a way that indicates it was understood. There are five important questions to ask when examining the quality of information devices:

1. If the message was received, was it read [heard]?
2. If it was read [heard], was it understood?
3. If it was understood, was it understood in the right spirit?
4. If it was understood in the right spirit, will it be acted on in a positive way?
5. How do you know?

An array of communication techniques and structures is available. The remainder of this chapter is a discussion of promising approaches.

Community Advisory Councils

The trend to greater autonomy at the school building level has brought with it increasing use by principals of community advisory councils. In some states, legislation establishing greater school unit autonomy and the concomitant greater principal accountability has also mandated that there be community advisory councils. Parents, teachers, and sometimes students are included in such councils.

Issues often arise about what is *policy advising* and what is *policy making*. Clearly, the reason for having advisory councils is so that there is a formally established way for community and faculty representatives to share information with the principal and suggest alternative approaches to the solution of problems of schooling. In the best of worlds, this provides the principal with additional expertise and useful insights that will result in maximum feasible decisions. Our point is that "advising" is not the same as "decisioning" although it would seem to be a foolish principal who found himself or herself always operating contrary to the advice of the council.

Membership on the Advisory Council. State law or local district policy may prescribe the nature of membership of the council and/or how members are to be selected. Lacking this, it would seem fundamental that members, whether elected or appointed by the principal, should represent a cross-section of the local community.

Achieving Maximum Output from an Advisory Council. Lack of clarity and understanding about the role of council members and about the difference between helping to make policy and policy implementation can become a source of conflict. People work best when they know what the expectations and limitations are. To establish a framework to guide advisory council activities, the school principal should:

1. Establish the essential conditions that any solution, action plan, or policy must meet if it is to be acceptable. That is, are there financial, legal, or district policy considerations that must be taken into account? Are there things that are known to not be in the best interests of learners? Are there things that, in good conscience, the principal would not carry out?
2. Help the group establish a specific time line and a set date for task completion.
3. Indicate what resources are available to the group.
4. Specify what specific outcomes are desired.
5. Establish the limits of the group's authority in the issue at hand. That is, is the principal asking for a final decision, for some alternative decisions, or simply for some advice?

Focus Groups

Research bureaus, professional associations, and advertising agencies, among other organizations, have used focus groups for years to define issues, anticipate problems, explore reactions to potential problems, develop alternative scenarios, and plan leaps into the future. A focus group is an example of a *nonprobability sampling* technique. The technique employs directional rather than quantitative data and can be used to great effectiveness as both a school public relations technique and a creative problem-solving technique. Focus groups, however, are not decision-making bodies nor are they even advisory bodies. They are groups of community members whose opinions about an issue the principal wants to learn. The purpose is both problem sensing and problem solving, but the problem "sensor" and the problem "solver" is not the focus group. The focus group is to provide feelings, attitudes, and information.

Focus groups are composed of a small number of people—8 to 10 is the recommended number—each group representing a segment of the school-community population. The purpose of meeting with focus groups is to gain an assessment of how people feel about a school-related issue or problem—or anticipated problem. Typically, the meetings last no more than an hour and no more than four questions are asked of the group. A moderator takes notes on the discussion, noting the key concepts, levels of intensity, and new information. Verbatim comments are recorded to the degree possible, absent editing. It is not important that the group meet in the school. Union halls, church basements, or apartment complex hospitality rooms might be a more convenient and comfortable choice for meetings.

Business and Other Community Partnerships

Many benefits are to be gained from well-organized business/industry/education partnerships. Such benefits include:

- Getting important people engaged in the important work of educating children. For example, in one of the author's cities, the executives of a leading business have developed a training program in ethics and give their top staff released time to work with children in this program; a local psychiatric hospital offers free counseling services to its "adopted school"; a leading manufacturer of computers releases its personnel to work with teachers and students in more effective use of computer technology (and not just in the use of the manufacturer's own computers, either); another business sends school principals to its executive training program; still another employs science teachers in its research and development department during summers and at other times; still others offer in-service programs as well as tutorial services; another provides work opportunities for students who need financial help to stay in school; and the list could go on.

- Helping community leaders better understand the complexities of educating a child and helping them develop an appreciation for the problems and pleasures of teaching.

- Capitalizing on the technical expertise that is available in the community and using that expertise for staff updating as well as for program analysis and student tutoring.

To be maximally effective and to avoid costly misunderstandings, cooperative programs must be well coordinated. Although the principal doesn't need to be the one who manages the program, he or she is responsible for making sure that the program is well coordinated. Figure 15.5 provides guidance for the development of productive school-business partnerships.

FIGURE 15.5 Guidelines for Productive School-Business Partnerships

1. Be certain that the program that is implemented is objective and balanced, and that the goals of the business and the school are compatible. Just because it's "free" doesn't mean it is in the best interests of the students and staff of the school.
2. Focus only on that part of the curriculum about which the business partner has an interest or understands. The key word is *focus*. Businesses can't solve all of the problems of the school, and may have difficulty staying interested in problems that are too broadly based.
3. Don't overlook staff development as a school need. Materials and equipment for the school is good. Instructional assistance is good. Dollars for special projects are good. But so are expertise, materials, and money earmarked for projects that expand the abilities of teachers and administrators. These have a multiplier effect.
4. Appoint a school-based coordinator. More good ideas have been bungled by poor management and bad communication than for any other reason. If it is worth doing, it is worth appointing a person with good management and public relations skills to oversee.
5. Give the business partners credit for their efforts. Give praise to your partner at every opportunity and do this publicly and often.

Key Communicators

Many principals capitalize on their knowledge of the community influence structure and develop a list of "key communicators." These are the persons to be contacted when there is a need to disseminate information quickly about the school. Key communicators are influential people in the immediate community who have an identified interest in the school. These people are influential because they interact with large numbers of other people and are trusted. A loose organization of such individuals is easily formed. From time to time, the group might meet with the principal and other professionals in the building to discuss what is going on at the school that would be of general community interest. After an initial meeting, the key communicators are kept informed about such things as school budgets, new curricula, teacher turnover, and new construction. The group, as individuals and in collective feedback sessions, keeps the principal informed about "rumblings and rumors" in the community.

This group is simply a collection of important people. As always, care should be taken to see that all dimensions of the school community are tapped. The notion of using key communicators capitalizes on communications research which continues to indicate that individual members of a community get most of the information from which attitudes and beliefs are formed in a word-of-mouth fashion—even in this mass media age.

Principal-Organized Interaction Sessions

In high-performing schools, principals often have regular "tell-it-to-the-principal" interaction sessions. Concerned about establishing and maintaining good relationships with students and parents, principals have initiated two kinds of sessions. One is a student-principal program conducted regularly in the principal's office or over lunch in a more secluded part of the school cafeteria. Attendance is limited to 8 or 10 students. It is important that a representative sample of the students participates. In these open-forum sessions, students express interests and discuss grievances they have, making suggestions about the general improvement of the school.

The same sorts of session can be scheduled for parents and other community members. Patrons are invited to the meeting, with the secretary taking reservations for a dozen or so patrons. Special invitations are necessary to ensure representativeness.

The rules for the meeting are that "anything goes," except personal complaints about individual teachers. (These latter issues must be reserved for private individual sessions.) Two or three hours will provide an opportunity for an informal exchange of ideas. For the principal, it's an excellent sensing mechanism to find out what patrons are concerned about and to get some notion of impending problem situations. For the patrons, it's a good opportunity to learn about the operation of the school and to raise questions about the educational practices.

One of the difficulties in engendering community support is the inadequacy of the information exchange between the school and the home. Organized, yet informal, parent-principal forums help. Complex ideas are difficult to express in the usual one-way bulletins or news stories that frequently serve as major sources of information for parents and other community members. Complex ideas are best tested in a face-to-face setting.

Parent-Teacher Conferences

Planned parent-teacher conferences can be an important element in a school-community relations program. Thought must be given about such things as working parents, one-parent households, a parent's occupation that would preclude attendance at parent-teacher conferences scheduled during the normal school day, the language spoken, and transportation difficulties, among other factors, influencing the success of the endeavor. These and other constraints can be overcome with diligent work on the part of school personnel.

Parent-Teacher Organizations

Historically, a PTA or PTO has served as the main, and sometimes only, organized school outreach program. Principals should use whatever devices are available to facilitate a two-way flow of information, but in the case of parent-teacher organizations, the effectiveness has varied markedly throughout the country.

Nothing good automatically happens just because an organization is labeled in such a way as to suggest a formal relationship with the school. Parent-teacher organizations can provide a useful avenue for interaction between school and community if the meetings are organized to provide an opportunity for both formal and informal interaction and if the organization is given important tasks to perform. The key would seem to be *active involvement in tasks*. Parent organizations, just like other community organizations, are competing for the time of their members. Whether a parent or a teacher elects to spend Thursday evening at a PTO meeting will depend on whether that time is viewed as productively occupied.

A good parent-teacher organization will spend less time meeting formally and more time in subgroups considering important tasks to be performed around the school and the community. Organizing business-industry-education days for the career development program in the school, developing after-school programs for children and adults in the community, recruiting and training paraprofessionals, and working on curriculum review teams are the kinds of activities in which an effective parent-school organization engages.

One common problem that inhibits the usefulness of a parent-teacher organization as a communication device is the unevenness of the membership makeup. Even though the school may serve a heterogeneous population, the active membership is often composed almost entirely of those from only one thread in the societal fabric. Thus, the principal should examine the membership rolls of the parent organization carefully. If these organizations are to be used as effective communication devices and the school community is heterogeneous, a membership that reflects the school community at large becomes most important. If not, then it is likely that important opinions are not being heard and the organization is not serving to promote an information exchange with the broader community.

In those schools that are "magnets" and that draw a substantial number of students from widely dispersed areas, a traditional parent-teacher organization may be difficult to maintain, even with the most intense efforts. Under such a circumstance, energy might be directed more efficiently to other involvement techniques.

Community Surveys

Surveying community attitudes and opinions can be effective, especially as a school district enters an evaluation phase in an effort to establish or review educational goals, objectives, and priorities. Such a survey can lead to numerous community committees and a revitalization of community involvement in educational policymaking.

Educational surveys may be conducted in a variety of ways. Mailed questionnaires to a random sample of the population living in a particular school attendance area is the most common. A better technique to employ, if the time and person power are available, is to conduct house-to-house interviews using a structured interview technique, calling on a random sample of the population, making sure that all parts of the community are included in the sample. Telephone surveys may also provide a reasonable alternative.

When done right, however, surveys are expensive to conduct. Often, too, the number of responses is disappointingly small—so small or so unrepresentative that the results are unreliable. However, finding out periodically and regularly what community members think is very important. Demographics change—often rapidly, public opinion is fluid, and good information is essential to good administrative decision making. At the very least, the principal does not want to be blindsided. A crisis rarely occurs without some early indications, unrest, and dissatisfaction. "Be prepared" is a good motto.

SUMMARY

People in the community have a right not only to be informed about school happenings but also to be engaged in these happenings. If school principals do not use available means to interact with members of the community, the school will become static and unresponsive to changing community and societal needs.

Principals need to analyze their existing public relations activities in light of the community being served. Are there both one- and two-way programs? Is membership and attendance at parent-teacher organizations, "booster groups," or other school organizations representative of the school population? Are there focus groups and advisory committees? Are there partnerships with other agencies?

The skilled principal will analyze the existing public relations program and the community that is to be served. Modifications in the public relations program should be based on that analysis.

ACTIVITIES

1. Discover and list the kinds of public relations activities in which your school is currently engaged. Are any of these activities "two-way" in nature?

2. Collect some demographic data about the community your school serves and the makeup of the student population. Racial and ethnic data for both the community and the student population will provide a starting point, but go beyond this. Check census tract data. Do a drive-about of the attendance area. Note housing types, dwelling areas, kinds of neighborhoods, and commercial centers both by location and type.

   Examine the rolls of important school groups—advisory councils, booster clubs, PTA/PTO, and so on. To what degree does the active membership in the groups you have identified reflect the nature of the community population and the student population?

   Find a map of the attendance area. Color code the location of the people who are active members of the identified groups. Does this reveal anything that might suggest public relations problems that need to be addressed? Does it suggest that a greater array of techniques needs to be engaged in? What new efforts seem to be suggested?

3. Analyze Case Studies 6, 11, 20, and 22 at the end of this book. What approach will you take in these community relations situations? What concepts presented in this chapter might assist you in your analysis?

4. Turn to the ISLLC Standards found in Appendix B. Review the knowledge, dispositions, and performances listed with Standard Six. Reflect on which of the standard items relate directly to the material presented in this chapter. How would you use the concepts and skills of ISLLC Standard Six to help develop the vision and mission of the school proposed in Standard One? Identify one knowledge area, one disposition, and one performance to link directly to a concept or idea discussed in Chapter 15.

ENDNOTES

1. Larry W. Hughes and Don W. Hooper, *Public Relations for School Leaders* (Boston: Allyn and Bacon, 2000) p. 76.

2. Jesse Bernard, *American Community Behavior* (New York: Holt, Rinehart and Winston, 1965), p. 358. The ideological unity of *blut und bod* groups makes such groups at once powerful forces on any given issue about which they care.

3. See Chapter 16 for a discussion of this issue.

4. "The powers not delegated to the United States by the Constitution, nor prohibited by it to the States, are reserved to the States respectively, or to the people."

5. As with most such social legislation, these two acts came about as a result of much concerted action on the part of informal sectors of society that exerted much pressure for federal action.

SELECTED READINGS

Blank, Mary Ann, and Cheryl Kershaw. *Design Book for Building Partnerships: School, Home, and Community* (Lanham, MD: Scarecrow Press/Technomic Books, 2000).

Dolan, G. Keith. *Communication: A Practical Guide to School and Community Relations* (Belmont, CA: Wadsworth, 1996).

Davis, Donald. "Schools Reaching Out." *Phi Delta Kappa 72,* no. 5 (January 1991): 376–380.

Hughes, Larry W., and Don W. Hooper. *Public Relations for School Leaders* (Boston: Allyn and Bacon, 2000. Part I deals especially with policy development.)

Kowalksi, Theodore J. *Public Relations in Schools,* 2nd ed. (Upper Saddle River, NJ: Prentice-Hall, 2000).

Lueder, Donald C. *Creating Partnerships with Parents: An Educators Guide* (Lanham, MD: Scarecrow Press/Technomic Books, 2000).

CHAPTER SIXTEEN

LEGAL RIGHTS AND RESPONSIBILITIES OF STUDENTS AND STAFF

Shifting the locus of authority to the individual campus unit is accompanied by a concomitant extension of legal responsibility. Administrative decision-making at the building level involves relationships with fundamental issues that involve parents, students, faculty, and other employees. The administrator functioning at the building level must be prepared to lead the instructional program effectively while administering a plethora policies, regulations, state statutes, and federal law controlling various facets of behavior behaviors exhibited by various student and professional personnel.

—Richard D. Strahan[1]

Society today has become increasingly litigious. More and more, principals and teachers are held directly accountable for what occurs at the school site. As Strahan, above, puts it, with increasing decision authority vested at the building level, the concomitant is greater responsibility to behave in legally defensible ways. But, even in those days of less decentralized authority, this was so. It's just that now citizens—all citizens—seem to be greatly aware of certain rights and ever more conscious of perceived transgressions of these rights. Threats of lawsuits have seemingly become as common place as PTO potlucks. What is required is good preparation and a thorough understanding of the laws undergirding the operation of the school.

Although students, parents, community members, and staff may not always *be right,* they always *have rights.* They also have responsibilities. This chapter is about those rights and responsibilities and about the legal and ethical framework within which school leaders must operate to provide at once the lawful and humane school environment.

We do not intend to replace with a single chapter the need for aspiring and practicing school leaders to take coursework in school law and to continually update themselves about new laws and court decisions. But we do intend to establish certain legal bases for an effective school operation and to examine those legal issues with which a school leader will most likely have to contend.

This chapter comprises four sections. We begin with an analysis of the legal foundation of schools in the United States. Subsequent sections focus on the specific rights and responsibilities of staff and students. Attention is directed to issues of due process, educational equity, including the rights of the disabled, sexual harassment, concerns of religious groups, and matters of tort liability.

LEGAL BASES FOR SCHOOLS: A FEDERAL, STATE, AND LOCAL PERSPECTIVE

Historically, schools are creatures of the states, but in practice, the support and control of schools has been a partnership between local, state, and federal governments. Even private and parochial schools and school systems do not exist as autonomous entities, because these too must meet certain state curriculum and teacher certification standards. Also, certain federal regulations impinge when these schools accept available federal funds.

The legal framework within which school systems operate is manifest in the acts passed by federal, state, and local legislative bodies, court decisions, constitutional law, and rules and regulations enacted by regulatory and administrative bodies such as the state departments of education or other governmental departments. A further source of legal guidelines is the opinions of various attorneys general that stand until tested in a court of law or modified by subsequent legislative acts. An extralegal impingement also exists: community sanctions, attitudes, and belief structures that modify, often very directly, the development and implementation of local policies. Within this framework, local administrators have latitude in the development of policies, rules, regulations, and procedures.

Limitations on local authority depend also on prevailing court philosophy in any state. In some states, the prevailing philosophy is that boards of education may adopt any reasonable policy not specifically prohibited by statute. In other states, courts insist that there be specific statutory permission before a particular policy can be adopted. Generally speaking, courts have tended to uphold the rule of reason—that boards of education may adopt any reasonable policy within the law. Courts in all states do insist on strict adherence to laws concerning management of public funds, however. School boards and administrators must find clear statutory authority for the expenditure of funds derived from public revenues.

It is at the school building level that the policies of the school board and the laws governing education are most often implemented. It is also at the school building level that most of the litigation involving a school system begins.

Most of the individual rights enjoyed in this country derive from the Constitution of the United States and are largely located in the first 10 amendments of the Constitution (the Bill of Rights) and in some subsequent amendments, notably the Fourteenth Amendment. Those amendments of special relevance to the operation of schools are:

> *Amendment One* deals with freedom of religion and expression and rights to peaceful assembly and petition. It grants the rights of all citizens to assemble peacefully and to petition the government for redress of grievances. Amendment One has often been cited in civil rights cases involving students and teachers.
>
> *Amendment Four* focuses on the rights of persons and states that the people and property shall be protected against "unreasonable searches and seizures," meaning that appropriate warrants must precede such police action. The educational implications here affect the confidentiality of records, interrogation of pupils, and the proceedings of juvenile court.
>
> *Amendment Five* guarantees the due process of law. It says that certain rights to life, liberty, and property are inviolate, and that people cannot be deprived of them without due process of law.
>
> *Amendment Six* provides for judicial procedure and guarantees a speedy public trial, an impartial jury, information about the nature of the charge, confrontation by witnesses against the party, the right of the accused to obtain witnesses in his or her own behalf, and the right to have counsel.
>
> *Amendment Eight* prohibits cruel and unusual punishment and excessive bail. The educational implications are clear, especially with regard to the question of corporal punishment although undue mental anguish has also been cited as a "cruel and unusual" punishment.
>
> *Amendment Nine* guarantees the "rights of the people" and states that the enumeration in the Constitution of certain rights shall not be construed to deny or discourage other rights retained by the people. This simply means that even if the Constitution is silent, it does not imply that other rights are not enjoyed.
>
> *Amendment Ten* indicates that the powers that are not delegated to the United States by the Constitution nor prohibited by it to the states are reserved to the states respectively or to the people.

After the Civil War, the Fourteenth Amendment, the "States' Bill of Rights," was adopted. It states that "no state shall make a law which abridges the rights of citizens in the United States nor deny anyone the equal protection of the law." It states further that all persons, whether born or naturalized in the United States and subject to the jurisdiction thereof, are citizens of the United States and of the state wherein they reside. Thus, each state must guarantee the same rights to its citizens that are guaranteed by the U.S. Constitution. It is important to call attention to the phrase "all persons." The amendment does not say all adults; it says all persons, and that includes children.

The courts have made it clear that constitutional protections apply to students both in and out of school. Freedom of expression and other basic rights, if not always clearly defined in the schools, are well established in the law. As the Supreme Court pointed out in *Tinker* v. *Des Moines School District,* "Students do not surrender their rights at the school house door."[2] Courts require specified procedures to safeguard those rights against the abuse of institutional authority. The matter of procedural due process, which will be discussed more completely later in this chapter, guarantees certain rights by the fair application of rules and regulations.

Nevertheless, even though students do have rights at school, these are balanced against the rights and responsibilities of administrators and teachers to maintain order and provide a good learning climate. The courts have been particularly careful to ensure that the school has the ability to effectively carry out the educational mission.

Application of the Laws

Of course, some rules of law are not universally accepted. Different courts often hand down conflicting decisions in seemingly similar cases, even within the same state. Also, the opinions of attorneys general will vary over the years and between states. At the federal level, a change in the party controlling the executive branch will often affect the rigor and vigor with which an attorney general or the Justice Department interprets and enforces the law and how the federal courts interpret a law.

Legislative acts at both state and federal levels vary from term to term as this or that current concern becomes law, or is countermanded by superseding law, or reaches a "sunset" provision. Also, the interpretation and the application of laws sometimes change over the years.

For these reasons, it is important for the principal to continually keep abreast of new developments on the legal front. This chapter will help, but the legal framework is constantly evolving. Subscribing to a legal update service provided by many of the professional associations, as well as attention to the day-to-day occurrences in one's community and state, is good advice for any educator.

DUE PROCESS

The right to a fair warning and a fair hearing before a transgression is acted on is basic in American law. The general issue addressed by due process considerations is that of the constitutional rights of personnel and students balanced against the duty of school officials to control and protect the school system and to protect the rights of students to obtain an education. Two kinds of due process—substantive and procedural—must be considered and implemented.

Substantive Due Process

Substantive due process is concerned with the basic lawfulness of a legislative enactment. School policies, rules, and regulations must stand the test of substantive due process. A person punished or denied the right to behave in some way by an existing law, rule, or regulation when that law, rule, or regulation is itself contrary to certain constitutional guarantees has legal recourse to set aside the punishment or denial and make the rule invalid. Moreover, substantive due process requires that there must be sufficient evidence or documentation of violation to warrant action by school officials or sufficient reason to believe that, if the rule is not invoked, current or subsequent acts by the parties involved will result in disruption of the educational process. The burden of proof rests with the school officials, not the transgressor.

Tinker is often cited in reference to presumed disruptions.[3] Rules are invoked because the school principal says, in effect, "If this rule is not enforced and obeyed, the process of education in the school will be impeded." In *Tinker,* two important legal principles of a substantive nature were applied by the Supreme Court in holding for the students: There was no disruption; therefore, the presumption of the rule was false and students had the constitutional right to defy the rule. The wearing of the armbands was analogous to free speech (a First Amendment guarantee) and the students had the right to express themselves.

The two rules of thumb that must be applied are: Will the behavior cause substantial disorder to the education process or normal operation of the school? and Will the behavior be an invasion of the rights of others? The burden of proof rests on the principal. Courts are critical of administrative action predicated on presumption. The collection of sufficient evidence to show reason for administrative action is essential.

Guidelines to Ensure Substantive Due Process. School policies, rules, and regulations, as well as the administrative actions enforcing them, should be subjected to the following guidelines:

1. *Legality*. Is there a basis in state and federal constitutional and legislative law for the policy, rule, or regulation? Are the constitutional rights of those for whom it was written protected?
2. *Sufficient Specificity*. Are the conditions under which the policy, rule, or regulation will be invoked detailed? Are the terms and phraseology used definitive? Vague and unclear statements are sufficient to cause the courts to abrogate.
3. *Reason and Sensibleness*. Does the rule or regulation really enhance the educational climate; that is, is it really necessary? Is there sufficient reason to believe that without the rule, the rights of others will be unprotected or the school will be disrupted? A rule may be declared unreasonable in and of itself or in its particular application.
4. *Adequate Dissemination*. Has information about the rule been distributed in such a way that persons affected can be expected to know about it, know what it means, and know what the penalties are?
5. *Appropriate Penalties*. Are the punishments appropriate to the nature of the infraction? Severe penalties for minor transgressions must be avoided.[4]

Procedural Due Process

Procedural due process is an orderly, established process for arriving at an impartial and just settlement of a conflict between parties. It entails fair warning and fair hearing.

Fair Warning. Fair warning simply means that a person must be aware of the rules to follow, or behavior that must be exhibited, and the potential penalties for violation.

The age of the person must be taken into consideration as well. Moreover, there must be a correlation between the severity of the penalty and the rule that has been broken.

Fair Hearing. A fair hearing is composed of the following specific aspects:

1. *The individual must be given a written statement of the charges and the nature of evidence*. This is often called a "Bill of Particulars." Clarity is very important. The accused, and, in the instance of pupils, the accused's parents, must comprehend the contents of the written statement. The background and educational level of the individuals involved and the complexity of the statement should be taken into account. A personally delivered statement to the parents would provide an opportunity for clarifying charges and would be appropriate at times. The precise nature of the charges and the evidence must be incorporated in the statement. Vague rules and imprecise charges have resulted in the reversal of more school board and administrative decisions than any other defect.[5]
2. *The individual must be informed of certain procedural rights*. Having rights but being kept unaware of them is the same as not having rights. Individuals must be provided information specifying the appeal and defense processes available. Information such as to whom the appeal should be made, the time limit under which the appeal can be advanced, and other elements of procedural due process is necessary.
3. *Adequate time must be provided to prepare a defense*. In serious issues, ordinarily a minimum of 5 days should be provided for an individual to prepare a defense; 10 days almost certainly will sustain a court inquiry.[6]
4. *There must be an opportunity for a formal hearing*. Five components comprise a proper formal hearing:

    - The case must be presented to an impartial hearer. The school official bringing the charge may not also serve as hearer.
    - The individual must have the opportunity to present evidence.
    - The individual has the right to know and confront whoever brought the charges and to question that person or those persons.
    - The individual has the right to produce witnesses and to cross-examine witnesses. The individual must have the opportunity to disprove the accusations of a hostile witness and include testimony of those who can explain the defendant's side of the issue.
    - The individual has the right to counsel. This does not necessarily mean an attorney, but there is no reason why it could not be. It may be simply a friend, parent, or citizen on whose advice the defendant wishes to rely.

ISSUES OF EQUITY

Increasing attention has been placed on the need to assure that all persons have equal access to the fruits of education, irrespective of their gender, race, ethnicity, or any disabling condition. A host of laws, often federally generated, have been promulgated and much litigation has occurred in the effort to ensure equity. Of special relevance to the school principal are the laws, court decisions, and educational guidelines with respect to sex discrimination, desegregation, provision of the least restrictive educational environment for students with disabilities, and employment opportunities for people with disabilities who are otherwise qualified.

Gender Discrimination

The issue of gender discrimination has arisen in both academic matters and cocurricular matters. More frequently in recent years, issues of gender discrimination have been located in the cocurricular realm.

In academic matters, gender discrimination has been found to occur most often in class assignments and admission to programs or schools. Gender has been determined to be an illegal criterion for assignment and admission. It has been held also to be a violation of the equal protection clause of the Fourteenth Amendment to use higher admission standards for females than for males for admission to an academic school. The circuit court, in *Berkleman* v. *San Francisco Unified School District,*[7] said that merit is the only sound basis for admission, not such "unsupported" needs suggested by the school district officials' position that "an equal number of male and female students is an essential element in a good high school education."[8]

Nevertheless, the "separate but equal" concept with regard to schools for boys and girls is still viable where a school district (or any educational unit) can show that genuinely equal educational opportunities are provided to students in these schools, when these schools are compared to all other schools or units in the system.[9] The burden of proof is on the school system, however.

In some schools, too, females have been excluded from certain specialized vocational and prevocational courses. This practice has been challenged, and in most such cases, women were admitted to the courses before the cases came to trial. Clearly, even though there is little in the way of case law, such exclusion practices are contrary to the current thrust of the law. Unless the school administrator or the school board can show some rational basis for excluding one gender or the other from a course or program, there should be no policy that would differentiate the enrollment. It is doubtful that such a basis could be developed; few human activities are physiologically determined.

Most of the recent litigation focusing on gender discrimination has had to do with participation in cocurricular activities, specifically participation in athletic competition. Title IX of the Education Amendments of 1972 (PL 92-318) is a bulwark against gender discrimination in the cocurricular realm. Title IX established, among other things, that organized athletic programs in the public schools must be accessible irrespective of the gender of the aspirant.

There are two situations in which claims have arisen. The first is the failure of a school district to fund and provide a team for a specific sport for its female students, and then, while not providing a team, also prohibiting females from participating on the team it does have. The issue in these cases is not whether a female has a constitutional right to participate in a particular sport but whether the state, having provided an athletic program, can deny an opportunity to participate to members of one gender. The asserted protective purpose in maintaining separate teams is frequently stated this way: Girls cannot compete effectively with boys in sports because of the inherent physical differences between the sexes; thus, it is argued frequently, separate teams are reasonable and indeed even necessary. Several courts have accepted this conclusion but have held that they could not sanction a failure to provide a separate athletic program for girls.[10]

Separate but equal athletic programs are also statutory law in section 86.41 of Title IX(B), "Administration of Athletics." But, there is a provision that states if a school district does not fund and offer separate athletic programs, it must allow members of the excluded sex to try out for the team it does have, unless the "sport involved is a contact sport."

Some courts have determined that even in cases of contact sports, a school must allow a girl to participate if there is no girls' team. For a school to maintain different teams for boys and girls, the reason for the disparity in treatment must be "substantially related" to the achievement of an important government objective; however, "overbroad and archaic" generalizations about differences in the genders are not acceptable.[11]

When a school attempts to use safety as a rationale for forbidding coeducational teams, the school must show that there is a sufficient relationship between the announced goal of safety and a rule that would automatically exclude one gender.[12] Accordingly, girls must be given the opportunity to demonstrate that the presumption they are more prone to be injured is invalid. "They must be given the opportunity to compete with boys in interscholastic contact sports if they are physically qualified."[13]

Elementary and Secondary Education Act (Reauthorization)

The reauthorization of ESEA contains some new wrinkles, most of which focus on expanding educational equity. Title I has been redesigned to address the National Education Goals in a more specific manner. Addressed is the belief that all students can achieve high standards of excellence and that local districts should have greater flexibility in designing programs to increase achievement.

The funding formula for Title I has been revised to target more dollars to schools with the highest concentration of poverty. Equally important is the provision that permits schools to use Title I money to upgrade the entire school's educational program. Title I money may be combined with other resources, as well. Under the provisions, a school may develop a program to include the entire school *if* 50 percent or more of its students come from low-income families.

Among other provisions are grants for projects designed to focus on the unique problems of urban and rural schools with high-poverty populations. The projects must focus on ways to close the achievement gap between disadvantaged students and students in more affluent areas.

Providing for the Disabled

Public schools historically have been involved in the education of youngsters who are disabled, but in the last several years, such activities have taken on a more precise and legally defined basis. Legislation culminating with the Education of All Handicapped Children Act of 1975 (PL 94-142) has mandated the provision of the "least restrictive learning environment" for children who are disabled. Public Law 94-142 provides for ready access to appropriate public education for these children between the ages of 3 and 21 and mandates the integration of these children into settings that formerly may have been limited to nondisabled children.

Public Law 94-142 is buttressed by other federal laws: PL 94-143, the earlier PL 93-112, and the Individuals with Disabilities Education Act (1990), which have established certain rights to education and fair treatment for children with disabilities.[14] These rights include:

- Right to a free appropriate education at public expense, without regard to severity of disability
- Right to service in the least-restrictive setting when the disability requires service in something other than the normal school setting
- Right to prior notice before any decision is made to change services given to a child
- Right of parents to give consent before their child is evaluated, placed in a special program, or changed in placement
- Right to full due process, including representation by legal counsel, right to confront and cross-examine school personnel, right to a verbatim transcript, right to appeal, and right to be heard by an impartial hearing officer (not a school employee)
- Right to assignment without discrimination on the basis of sex, race, or culture
- Right to program placement without discrimination on the basis of sex, race, or culture, and to placement in a facility that is comparable to that offered to nondisabled clients of the system
- Right to be served in accordance with an individual program plan that states annual goals, measurable intermediate steps, the names of persons who will provide services and their qualifications, a timetable for beginning each step in the service and its anticipated duration, a schedule for evaluating the success of the program, and the right to be transferred if the program is failing
- Right to be protected from harm through the use of unregulated experimental approaches, untrained staff, inclusion in a program with others who are physically assaultive, freedom from unreasonable corporal punishment, and freedom from work assignments without compensation
- Right to see all records and to contest them in a hearing, with the right to place in the record information that the client feels presents a balanced picture

Thus, "separate but equal" as a concept appropriate to the education of children with disabilities has been found to be generally unacceptable.

The passage of PL 94-142 was the culmination of many years of litigation and legislation to protect the civil rights of children who are disabled. The legislative act ensures specified substantive and procedural provisions for such children, as well as an escalating funding formula to ensure a free and appropriate public education for all students who are disabled.

Of specific importance to school principals is that the law insists on:

1. A zero reject policy
2. Specific due process procedures
3. Nondiscriminatory testing
4. A written and promulgated individual educational plan for every child who is disabled (to be developed jointly with parents and reviewed at least annually)
5. Provisions for a least-restrictive environment

The act's "stay-put" provision directs that a child who is disabled "shall remain in his or her then current educational placement" pending completion of any review proceedings, unless the parents and state and local educational agencies otherwise agree.

The stay-put provision prohibits school authorities from unilaterally excluding children with disabilities from the classroom for dangerous or disruptive conduct growing out of their disabilities *during the pendency of review proceedings*. The act is unequivocal in its requirement that the "child *shall* remain in the current educational placement."

Doe and Smith, students who were emotionally disturbed, were suspended indefinitely for violent and disruptive conduct, pending the completion of expulsion proceedings by the school. In *Honig* v. *Doe and Smith,*[15] it was held that the implementing regulations under the act allow the use of normal, nonplacement-changing procedures, including *temporary* suspensions for up to 10 school days for students posing an immediate threat to others' safety, and allows for interim placements where parents and school officials are able to agree. Further, the act authorizes schools to file a suit for "appropriate" injunctive relief where such an agreement cannot be reached. In such a suit, there is a presumption in favor of the child's current placement, but school officials can rebut only by showing that maintaining the current placement is substantially likely to result in injury to the student or to others.

The Individualized Education Program. For each child there must be developed a formal individualized educational plan (IEP). The IEP is developed by a team, including the appropriate professional educators (diagnosticians, teachers, psychologists, and principals, for example) and the child's parents. Parents must give consent before a child with disabilities may be placed in a program. The IEP must contain:

- The child's current level of performance
- A statement of goals and objectives
- The nature of the educational services to be provided
- The place(s) and time(s) the services will be provided

- The person(s) who will be working with the child

The litmus test is whether the IEP is "reasonably calculated" to enable the child to advance from grade to grade.[16] Moreover, removing a child who has a disability to a disciplinary setting may be a change in placement and thus requires that the school comply with the act's procedures.[17] If the school cannot meet the needs of the child in the 180-day school year, the act requires a program longer than the normal year.[18]

The Supreme Court has held that schools may be required to reimburse parents for expenditures incurred in private school placement if the court ultimately determines that the private school placement is proper and that the school district's proposed IEP is not proper under the act.[19]

Individuals with Disabilities Education Act (IDEA). Passed by Congress in 1990, this is the so-called inclusion act. It requires that the educational placement of each child who has a disability is to be determined at least annually, that the plan is based on the child's individualized education program (IEP), and that the child is educated as close as possible to his or her home. Unless the IEP requires some other arrangement, the child is to be educated in the school that would have been attended had there been no disability. In selecting the least-restrictive environment, consideration is to be given to any potential harmful effect on the child or on the quality of services needed.

Simply put, these regulations require the school to make a substantial effort to find an inclusive solution for the child. Federal courts have held that this act requires that children with very severe disabilities must be included in the regular classroom they would otherwise attend if not disabled (even when they cannot meet the academic expectations of the class) *if* there is a potential social benefit, *if* the class would stimulate the child's linguistic development, or *if* the other students could provide appropriate role models for the student.[20]

Parents are increasingly aware of these rights and have shown a willingness to go to the courts to force school districts to include their child in "regular" classes even when the child who is disabled may not be able to keep up with the standard work of the class. The burden for showing both the parent and the court how exclusion is in the best interests of the child rests on the school.

Aside from the legal implications of IDEA and PL 94-142, the implications of these acts with regard to teacher training and in-service development are immense. Inclusion is clearly a way of reconceptualizing the method by which special services are delivered to children with disabilities. Rather than sending the child to a special class full time or to a school in the district that houses only special classes, the new model requires that the special education services be brought to the child.

Employment Issues. School administrators have the responsibility to practice fair employment policies and provide equal opportunity for job aspirants. Increasingly, in these days of greater authority for employment decisions to be made at the school site level, there is a need for the principal and the school staff to be aware of the federal and state laws and court decisions that regulate decision making about personnel selection and termination.

At the federal level, the Equal Employment Opportunity Commission (EEOC) is specifically charged with the enforcement of Title VII of the Civil Rights Act of 1964 (race, color, religion, sex, and national origin); the Equal Pay Act of 1963; the Age Discrimination in Employment Act of 1967; the Rehabilitation Act of 1973; the Americans with Disabilities Act of 1990; and the Federal Civil Rights Act of 1991. The EEOC actively follows up complaints to obtain full compensation and benefits for employees who have been discriminated against in an unlawful manner.

Frels[21] points out:

> Site-based management gives the principal and others who share decision making a greater say in who joins the school as teachers or in other staff positions. The rationale for school-based staff selection is based on the premise that the principal should not be held responsible for what teachers do when the principal has little or no voice in the selection of staff...[But] with the right of the principal and others at the campus level to make more staffing decisions comes greater legal risks that discrimination in hiring will occur.

Frels[22] also identifies five important steps that should be taken to lessen the legal exposure of principals in personnel matters:

1. Non-discrimination criteria for selection must be mandated.
2. Those who are involved in staff selection should receive adequate training.
3. Pools of qualified candidates can be screened centrally, with ultimate selection at the campus level.
4. The termination process should afford the necessary due process and have enough *systemwide uniformity* to guard against claims of unequal treatment individually and on a class basis [emphasis supplied].
5. Some centralized authority should retain oversight and control of the employment and termination process to ensure non-discriminatory treatment.

Americans with Disabilities Act (ADA). This 1990 piece of federal legislation specifically protects the employment rights of the disabled. The law is sweeping in its protection for such persons in employment and in state and local government services. Organizations in both the public and private sectors come under the act, whether or not the particular entity receives any federal funds. Students and employees are covered and certain accommodations are required. Generally speaking, the following guidelines apply to employment practices:

1. All positions are open to qualified applicants with disabilities.
2. Position openings must be posted in places that can be reached by people who are disabled.
3. Applicants may not be asked if they have a disability or how it was caused. Only those questions that have to do with the ability to perform essential job functions should be asked.
4. Medical information on an employee's disabilities must be kept in a separate file.

5. Employers must accommodate employees who are disabled unless the changes would impose an "undue hardship." (Widening doors and lowering chalkboards, for example, have not been found to be unreasonable accommodations.)
6. Readers, interpreters, and attendants should be provided unless that would be a "hardship."
7. Preemployment testing cannot discriminate against persons with sight, hearing, or speaking limitations.

The implications of the act to the school administration seem clear. Essential job skills will need to be even more carefully established and demonstratively related to the tasks that need to be performed before an otherwise qualified person with disabilities is denied employment because of a presumed inability to carry out job responsibilities. The burden for showing this will rest with the school district and the school administrator.

FIRST AMENDMENT RIGHTS

The school's power to control students is not broad enough in scope to proscribe protected speech. In the *Tinker* case,[23] three students wore black armbands to publicize their objections to the Vietnam conflict. The Supreme Court held that wearing the armbands was protected because it was closely related to protected political speech. Political speech must be encouraged and protected because open speech is the basis of our national strength and of the "independence and vigor" of Americans. First Amendment rights, when allowed "in light of the special characteristics of the school environment, are available to teachers and students." Where there is no proof that the student has interfered with the school's work or the rights of other students, the school may not limit free expression merely because they fear a disturbance. The Constitution requires the risk of dispute to foster the democratic system.

Freedom of Expression

There are limits on students' and on teachers' rights to freedom of expression in the school. In *Bethel School District No. 43* v. *Fraser* (106 S.Ct. 3159), the Supreme Court held in 1986 that a student's "lewd and indecent speech" is not protected by the First Amendment.[24] Similarly, a teacher's rights to freedom of expression may be circumscribed. Several kinds of classroom speech are not within the protections of either academic freedom or the First Amendment. The repeated use of profanity in the classroom has been found not to be protected (*Martin* v. *Parrish,* 1986)[25] nor has using the classroom as a forum for criticizing school administrators or school policies (*Robbins* v. *Board of Education of Argo Community High School District 217*).[26] Political views and personal views unrelated to class subjects or the curriculum are also subject to proscription.[27]

Limits on student expression extend to slogans, matter that appears on clothing, and jewelry that may signify gang membership. For example, *Olesen* v. *Board of Edu-*

cation (1987) upheld an antigang rule that prohibited the wearing of earrings by male students.[28] Similarly, dress codes that prohibited certain clothing that identified professional sports teams was upheld when the school showed that gangs wore these articles of clothing and that there was a large amount of gang activity in the school.[29] T-shirts and articles of clothing that depict lewd scenes or expressions have been found not to be within the bounds of student freedom of expression.[30] Where regulations are established for the purpose of protecting health and safety or for maintaining discipline, the courts are likely to be sympathetic. It is the responsibility of school officials to show that the rule bears a rational relationship to a legitimate state interest, however.

We turn now to a discussion of First Amendment rights as these relate to student publications.

Student Publications

Since scholastic newspapers fall within the ambit of the First Amendment's prohibition on censorship, a court would require a strong showing on the part of the school to uphold any censorship. The school would have to show that publication of the forbidden articles would materially and substantially interfere with the requirements of discipline in the operation of the school. Students are *not* free to publish without supervision, however, and administrative review has been held to be appropriate. In *Nicholson* v. *Board of Education, Torrance County Unified School District,* for example, the court held:

> Writers on high school newspapers do not have an unfettered constitutional right to be free from pre-publication review. The special characteristics of the high school environment particularly one involving students in a journalism class that produces a school newspaper, call for supervision and review by faculty and administration. The administrative review of a small number of sensitive articles for accuracy rather than for possible censorship or official imprimatur does not implicate First Amendment rights.[31]

This same court also held that the school possessed a substantial educational interest in teaching young student writers journalistic skills that stressed the tenets of accuracy and fairness.

A banner case involving the First Amendment rights of students was decided by the Supreme Court in *Hazelwood School District* v. *Kuhlmeier*.[32] Former high school students who had been staff members on the school newspaper filed suit in federal district court, alleging that their rights had been violated by the deletion of two pages from an edition of the paper. Included in the deletion were two articles. One of the articles described school students' experiences with pregnancy; the other discussed the impact of divorce on students at the school. The newspaper was written and edited by a journalism class and the class was a part of the regular school curriculum.

Pursuant to the school's practice, the teacher in charge of the class had submitted page proofs to the principal, who subsequently objected to the pregnancy story. He objected because, even though no names were used, he believed that the pregnant students might be identified from the text and because he believed that the references to sexual activity and birth control were inappropriate for some of the younger students.

He objected to the article about divorce because the page proofs he had been furnished identified by name (deleted by the teacher in the final version) a student who complained of her father's conduct. The principal indicated he thought the parent should have been given an opportunity to respond to the remarks or to consent to their publication. Believing that there was insufficient time to make the changes if the paper was to be issued before the end of the school year, he directed that the pages be removed even though other unobjectionable articles were included on the same pages.

The Court held that the First Amendment rights of the students had not been violated; that such rights were not automatically coextensive with the rights of adults in other settings, and must be applied in light of the special characteristics of the school environment. In the opinion of the Court, the school need not tolerate student speech that is inconsistent with its basic educational mission even though the government could not censor similar speech outside of the school.

School newspapers cannot be characterized as a forum for public expression. School facilities may be deemed to be public forums only if school authorities by policy or by practice have opened the facilities for any indiscriminate use by the general public, or by some segment of the public, such as student organizations. Otherwise, no public forum has been created and reasonable restrictions may be imposed on the speech of students, teachers, and other members of the school community. The school, in this case, was found not to have deviated from its own restrictive policies.

School Library Books

To what extent do school boards (and, by implication, administrators) have discretionary authority to remove books and materials from a school library? Courts have held that although a school board has broad discretion in adding books to a school library, it may not remove books simply because it dislikes the ideas contained in those books. The school may not remove books in order to "prescribe what shall be orthodox in politics, nationalism, religion or other matters of opinion."[33] The question of whether the removal of the books is an unconstitutional abridgment of a student's First Amendment rights is decided on an analysis of the board's intention. The board may not remove books in order to prevent access to ideas that it disapproves of or when those ideas fall under the protection of the First Amendment. The circumstances that permit exception to this principle are narrow. However, it would be permissible to remove books that were "pervasively vulgar" or educationally unsuitable.

These latter issues require definition, of course. The wise principal will work with the staff to develop criteria to determine "educational suitability." Help is available from the National Council for the Teaching of English and from the American Library Association. Whatever the court meant by "pervasively vulgar" in unknown—such phrases lack definition and are useless to the school leader.

Required Reading Materials

In *Grove* v. *Mead School District No. 354,*[34] a student and her parents argued that the use of a particular book that was a part of the English curriculum violated the First Amendment's prohibition of state establishment of religion. The court held that the factors that must be considered were whether there was a heavy burden on the individual's exercise of religion; if there was a compelling state interest justifying that burden; and if there could be some accommodation that would not impede the school's objective. The court decided that the burden on the student's exercise of religion was minimal because she was allowed to read an alternative book and avoid the classroom discussions of the other book.

This accommodation was made in order to allow the school to continue to provide a well-rounded public education; to do otherwise would have critically impeded the school's function. When there is no coercion used with the student, and the school is pursuing a valid end of public education, such an accommodation does not violate the student's right of free exercise of religion.

Searching Students

A particularly difficult legal issue is that of conducting searches of students and their property. Freedom from unreasonable searches and seizure of property is a Fourth Amendment right. The Fourth Amendment's prohibition of unreasonable searches and seizures applies to searches conducted by public school officials. In carrying out searches and other disciplinary functions pursuant to school policies, administrators act as representatives of the state, not merely as surrogates for the parents, and they cannot claim the parents' immunity from the strictures of the Fourth Amendment.

Although school officials may search students or their possessions when it is "reasonable" to do so, the court has not given specific examples of what is reasonable although "possible cause" is a common determinant. Whether a search is reasonable depends on the factual context of the search. The search of a child's person or property is a violation of the expectation of privacy of the student; however, this expectation of privacy is balanced against the interest of teachers and administrators in maintaining discipline and security.

These principles lead to the following test of the legality of a search: Is the search reasonable under all of the circumstances of the search? More specifically, is the search justified at its inception, and is the search related in scope to the circumstances that justify the interference in the first place?

Under ordinary circumstances, a search by a school official will be justified at its inception when there are reasonable grounds for suspecting that the search will show that the student has violated or is violating either the law or the rules of the school. The severity of the violation is a factor, however. One shouldn't search a student for minor infractions.

Religion in the Schools

As noted earlier, the First Amendment to the Constitution states, "Congress shall make no law respecting an *establishment* of religion, or prohibiting the *free exercise* thereof (emphasis added)." The federal and state courts have held in many cases that every governmental body (including school districts) must remain neutral with respect to religion. Schools are prohibited from taking any kind of action that tends to either "establish" or support religious beliefs, *or* tends to prevent the "free exercise" of religion. The courts mean that public school personnel may not require, lead, or encourage the study or discussion of scripture or any other religious activities during the school day or in connection with school-sponsored extracurricular activities.

May students study about religion when it is directly related to curricular offerings? Generally, yes. For example, a history teacher developing a lesson about the early settlement of what became the United States could certainly examine the centrality of religious beliefs to the migration of the Pilgrims to this continent and the degree to which those beliefs affected their lives. Also, for example, it would seem impossible not to discuss the Spanish Inquisition or the effect of the spread of Islam on the development of the Mediterranean region, including parts of southern Europe, if a class was engaged in a study of western civilization. And, how could one introduce such plays as *The Crucible* without examining the basis for the Salem witch trials?

Religious Clubs. If the school has an "open forums" policy, and the formation of after-school clubs of a noncurricular nature that meet on school grounds is permitted, then such nonschool-related clubs as chess clubs, science fiction clubs, and bible study groups are permitted. But this is permitted only to the extent that the groups are student sponsored and not school sponsored and are not held during school hours.[35]

Students may also distribute religious tracts on school grounds *if* other groups are permitted to distribute materials about their organizations. If a school regularly permits students to distribute noncurriculum, nonreligious materials in the hallways, then it must allow students to distribute religious materials. Our advice is to not permit any noncurriculum materials to be distributed by students. Such a policy will prevent a lot of unnecessary headaches and hurt no one.

Objectional Materials. What about objections of this or that religious group to instructional materials being used or to certain ceremonies such as Halloween parties (don't forget those Halloween demons and satanic creatures!). In an elementary school in Wheaton, Illinois, a new supplementary reading program for K–5 students was introduced after a curriculum review committee screened the series for educational suitability and quality. The series included the work of Dr. Seuss, C. S. Lewis, Ray Bradbury, Maurice Sedak, A. A. Milne, and other noted authors. Some parents filed suit and alleged that the series fostered a religious belief in the existence of supernatural beings including "wizards, sorcerers, [and] giants." They further alleged that the material "indoctrinates children in values directly opposed to their Christian beliefs by teaching tricks, despair, deceit, parental disrespect and...denigration of Christian symbols of holidays." Lately, the *Harry Potter* books by C. K. Rowling have been assailed by the Christian religious right.

Ultimately the courts held that the burden on the parents was, "at most, minimal"; they were free to provide religious instruction on their own, and "the use of the series did not compel their children to affirm or deny any religious doctrine." The teaching of reading and creativity was viewed by the court as a fundamental and compelling governmental interest, and the court noted that the tolerance of religious diversity is among the appropriate values for public schooling.[36]

The selection and use of instructional materials should always be subjected to careful review by teachers. Moreover, good educational practice requires that the development of new curriculum be subjected to such criteria as suitability and quality, and that the formation of curriculum review committees only makes good sense in any case. Although prudence and sensitivity are always important, principals and teachers should not be intimidated by parent's religious beliefs. Efforts to "cleanse" the curriculum by this or that religious group in accordance with any particular religious orthodoxy may be very harmful—indeed, it may be at extreme cross-purposes to the very reason that schools exist. This does not mean that a discerning excusal policy may not be advisable, but it does mean that wholesale elimination of educational materials in the face of parental complaint is a dereliction of duty and contrary to good educational practice. For advice, use a review committee.

Now to Halloween and other such celebrations: The schools have also been accorded latitude here in the instance of parental objection on religious grounds. In Florida, some parents objected to Halloween celebrations as satanic celebrations that inculcated a belief in witches. The court held that "witches, cauldrons, and brooms in the context of school Halloween celebrations appear to be nothing more than a mere 'shadow,' if that, in the realm of establishment clause jurisprudence."[37]

SEXUAL HARASSMENT

Complaints of sexual harassment between adults and between adults and children have increased exponentially, it seems. It is a serious issue and truly one of the fastest-growing areas of potential school district and school administrator liability. Failure to respond to allegations of sexual harassment most frequently gets school officials into difficulty.

Strahan[38] writes, "Sexual misconduct by a professional employee . . . is a fact situation that often results in both contract termination and a criminal complaint." The situation becomes especially electric when the allegations involve a teacher or an administrator and a student. Those instances where cases have been about teachers permitting one student to sexually harass another, or a teacher being sexually involved with another student, or even a faculty member dating a student have been resolved against the professional staff member.[39]

The *Davis* v. *Monroe* case (1999) is especially interesting because of some far-reaching implications.[40] In this case, a fifth-grader revealed that she was sexually taunted by a male classmate, including suggestions to come to bed with him and being touched on her breasts. Despite repeated complaints by the girl's mother, school officials failed to do anything to stop the boy. (The local sheriff had also been advised of her complaint.)

In 1994, Davis sued the board of education under Title IX of the 1972 Education Amendments, which covers public education at all levels. The school board won in lower courts but, because it was only one of a myriad of peer sexual harassment suits filed nationwide and these suits had yielded conflicting judicial opinions, the Supreme Court took the case on appeal. The Supreme Court ruled that in the case of harassment, a student could sue under Title IX if it could be shown that school officials knew of and were deliberately indifferent to the misconduct.

What is the lesson of these and other harassment allegations? School leaders must review every allegation, investigate the basis for those, and be prepared to take appropriate action. Indifference clearly will not be tolerated. The ridicule of overreaction, of course, offers some measure of restraint.

Interestingly, the implications of the *Davis* case extend well beyond the particulars. Title IX as a legal point—a prohibition against sex bias in schools that receive federal aid—was the issue. Women's rights groups applauded the decision as a victory, as did gay rights groups who now hope to use Title IX to fight abuse of gay and lesbian students by their peers.

COMMON TORT LIABILITY SETTINGS

A tort is an act *or an omitted act,* including breach of contract that results in damage, injury, or loss to the injured person(s), who then may seek relief by legal action. Torts may be intentional, may result from negligence, or may be caused by carelessness. School employees are liable for their failure to carry out prescribed duties or the failure to carry out these duties correctly. Individual staff members are expected to behave in a reasonable manner in the discharge of their duties, avoiding acts that are capricious, arbitrary, or negligent.

Tort liability suits usually require adequate evidence of the following:

- A prescribed or implicit duty on the part of the defendant for the care of the plaintiff
- An error of commission or omission by the defendant
- Damage, loss, or injury sustained by the plaintiff
- Indication of a cause-and-effect relationship between the error and the circumstance at issue
- Absence of contributory or offsetting comparative negligence on the part of the plaintiff [41]

The best defense against law suits is precaution. Principals and teachers cannot be expected to be prescient but they should anticipate possible dangers. The discussion that follows will examine common liability settings and describe certain aspects of the legal environment.

Pupil Injuries

A school is not usually a hazardous place, but children frequently do sustain injuries in and about the school. Most of these injuries are accidental and minor, the result of normal behavior. Nevertheless, teachers and administrators do have a responsibility to provide reasonable and prudent protection for their charges, and they are legally liable in tort for injuries arising from their negligence.[42]

The main test of negligence is "foreseeability." That is, the behavior of an individual would be called negligent if an ordinarily prudent person would have foreseen that certain actions, or a failure to act, would lead injury to another. The principles of sovereign immunity or statutory immunity may protect educators in some instances. However, the scope of that immunity varies from state to state.

The principal is responsible for taking all steps to promote the well-being of the children within the school and to guard the welfare of the staff. Therefore, to both staff and students, the principal has a particular duty to plan and supervise in a manner that will minimize the possibility of injury. At the very least, this involves providing information to staff members about their legal responsibilities and developing a set of rules and regulations that, if carefully followed, will result in protection for students.

Schools should be especially cautious in instances where it is "foreseeable" that student injury might result. Certain parts of the school environment present particular problems.

Physical Education, Field Trips, and Other Extracurricular Programs. Field trips, other extracurricular programs, and physical education are inherently more hazardous than the regular academic program. Greater supervision is required to avoid liability as a result of negligence. Carefully developed and well-understood written rules and regulations for the governance of these activities are important.[43] Adequate regulations cover such categories as pupil conduct while a participant or spectator, medical examinations for participants, medical care for sick and injured participants, transportation to and from the activity, duties of teachers and other supervisors, and notification and approval in advance by a parent or guardian.[44]

Laboratories and Shops. These two instructional areas present more hazards than any other in the school. Even general science classes frequently engage in experiments within the classroom, often involving chemicals as well as common electric- or gas-powered laboratory equipment. Moreover, good educational practice in teaching science involves such outside classroom events as off-campus field trips and on-campus outdoor activities.

Similarly, greater emphasis on career education and career exploration means that more and more middle and elementary schools are developing prevocational shops with at least rudimentary power equipment as well as common hand tools. In addition, classes such as cooking and sewing continue in popularity and require power- and hand-operated equipment.

Constant and immediate supervision is expected of teachers functioning in these instructional spaces. Teachers must adequately instruct students in the care and use of equipment they will be operating. If there is evidence that a student has been permitted to use a particular tool, or perform an experiment before being trained and told the consequences of improper usage, negligence will be difficult to disprove. Greater care is expected of teachers supervising students who are exposed to dangerous equipment. Even a brief teacher absence from a room where a class in engaged in hazardous activities is very risky.[45]

Playgrounds. Where supervision is regular, planned, reasonable, and proper, a negligence charge in case of pupil injury on the playground is not likely to be sustained. Consideration should be given to the kind of playground equipment in use, the size of the playground, and the number and age of the pupils to be supervised.

The courts generally appreciate the fact that a teacher is unable to keep every child within view and out of hazard at all times. Nevertheless, negligent supervision is often held to be the proximate cause of injury. If, for example, a teacher permits a child to leave a supervised group and the child is injured in a known, existing hazardous condition, then the teacher may be liable. If a teacher assigned to playground duty leaves a post for no good cause and a child is injured in a known or foreseeable dangerous condition, there may be tort liability because of negligence. Also, although teachers would not be expected to repair playground equipment, permitting pupils to use equipment known to be faulty, or beyond the maturity level of the child, could result in a claim of negligence.

The principal has three major responsibilities. First, proper rules of behavior, consistent with good safety practices, must be developed and implemented. Second, adequate adult supervision on the playground should always be provided when children are present. Third, the principal must arrange for frequent and regular inspection of the playground and playground equipment and a reporting system about any hazardous conditions. Staff and students must be apprised of these, and action should be taken to have the conditions corrected.

The Classroom. Teachers are normally in charge in the classroom and thus are most frequently held responsible for the safety of the children there. However, the principal has some responsibilities that, if not met, may result in a charge of negligent behavior. The primary responsibility of the principal with regard to classroom activities is to ensure that there is a teacher or a responsible adult present at all times. The principal should always be aware of a teacher's absence from the classroom. Failure to have a plan to provide for pupil supervision when a teacher becomes ill or is tardy to class could cause the principal to be charged with negligence if an injury resulted while the students were unsupervised. A common practice is to have a check-in sheet for teachers in the morning so that the principal can know immediately of any unanticipated absence or tardiness of personnel who have responsibility for the supervision of students.

Generally speaking, however, the temporary short-term absence from the classroom by a teacher would not, in and of itself, be considered a negligent act of general supervision. If, for example, a student misbehaves and in so doing injures another student during a teacher's brief absence from the room, a court would not ordinarily find negligence, because the teacher's absence was not the proximate cause of the accident. However, in all cases, the age, maturity, and intelligence of the student will bear on the question of teacher negligence in such absences. The best rule is not to leave students unattended.

Regulating Student Conduct

In even the best-run schools, students misbehave. Principals and teachers may prescribe reasonable controls against the misconduct of children. Many kinds of disciplinary action are available to school administrators and teachers when pupils violate school policies and rules. These include such minor punishments as short-term removal from the classroom, withholding certain privileges, detention after school, isolation from the rest of the class, being sent to the principal's office, and so on. The courts have generally upheld the right of school administrators and teachers to impose such minor punishment. Other forms of disciplinary action, however, such as suspension and expulsion from school[46] or the use of corporal punishment, are more often tested in the courts, and school administrators and teachers must take great care in the prescription of these punishments. Figure 16.1 depicts a basic information form to document disciplinary action.

In any case, the question of both substantive and procedural due process is extremely important.[47] The reasonableness and legality of the rule or regulation violated must be examined with care, and the legal issue of whether the student has a right to a prior hearing is important. Clearly, administrators should take care in imposing minor as well as major punishments to ensure that pupils or personnel are treated fairly and are not victimized by capricious or arbitrary action.

Corporal Punishment. *Corporal punishment* is disciplinary action by the application of physical force. As a means of modifying behavior, it is probably the oldest disciplinary tool. It also is one of the least efficacious. Acts of corporal punishment are probably the cause of more court cases than anything else.[48] However, under *in loco parentis,* the courts continue to uphold the right of teachers and principals to use "reasonable" force to ensure proper conduct or to correct improper conduct.[49]

In the *Baker* case,[50] the court held that corporal punishment may never be used unless the student was informed beforehand that specific misbehavior could occasion its use. The court also said that corporal punishment should never be employed as a first line of punishment. Another official also must be present and be told of the wrongful act before the student, to give the student an opportunity to protest spontaneously. A written explanation must then be sent to the parent, stating the reasons for the punishment.

Important guidelines must be followed if the use of corporal punishment is to be adjudicated as prudent and reasonable. Corporal punishment is generally held to be prudent providing:

- The state law and the local policy permit it.
- The punishment takes into consideration the age, size, gender, and health of the student and is not excessive.
- There is no malice; the punishment is given for corrective purposes only and is not immoderate.
- The student understands why punishment is required.
- An appropriate instrument is used.

Sometimes courts consider other attendant circumstances such as whether there was permanent injury suffered as a result of the punishment.

To ensure the fairest treatment possible for the student, it is important for the principal and the teacher to establish reasonable rules and to make sure that the punishment

FIGURE 16.1 Report of Disciplinary Action: Robert Craig Junior High School

Date: ___________________

Student's Name: __________________ Homeroom: ____________ Grade: _______
Time: ______________
Person Reporting: ____
Title of Person Reporting: _____________________________________
Nature of Offense:

Student's Account:

Action Taken:

I have had a chance to tell my side. ____
(Student Signature)
Date of Hearing: _________ Person Conducting Hearing: _______________________
Time: _________________ Other Person(s) Present: _________________________
Infraction: State Law: ______________________ School Policy: _______________
Board of Education Policy: ____
Central Office Policy: ____
Teacher Rule: ______________ Common Sense: ______________________________

for breaking these rules is suitable. It is also important to reasonably administer the rules and apply them equally to all students. It is possible to administer a reasonable rule so improperly that it becomes unreasonable. Any vindictiveness or viciousness in administering corporal punishment must be avoided. If the teacher or the principal knows that he or she is uncontrollably angry, then it is not time to punish the child corporally—or in any other way.

Suspension/Expulsion. *Suspension* is a dismissal from the school for a specific, but relatively short, length of time. *Expulsion* means permanent or long-term dismissal from school and, in most states, can be accomplished only by the board of education; permanent exclusion from school is outside the authority of the school administrator.

Attendance at a public school is generally viewed as a right rather than a privilege, but the enjoyment of this right is conditioned by the student's willingness to comply with reasonable regulations and requirements of the school. Violations of these may be punished by suspension or, in extreme cases, by permanent exclusion. Under a suspension, a student is usually required to meet some set of conditions established by the administrator before being readmitted.

The dividing line between a short- and a long-term exclusion from school is not clearly defined, but as a result of *Goss* v. *Lopez* has probably been established as 10 days.[51] In *Goss,* the court clearly established the right of school administrators to suspend students to maintain order in the school system. However, in this case, the court did find that school officials had violated the student's constitutional right to procedural due process. Nine students were temporarily suspended from school *without a hearing* and thus were held to be denied due process. The school board had contended that due process was not applicable to suspensions because there was not a "constitutional right" to public education. The court disagreed with this, saying:

> Although Ohio may not be constitutionally obligated to establish and maintain the public school system, it has nevertheless done so and has required its children to attend. Those young people do not "shed their constitutional rights at the school house door. . . ." The authority possessed by the State to prescribe and enforce standards of conduct in its schools, although concededly very broad, must be exercised consistently with the constitutional safeguards.[52]

Second, the school board had argued that even if public education was a right that was protected by due process, in this instance the due process clause should not apply because the suspensions were limited to 10 days and this was neither a severe nor a grievous infringement on the students' right to an education. The court disagreed here also and faced the question of what kind of process is due in the instance of short-term student suspensions. The court held that only rudimentary process was required to balance student interests against the educator's need to take quick disciplinary action. The court said:

> The student [must] be given a written notice of the charges against him, if he denies them, an explanation of the evidence the authorities have and an opportunity to present his side of the story. . . . There need be no delay between the time "notice" is given and the time of the hearing. In the great majority of cases the disciplinarian may informally discuss the alleged misconduct with the student minutes after it has occurred. We hold only that, in being given an opportunity to explain his version of the facts at this discussion, the student first be told what he is accused of doing and what the basis of the accusation is.[53]

This is important because it implies that while due process provisions must always be present, even in less than major punishment, the nature of the punishment and the infraction will determine the degree to which one must engage in elaborate vestments of due process. In minor infractions it would be necessary only to provide rudimentary forms of hearing. Even here, however, the important lesson is that the child to be punished must in all instances be treated fairly and that there must be clear indication of the absence of capricious action. Expulsions are a different matter. In the case of an expulsion, it would seem clear that all of the vestments of due process be clearly applied.

Opposition to the use of suspensions and expulsions as punishment for misconduct is growing. More often, schools are developing a disciplinary procedure called *in-school suspension* as a means of avoiding the disruption and negative effects cited above. The in-school suspension usually involves taking the student out of the regular classroom for a period of time and placing the student in another learning situation within the school building, either in an independent learning situation with supervision or in a designated special class. When this procedure is coupled with counseling by the principal, the guidance counselor, or some other clinician to diagnose and treat the problem, it is a sound practice.

Detention. It is well established that principals and teachers do have the authority to temporarily detain students from participating in extracurricular activities and even to keep children after school as a punishment, providing, of course, that the student has a way of getting home. As in other punishments, the detention must be reasonable. False imprisonment may be claimed if the principal or a teacher either wrongfully detains a student or detains a student for an unreason able amount of time as a punishment. In this, as in all other punishments, the main test is one of fairness. If school officials act fairly and in good faith in dealing with students, their actions will probably be upheld by the courts.

PRIVACY AND CONFIDENTIALITY OF STUDENT RECORDS

The question of the confidentiality and accuracy of student records is important, and since the passage of Public Law 93-380, Family Educational Rights and Privacy Act of 1974 (FERPA), the issue has been legally clarified. This act states that students and parents are permitted to inspect and review records and must be given a copy of any part or all of the educational record on request. It also requires that in any dispute concerning the contents of a student's educational record, due process must be provided. Where a record is found to be inaccurate, the inaccuracies must be expunged.

The act essentially requires that the schools and other agencies permit an individual to determine what relevant records are maintained in the system of records; to gain access to relevant records in such a system of records; to have copies made; and to correct or amend any relevant record.

Further, the records about an individual may not be disclosed to outsiders except by the consent of the individual in question. The consent must be in writing and must be *specific* in stating to whom the record may be disclosed, which records may be disclosed, and, where applicable, the time frame during which the records may be disclosed.

In some instances, disclosures may be made without the consent of the pupil or the pupil's parents. Information may be disclosed within the school to teachers or guidance counselors who have a "need to know"; where there is a court order; where there is required disclosure under the Freedom of Information Act; and for routine usage, such as the publication of names of students who made an honor roll or information for a directory such as class lists or sports brochures, which might include such information as the student's name, address, gender, or birthplace. Even in this latter instance, however, it would be best to get prior permission through some sort of routine process. The district may be held liable for a common law tort for the disclosure of private facts about a student without consent if the disclosure results in any unwarranted publicity.[54]

Guidelines to assist principals in developing fair policies about student records include:

1. Develop procedures to ensure that parents and students know what kind of information is contained in school records at a given time and are informed of their rights concerning control over the process of information collection and recording.

2. Encourage mature students and their parents to inspect the records. The rights of parents to do this are now well established, but most parents are unaware of these rights. Increased communication and greater trust on the part of the parents will be a major benefit and such a policy might provide a substantially more accurate record.

3. Develop systematic procedures to obtain explicit and informed parental or pupil consent before information contained in school records is released to outside parties, regardless of the reasons for such release or the characteristic of the third party. Most schools will, on occasion, give out information to law enforcement or other agencies without obtaining consent from the student or the parents. Aside from the possible legal implications of a violation of privacy, this practice can have no other effect than that of discouraging a trustful relationship among the parent, the child, and the school.

SUMMARY

The constitutional roots, case law, and legislative bases on which the interactive relationships of students, teachers, parents, and principals legally occur has been the subject of this chapter. A working knowledge about the legal principles, important court decisions, and current law is essential. Understanding the laws governing the operation of schools is important—not just in order to stay out of court but also, and perhaps more importantly, to provide the kind of orderly, productive, and humane school basic to the continuation of a democratic society.

ACTIVITIES

1. Case Studies 7, 13, 16, 18, and 22 contain problems that have legal as well as instructional, curricular, and public relations implications. Review these cases, keeping the concepts presented in this chapter in mind. What questions of law seem to arise? How would you go about addressing these questions? What additional information, if any, do you need? Where would you get this information? Considering just the information you have from this chapter, the case, and your own experience, what solutions do you suggest?

2. Turn to the ISLLC Standards found in Appendix B. Review the knowledge, dispositions, and performances listed with Standard Six. Reflect on which of the standard items relate directly to the material presented in this chapter. Why is it important to know "the law as related to education and schooling? Identify one knowledge area, one disposition, and one performance to link directly to a concept or idea discussed in Chapter 16.

ENDNOTES

1. Richard D. Strahan, "Building Leadership and Legal Strategies," *The Principal as Leader* (2nd ed.), ed., Larry W. Hughes (Upper Saddle River, NJ: Prentice-Hall, 1999), p. 292.

2. *Tinker* v. *Des Moines Independent Community School System,* 393 U.S. 503, 89 S.Ct. 733 (1969).

3. Tinker, op. cit. See also *Burnside* v. *Byars,* 363 F. 2d 744 (5th Cir. 1966).

4. Procedures and punishments must be tailored to fit the offender and the offense. See, for example, *Rhyne* v. *Childs,* 359 F. Supp. 1085 (1973), affd, 507 F.2d 675 (5th Cir. 1975).

5. Full disclosure requires an explanation of the evidence the school officials have against the student. See *Goss* v. *Lopez,* 419 U.S. 565; *Board of Curators of the University* v. *Horowitz,* 435 U.S. 78 (1978); *Keough* v. *Tate County Board of Education,* 748 F. 2d 1077 (5th Cir. 1984), for example.

6. Although procedural due process is required by the U.S. Constitution, the courts have a different fact pattern in each case. There is no set formula for what is sufficient procedural due process. Too, the various district and circuit courts have given slightly different variations of the test for what is adequate. It is important to remember that while this process appears to take on the vestments of a court of law, it is *not* a court of law. It is simply a procedure for fair and impartial treatment. After the process is complete, the individual still has the right to take the issue to civil court if he or she feels the issue was decided wrongly or the punishment to severe.

7. 501 F.2d 1264 (9th Cir. 1974). See also *Bray* v. *Lee,* 337 F. Supp. 034 (D. Mass 1972).

8. Ibid. at 1269.

9. *Vorcheimer* v. *School District of Philadelphia,* 532 F.2d 880 (3d Cir. 1976).

10. For example, *Brenden* v. *Independent School District,* 343 F. Supp. 1224 (D. Minn. 1972), aff'd. 477 F.2d 1292 (10th Cir. 1973); *Herver* v. *Meiklejon,* 430 F. Supp. 164 (D. Col. 1977).

11. See *Clark* v. *Arizona Interscholastic Association,* 695 F.2d 1129 (9th Cir. 1982).

12. *Force by Force* v. *Pierce City School District,* 570 F. Supp. 1020 (W.D. Mo. 1983).

13. *Yellow Springs Exempted Village School District Board of Education* v. *Ohio School Athletic Association,* 433 F. Supp. 753 (S.D. Ohio 1978).

14. PL 94-143 is entitled "Developmentally Disabled Assistance and Bill of Rights Act"; PL 93-112 is "Rehabilitation Act" and was enacted in 1973.

15. 484 U.S. 305; 108 S.Ct. 592; 98 L.Ed.2d 686 (1988).

16. See *Board of Education of Hendrick Hudson Central School District* v. *Rowley,* 458 U.S. 176 (1982).

17. See *Adams Central School District* v. *Deist,* 334 N.W.2d 775 (Neb. 1983).

18. See *Board of Education for the City of Savannah* v. *Georgia Association of Retired Citizens,* 52 U.S.L.W. 3932 (June 26,1984).

19. *School Committee of the Town of Burlington, Mass.* v. *Mass. Dept of Education,* 53 U.S.L.W. 4509 (April 30,1985).

20. For example, in *Board of Education, Sacramento* v. *Holland* (786 F.Supp. 874 [ED Cal. 1992]), the court ordered the school district to place a child with an IQ of 44 in a regular second-grade class and rejected the district's complaints about expenses as exaggerated. In *Oberti* v. *Board of Education of the Borough of Clementon School District,* (789 F.Supp. 1322 [D.N.J. 1992]), the court rejected the claim of the school district that a child would be so disruptive as to significantly impair the education of the other children.

21. Kelly Frels, "Legal Aspects of Site-Based Management," *School Law in Review,* 1992 (Washington, DC: National School Boards Association, 1992), p. 5.

22. Ibid.

23. *Tinker,* loc. cit.

24. 106 S. Ct. 3159.

25. 805 F. 2nd 583.

26. 313 F. Supp. 642.

27. *Goldwasser* v. *Brown,* 1969 (417 F. 2nd 1169); *Moore* v. *School Board of Gulf County Florida,* 1973 (364 F. Supp. 355).

28. 676 F. Supp. 820.

29. *Jeglin II* v. *San Jacinto Unified School District* (1993) 827 F. Supp. 1459.

30. See, for example, *Pyle* v. *Hadley School Committee* (1994), 861 F. Supp. 157 and *Gato* v. *School District 411* (1987), 674 F. Supp. 796.

31. 682 F.2d 858 (9th Cir. 1982).

32. 108 S.Ct. 562 (1988).

33. *Board of Education, Island Trees Union Free School District No. 26* v. *Pico,* U.S. 853 (457 1982).

34. 735 F.2d 1528 (9th Cir. 1985).

35. *Lamb's Chapel* v. *Center Moriches Union Free School District,* 124 L. Ed. 2d 352 (June 7, 1993). See also *Westside Community School Board* v. *Mergens* (496 U.S. 226 [1990]) for a definition of a *noncurriculum-related school group*. In the latter judgment, such a group was defined broadly to be any student group that does not directly relate to the body of courses offered by the school. If a school permits student groups such as a scuba diving club, a political club, and so on, to meet at school facilities during noninstructional time (before or after the school day), it must also permit a *student-organized* religious group to meet. The only way a school could deny access to a group that wished to advance the teachings of Mohammed or Karl Marx or Jesus or Confucius would be an open forum or public forum policy. The only way it can deny access is to convince a judge that the group advocates the violent overthrow of the government or that the group's presence will lead to violence, damage to property, injury to persons, and the like.

36. *Fleischfresser* v. *Directors of Sch. Dist.* 200, 15 F. 3d 680 (7th Cir. 1994). See also *Mozert* v. *Hawkins County Pub. Sch.* 827 F. 2d 1058 (6th Cir. 1987), *cert denied* 108 S.Ct. 1029 (1988).

37. *Guyer* v. *School Bd.,* 634 So.2d 806 (Fla. Dist. Ct. App. 1994).

38. Strahan, op. cit. p. 313.

39. See, for example, *Board of Education of Santa Fe Schools* v. *Sullivan,* 740 F.2nd 119 (New Mexico, 1987), *Katz* v. *Amback,* 472 N.Y.S.2nd 492, and *Davis* v. *Monroe County School Board,* 119 S.Ct. 791; 142 L.Ed 2nd 655 (1999).

40. Ibid.

41. Contributory negligence is determined by whether or not the party who was injured exercised the degree of caution others of the same age, sex, maturation level, and experience would have exercised under the same conditions. Comparative negligence requires that the plaintiff be charged with proportional liability for his or her acts that contribute to the injury when the plaintiff is old enough to be held accountable for those actions.

Obviously, more supervision is expected of those in charge of young children. Personnel in elementary schools are less likely to be able to claim contributory negligence than those who supervise older students. Nevertheless, whatever the age, a student who disregards or acts in direct defiance of an admonishment of a supervising adult would probably be found guilty of contributory negligence if the refusal to follow directions resulted in the injury.

42. Of course, not all injuries to students are actionable; some are simply unavoidable, the result of pure accident. Only those injuries resulting from negligence provide an actionable basis.

43. For example, the failure to provide safety equipment when playing sports is negligence (*Berman* v. *Philadelphia Board of Education,* 310 Pa. Super. 153; 456A.2d 545, Pa. Super. Ct. 1983) or the failure to give proper instructions in the way to perform physical ability tests (*Ehlinger* v. *Board of Education of New Hartford Central School District,* 96 AD 2d 708; 465 N.Y.S. 2d 378, N.Y. App. Div. 1983).

44. However, advance approval by a parent or guardian for a child to go on a field trip does not foreclose the right to sue if the child is injured.

45. Greater than usual care is required. For example, in a New York case where student employees dropped chemicals from a laboratory window and those chemicals were later retrieved by a young child who was injured by them, the failure to either keep the chemicals under lock and key or to supervise the student employees was held to be negligence. *Kush by Marszalek* v. *City of Buffalo,* 59 N.Y. 2d 26; 449 N.E. 2d 725; 462 N.Y.S. 2d 26 (1983).

46. *Suspension* is generally defined as dismissal from school for a specific, although relatively short-term, period of time. The term is two or three days and often the maximum of a week. Usually, the principal of the school has the right to suspend. *Expulsion* is defined to mean permanent dismissal and normally is an action that legally can be taken only by a school board.

47. In the instance of suspension, one of the most limiting cases was that of *Mills* v. *Board of Education,* 348 F.Supp. 866 (1972), in which the court ordered that there must be a hearing prior to a suspension invoked for any period of over two days. In *Goss* v. *Lopez,* 95 S.Ct. 729 (1975), the Supreme Court ruled basically that school officials must accord students and school employees their constitutional right of due process even in routine disciplinary actions. *Goss* held that a

junior high school student suspended for as much as a single day is entitled to due process. In *Wood* v. *Strickland,* 95 S.Ct. 992 (1975), the Supreme Court ruled that school board members and school officials can be held personally liable for pecuniary damages when students are denied constitutional rights, even by accidental omission.

48. If a teacher or a principal uses excessive force or causes untoward injury he or she may be held liable for battery. There is often confusion about the terms *assault* and *battery*. Battery is the actual unlawful inflicting of physical violence on another. Assault is a threat to commit battery. There can be assault without battery.

49. The Supreme Court has affirmed the right of school personnel to use corporal punishment as long as there is no state law or local policy to the contrary. A lower court ruling upheld that corporal punishment may be administered provided that only "reasonable force" is used and provided that students knew beforehand that certain behaviors could result in physical punishment. *Ingraham* v. *Wright* 430 U.S. 651 (1977), and *Baker* v. *Owen,* 385 F. Supp. 294 (1975).

50. *Baker,* op. cit.

51. *Goss* v. *Lopez,* 95 S.Ct. 729 (1975).

52. Ibid., 736.

53. Ibid., 740.

54. *Klipa* v. *Board of Education of Anne Arundel County,* 54 Md. App. 644, 460 A 2d 601 (Md. App. 1983).

SELECTED READINGS

Alexander, Kern. *American Public School Law,* 4th ed. (St. Paul: Wadsworth, 1998).

Cases in Point, a legal update service provided to members by the National Association of Secondary School Principals, 1904 Association Drive, Reston, VA 20191-1537. <http//www.nassp.org>

Hughes, Larry W. (Ed.). *The Principal as Leader,* 2nd ed. (Upper Saddle River, NJ: Prentice-Hall, 1999). See especially Chapter 12.

Imber, Michael, and van Geel, Tyll. *Education Law,* 2nd ed. (Thousand Oaks, CA: Erlbaum, 2000).

Rogers, Joy. "The Inclusion Revolution." *Research Bulletin,* 11. Bloomington, IN, Center for Evaluation, Development and Research, Phi Delta Kappa, 1993.

Shelton, Maria M. "The Americans with Disabilities Act: A Primer for Principals." *The Principal 73,* no. 2 (November 1993): 35–37.

Yodorf, Mark G., David Kirp, and Betsy Levin. *Educational Policy and Law,* 3rd ed. (St. Paul: West, 1992).

APPENDIX A

CASE STUDIES IN SCHOOL LEADERSHIP AND MANAGEMENT

PROBLEM ANALYSIS, DECISION PROCESSING, DECISION MAKING: INTRODUCTION TO THE CASES

In order to arrive at the maximum feasible decision, it is first necessary to define the problem correctly. Then, one needs to think about the decision processes that are available in order to resolve the problem. Many response patterns are open to any executive. Selecting the right one will determine whether the problem will be resolved or at least mitigated or whether even greater problems result. Anticipating the consequences of any particular process or act is more than an intellectual exercise.

A school leader's day is characterized by one encounter after another with staff members, students, parents, community members, politicians, and others—the kinds of individuals or subgroups are myriad and diverse. For the school principal, a simple walk down the hall from the office to resolve a problem in the cafeteria may result in half a dozen or more encounters with this or that teacher, custodian, parent, or child, all of whom have questions and requests and problems that the principal is asked to solve. Hurried answers are shouted over the shoulder. The principal is thrust into a maelstrom during the routine of most days. The rapidity and intensity of encounters and the life span of the problems will vary. Frequently, the time frames will be short and the databases will seem too meager.

The fact is, though, few problems have to be solved at the moment. There is almost always some time—albeit often not much—to reflect on the nature of the problem and the likely decision process that will result in a satisfactory solution. The fundamental questions to be asked are:

- Do I have at hand the information necessary to solve this problem?
- Whose support will be necessary in order to effect a long-term solution?
- How likely is it that I will get this support if I go ahead and make the decision on my own?
- Does this problem need immediate attention?
- On what rationale, value, or theory am I basing my decision?

On the pages that follow are case studies about problems that occur in and around schools—student problems, angry clients, budget crunches, maintenance issues, staff appraisal difficulties, dilemmas about curriculum, conflicts about a multitude of issues—most not simple. In any given case, select analytical processes that seem to you to be most appropriate. The Maier and Vroom-Jago models (Chapter 3) may be especially helpful, but whatever approach you choose, be prepared to defend your reasoning.

As you analyze the cases, make only those assumptions that are reasonable, given the limited number of facts that are provided. But remember, *you* are the executive who is confronted by the issue—not someone else. It is *your* problem. You don't have to solve the problem, however. Your task is to analyze the issue and set in motion a process that you believe will result in a good solution. Determine what you believe is the main problem or issue and indicate any subproblems or issues (and, stay out of the garbage can!).

Case Studies: Primary Subject Matter and Decision Level

CASE	ISSLC STANDARD	CURRICULUM	PERSONNEL	STUDENTS	PUBLIC RELATIONS	FINANCE
1	2, 5	X	X			X
2	2	X				
3	2, 3, 4	X			X	X
4	1, 2, 4		X	X	X	
5	1, 2	X		X		
6	1, 4	X			X	
7	3, 5		X			
8	1, 2	X	X			
9	5		X			
10	3					X
11	4, 5, 6		X	X	X	
12	2, 5		X		X	
13	1, 4, 6			X	X	
14	1, 4	X	X		X	
15	3, 5					X
16	2, 5		X			

17	2, 4		x		x	
18	4, 5	x		x	x	
19	2, 3		x			
20	1, 2	x			x	
21	2, 5			x		
22	1, 4, 5	x			x	
23	3, 6			x	x	
24	3, 6		x	x	x	

Table of Contents

CASE 1: THE PROJECT IS LATE

You have accepted an assignment as principal of one of the largest schools in the district. The school is widely recognized as being a trouble spot. Antagonism between teachers and administrators abounds. Even the department heads show antagonism toward the administration. They identify with the teachers. And no one, including yourself, is especially pleased with a new state mandate with regard to pay for performance. (You know it's going to be difficult to implement under any circumstance.)

This is your first principalship and you are anxious to do well. However, during your first month on the job, you have not had much success in gaining the acceptance of the eight department heads. They seem friendly in the interactions with each other but noticeably cool and suspicious toward you.

Today, you received a visit from your superintendent. One of the curriculum projects on which your group is working is six months overdue. Unless it is completed soon, outside funding ("seed money," which is desperately needed) will be in jeopardy. You were previously unaware that this problem was so severe and your boss now indicates that immediate action is required.

You know that some of the department heads are skeptical of the value of the project in question. It will require a complex organizational change. Ultimately, it will probably result in the collapsing of two departments into one budgetary unit, the reassignment of one department head, and a reduction of six teachers and one paraprofessional.

CASE 2: YOUR KIDS DON'T READ WELL ENOUGH

You are the principal of a K–6 school. The children in grades 4 through 6 do not seem to be reading as well as might be expected.

There are a number of troubling indicators. As you review scores on the standardized reading tests used, you see that your students are, in the main, well below the norms for your school district as a whole, as well as for the nation. Various teachers have expressed concern about the reading skills of their students. The librarian has mentioned the low circulation rate of even the usually more popular trade books. Junior high school and senior high school principal colleagues have remarked to you frequently that students from your school don't do very well at their schools.

Your school has a heterogeneous student population with slightly more children from homes at the lower end of the economic continuum. Staff turnover is about average for the district.

CASE 3: DON'T MESS WITH MY BUDGET

You are the principal. As you conduct a review of the school's science program, you are aware of the following:

1. Students from your unit do not do well on the SAT or similar tests and complain about not being able to get into prestigious colleges and universities.
2. Enrollments in advanced science classes have been dropping steadily over the past five years.
3. Many of your science teachers did not major in science; it is their second teaching field.

4. Some members of the community have been clamoring for "a better science program."
5. The superintendent of schools and the deputy in the district's division of instruction have just mounted an effort to persuade the board of education that massive additional resources need to be expended on the reading program in the middle schools.
6. Principals in your district have considerable latitude in the development and implementation of an instructional budget.
7. The amount of your instructional budget is determined by a basic allotment plus a factor, which is largely a result of the average daily attendance in the previous year.
8. There is a good bit of jealousy among the academic departments about matters of budget.
9. A change of attendance zone boundaries has recently occurred because a new freeway displaced several hundred families. The impact of this on your school is a 10 percent increase in students from homes in which English is not the primary language.
10. No overall increase in your budget for next year can be expected. Your average daily attendance is about the same from year to year.

CASE 4: TROUBLE BREWING AT HUGHES MIDDLE SCHOOL

You are the new principal of Hughes Middle School. The school has had three different principals in the past five years. It is August 1 and school will be opening in a few weeks. You have the following facts at hand:

1. Enrollment is 1,200 students in grades 5 through 8 and the school is in an urban setting.
2. Although the total population of the school is relatively stable, there is much transience. About 35 percent of your students will "turn over" in any given year, some leaving and returning within the year, many just leaving or entering.
3. Your student population is 30 percent African American, 20 percent Hispanic, and about 10 percent Asian, mostly Vietnamese. Projections are for an increasingly declining white population. Many of the white parents in the attendance area send their children to one of two private schools, one of which is parochial.
4. A little over one-quarter of the students come from a nearby public housing project.
5. About one-fourth of the students are bused in because of a special extended day program that your district maintains in a few of its middle schools.
6. The attendance area that your school serves has an adult population composed of 65 percent white, 12 percent black, 13 percent Hispanic, and 5 percent Asian. Socioeconomic status (SES) indicators suggest a wide range of economic levels.

Housing ranges from luxury class to substandard housing. Recently, young married couples with no children have been taking advantage of some housing bargains in one of the neighborhoods and there has been a substantial in-migration of these couples.

7. The teaching staff has a 20 percent annual turnover and is bimodal in teaching experience—that is, a large number are in their first three years of teaching and a large number have over 15 years of experience. Only a few of your teachers are in their intermediate years.
8. There doesn't seem to be a very active PTO.
9. Your predecessor left no plans for the three-day staff in-service program that is to begin each school year.

CASE 5: THE CURRICULUM IS NOT WORKING; FIX IT

You are the principal of a large elementary school (average daily attendance = 925). Your school district has always searched for ways to increase student learning and has frequently been on the "cutting edge" statewide in its efforts to do this. Recently, the district has adopted the whole language approach as a curricular and instructional thrust. To the surprise of everyone, including yourself, the expected increase in student learning as evidenced by the results on state and national standardized tests has not been realized in your school. In fact, scores have dropped significantly in English, reading, and social studies. Moreover, your staff turnover rate has increased greatly over what it was just two years ago.

You are puzzled. Other schools in the district have not experienced this decline and nearby districts who have a similar curriculum are successfully implementing it. You have had consultations and visits from instructional specialists from the district office and they have reported that the materials seem to be used appropriately and your teachers seem generally well qualified and satisfied with the curriculum.

You suspect that there must be at least some parts of the new curriculum that are responsible for the lack of success of your students. Also, you are not all that satisfied that some of your teachers are working hard to fully implement the program. This view is not widely shared among your immediate subordinates—department and grade-level chairs or your dean of instruction. Most of them attribute the problem to poor in-service training of the teachers, to a lack of additional resources to provide for the extra time teachers say the program requires, and to generally low morale on your staff. There is a considerable depth of feeling on the part of your staff and much potential disagreement among subordinates about the issue. Some are angry with the students for the poor test scores; others are becoming openly hostile about the "extra" time they say the program is taking; still others resent the implication that they are not doing a good job.

This morning you receive a phone call from your district superintendent. The superintendent has just reviewed the test scores for the district, school by school, and is calling to express concern. The superintendent indicated that the problem was yours to solve in any way you think best, but wants to know within the week what steps you plan to take.

You share the superintendent's concern and know that many of your people are also concerned.

CASE 6: VALUES CLARIFICATION DISPUTE

You are the principal of a large middle school located in a large city. An aspect of the districtwide guidance program is a values clarification unit. One of your 12-year-old students, a participant in the program, requested help with his assignment from his mother. The mother is furiously angry about the program now.

The sixth-grade worksheet the student was working with read as follows:

> "Your oldest sister loves and trusts her husband. You see him coming out of a restaurant with another woman. He and the woman get in a car and drive away together. What would you do?"

The mother was nonplused and decided to find out what it was that the students were being "guided" to do. She relates, "I did not go to the school as an outraged person; I just wanted to find out what was going on." She secured a copy of the guidance program in values clarification from the director of guidance and now she is really upset. She points to lessons that deal with who should be allowed to live in the case of a limited number of dialysis machines, and other lessons that ask the student to respond to such questions as "One time I cheated and it was OK; another time I cheated and it was wrong."

The mother states, "I have always trusted the school and the teachers but these are areas that they have no business being in. They attack the values the parent is trying to instill. I'm really bothered that none of the parents I talked with has any idea that this sort of thing is going on."

Asked for his opinion, the president of the Teachers' Association remarked that the class is a waste of instructional time. "It's the biggest waste of time we have in the district. Our teachers complain that they aren't provided time enough for remedial work with students who need academic help but 30 minutes or more a week is spent on Mickey Mouse activities like this. The teachers hate it and are embarrassed to have to present it."

The newspaper has picked up the story.

CASE 7: REDUCTION IN FORCE

You are principal of a small elementary school (primary grades only) with a faculty numbering 19. The formal education and teaching experience of your staff is quite similar, permitting you to use them interchangeably at various grade levels and in various "teaming" arrangements. During the past two years, your student enrollment has decreased. This has probably stabilized for the time being, but the result has been a very favorable teacher-pupil ratio. In fact, you are slightly overstaffed. Your teachers have begun to worry about possible reassignments to other schools and have expressed this concern to you. Basically, they are happy where they are.

Yesterday, you were informed by your superintendent that a request had been received by the personnel office from one of your colleagues in another primary school unit. Her school is experiencing rapid growth in the number of students and her data justify her request for at least four additonal faculty. Even with these four additional staff members, her pupil-teacher ratio will still exceed yours. There is a "budget crunch" and a districtwide hiring freeze. The superintendent indicates that your colleague's faculty needs must be met from the ranks of your teachers.

All of your teachers are capable of handling the new assignments, and from the standpoint of present and future changes, there is no particular reason why any one more than any other should remain on your faculty. The problem is complicated even further because the school to which the reassignments will be made is in what is generally regarded in the district as a highly undesirable location.

CASE 8: WHICH TEXTBOOK WILL IT BE?

You are the principal of a middle school, grades 6 through 9, and there is need to review the social studies series currently in use. You have a strong opinion that the current series does not adequately depict the contributions made by minorities and women. Because your own teaching field is social studies, you have more than a casual interest in and knowledge about the issue. The social studies department seems split on the matter. Two teachers do not want to use any text at all, several teachers are satisfied with the current text, and three others favor at least two other series. The board requires one adopted text series but does permit supplemental works when it can be shown that there is good reason to do so. It is now January; a recommendation is due in the central office one month from today.

The chairperson of the department is undecided on the matter and requests that you "do something." A review of staff evaluations reveals that one of the teachers who wants no text at all is among the top-rated teachers in the school. She is unhappy with the more conservative posture of many of her colleagues and has indicated that unless a more positive stand on the multicultural nature of society is taken by the department, she will go elsewhere. A *cause célèbre* looms.

CASE 9: THAT'S MY PARKING PLACE!

You have recently been appointed principal of a new school currently under construction. Your team of five department heads and two assistant principals has been selected and they are now working with you to help select staff, purchase equipment, and generally anticipate the problems that are likely to arise when the building is opened in the fall—3½ months from now.

Yesterday, you received a final set of architectural plans for the building and for the first time you examined the parking facilities that are available. There is a large lot across the road from the school intended for teaching staff, support personnel, and students. In addition, there are 12 parking spaces immediately adjacent to the school intended for visitors, disabled, and reserved parking. School-district policy requires a minimum of 3 general visitor spaces and 2 spaces for the disabled. This leaves you with only 7 spaces to allocate among yourself, 5 department heads, and 2 assistant principals. There is no way to increase the number of spaces without changing the structure of the building.

Up to now, there have been no obvious status differences among your team who has worked together extremely well in the planning phases. To be sure, there are salary differences, but experience and degree levels are the primary cause of this. One of your people has her doctorate; four others have master's degrees. Each has just recently accepted the new position and expects reserved parking as a privilege of the new status.

CASE 10: THE NEW PHOTOCOPIER

Losses in enrollments because of population shifts and an eroding tax base have resulted in deep budget cuts. You, as the principal, must trim all nonessential expenditures. You have decided to investigate whether your office needs the large, fast, highly flexible copier currently in use. It could be replaced with any of a number of cheaper machines on the market and a substantial cost savings effected. You have the specifications for both the current and the smaller machines and the salespersons have advised you of the various features of each, including fidelity of reproduction, copies per minute, number of copies collated (if at all), and other features. Other useful information is readily available from your staff as well as the business office.

It is clear that your support staff prefers the current machine, some outspokenly so. They are not as concerned as you are about costs and are well aware of the many advantages the current machine has in making their own workload easier. Moreover, if you had a smaller machine installed, there would be the need to improvise on some of the larger jobs, or, from time to time, to take work over to the district office. Some of the staff could make life more difficult for you by making up reasons to take work "downtown." It would not be possible to develop a policy to fit every contingency, so you would either be in position of constantly monitoring the reproduction tasks or of running the risk of flagrant misuse of the district's equipment, which would be charged against your operating budget, as well as a waste of time of some of your support staff.

Nevertheless, even though they will all be affected, the staff knows that a substantial amount of money is involved. Most also believe that making these kinds of decisions is what you are being paid for.

CASE 11: HOW SAFE IS THE SCHOOL?

You are principal of an urban high school. Numerous break-ins and incidents of violence have characterized several of the high schools in the district. Your high school is one of these. The window breakage alone in the district required $375,000 for repairs last year. Beyond this, the costs for repainting and other building repairs exceeded national averages by far.

Teachers are complaining that they do not feel safe, and some parents complain that their children have had money extorted from them by other "students" on their way to and from school as well as on the school grounds. Also, within recent months, there was a parking lot incident in which a teacher was shot at by an unidentified youth.

The restroom walls always seem to need cleaning; spray-painted scatology abounds in the restrooms and on sidewalks. School equipment doesn't seem to last long—it breaks or it disappears.

And now, an enterprising news team from a local TV station has started a well-watched series on "How Safe Are Our Schools?"

CASE 12: MRS. DAVIS IS A BAD TEACHER

You are principal of Ubben Elementary School, a prekindergarten through grade 5 school with a population of 530. It is nearly the end of the school day and you are reviewing your mail. A handwritten letter from a parent captures your attention. It reads as follows:

> Dear Principal, Assistant Principal, and School Board:
>
> My husband and I, as parents of a third-grader and a fourth-grader at Ubben Elementary, would like to bring to your attention some problems in Mrs. Davis's class. Our daughter Samantha is in Mrs. Davis's third grade. In the past few weeks, our conversations with Samantha have turned up some disturbing facts about Mrs. Davis's interactions with her students. Among other things that Samantha reports are the following: The entire class is denied recess if any one child misbehaves. Mrs. Davis repeatedly tells her class that they are "dumb," "stupid," "ignorant fools," and that their behavior is much worse "than her two-year-old."
>
> We concede that an eight-year-old's perceptions can be very different from that of an adult—after all, missing recess on several occasions for something you didn't do is very upsetting for an eight-year-old. However, I have sat in on Mrs. Davis's class and have observed her behavior in the classroom. On one occasion, she and the class were returning from lunch and some of the children were talking and moving about, which I think is normal for eight-year-olds. She yelled at the children to sit down and then screamed, waving her arms. Everyone sat down. As an adult, I was fright-

ened. Can you imagine what an eight-year-old would feel? If she demonstrated that kind of behavior while I was present, I can't imagine how she is when she is alone with the children. We also have evidence of unfair grading practices.

We are requesting that Samantha be transferred out of Mrs. Davis's class immediately. This, of course, is only a partial solution—it won't solve the problem for the rest of the class. There is a complete lack of a positive learning climate.

Verbal abuse is just as destructive as physical abuse. We have always had a high regard for the district and we are shocked that someone like Mrs. Davis could be employed. Surely others have complained.

We would like to hear from you immediately.

Sincerely,

Janet and Ralph Davis

CASE 13: RICKY

You are an assistant principal of a large junior high school (1,000 students). One of your duties is to chair special education Admission, Review, and Dismissal meetings (ARDs) for students who are emotionally disturbed. Ricky, who has a long history of being disruptive in school, has once again come to your attention. He is on medication for hyperactivity, but recently it seems to have a diminishing effect. Ricky is entering adolescence and is currently being retested by his physician. His behavior has been getting progressively worse.

Ricky is now scheduled to be in a self-contained classroom all day. However, the school also houses a regular school program and most students who attend are "normal" adolescents or near adolescents. This permits Ricky and his emotionally disturbed colleagues opportunities for interaction with the rest of the student body during lunch periods, in halls and restrooms, and before and after school in schoolwide organized activities. Regardless of the situation, Ricky doesn't get along. He fights, bites, and scratches his fellow students and screams at teachers and students alike. His behavior problems show little sign of improving. The school year is about half over.

A districtwide Central Unit for the Emotionally Disturbed has just opened. You mention this possibility to Ricky's parent and indicate that you are scheduling a midterm ARD for next week. The parent becomes very upset. "You will turn Ricky into a hoodlum; he'll only become worse" is her response. She also says she wants Ricky "mainstreamed" into the regular program "as PL 94-142 requires" and threatens to file a lawsuit unless this is done. She also states that both the principal and Ricky's teacher are "against Ricky" and that no matter what happens she insists that her child be removed immediately from the current class.

CASE 14: BACK TO THE BASICS

You are the principal of a large junior high school. Your school system is on a "back-to-the-basics" mode, reflecting the outspoken criticism of several board members and their constituencies. This, coupled with a new educational reform bill passed in the state legislature, is having a negative effect on your district's highly successful prevocational education program and, to a significant degree, on the fine arts program. Your school has achieved special state recognition for its efforts and achievements in both. Nevertheless, the school board has decided that prevocational education should be eliminated and has reduced the budget amounts to be spent districtwide in the fine arts to the barest of minimums.

You are now faced with counselors, teachers, and parents who are very concerned about the demise of the career education program. Counselors are concerned that the career counseling load will now fall on them. They say, "I don't know much about that." Parents are asking, "What courses should my youngster sign up for next year?" And the superintendent expects that even though the program is going to close, the obligation of the school is still to provide career guidance services and prevocational experiences.

Also complicating the matter is what to do about the current full-time career counselor. She relates very well to adolescents and has been able to "turn tough kids around." Parents are very supportive as well. Her teaching fields are history and Latin. Latin has not been offered in years at your school and the history department "runneth over." You would hate to lose this fine teacher. The parents are upset on several counts, not the least of which is the lack of attention to the fine arts program.

Your superintendent is waiting for your staffing plan and budget proposals for next year. These are due in two weeks.

CASE 15: WHERE IS THE MONEY?

You are the new principal of a middle school with an enrollment of 1,400 students. Your predecessor resigned the position six weeks ago to accept a similar position at a higher salary in a district across the state.

One of your teachers has come to see you about a problem he has just discovered. The teacher has been recently transferred to his present position to replace a teacher who suddenly resigned. The teacher who is conferring with you has been with the district 11 years but only in your school since the beginning of the semester.

He is in the process of preparing his students for a statewide industrial arts exhibition and contest to be held in the capital city, 125 miles away. He has discovered that $1,345.00 he had assumed to be in the "Ind-Art" account was never deposited. The money had been earned from several special student activities (car washes, bake sales, etc.) designed to raise sufficient funds to pay student and faculty expenses for the exhibition. Without the money, students and faculty will be unable to attend.

CASE 16: HOW COME I'M NOT A MASTER TEACHER?

You are Kym Nyberg, principal of a large high school in a medium-sized school district (ADA = 2,100). You are reviewing the morning mail. Among the memos and letters is the following:

> TO: Kym Nyberg
> FR: Kelli Jones
> SU: Career Ladder—Level III: Master teacher
>
> As you know, I did not qualify for Level III on the career ladder. I was and still am deeply hurt. And in addition to being hurt, I am now very angry.
>
> I came to this district 14 years ago. I have always been so proud of our district and considered it the best in the state. I have never felt the district was unfair to me in any way until now. In those 14 years, I have been told by evaluators that I was doing a good job and that I was a "master teacher." I have always gotten good evaluations. I was told last year by an evaluator that I qualified for Level III. I am now told I do not qualify.
>
> As I am doing the best I can, obviously I need help to improve. In order to help me improve my teaching performance, I respectfully ask three things from you and the other administrators:
>
> 1. A computer printout of my evaluation scores for the past five years
> 2. A list of the Level III teachers on the secondary level and permission to observe these teachers so I can determine what they are doing right and I am doing wrong
> 3. A written growth plan to help me become a Level III teacher

CASE 17: WELCOME: PLEASE CHANGE JANIE'S TEACHER

You are the new principal of Selter Elementary School. It's the third day of school and you've had a reasonably smooth opening. Selter is a large elementary school (ADA = 790) and houses grades 1 through 5. Your predecessor retired after a 30-year career in the district and is now enjoying the fruits of a successful tenure. She is on a world-spanning vacation after which she will relocate in a small town some distance away.

You are reviewing your mail and come across a letter from the president of the PTO, whom you have met but once, briefly, at a preschool opening reception. She welcomes you in her first couple of lines and then turns to another subject. The final paragraph of the letter reads:

> "Oh yes, I am not happy with Janie's class assignment. You have placed her with a Level I teacher—a Miss Burket. Lovely person, so young and pleasant. But Janie requires some special help, as I'm sure you've seen from her

records. Certainly a novice is ill prepared to deal with these. I know you have a number of Level II teachers but I especially admire Dr. Norris who is a Level III "Master Teacher." Janie and I were most disappointed that she was not assigned to her class. Your predecessor had indicated that this would be done. Could you arrange for Janie to be placed with Dr. Norris, please? Thank you very much."

CASE 18: WE OBJECT!

You are principal of a high school (grades 9 through 12) with an enrollment of 1,500. It is mid-November. You have been at a statewide professional meeting for the past three days and have just returned to your office. The letter below is among other first-class mail that you find in your in-box. The letter arrived on Monday; today is Thursday.

Dear Principal:

We, John and Grace Michael, request that our daughter Heather be dismissed from her fifth-period class, Health, for the remainder of the semester. We are basing our decision on the fact that materials used in the classroom and methods of teaching are in complete disharmony with the values and beliefs we have tried to implement in our home. At such a vulnerable time in their lives, it is difficult, at best, for young people to be strong in the beliefs they have been taught and then stand up against the pressure of their peers. But it's something the youth of today face on a daily basis and we parents, as a collective group, hope and pray that our youth make the right choices and develop a stronger character because of those choices.

But when the adults who have a direct influence on our child, through teaching, begin to promote a value system that has been rejected in our home, just consider the impact on our child (or any other) and how it will affect the decision-making process when that young person is once again faced with peer pressure.

During a recent conversation with Ms. Blackstone and Ms. Weaver, it was interesting to us how we were told repeatedly that teachers cannot tell students what is right and what is wrong; they must choose for themselves. Yet, in the same conversation, we were told that because many students have sex and many students drink, it is okay to teach "safe sex" and "responsible drinking." If this isn't at the very least a contradiction, then certainly you must agree that it is a compromise in values. As it has become obvious to us, it must also be obvious to you that we simply do not agree with the standards being practiced and taught. It is at this point that we have reached the conclusion that Heather should be removed from this course.

Sincerely yours,

John and Grace Michael

CASE 19: MIKE IS THE BEST YOU HAVE

Mike Flynn is your best mathematics teacher. His students always excel and he doesn't always get the best students to begin with. His classes range from Algebra I to a special advanced placement group in concepts well beyond calculus and differential equations. Parents of all students are highly supportive of Flynn. Moreover, he is frequently used by the district as an in-service training leader.

For as long as anyone can remember, Mike has had first period as his planning period. He comes to school late every morning because of his avocation, which is raising roses and doing other kinds of hybrid gardening. "Early morning hours work best for this," he says. "Especially for watering, pruning and fertilizing."

You are Mike's new principal. Two teachers have come to you within the past few days, each complaining of the "favoritism being shown Mr. Flynn." Each has asked why they cannot leave school during their planning period to tend to their personal business. Also, each has further suggested that "first period off" privileges should be extended to everyone. "Nobody else gets to do this," they say.

CASE 20: THE RESTRUCTURED SCHOOL

After a two-year study, the decision has been made by the professional staff of Cynthia Norris Middle School to implement the concept of "continuous progress" programming. Several professional task forces engaged in such activities as material selection, leveling, scoping and sequencing, and staffing patterns. The school is now characterized by flexible scheduling, teaming, independent learning contracts, a new reporting system, and other new processes. In general, staff members are at Norris because that is where they want to be. Teachers who were not favorably disposed to the restructuring were given the option to join other more traditionally organized schools. The program at Norris has been in operation for two years.

Almost from the start, some parents complained about the program. The complaints were manifest at first in phone calls to the principal, then in some heated discussions at PTO meetings, letters-to-the-editor of a local newspaper, a spurious mimeographed neighborhood newspaper called "The Guardian," and ultimately in the formation of a "Return to the Basics" community group.

Members of this group have now called for a public meeting about the program and you, as principal, have agreed to host the meeting. The group's position is that the program is not providing an adequate education for their children.

Specifically, the charges are:

1. The children are not learning the basic skills.
2. The children are confused by so much independence.
3. The current report card reveals only individual progress; it does not tell parents how their child compares with others in the school system or the nation. Thus, "we parents cannot set realistic goals for our children."
4. Discipline is missing; the students are running amok and not "learning respect."

5. Children need a home base—a single teacher who knows them well, not an impersonal team of teachers.
6. Students are not happy with the new program. Some say, "I can't get help from my teachers because there are too many other kids and they get help first."
7. It's a "fuzzy-headed" idea thought up by left-leaning educators. Children should not be put in charge of their own learning. That's what teachers are paid to do.

The meeting will occur three days hence.

CASE 21: I WISH I WAS DEAD

You are principal of a prekindergarten through grade 5 elementary school with an enrollment of 530. It is ten o'clock and you have just returned from a morning tour of the building. You are reviewing mail, memos, and notes from various staff that have accumulated since late yesterday afternoon when you were attending an all-district administrators' meeting at the central office.

Among other things, there is a short note from one of your fifth-grade teachers, written the afternoon before. It reads: "I thought you ought to see this." Stapled to the note is a piece of tablet paper containing the last part of an essay by one of her students, a boy named Timmy. The assigned topic for the essay was "My Favorite Things." Timmy's essay concludes, ". . . but I'll never get to have these things. Sometimes I wish I was dead. Sometimes I want to kill myself."

CASE 22: GET RID OF THAT BOOK!

You are principal of Selter Elementary School, which houses kindergarten through sixth grade and has an enrollment of 640. It's the end of the day and it's Friday. All of the children, your secretary, and most of your staff have left. You're looking forward to the weekend. You haven't had time to look at the day's incoming mail and that's what you do before going home. The last piece of mail is a letter from a parent:

Principal
Selter Elementary School

Dear Principal:

My son Brian came home Wednesday with a book entitled *Coming of Age* written by David Thomas. Brian got the book at the Selter school library and was reluctant to show it to me when I asked about it. Small wonder! I had heard some of the other parents talking about this at PTO just the other night. It's disgusting. I can't express how bothered I am that such a book is being circulated to young children.

Here's some of what it contains:

- On the second page, just after the title, there is a frontal shot of a nude baby.
- On page 17, there is another picture of a nude baby (the same shot that is on the title page).
- On page 48, human sexual intercourse is described.
- On page 60, there is a drawing of a baby in utero.
- On page 67, there is a picture of a mother breastfeeding a baby.
- On page 81, there is a photo of a statue of a nude woman and on the opposite page there is a similar photo of a nude man, showing genitals.

I'm no bluenose but this book shouldn't be available to grade-school children. You ought to be aware of the popularity of this book among the children and the kind of talking that is going on. Why should such a book be on our library shelves?

I know that school-district policy places the responsibility for the selection of books for general circulation in the hands of the school librarian, but you must have the authority to override such decisions. I hope you will agree with me that this book needs to be removed from the library.

Sincerely,

Scott L. Hughes, Parent

CASE 23: GUN IN THE SCHOOL

You are the assistant principal of Ubben High School, a school with an enrollment of 1,500 students. Ubben has a multiethnic student body and is located in a small city. It's Friday.

Two students approach you during second period and say a girl has brought a gun to school because she wants to scare a boy who continues to sexually harass her. The girl is in a class on the second floor; the student who allegedly has been harassing her is not in that class. The bell to change classes will ring in 15 minutes.

What do you do?

CASE 24: MR. BISHOP GRABBED ASHLEY JANE

Principal
Norris Middle School

Dear Principal:

Last Thursday my granddaughter Ashley Jane came home all upset and wouldn't tell me what had happened. Later that evening I found out that Mr. Bishop grabbed Ashley from her seat and proceeded to shake her by the shoulders for not doing her math homework! I don't care what a child does in school, no teacher has the right to lay his or her hands on my child, especially a male teacher!!!

Ashley said he told her that he was tired of her taking advantage of him. Who is taking advantage of who? There are times when Ashley does not get all of her work done because she has to babysit her younger brother some nights when I have to work. Even so, I make sure she keeps busy and I help her with her work when I can. She is a good student!

I am willing to take a day off next week to talk to you and Mr. Bishop to straighten this out. In the meantime, my granddaughter has my permission to leave class if she feels she is being picked on, and if Mr. Bishop has any problems, he is not to lay a hand on her but call me and I will handle it. My next step is the police. Male teachers should not be touching little girls.

Thank you.

Phyllis Selter Hughes

P.S. If you need to reach me, my work number is 123-4567, ext. 890.

APPENDIX B

ISLLC STANDARDS

<table>
<tr><td colspan="3">Standard 1: A school administrator is an educational leader who promotes the success of all students by facilitating the development, articulation, implementation, and stewardship of a vision of learning that is shared and supported by the school community.</td></tr>
<tr><td>KNOWLEDGE</td><td>DISPOSITIONS</td><td>PERFORMANCES</td></tr>
<tr><td>The administrator has knowledge and understanding of:
■ Learning goals in a pluralistic society
■ The principles of developing and implementing strategic plans
■ Systems theory
■ Information sources, data collections, and data analysis strategies
■ Effective communication
■ Effective consensus-building and negotiation skills</td><td>The administrator believes in, values, and is committed to:
■ The educability of all
■ A school vision of high standards of learning
■ Continuous school improvement
■ The inclusion of all members of the school community
■ Ensuring that students have the knowledge, skills, and values needed to become successful adults
■ A willingness to continuously examine one's own assumptions, beliefs, and practices
■ Doing the work required for high levels of personal and organization performance</td><td>The administrator facilities processes and engages in activities ensuring that:
■ The vision and mission of the school are effectively communicated to staff, parents, students, and community members
■ The vision and mission are communicated through the use of symbols, ceremonies, stories, and similar activities
■ The core beliefs of the school vision are modeled for all stakeholders
■ The vision is developed with and among stakeholders
■ The contributions of school community members to the realization of the vision are recognized and celebrated
■ Progress toward the vision and mission is communicated to all stakeholders
■ The school community is involved in school improvement efforts
■ The vision shapes the educational programs, plans, and actions
■ An implementation plan is developed in which objectives and strategies to achieve the vision and goals are clearly articulated
■ Assessment data related to student learning are used to develop the school vision and goals
■ Relevant demographic data pertaining to students and their families are used in developing the school mission and goals
■ Barriers to achieving the vision are identified, clarified, and addressed
■ Needed resources are sought and obtained to support the implementation of the school mission and goals
■ Existing resources are used in support of the school vision and goals
■ The vision, mission, and implementation plans are regularly monitored, evaluated, and revised</td></tr>
</table>

Reprinted with permission from Council of Chief State School Officers (1996), *Interstate School Leaders Licensure Consortium: Standards for School Leaders* (Washington, DC: Author).

Standard 2: A school administrator is an educational leader who promotes the success of all students by **advocating, nurturing, and sustaining a school culture and instructional program conducive to student learning and staff professional growth.**

KNOWLEDGE	DISPOSITIONS	PERFORMANCES
The administrator has knowledge and understanding of: ■ Student growth and development ■ Applied learning theories ■ Applied motivational theories ■ Curriculum design, implementation, evaluation, and refinement ■ Principles of effective instruction ■ Measurement, evaluation, and assessment strategies ■ Diversity and its meaning for educational programs ■ Adult learning and professional development models ■ The change process for systems, organizations, and individuals ■ The role of technology in promoting student learning and professional growth ■ School cultures	*The administrator believes in, values, and is committed to:* ■ Student learning as the fundamental purpose of schooling ■ The proposition that all students can learn ■ The variety of ways in which students can learn ■ Life-long learning for self and others ■ Professional development as an integral part of school improvement ■ The benefits that diversity brings to the school community ■ A safe and supportive learning environment ■ Preparing students to be contributing members of society	*The administrator facilitates processes and engages in activities ensuring that:* ■ All individuals are treated with fairness, dignity, and respect ■ Professional development promotes a focus on student learning consistent with the school vision and goals ■ Students and staff feel valued and important ■ The responsibilities and contributions of each individual are acknowledged ■ Barriers to student learning are identified, clarified, and addressed ■ Diversity is considered in developing learning experiences ■ Life-long learning is encouraged and modeled ■ There is a culture of high expectations for self, student, and staff performance ■ Technologies are used in teaching and learning ■ Student and staff accomplishments are recognized and celebrated ■ Multiple opportunities to learn are available to all students ■ The school is organized and aligned for success ■ Curricular, cocurricular, and extra-curricular programs are designed, implemented, evaluated, and refined ■ Curriculum decisions are based on research, expertise of teachers, and the recommendations of learned societies ■ The school culture and climate are assessed on a regular basis ■ A variety of sources of information is used to make decisions ■ Student learning is assessed using a variety of techniques ■ Multiple sources of information regarding performance are used by staff and students ■ A variety of supervisory and evaluation models is employed ■ Pupil personnel programs are developed to meet the needs of students and their families

Standard 3: A school administrator is an educational leader who promotes the success of all students by **ensuring management of the organization, operations, and resources for a safe, efficient, and effective learning environment.**

KNOWLEDGE	DISPOSITIONS	PERFORMANCES
The administrator has knowledge and understanding of: ■ Theories and models of organizations and the principles of organizational development ■ Operational procedures at the school and district level ■ Principles and issues relating to school safety and security ■ Human resources management and development ■ Principles and issues relating to fiscal operations of school management ■ Principles and issues relating to school facilities and use of space ■ Legal issues impacting school operations ■ Current technologies that support management functions	*The administrator believes in, values, and is committed to:* ■ Making management decisions to enhance learning and teaching ■ Taking risks to improve schools ■ Trusting people and their judgments ■ Accepting responsibility ■ High-quality standards, expectations, and performances ■ Involving stakeholders in management processes ■ A safe environment	*The administrator facilitates processes and engages in activities ensuring that:* ■ Knowledge of learning, teaching, and student development is used to inform management decisions ■ Operational procedures are designed and managed to maximize opportunities for successful learning ■ Emerging trends are recognized, studied, and applied as appropriate ■ Operational plans and procedures to achieve the vision and goals of the school are in place ■ Collective bargaining and other contractual agreements related to the school are effectively managed ■ The school plant, equipment, and support systems operate safely, efficiently, and effectively ■ Time is managed to maximize attainment of organizational goals ■ Potential problems and opportunities are identified ■ Problems are confronted and resolved in a timely manner ■ Financial, human, and material resources are aligned to the goals of schools ■ The school acts entrepreneurially to support continuous improvement ■ Organizational systems are regularly monitored and modified as needed ■ Stakeholders are involved in decisions affecting schools ■ Responsibility is shared to maximize ownership and accountability ■ Effective problem-framing and problem-solving skills are used ■ Effective conflict resolution skills are used ■ Effective group-process and consensus-building skills are used ■ Effective communication skills are used ■ There is effective use of technology to manage school operations ■ Fiscal resources of the school are managed responsibility, efficiently, and effectively ■ A safe, clean, and aesthetically pleasing school environment is created and maintained ■ Human resource functions support the attainment of school goals ■ Confidentiality and privacy of school records are maintained

Standard 4: A school administrator is an educational leader who promotes the success of all students by **collaborating with families and community members, responding to diverse community interest and needs, and mobilizing community resources.**		
KNOWLEDGE	**DISPOSITIONS**	**PERFORMANCES**
The administrator has knowledge and understanding of: ■ Emerging issues and trends that potentially impact the school community ■ The conditions and dynamics of the diverse school community ■ Community resources ■ Community relations and marketing strategies and processes ■ Successful models of school, family, business, community, government, and higher education partnerships	*The administrator believes in, values, and is committed to:* ■ Schools operating as an integral part of the larger community ■ Collaboration and communication with families ■ Involvement of families and other stakeholders in school decision-making processes ■ The proposition that diversity enriches the school ■ Families as partners in the education of their children ■ The proposition that families have the best interests of their children in mind ■ Resources of the family and community needing to be brought to bear on the education of students ■ An informed public	*The administrator facilitates processes and engages in activities ensuring that:* ■ High visibility, active involvement, and communication with the larger community is priority ■ Relationships with community leaders are identified and nurtured ■ Information about family and community concerns, expectations, and needs is used regularly ■ There is outreach to different business, religious, political, and service agencies and organizations ■ Credence is given to individuals and groups whose values and opinions may conflict ■ The school and community serve one another as resources ■ Available community resources are secured to help the school solve problems and achieve goals ■ Partnerships are established with area businesses, institutions of higher education, and community groups to strengthen programs and support school goals ■ Community youth family services are integrated with school programs ■ Community stakeholders are treated equitably ■ Diversity is recognized and valued ■ Effective media relations are developed and maintained ■ A comprehensive program of community relations is established ■ Public resources and funds are used appropriately and wisely ■ Community collaboration is modeled for staff ■ Opportunities for staff to develop collaborative skills are provided

<table>
<tr><td colspan="3">Standard 5: A school administrator is an educational leader who promotes the success of all students by acting with integrity, fairness, and in an ethical manner.</td></tr>
<tr><th>KNOWLEDGE</th><th>DISPOSITIONS</th><th>PERFORMANCES</th></tr>
<tr>
<td>The administrator has knowledge and understanding of:
■ The purpose of education and the role of leadership in modern society
■ Various ethical frameworks and perspectives on ethics
■ The values of the diverse school community
■ Professional codes of ethics
■ The philosophy and history of education</td>
<td>The administrator believes in, values, and is committed to:
■ The ideal of the common good
■ The principles in the Bill of Rights
■ The right of every student to a free, quality education
■ Bringing ethical principles to the decision-making process
■ Subordinating one's own interest to the good of the school community
■ Accepting the consequences for upholding one's principles and actions
■ Using the influence of one's office constructively and productively in the service of all students and their families
■ Development of a caring school community</td>
<td>The administrator:
■ Examines personal and professional values
■ Demonstrates a personal and professional code of ethics
■ Demonstrates values, beliefs, and attitudes that inspire others to higher levels of performance
■ Serves as a role model
■ Accepts responsibility for school operations
■ Considers the impact of one's administrative practices on others
■ Uses the influence of the office to enhance the educational program rather than for personal gain
■ Treats people fairly, equitably, and with dignity and respect
■ Protects the rights and confidentiality of students and staff
■ Demonstrates appreciation for and sensitivity to the diversity in the school community
■ Recognizes and respects the legitimate authority of others
■ Examines and considers the prevailing values of the diverse school community
■ Expects that others in the school community will demonstrate integrity and exercise ethical behavior
■ Opens the school to public scrutiny
■ Fulfills legal and contractual obligations
■ Applies laws and procedures fairly, wisely, and considerately</td>
</tr>
</table>

<table>
<tr><th colspan="3">Standard 6: A school administrator is an educational leader who promotes the success of all students by understanding, responding to, and influencing the larger political, social, economic, legal, and cultural context.</th></tr>
<tr><th>KNOWLEDGE</th><th>DISPOSITIONS</th><th>PERFORMANCES</th></tr>
<tr><td>The administrator has knowledge and understanding of:
■ Principles of representative governance that undergird the system of American schools
■ The role of public education in developing and renewing a democratic society and an economically productive nation
■ The law as related to education and schooling
■ The political, social, cultural, and economic systems and processes that impact schools
■ Models and strategies of change and conflict resolution as applied to the larger political, social, cultural, and economic contexts of schooling
■ Global issues and forces affecting teaching and learning
■ The dynamics of policy development and advocacy under our democratic political system
■ The importance of diversity and equity in a democratic society</td><td>The administrator believes in, values, and is committed to:
■ Education as a key to opportunity and social mobility
■ Recognizing a variety of ideas, values, and cultures
■ Importance of a continuing dialogue with other decision makers affecting education
■ Actively participating in the political and policy-making context in the service of education
■ Using legal systems to protect student rights and improve student opportunities</td><td>The administrator facilitates processes and engages in activities ensuring that:
■ The environment in which schools operate is influenced on behalf of students and their families
■ Communication occurs among the school community concerning trends, issues, and potential changes in the environment in which schools operate
■ There is ongoing dialogue with representatives of diverse community groups
■ The school community works within the framework of policies, laws, and regulations enacted by local, state, and federal authorities
■ Public policy is shaped to provide quality education for students
■ Lines of communication are developed with decision makers outside the school community</td></tr>
</table>

INDEX